HERE IS THE WAY IT WAS

in the great crucible of the E.T.O., from 1940 to 1945.

Some of these accounts of battle are written by skilled war correspondents like Eric Sevareid and Alan Moorehead, some are taken from personal reports of the infantrymen who took the ground, yard by bloody yard.

In addition, there are maps, and a running commentary which establishes the background and chronology of the war in Europe, and sets each report in its context.

The introduction is by a man who served as a reporter and editor for YANK, The Army Weekly, in Europe.

This is a companion volume to COMBAT: PACIFIC THEATER.

COMBAT

EUROPEAN THEATER

WORLD WAR II

Edited by DON CONGDON
Introduction by MERLE MILLER

A DELL FIRST EDITION
an original volume

Published by
DELL PUBLISHING CO., INC.
750 Third Avenue
New York 17, New York

Designed and produced by
Western Printing & Lithographing Company

Cover painting by Robert Shulz

COPYRIGHT NOTICES AND ACKNOWLEDGMENTS

First printing—December, 1958
Second printing—February, 1959

Printed in U.S.A.

Contents

INTRODUCTION

The presses on which the Continental Edition of *Yank* was to be printed were warm when this one-time editor got to Paris in late August 1944. The editors of another army publication, *Wehrmacht* by name, had just left town in something of a hurry.

There were a lot of old copies of the German publication lying around the press room, and with the eager help of a tri-lingual Frenchman I was able to make out the kind of publication the Germans put out for their soldiers.

However, I didn't get to read as much of *Wehrmacht* as I wished. My translator, a man who oozed love for democracy and passion for the United States from every pore, turned out to be a collaborator and an informer, and he was hauled off to jail. I heard later that he was shot without much of a trial, and it is possible. The French were impatient with traitors in those impatient days.

Nevertheless, my French buddy-buddy had translated enough stories in the German publication for me to catch on to the fact that its editors kept telling the troops that if they were lucky enough to get knocked off in the Third Reich's war to make the world safe for mass murder, they were assured of a place in Valhalla, probably very near to the right hand of Der Fuehrer himself, though *Wehrmacht* hinted strongly that Hitler was probably going to turn out to be immortal.

The writers and editors who were responsible for *Yank* decided in the very beginning that their simple (but often difficult) duty was to tell the truth whether you were where the shooting was—in the early days at, let us say, the Kasserine Pass or in and around Henderson Field on Guadalcanal—or waiting in line for a short-arm inspection at Fort Benning.

I remember with dismay that early in the war we ran a story which was a sort of testimonial for K rations, and there are other examples of human fallibility in the *Yank* files, but we very often succeeded in our aim—contending as best we could with the brass, which was sometimes capricious, occasionally arrogant, frequently imbecilic, but often helpful and understanding. There was a major in Paris who kept insisting that he was Jesus Christ, though in what is perhaps going to turn out to be the proudest moment in a largely misspent life I told him to go to hell. Also there was a colonel who thought that an immortal (I think) cartoon concerning the Sad Sack and a dream he had involving a curvy young lady would tend to corrupt the troops. The colonel, who ended the war as a brigadier general, lost to the Sad Sack, who ended the war as a private, but then the colonel was demonstrably less appealing than the Sad Sack.

Because of what I have always considered the conspicuous success of *Yank* in covering the Second World War, I was surprised to learn that there is only one piece from the enlisted men's magazine either in this volume or in its companion, *Combat: Pacific Theater—World War II*. The exception, which is contained herein, is a short, heart-breaking piece about the Huertgen Forest, possibly the single most costly battle of the Second World War. It was written by Sergeant Mack Morriss, whose genius for capturing the mood of the infantryman was perhaps possible because Mack had been an infantry line soldier and remained one in heart throughout the war.

Now that I have read all of the reports in this book and the other I realize that *Yank* has not been slighted but has, in fact, been honored.

In the years that have passed since the peace was signed in the Pacific, many thousands of books and tens of thousands of magazine pieces and stories have been written about the most profusely reported war in history. Don Congdon, who has so brilliantly edited this volume and the one about the Pacific war, has chosen only the best and truest words from the several million he must have read.

As a result, the pieces in both books have a very wonderful quality. It is this: No matter where you were at the time the battles described here were going on, no matter what you were doing, you will *know* when you have read this book that this is the way it was. You may not be able to explain how you know, but you will be absolutely certain. Just as you do not have to have been in the Civil War to be positive that Stephen Crane got it down right when he told how a very young man felt going into battle; or that Count Leo Tolstoy's account of what went on at Austerlitz is absolutely accurate.

Of course, both *War and Peace* and *The Red Badge of Courage* are fiction, and the sixteen pieces in this book are factual, but the quality of the writing is the same. It is a very rare quality, and it is particularly rare in writing about combat, which is the most personal experience there is. Capt. Laurence Critchell, a line officer in the 501st Parachute Regiment of the 101st Airborne Division and the author of two fine pieces in this book, says this, "Combat is foreign to all other experience. Nothing in ordinary life reminds one of it."

When a man faces death on the battlefield—or in the air or on the ocean—all he has is what he brought with him. Knowing that, he always wonders how he will act under fire, and he hopes and prays that he will act well. A thoughtful man will realize that he will be afraid and that he very probably will be tempted to run away as Mr. Crane's youth did. At first.

Most men do not run away. The reason, I suppose, is that men realize that if they run and thus survive the day of battle, they will have to return and spend more time with the men on either side of them, and they will have to spend the rest of their lives with themselves.

At such moments it does not seem to matter which side a man is on, or even whether the cause for which he fights is just.

As this is written men are dying—in small numbers, to be sure—both on the coast of China and on two tiny islands off its shore. The fact that they will not have much company at the end does not matter a great deal, nor, while they are waiting to die, will they do much thinking about the reason they were called on to do it.

The slogans are always forgotten at the last, and a man faces only the fact that in the increasing darkness, he wants it to be light again; he wants desperately to live. This is particularly true of young men, and that is what most soldiers are.

Now neither the men who wrote the pieces in this book nor Mr. Congdon, who has written the passages which connect the various battles and give the whole a coherent pattern, have dealt with the semantics dreamed up by the fellows in the Pentagon. I refer to the fellows who fairly late in the Second World War decided that *reinforcement* would be a more palatable word than *replacement* and passed the word along to the officers sending men out to die from places like the combined replacement center-concentration camp they had at Litchfield in England at the time; and to the officer, long since retired to a richly deserved obscurity, who, in the cold, awful winter of 1944 in Europe, thought that *The Stars and Stripes* absolutely had to print this question every twenty-four hours: "Have you killed your German today?" The question seemed in poor taste in Paris; where the fighting was going on, it was obscene.

No, there is none of that in this book; in this book words have been used only for the purpose for which words are presumably meant, to communicate the truth, not to inflame or mislead or confuse, which is what words very often are used for. I hope that does not sound solemn; this is a serious book, but it is never a solemn one.

One way to illustrate what I mean is to use an example from the moving account of the events in and around Bastogne in December 1944. It was written by Capt. Critchell. Capt. Critchell tells what happened when General McAuliffe's renowned one-syllable reply to the German demand for surrender was handed to a German officer by a Colonel Harper, a medical officer of the 101st.

The German captain and the major who was with him just couldn't seem to get the drift of General McAuliffe's answer.

Finally, in exasperation, Colonel Harper said, "If you don't understand what 'nuts' means, in plain English it is the same as 'Go to Hell.' And I will tell you something else —if you continue to attack, we will kill every goddamn German that tries to break into this city."

The German major and captain saluted very stiffly. The

captain said, "We will kill many Americans. This is war."

"On your way, bud," said Colonel Harper.

Well, there you have it; that small, beautiful exchange tells a great deal about the difference during the Second World War between the attitude of a German officer and that of an American.

More than that, it has the wonderful, melodic sound of truth, which is the case with every word in this book, from the time Capt. Russell Grenfell describes one of the greatest sea hunts of all time to the moment when Lt. Col. Wallace Cheves, who was there at the time, tells how it felt to be fighting your way into the Siegfried Line.

I expect that for a great many readers the pieces in this book will be a reminder, sometimes awful but always real. For example, there is a harrowing article by Capt. Andrew Wilson, who fought the war in a British Crocodile tank, which was used to flame the most heavily entrenched positions.

Of one day in Holland, Capt. Wilson writes:

"For the first time Wilson felt sure of himself in battle. More than that, he was elated. He'd led in the infantry, flamed an anti-tank gun, burned down half a dozen buildings which might or might not have held enemy, switched tanks, knocked out what was generally thought to have been a Mark IV in a haystack, and seen a Tiger long enough to fire at it.

" 'Well,' said Barber. 'Did you have a good time?'

" 'Fine,' said Wilson."

A little later Wilson decides to see what has happened where he has flamed. He has never done so before; since he landed in Normandy he has just not had the time. Wilson goes to a trench where he has burned all the underbrush away. There he sees a mass of charred fluff, and he decides that it is the remains of some looted bedding.

"Then, as he was turning to go, he saw the arm. At first he thought it was the charred and shrivelled crook of a tree root; but when he looked closer, he made out the hump of the body it was attached to. A little way away was the shrivelled remains of a boot."

What that sight did to Captain Wilson can perhaps only be fully understood by other men who have seen such things for which they were responsible.

After some of the sickness and some of the enormous disgust at his deed had gone away, Wilson made his decision: ". . . that either one threw up everything and made one's protest . . . or else one did everything more thoroughly and conscientiously than ever before, so that there was no time to think."

Such decisions were made by many of the men whose courageous deeds are recounted here. The telling has in a few cases been done by historians, sometimes by correspondents, but largely by men who were on hand while the battle was being fought.

I cannot possibly introduce everybody. There simply isn't the time. You have not met Second Lieutenant Karl Timmermann, the first American officer to cross the bridge at Remagen in March 1945. Lieutenant Timmermann, a fellow who had quite a bit of trouble in high school at West Point, Nebraska, and never got to the trade school of the same name on the Hudson, is my favorite lieutenant encountered either in real life or in print. You will understand why when you read about him.

The choice of Timmermann was not easy, though; there is a Lieutenant Hugo Sims of Orangeburg, South Carolina, who in Holland led what in this book is in masterly understatement referred to as "The Incredible Patrol." Also there is in the Pacific volume a Marine platoon leader on New Britain with the improbable name of Elisha Atkins, who appears to have had all of the attributes that have won wars since considerably before Thermopylae, including selflessness and courage and great gentleness.

This must also be said before you start in on the riches just beyond. You can *trust* what you read in this book. You are not being told the way it might or the way it ought to have happened; you are told the way it did happen. This is very unusual in these odd times.

A few years back in that never-never land in Southern California they pasted together a sort of Tab Hunter spectacular, one in which Tab finished off those few Japanese left by Errol Flynn. There was even a little Technicolor blood when Tab nicked his pinkie. He suffered mightily, and in stereophonic sound at that.

Now I know a couple of ex-Marines who went to that movie, men who had carried guns on Guadalcanal and had done damage with them, but they came out of that movie saying that it was a damn fine movie. They said, yes, as they remembered it, that was pretty much the way it had been on the Canal.

Oh, my. What curious, frightening things people's memories sometimes do. Because not everybody's memory can be trusted, almost all war movies do a great disservice to the Second World War and to the men who won it.

Some of the fellows out in Far Hollywood seem determined to create several myths about the Second World War: one, that it was easy; two, that it was *fun;* and three (and perhaps most dangerous), that there were absolutely no Nazis in Germany during it—with the possible exception of Adolf Hitler, who is presumed dead, and thus unable to plunk down the price of admission to a movie.

It is the admission money which interests most of the fellows who make most of the war movies, and German marks are just as good as American dollars.

If there is profit in the truth, the men who make these movies do not object to telling the truth, but if a lie looks as if it will bring in more loot, a lie will have to do. That is the reason we recently saw Marlon Brando playing a sort of *cuddly* German soldier. He absolutely hated Hitler, you understand, and Marlon wasn't ever an honest-to-God Nazi. What Marlon was was a crazy, mixed-up, lovable kid who happened to be German.

Eventually, if this myth that there were no bad Germans keeps on being repeated, it will grow, as myths have an uncomfortable habit of doing, and pretty soon it is going to be impossible to understand who was responsible for the murder of six million Jews.

I apologize. I started out to write an introduction to a book containing sixteen superb pieces about a war that is long past, and I have ended up with a criticism of those patriotic citizens, the Warner Brothers.

Maybe it was all too long ago to bother. A friend swears that when her son came home from school the other day, she asked him the usual question, namely what he had studied.

And she also swears that he said, "Oh, it was all about some jerk named Adolf Hitler."

That dates me, and it probably dates you, and, anyway, this is just about where I came in, and I have still not said that I figure I have read about a thousand books concerning the Second World War, and that this one, and its companion volume about the fighting in the Pacific, are among the half dozen best. They are among the best because they were put together with great understanding and skill and with the proud concept that the business, indeed the awesome duty, of a man who puts words on paper is to tell the truth at whatever the cost to himself or to anyone else.

The authors of these pieces had done just that, and they have done it with great feeling, which is something else good writing is all about.

What this book says over and over and in many different ways can best be summarized by a paragraph Capt. Critchell once wrote. Since I could not come even remotely close to saying it as well, I set it down here:

"We who had fought this war could feel no pride. Victors and vanquished, all were one. We were one with the crowds moving silently along the boulevards of Paris; the old women hunting through the still ruins of Cologne; the bodies piled like yellow cordwood at Dachau; the dreadful vacant eyes of the beaten German soldiers; the white graves and the black crosses and the haunting melancholy of our hearts. All, all were one, all were the ghastly horror of what we had known, of what we had helped to do. . . .

"Face it when you close this book.

"We did."

—Merle Miller
Brewster, N. Y.

England Alone

When Hitler invaded Poland on September 1, 1939, he lit the fuse that set off World War II. England and France had guaranteed the borders of Poland by treaty; two days later, they were at war with Germany. Most of the world would be drawn into the conflict in the months to come.

The British and French armed forces were dangerously inferior to Germany's, their peoples were slow to accept the need to fight. The French sat passively behind their Maginot Line, believing the Germans would wear themselves out against its maze of defenses. The British hadn't begun to arm until after Munich, and weren't galvanized into real action until the disaster at Dunkirk. Both of the allies were waiting for the Germans to make the first move—waiting through the fall and winter of 1939, and into the spring of 1940, a time that became known as the "phony war."

The war was no longer "phony" in April; Germany occupied Denmark and Norway, swept through Holland, then overran Belgium. The French and British armies in Belgium were split in two, the battered remnants rolled up against the coast at Dunkirk; by June 4th, the British had carried out the famous evacuation, rescuing more than 300,000 troops from the beaches.

Hitler could have tried to drive these troops into the sea before they escaped, and then quickly leapfrogged across the Channel to Britain; instead, he aimed straight for Paris. Outflanking the Maginot Line, he massed more than 100 divisions along the French border against half as many French divisions, and a pitifully small French air force. The "blitzkrieg" tactics of the Wehrmacht had stunned the French, and their government was indecisive; already some members of the French cabinet were discussing an armistice. The French armies steadily withdrew toward Paris, fighting a delaying action. Then Paris was given up without a fight. On June 23rd, the war in France was suddenly over—the aged Marshal Pétain had signed an armistice.

(On June 10th, Italy had declared war on France and England. Mussolini, not willing to risk anything but oratory before, now announced to his generals, "In September everything will be over, and I need some thousands of dead to be able to sit at the peace table as a belligerent.")

The coast of Hitler's Europe now stretched from the borders of Spain to the Arctic. Only England, across the Channel, was unconquered, and she seemed in a state of shock; the island was defenseless, having lost great quantities of arms and supplies at Dunkirk. (At that moment, the British could muster less than 290 tanks and 500 field guns in the home islands; ammunition of all kinds was scarce as hens' teeth.)

If Hitler had been ready to bridge the Channel, if he had been willing to risk big casualties on the beachheads of Britain, the British might have been overwhelmed then and there. The only substantial fire power between Hitler and the coast of Britain was the British Navy. Fortunately, Hitler hadn't enough amphibious craft (by September he would have assembled 3,000 self-propelled barges in European harbors, but by then it would be too late); his navy was crippled and in no shape to give adequate support to landings, and Goering was clamoring that the Luftwaffe could, given a chance, bring Britain to her knees by bombing attacks alone.

Hitler himself was busy with plans to invade Russia. If the invasion of Britain couldn't be brought off quickly, he would be caught fighting on two fronts. So Goering was given the signal to throw the Luftwaffe at the British; the U-boats were to tighten the noose around the supply lines to the British Isles and, if all went well, the German command could plan for an invasion of Britain in the fall.

The air battle over Britain aroused the whole world; there was horror at the first extensive bombing of civilians, and admiration for the gallant defense put up by the British Spitfire squadrons. But the British also had a "secret weapon," which mystified the Germans for weeks; how did the British get their Spitfires into the air and in position before the German raiders arrived at target? The British had discovered and developed radar (their experiments before the war had been a closely guarded secret). Later, radar would help the British defeat the German U-boat campaign against Allied shipping.

By the end of September, Goering was forced to admit he wasn't accomplishing any of his objectives—he hadn't even knocked out the R.A.F. And bombing the British cities had done nothing but make the British spit on their hands and fight back harder. Hitler was astounded; he had been sure the "decadent" British would ask for an early armistice. Had he realized that the effect was just the opposite, he might have invaded England before turning on Russia. Instead, he ordered the U-boat campaign intensified, and the Battle of the Atlantic began in all its fury. The first combat report in this book concerns that battle.

Action in the Atlantic

The U-boats were not the only menace to shipping; the Germans had built a force of surface raiders, including pocket battleships and battle cruisers, which could now operate from bases along the coast of Europe; from air bases in France, their aircraft could bomb and strafe the approaches to the British ports. In 1940 and 1941, eight million tons of shipping were destroyed.

The U-boats were responsible for the major losses, while the surface raiders cost the British little more than three-quarters of a million tons; but the pocket battleships and cruisers in European coastal harbors were major threats to the convoys converging on the British Isles. A pocket battleship in an unprotected convoy could produce a slaughter like a wolf among sheep. The British Admiralty was forced to keep battleships in the Home Fleet, though they were badly needed for convoy duty, against the day when a raider sallied out into the Atlantic.

The British caught the pocket battleship *Graf Spee* off South America in December, 1939, and crippled her so badly the Germans had to scuttle her to avoid capture. Both battle cruisers, *Scharnhorst* and *Gneisenau,* were kept bottled up and inactive by intermittent bombings. But, early in 1941, the Germans finished work on the *Bismarck,* their fastest battleship, with a displacement of 45,000 tons and an armament including eight 15-inch guns. On the 21st of May, the British Admiralty was signaled that the *Bismarck,* plus the light cruiser *Prinz Eugen,* had been sighted escorting a convoy to Bergen. Because of bad weather, both ships got out of the Norwegian harbor undetected by British air patrols. The British were certain they were out to raid Atlantic shipping routes—but where? *

* At this time, shipping losses had become so serious the British War Cabinet was on the point of not publishing monthly tonnage figures of sinkings.

Admiral Tovey, Commander of the British Home Fleet, had the battleships *King George V* and the *Prince of Wales* (newest and fastest ship in the British fleet), the battle cruisers *Hood* and *Repulse,* and the carrier *Victorious,* all at Scapa Flow. Two cruisers, *Norfolk* and *Suffolk,* were on patrol in Denmark Strait between Greenland and Iceland, and were alerted. Tovey then sent the *Prince of Wales,* the *Hood,* and six destroyers to intercept the *Bismarck* if and when it emerged from Denmark Strait; some hours later another force consisting of *King George V,* aircraft carrier *Victorious,* four cruisers and seven destroyers was sent to cover other approaches south of Iceland. Another force at Gibraltar, which included the aircraft carrier *Ark Royal,* was speeded northward.

The two German ships *had* sailed into Denmark Strait; they were sighted there on May 23rd, and carefully trailed by the two British cruisers (the heavier guns of the *Bismarck* had to be kept at a safe distance). At 5:35 a.m., May 24th, the battleships *Hood* and *Prince of Wales* sighted the *Bismarck* and *Prinz Eugen,* and closed for action at 25,000 yards.

The *Bismarck* straddled the *Hood* with her first salvo.* Within minutes, the *Bismarck*'s very accurate shooting broke the *Hood* in two; she sank so fast only three survivors were picked up. The *Prince of Wales,* crippled soon after, was forced to pull out of action.

The news of the *Hood*'s loss was a shock to the Admiralty, but they quickly called for other ships in the Atlantic area to join the hunt. They knew the *Bismarck* had been hit, because the *Norfolk* and *Suffolk,* still trailing, reported a broad oil slick behind her. As the hours went by, the *Bismarck* was lost sight of, then picked up again on the 25th; from

* Capt. Russell Grenfell, *The Bismarck Episode*—"The principal guideposts in modern navel gun battles are the splashes made by shells hitting the water. These splashes leap up to a great height (in the case of large shells about 200 feet) and are the means whereby gun control officers know where their shots are going. Splashes off the target indicate how corrections are to be made. What the control officer wants is a straddle. That is to say, one or more splashes over and one or more splashes short. He then knows he is 'on the target' and there may be one or more hits. As a rule he will not see those hits. With delayed action fuses, they may crash through the ship side or deck and penetrate deep into a hull before exploding."

her course, the British were certain she was steaming for Brest, a naval port on the French coast.

The *Bismarck* might have made it, with her great speed, but she was losing fuel, and her steering mechanism was damaged, too. Without these mishaps the British battleships would never have been able to get into range.

The chase was to cover nearly 3,000 miles, from the fringe of the Arctic Circle almost to the Bay of Biscay, before the *Bismarck* was cornered. The British themselves were faced with a fuel problem. But Churchill gave orders to keep hard on the scent, even if the battleships had to be towed home.

On the night of the 24th, the *Prinz Eugen* was sent off to rendezvous with an oiler, leaving the *Bismarck* to meet her fate alone. The British ships now moving in for the kill were the *King George V*, with Admiral Tovey aboard, joined by the battleship *Rodney*, plus the *Norfolk*, all pursuing the *Bismarck* out of the northwest; the carrier *Ark Royal*, the cruisers *Sheffield* and *Dorsetshire*, from the south; and a small force of destroyers approaching from the east. Other ships were in the pack, but would not be prominent in the action to follow.

The *Ark Royal* was the first to get within striking distance. Unluckily, the first attack by her Swordfish torpedo-bombers mistook the British cruiser, *Sheffield*, for the target—but no damage resulted. Capt. Russell Grenfell supplies the full account of the battle as it developed from there.

THE CHASE OF THE BISMARCK

by Capt. Russell Grenfell

After emerging safely from the disconcerting episode of the Swordfish attack, the *Sheffield* had gone on to find the *Bismarck*. On her bridge, everyone was scanning

This selection is made up of three chapters slightly condensed from the author's *The Bismarck Episode*.

the horizon ahead for a sign of a ship, and the lookouts had been promised two pounds to the first man to sight her. At 5:40 p.m., on May 26th, the officer of the watch said: "I think I can see something on the port bow." All binoculars were raised to look in that direction and, sure enough, a dim grey shape could just be made out on the misty horizon. Was it the *Bismarck?* At first it was difficult to say, but as the *Sheffield* came closer the silhouette of the *Bismarck* became unmistakable. Once again, a shadowing warship was in contact after an interval of more than a day and a half.

Captain Larcom, of the *Sheffield*, did not want to be seen if it could be avoided, and he altered course away and began to work round to get astern of the enemy at a distance of seven to ten miles. He began also to send in the usual shadower's reports of the enemy's position, course and speed. These reports were supplementing those going out from the *Ark Royal*'s shadowing aircraft who, in successive pairs, had been keeping a continuous watch on the *Bismarck* since 11:15 a.m.

Whether or not the *Bismarck* could see the *Sheffield,* she made no hostile move. Possibly she felt that, as she was obviously being reported by aircraft, it would serve no useful purpose and be only a waste of ammunition to try to drive away the cruiser, anyway during daylight.

Meanwhile, feverish activity was going on in the *Ark Royal* to get the next striking force ready to go. There was no time to be lost and everyone was working at top speed. With the ship rolling heavily, aircraft were refuelled and more torpedoes got ready. This time, too, there would be no mistake about the *Sheffield.* To make assurance extra sure, the aircraft were told to contact that ship on their way to the *Bismarck,* and the *Sheffield* herself was told that they would do so.

By 7 p.m. the striking force was up on deck and ranged. There were fifteen Swordfish, every single torpedo-bomber that remained in the ship. It was still blowing hard. Visibility was exceedingly variable, cloud was at about 600 feet or less, and rainstorms covering very large areas were sweeping across the sea. Once more the ship was turned into the wind and once more the aircraft careered unsteadily along the heaving deck before they rose clear into storm-swept sky. As they formed up in the air and disappeared in the direction of the enemy, everyone in the *Ark Royal* knew that they meant to succeed this time.

About forty minutes later, just before 8 p.m., the *Sheffield* sighted them coming. She made to them "the enemy is twelve miles dead ahead," and they were seen climbing into the clouds. Half an hour later they were back to ask for another bearing, having apparently failed to find the *Bismarck*. Redirected, they departed once more in the enemy's direction. There was too much rain and low cloud about for the *Sheffield*'s people to keep them long in sight. But after an interval there came an outburst of gunfire off the starboard bow and the bright winking of numerous shell bursts in the air which showed plainly that the attack was starting.

The distant display of anti-aircraft fire flashed and sparkled away for some minutes and then died away. There was a pause, and then those on the bridge of the *Sheffield* saw first one and then two more Swordfish flying towards them. They came past very low on a level with the bridge. It could be seen that their torpedoes had gone, and as one Swordfish flew by very close the crew were smiling broadly and had their thumbs held upwards. All those on the *Sheffield*'s bridge and upper deck took off their caps and gave them a cheer as they passed.

The attacks went on, and owing to the bad weather conditions were somewhat protracted. Mostly, the *Sheffield* could see little of what was happening, but at times, in a clear patch, her people saw the *Bismarck* spurting flame from every anti-aircraft gun, while through binoculars it was occasionally possible to spot some of the aircraft as they dived down and flattened out low over the water to drop their torpedoes.

Had the day been fine and clear, a simultaneous assault by the whole force would doubtless have been delivered. As it was, on nearing the enemy's position the aircraft encountered a thick bank of cloud, rising 6,000 to 10,000 feet above its base a few hundred feet from the sea. Inside this cloud bank the striking force got split up. Some aircraft went straight on at the same level till they reached what they estimated to be the correct attacking point. Others spent time in climbing several thousand feet before diving down. Those that did this experienced varying degrees of icing. On breaking cloud cover, some aircraft did not find the enemy where expected and had either to work round in the open or go back into cloud for another approach. One pair and one single aircraft lost the enemy completely and separately went back to the *Sheffield* for redirection. One aircraft found the flak so heavy that it gave up the attack and jettisoned its torpedoes before returning to the carrier. Altogether, the attacks were spread out over about half an hour, from 8:55 p.m. to 9:25 p.m.

While the attacks were still proceeding, those on the *Sheffield*'s bridge noticed that the *Bismarck* was altering course. She would naturally swerve about a good deal to dodge the torpedoes being dropped at her. Now she was getting almost broadside on to the *Sheffield*. Then suddenly from the distant enemy ship there came four rippling yellow flashes from her turret guns. As if stung to fury by the air attacks against her, she had opened fire on the only British ship she could see.

The shells fell a long way, perhaps more than a mile, from the *Sheffield;* and someone on her bridge made a derisory remark about the shooting. He spoke too soon. Again the enemy's turrets spurted their bright tongues of flame, and about fifty seconds later there were some piercing cracks as four 15-in. shells fell very close on either side of the British cruiser, exploding on hitting the water. Huge splashes shot up alongside, and the air was filled with whizzing shell splinters. Captain Larcom went on to full speed, put the wheel over to get clear, and gave the order to make smoke. But before that last order had produced any result four more enemy salvoes had fallen unpleasantly close.

The splinters from the second one had caused casualties among the anti-aircraft gun crews, twelve men being wounded, three of whom died. They had also destroyed the ship's radar apparatus, an awkward piece of damage, as it meant the *Sheffield* could now only shadow by eyesight, and would therefore be ineffective for that purpose after dark.

It was a hectic few minutes, with the sudden outburst of shellfire, the hurried giving of orders, the frantic rolling of the ship as she came beam-on to the sea, the swish and smack of the incoming spray and the rising howl of the gale as she turned at high speed into the wind; and at last, none too soon, the dense volumes of jet-black smoke pouring out of the funnels, blotting out the *Sheffield* from the vicious enemy's sight. The moments had been too crowded for a calm and leisurely observation of the *Bismarck*'s behavior. But she had been seen to continue her turn into the wind. As he swung round away from her gunfire, Captain Larcom ordered a signal to go out that she was steering 340° (NNW). What had been the *Bismarck*'s game? Had she thought this was a good moment to drive away her one surface shadower before dark, when the air attacks were in any case compelling her to twist and turn? Or was there some other explanation? Captain Larcom could not tell.

Many miles below the horizon, Sir John Tovey had even less means of knowing. All he had to go on was Captain Larcom's report that the *Bismarck* had almost reversed her course. What did it mean? In view of the shattering signal just previously received from the leader of the attacking aircraft it probably meant nothing. This signal had been short and very much to the point. It said: "Estimate no hits." It was assumed by the Admiral and indeed by all ships that took it in, that the signal referred to the attack as a whole and indicated that, like its predecessor, it had been a complete failure. The gloom thereby engendered was naturally abysmal. Captain Dalrymple-Hamilton told the *Rodney*'s company over the loudspeakers that no hits had been obtained and added that he very much feared there was now no hope of bringing the *Bismarck* to action. Commodore Blackman of the *Edinburgh* reached the same conclusion. He had been in sight of the *King George V* and *Rodney*, off and on, since early in the day. At about 5 p.m. he had crossed astern of them to make straight for the *Bismarck*'s reported position. But though he ran across both *Sheffield* and *Ark Royal* at different times and therefore must have got very close to the *Bismarck* herself, he did not succeed in sighting her. By this time, his fuel position was verging on the desperate, and the report that the second air attack had gained no hits decided him to give up the pursuit. He turned his ship for home.

To Sir John Tovey the "no hits" signal was the culminating rebuff. All was now clearly over. The *Bismarck* was practically certain to get away and there would be little left for him, Sir John, to do but to make his mournful way back to his base. Then another signal was brought to him. It was from one of the shadowing aircraft and it said that the *Bismarck* was steering due north. The *Bismarck* had undoubtedly turned right round. But this did not necessarily mean a great deal. Such a turn, drastic though it was, was not incompatible with the frustrating of an aircraft attack. The next report would surely show the *Bismarck* as back to east-south-east. But the next report, nine minutes later, did not. It made her still steering north-north-west. Another nine minutes passed, and again an aircraft report was handed to the Commander-in-Chief. Again it said that the *Bismarck* was heading about north-north-west. Sir John and his staff looked at each other with bewildered hopefulness. Could it really be true that the *Bismarck*, for no apparent reason, was steaming back on her tracks? Then, five minutes later, there came a second report from the *Sheffield*, in which the enemy's course was given as north.

There was now no room for doubt. The *Bismarck* was clearly moving in a general northward direction. But if she had not been hit, why was she behaving in this strange, and indeed suicidal, manner? It was to her vital interest to make every mile of progress she could towards the south-east. Yet here she was steering almost in the opposite direction for nearly half an hour. Was it possible that she had been hit after all? The thought was forming among Sir John Tovey and his staff that the *Bismarck*'s otherwise inexplicable movements might be due to her rudders being damaged and she herself being no longer under control.

Whatever the explanation, the situation had turned dramatically in the British favour. Two minutes after the *Sheffield*'s second report reached him Sir John led round to a course of south, directly towards the *Bismarck*'s position.

The *Sheffield* was still steering northward to open the range from the *Bismarck,* and just before ten o'clock she sighted some destroyers coming down from the north-westward. These were Captain Vian's five ships who had been steaming hard to overtake the *Bismarck* for the previous nine hours. They had already seen the *Renown* in the distance and had in turn been sighted by the *Ark Royal*'s aircraft on their way back from the attack. The sun was getting low towards the horizon. Yet even in the evening light, the destroyers made an inspiring spectacle as they came racing up, yawing about and heeling far over as they tore along down wind, the white of their foaming bow waves prominent even among the breaking seas. As they neared the *Sheffield,* Captain Vian asked her for the bearing of the *Bismarck,* and, receiving it, swept past and onwards towards the enemy.

The air striking force had begun to return to the *Ark Royal* at about 9 p.m., but they had a long way to go, and the last of them was not on board till an hour and a half later. Five had been damaged by gunfire. In one 127 holes were counted, the pilot and air gunner having both been wounded. But despite all this and the failing light, only one aircraft crashed.

It was a more cheerful lot of airmen who climbed out of their aircraft and went up to tell their stories. The crews were interrogated separately as they returned, and it was not until well after 10 p.m. that Captain Maund of the *Ark Royal* felt satisfied that one hit had been obtained amidships on the *Bismarck.* He signalled this over by lamp to Vice-Admiral Somerville, who passed it out by wireless at approximately 10:30 p.m. This report did not clarify the situation very much. If the hit had actually been amidships, it would be most unlikely to have been responsible for the *Bismarck*'s northerly course. Nevertheless, the report sufficed to bring the *Edinburgh* back towards the enemy.

Meanwhile, darkness had been coming on, and Sir John Tovey knew that the air shadowers would soon have to return to the *Ark Royal.* But he also knew that, thanks to Captain Vian's initiative earlier in the day, the latter's destroyers were now in the *Bismarck*'s vicinity and would presumably soon be taking over the watch.[1] To assist them in gaining contact, Sir John asked Vice-Admiral Somerville if the air shadowers could guide the destroyers to the enemy, and this instruction was passed to them via the *Ark Royal*. They seem to have left the *Bismarck* at about 10 p.m. and made a sweep in search of the destroyers. These they eventually found, but had by that time become too "lost" themselves to act as guides. Just before 10:30 p.m. they were recalled to the *Ark Royal*.

But Captain Vian was taking his destroyers in the right direction, and at ten minutes to eleven, after a silence of about three-quarters of an hour, the other British forces were cheered by a contact signal from the *Zulu*, showing that the destroyers were in touch. By now, Sir John Tovey was convinced that the *Bismarck* had been injured in such a way as to prevent her maintaining a continuous south-easterly course and to compel her frequently to come round head to wind, which by good fortune was blowing from the north-west. He was satisfied that she could not now escape him; and he therefore decided that, as night was falling, he would not seek an action at once but would wait for daylight. The positions of the enemy and of other British forces were none too certain and there was always the chance of an unfortunate incident if one of the latter was met unexpectedly in the darkness. At 11:36 p.m. Sir John altered course to about north-north-east to work round to the northward and westward of the *Bismarck*, with the object of having her silhouetted against the early morning light when he made his attack. He had hardly got round to his course when he received another signal from Vice-Admiral Somerville to say there had probably been a second hit on the *Bismarck*, on her starboard quarter. Apparently the signal was written out at 2240 (10:40 p.m.) since it bore that time of origin. But it was an hour later when it was received in the *King George V*.

[1] Sir John Tovey had intercepted a signal from the *Renown* saying that the destroyers had been seen passing her at 7 p.m.

The word "quarter" was highly significant,[2] and indeed was the sort of evidence for which they had all been waiting for two hours and a half. A hit on the quarter might well mean that the *Bismarck*'s propellers or rudder or both had been damaged, rendering her unmanageable. Sir John Tovey felt more confident than ever that he now had her at his mercy, and he made a signal that she appeared severely damaged and that he would be engaging from the westward at dawn. He also wrote a message to Captain Patterson, wishing the flagship good luck and victory in the coming fight.[3]

Meanwhile, the last aircraft shadowers had just got back to the *Ark Royal* with practically no petrol left, and in spite of the darkness and the lively pitching of the ship had somehow managed to make a successful landing. The crews had some important information to impart. It was that immediately after the aircraft attack the *Bismarck* had made two complete circles and had apparently come to a stop heading north, on which point of the compass she lay wallowing in the seas. This was the final link in the evidence needed to complete the whole chain. Captain Maund flashed it over at once to the *Renown*, and Admiral Somerville sent it on to Sir John Tovey by wireless at a minute before one o'clock, with a time of origin of 0046 (12:46 a.m.).

It was direct and invaluable confirmation of what Sir John had been suspecting for some time. The picture was now indeed reasonably clear to everyone on the British side. After the strain and anxieties of the past few days, culminating in the two wretched disappointments of the previous six hours, when hope of catching the *Bismarck* had declined practically to zero, the enemy's evident disablement seemed almost too good to be true. To the senior officers,

[2] The quarter is that part of a ship about halfway between the middle of her length and the stern.

[3] To *K.G.V.* The sinking of the Bismarck may have an effect on the war, as a whole out of all proportion to the loss to the enemy of one battleship. May God be with you and grant you victory. JT 26/5/41

particularly, the relief was immense. They, who had known the general strategical situation as their juniors had not, had previously almost despaired of getting the *Bismarck*. They had realized that the air attack which had done the vital damage was virtually the last hope of slowing the *Bismarck* up and thus preventing her escape; and that such a last-minute attempt should be an overwhelming success was beyond reasonable expectation.

All that Sir John Tovey now wanted to bring off his dawn attack were reports of the *Bismarck*'s position during the night, and these he was confident he would get from Captain Vian's destroyers. A few minutes after receiving the "circling" signal, he altered course right round to south-west. Sir John had also requested Sir James Somerville to take his Force H not less than twenty miles to the southward of the enemy. That would be quite close enough for the operation of the *Ark Royal*'s aircraft, and Sir John Tovey thought it best to keep the *Renown* well clear. An hour or two before, Sir James had suggested bringing her over to join the battleships. But Sir John was anxious to avoid any possibility of mistaking her for the enemy in the darkness, while he believed the *King George V* and *Rodney* quite strong enough for the job in hand.

To the north of the *King George V*, the *Norfolk* was still striving to catch up. She had shortened the distance the battleships were ahead of her during the day, but she was still behind them. Being seriously short of fuel, Captain Phillips had been hesitating to go too fast. But when the last air attack was due to be in progress, he could contain himself no longer. He put the telegraphs to full speed.

Another British warship was now speeding towards the *Bismarck*. Captain B. C. S. Martin of the cruiser *Dorsetshire* had been acting as the escort of Convoy SL 74 coming north. At 11 a.m. on the 26th, he and the convoy were about 600 miles west of Cape Finisterre, when the Admiralty's signal was taken in that the *Bismarck* had been sighted just before. The plot of the enemy's position made her 300 miles due north of the *Dorsetshire*, and Captain Martin realized that if the *Bismarck* were making for Brest, he could probably intercept her.

He made up his mind to leave the convoy and steer to meet the enemy. The intercepting course was about east and nearly down wind, which meant that the *Dorsetshire* could maintain a good speed. Captain Martin turned to east-north-east and went on to 26 knots. At 5 p.m., he altered course to east and increased to 28 knots.

When Captain Vian sighted the *Sheffield* ahead of him just before 10 p.m., his destroyers were spread in line abreast, two and a half miles apart, and the *Sheffield* on the opposite course passed through the line a quarter of an hour later. Learning from her that the *Bismarck* was not far off and when last seen was heading north to north-west, Captain Vian reduced speed. In the growing dusk and with heavy seas running, it might be dangerous to make the final approach too fast. It was expected to sight the *Bismarck* ahead of the centre destroyer. But at 10:38 p.m., she was seen a little on the starboard bow of the port wing ship, the *Piorun;* and shortly after the latter's next-in-line, the *Zulu,* also spotted her and was the first to get off a sighting report.

Within a very few minutes, the *Bismarck* sighted the *Piorun* and opened fire on her with both main and secondary armaments. Undismayed, the tiny *Piorun* returned the fire with her 4.7-in. guns. It is very unlikely that she did any good, and she herself, being frequently straddled, was in grave danger. But it was a most spirited display, and the *Piorun* actually kept up the hopelessly unequal contest for over half an hour before she ceased spitting fire at her armoured antagonist and hauled out of range.

Captain Vian had discovered the enemy he was seeking, and he now had to decide what policy to adopt towards him. As his destroyers drew closer and could make a better estimate of the *Bismarck*'s movements, it became apparent that she was proceeding at low speed and was steering erratically. Captain Vian concluded that interception by the British heavy ships was fairly certain in the morning, if not earlier, provided the enemy were successfully held during the night. He therefore made up his mind that his first duty was to shadow the *Bismarck* with a view to guiding the

King George V and *Rodney* to her position. He would, however, as a secondary duty, deliver torpedo attacks as opportunities offered, and provided this did not involve heavy losses among his ships.

Immediately after sighting the enemy, he had ordered his destroyers to take up their shadowing positions, and they were moving over to do that now. The *Maori, Sikh, Zulu,* and *Piorun* were to form a square round the *Bismarck,* one on each bow and one on each quarter; while the *Cossack,* Captain Vian's ship, would shadow from astern. It would take some time for all the destroyers to get into position, especially as the two detailed for the farther positions had to keep out of gun range while reaching them, involving something of a detour.

At about 11:15 p.m., however, the *Bismarck* made things easier by altering course in the destroyers' direction. Since they had first sighted her, she had seemed to be oscillating about a mean course of roughly north-east. She now swung round to about north-north-west. But it was nearly dark; and the outer destroyers did not immediately become aware of the *Bismarck*'s alteration, and so went on for a short time in the wrong direction.

At 11:24 p.m., Captain Vian made the signal for taking up preparatory stations for a synchronized torpedo attack. His plan, previously communicated to the other ships, was for three destroyers on one side of the *Bismarck* and for two on the other all to attack together, coming in on both the enemy's bows to fire their torpedoes at the same time. The weather was, however, unfavourable for an organized attack of this kind. It was blowing very hard and there was a big sea running. The destroyers could manage a fair speed down wind, but could make only moderate progress against it.

It very soon became clear, however, that the darkness was no handicap to the *Bismarck*. Time after time, she opened very accurate fire on the destroyers, evidently firing by radar and independent of visual sighting; moreover, she obviously intended to show the destroyers they would approach her at their peril.

The first destroyer to receive her attentions in this way

was Captain Vian's own *Cossack*. At 11:42 p.m., while she was still four miles away from the *Bismarck*, flashes of gunfire were seen from the latter's direction, and salvoes of large and small shells fell close alongside the *Cossack*, the splinters from which shot away some of her wireless aerials. The shooting was too good to be trifled with, and the *Cossack* was forced to sheer away.

Eight minutes later, the *Zulu* received the same treatment. She could just make out the *Bismarck* to the northward and had seen her shooting at the *Cossack*. Now the enemy's guns flashed out again; and a few seconds later a 15-in. salvo straddled the *Zulu* herself. Two more similar salvoes straddled her in quick succession, the splinters wounding one officer and two men. It was providential she was not hit and she made haste to turn away and get farther off. In this progress, she lost touch and did not regain it for more than an hour.

It was the first time in history that radar-controlled gunfire had been used against ships at night; and it was a weird and rather awe-inspiring experience for the destroyers to undergo. Had the *Bismarck* been using searchlights, it would have seemed less unnatural. But there was no such warning. Out of the darkness in the *Bismarck*'s direction would come a ripple of brilliant flashes, momentarily lighting up the sky. A ten- or fifteen-seconds' pause, and then the shriek of approaching shells and a quick succession of terrific, splitting cracks, as they hit the water. Simultaneously, a vast upheaval in the sea near the ship and a number of indistinct masses would tower up ghost-like and immense in the darkness alongside. Then another sudden glare of gunfire, momentarily revealing huge columns of cascading water close at hand.

From half-past twelve till one o'clock in the morning, the *Bismarck* seems to have been unshadowed, all destroyers having lost touch. There was a good deal of excuse. It was an inky-black night and, in addition to the gale and the heavy seas, frequent rain squalls were being encountered, in which the visibility was probably less than half a mile. To lose touch with a darkened ship under these conditions was only too easy. By this time, Captain Vian had come to the conclusion that no set-piece attack was possible. The *Bismarck*'s ability to keep his ships at a distance by radar-controlled gunfire had made the darkness a handicap rather than an advantage. In escaping from the enemy's broadsides, his destroyers had become scattered. If attacks were to be made at all, each destroyer would have to make her own, as best she could. He made a signal at twenty minutes to one that destroyers should attack when opportunities presented themselves.

On receiving this signal, Commander Graham of the *Zulu* at once went off to the westward by himself. As he did so, a star shell winked out into light on his port bow and began its slow descent to the sea. It was from the *Maori,* who was taking a look in the direction where she had last seen the enemy. But it revealed nothing. At about one o'clock, however, the *Zulu* sighted the black shape of the *Bismarck* on the starboard bow, steering apparently a little west of north. The *Zulu* was right astern of the enemy ship and had to get much farther up on or before her beam in order to fire torpedoes. Commander Graham therefore decided to run up on the *Bismarck*'s port side and went on to as high a speed as he could manage. The enemy must have been going very slowly, for it only took the *Zulu* about twenty minutes to get abreast of her, at an estimated range of 5,000 yards. At this point, the *Bismarck* opened a hot fire, and a minute or two later Commander Graham fired all his four torpedoes and then sheered away to open the range. So far as could be judged, none of the torpedoes hit.

The gunfire directed at the *Zulu* showed the *Maori* where the *Bismarck* was, and she steered in that direction. Judging by the gunflashes, the *Maori* was also astern of the *Bismarck;* and Commander Armstrong, like Commander Graham, determined to work forward on the enemy's port side. He got up to a position about 4,000 yards on the *Bismarck*'s port beam apparently without being seen. As it was very dark and he wanted to make sure of his aim, Commander Armstrong then fired a star shell to light the enemy up while he attacked; and as soon as it was burning, he fired two torpedoes. This was at 1:37 a.m.

The moment the star shell broke into light, the *Bismarck*

opened fire, and as usual made excellent shooting. Immediately after firing his torpedoes, Commander Armstrong had begun to turn towards the enemy. He fancied she was altering course towards him and he thought he would cross her bows and fire his other two torpedoes from her other side. The *Bismarck*'s fire was, however, much too fierce, and the *Maori* altered away to get clear, but the *Bismarck*'s salvoes followed her out to a range of 10,000 yards. As the *Maori* retreated those on board her were sure they saw a torpedo hit. A bright glow seemed to illuminate the enemy's waterline and shortly afterwards another vivid glare appeared to betoken a second explosion. A cheer went up from the men on deck.

While the *Bismarck* was firing westward against the *Maori,* Captain Vian in the *Cossack* was engaged in attacking from another direction. He had been stealthily making his way up on her starboard side, and was now in a position whence he could take full advantage of her preoccupation with her other assailant. From the *Cossack,* the *Bismarck* was clearly silhouetted against the glare of her own gunfire, and at 1:40 a.m., only three minutes after the *Maori* had fired two torpedoes, Captain Vian fired three at an approximate range of 6,000 yards. After an interval, the *Cossack* saw what they believed to be an unmistakable hit. Flames blazed up the *Bismarck*'s forecastle,[4] visible not only to the *Cossack* but to all adjacent ships.

The *Sikh* had been driven off by the *Bismarck*'s fire earlier in the night. Losing contact, she had taken in a report by the *Maori* that the *Bismarck* was steering south-west. It was probably a mistaken report for north-east, but it threw the *Sikh* out, and she went on for some time searching for the *Bismarck* in a south-westerly direction. Attracted, however, by the *Bismarck*'s firing in opposition to the other destroyers' attacks, the *Sikh* was now on the way back. The *Zulu* had just reported the *Bismarck* as being stopped, and the *Sikh* believed that this provided an opportunity for a long-range attack. At eighteen minutes past

[4] A possible but unusual indication of a torpedo hit, which, by letting water into a ship, is seldom accompanied by fire.

two, she fired her four torpedoes at a range of about 7,000 yards. After an interval for the passage of the torpedoes, it was thought that there was the sound of an explosion.

Sikh and *Zulu* had now fired all their torpedoes, *Maori* had two left, *Cossack* one, while *Piorun* had not yet attacked. All the first four destroyers had withdrawn out of range after making their attacks.

The *Bismarck* seemed to remain stopped or was only steaming very slowly for an hour from 1:45 a.m. Some of the destroyers were not always in contact, but they knew roughly where the wounded battleship lay.

At about half-past two, there came a signal from the Commander-in-Chief, whose battleships were presumably not far off, for the destroyers to fire star shells to indicate the *Bismarck*'s position. The Admiral was steering to get to the westward of the *Bismarck* for a dawn contact and was anxious for accurate knowledge of her position. His battleships and Captain Vian's destroyers had not yet been in sight of each other, and it was quite possible that, owing to natural variations of reckoning, the destroyers' positions relative to the flagship were appreciably different from what they purported to be. Moreover, the earlier succession of enemy reports had apparently come to an end an hour before. The firing of star shells by the destroyers might therefore give the Admiral a visual indication of the enemy's whereabouts. The destroyers began to comply with this order, but the unseen *Bismarck* quickly showed her resentment by opening an accurate fire on the star-shell firers; and Captain Vian did not think the Admiral would wish him to persist long with this explosive arrangement.

About 3 a.m., Captain Vian decided to take the *Cossack* in to fire her one remaining torpedo. The *Bismarck* was by now apparently under way again and proceeding slowly north-westward. Captain Vian worked round to the northward of her and, closing in, fired from about 4,000 yards. No hit was apparent.

After this attack, all certain contact with the *Bismarck* seems to have been lost till shortly before 6 a.m. But Captain Vian was confident he would find her as soon as it began to get light. It was obvious that she was in an unhappy state. She had been steering a course which varied between north-west and north-east since 11 p.m., at a very low speed. She would not have been doing that on purpose. Therefore daylight was bound to reveal her whereabouts, and it was questionable whether it was sound to court too deliberately any more of her extremely accurate gunfire. At 5 a.m., Captain Vian ordered the *Piorun,* whom he knew to be short of fuel, to return to Plymouth. Commander Plawski, who had been much hampered by rain squalls, was then searching north-west for the *Bismarck*. He went on for another hour before regretfully shaping course away.

Direct touch was first regained by the *Maori,* who sighted the black shape of the enemy battleship at 5:50 a.m., Commander Armstrong making her out to be zigzagging slowly in a direction north-north-west at about 7 knots. Having found her, he shadowed her till daylight. Half an hour later, the *Sikh* sighted her emerging from a rain squall about three and a half miles away. Darkness was gradually giving way to twilight. Just before sunrise when the visibility was getting fairly good, the *Maori* determined to get rid of her last two torpedoes. She closed in somewhat and fired them from a range of 9,000 yards, just before 7 a.m. There was no hit, but once more the *Bismarck* opened fire and straddled several times. It was her last smack at the destroyers that had been snapping at her all night.

With the coming of full daylight, Captain Vian stationed his destroyers in four sectors all round the *Bismarck,* and they continued to keep her in sight. They had had a sleepless and tiring night, keyed up at high tension from dusk to dawn. Each destroyer had been under accurate shellfire from the *Bismarck*'s heavy and lighter guns. All but the *Piorun* had indeed undergone that fiery ordeal at least twice and the *Cossack* had been through it thrice. They were frail craft and their officers and men were well aware that even one hit from the *Bismarck*'s 15-in. guns would probably make an end of them. Considering how often they had been straddled, it was astounding that not one of them had received a direct hit.

There can be little doubt that the periodical losses of contact during the night were mainly due to the accuracy of the *Bismarck*'s radar-controlled gunfire. But for her ability to drive the destroyers outside sighting distance by this means, it should have been a fairly easy matter for them to keep her continuously in sight, had they concentrated on doing so. At the same time, an unexpectedly difficult shadowing problem was still further complicated by the fact that the destroyers did not give it their whole attention. The decision to carry out torpedo attacks could not fail to have a prejudicial effect on the business of keeping the enemy under observation. Successful shadowing calls for the avoidance of damage and the careful maintenance of a suitable shadowing position. The attack, on the other hand, postulates a deliberate exposure to damage and a period of high-speed manoeuvring conducted with the single object of reaching a position for firing torpedoes, regardless of any other consideration. A shadowing destroyer which goes into the attack may emerge, if it emerges at all, five or ten miles from its shadowing station; and where, as in this case, the attacks are made piecemeal, the shadowing arrangements must soon be in disorder if not confusion. Shadowing and attacking by destroyers at night are, in fact, severely conflicting activities.

Nor does it seem that the hazarding of the primary object of shadowing was here compensated by the results achieved in pursuing the secondary object of attacking. It is true that several torpedo hits were claimed at the time. But according to the German records published by the British Admiralty, none were in fact scored. The German statement to this effect may not, of course, be true. On the other hand, the receipt of torpedo hits would probably be known throughout the target ship, and the Germans would appear to have had no incentive to suppress the record of such hits, had they occurred. If anything, rather the reverse; and in the absence of such incentive, the German evidence that there were no hits could well be more reliable than the British belief that there were two. It is very difficult for destroyers attacking at night to be sure that their torpedoes have got home. The tell-tale pillar of water going up alongside the torpedoed ship cannot be seen in the darkness, and the boom of the target ship's own guns firing at the attacking craft can very easily be construed into the roar of an exploding torpedo. The force of suggestion is very strong on such occasions. The officers and men of the attacking ships want to see or hear a torpedo hit, and can quite genuinely convince themselves that they have done so when they have not. Especially is this so when they have been through danger and strain to achieve their attacks.

Moreover, the circumstances in which these attacks were carried out were unquestionably most unfavourable to success. A single battleship is a poor target for destroyers at night. It is still poorer when the destroyers are attacking separately and not as a group. Admittedly, a favourable factor in this case was the *Bismarck*'s low speed, making quick avoiding action by her impossible. But against that were the long ranges at which many of the torpedoes were fired. To obtain good torpedo results against a single ship it is generally necessary to get in to about 2,000 yards before firing. Yet on this night, not one torpedo was fired at this range. Three were fired at 4,000 yards, four at 5,000 yards, three at 6,000, four at 7,000, and two at 9,000.

The torpedoing of the enemy was not the only consideration for the destroyers to keep in mind. The screening of the British battleships against submarine attack would be a matter of importance next day, when the danger of U-boat attack would obviously have to be taken very seriously. It was, indeed, for this main purpose that the destroyers had been detached from their convoy and ordered to join the Commander-in-Chief. Yet the performance of this duty would clearly have been impeded, if not prevented, by damage incurred during the night attacks.

It is, however, pertinent to note that Captain Vian's decision to attack was regarded with evident favour in the highest quarter at the time. Though he did not know it, the question of night destroyer attacks had already formed the subject of a communication from the Admiralty to the Commander-in-Chief. About 7 p.m., Sir John Tovey had received a signal, in a code the destroyers did not hold, asking whether he had considered ordering night destroyer attacks to be made. This signal, which the Commander-in-Chief can hardly have been over-pleased to get, was sent out before the *Ark Royal*'s attack and therefore before the *Bismarck*'s rudders had been hit. But it was not cancelled after the Admiralty must have become aware from intercepted signals that the *Bismarck* had probably been rendered unmanageable, nor after the reports of the destroyer attacks had begun to come through. It is therefore a fair assumption that Captain Vian's action in attacking had the full approval of the Naval Staff.

To those on board the two British battleships, the *King George V* and the *Rodney*, keyed up for approaching battle, the dawn seemed to be long in coming. Ships' companies were at action stations but were allowed, half at a time, to sleep at their posts. Neither of the two Captains left their compass platforms during the night, though each of them took an occasional doze, sitting in a chair and resting his head against some control instrument.

At last there came that faint awareness that the darkness was not quite as black as before, which meant that morning twilight was just beginning. Commander Robertson, the Admiral's Staff Officer (Operations), suddenly remembered that his steel helmet was down below in his cabin and he decided it was time he went to get it. As he went down the ladder into the cabin flat, an astonishing sight caught his eye. Round and round the flat were running in obvious terror four large rats. They took no notice of him but continued their frenzied roundabout, slipping and bumping into each other as the ship rolled. In the circumstances, it was not a very exhilarating spectacle, and Commander Robertson was glad to seize his helmet and get quickly back on deck.

Over in the *Ark Royal*, twenty to thirty miles away, the first aircraft shadowers had already been flown off. When they came up on the lift it was still pitch dark, and so strong was the wind down the flying-deck that the aircraft were seen to rise almost vertically past the bridge as they took off. As the daylight strengthened it revealed as stormy a scene as on the day before, while overhead there was the same mantle of ragged, leaden rainclouds driving across the sky. It was raining heavily and visibility was none too good.

Sir John Tovey was watching the weather conditions as they were gradually revealed. He had been up most of the night, examining the movements of the *Bismarck* reported by the destroyers. His main anxiety was how the destroyers' calculated positions corresponded with his. Neither his flagship nor the destroyers had seen the sun for several days and there was therefore plenty of room for errors of dead reckoning on both sides. It had been for this reason that the Admiral had told the destroyers to fire star shells in order to provide a visual bearing. But there was so much rain about that nothing was seen from the flagship and the firing ships reported they were being heavily shot at. The Admiral then ordered wireless transmission on medium frequency in the hope of obtaining wireless directional bearings. But for various reasons, this was no greater success than the star shells. As day began to dawn, the Commander-in-Chief was still full of uncertainty where his enemy was. This and the poor visibility of a stormy horizon convinced the Admiral that conditions were unfavourable for an immediate action, and that it would be better to wait an hour or two for full daylight.

Sir James Somerville had just come to much the same decision regarding the intended dawn air attack. In this vile weather, there was serious risk of the aircraft mistaking friend for foe, which made it prudent for this attack also to be postponed. Sir James was none too sure of the position of either the *King George V* and *Rodney* or of the *Bismarck;* and after the narrow squeak of torpedoing the *Sheffield* the day before, he wanted no more mishaps of that kind.

Shortly before sunrise, Sir John Tovey signalled across to the *Rodney* astern of him to tell Captain Dalrymple-Hamilton that in the forthcoming action he was free to manoeuvre independently, provided he conformed generally to the Admiral's movements. The *Rodney*'s two remaining destroyers had just been obliged to leave her for the return to their base for fuel. They had waited with her as long as they were able, but could wait no longer. Indeed, they had waited, as was to be shown later, rather too long.

The Commander-in-Chief's intentions, made known at this time to his Flag-Captain and Staff, were to close the enemy as quickly as possible to about 15,000 yards and then turn for a broadside battle. But first of all the *Bismarck* had to be located, and there was doubt as to her exact direction. The solution to this urgent problem was provided by the *Norfolk*. She had been rushing south in desperate haste all night, fearful of being too late for the final drama. At a quarter-past eight, she sighted a battleship about eight miles ahead and nearly end-on. Thinking it was the *Rodney*, Captain Phillips ordered the challenge to be made. Getting no reply, he had a more careful look and then realized that the vessel he was approaching at 20 knots was none other than the *Bismarck* herself. Once more the *Norfolk*'s wheel was put hurriedly over, as it had been on the evening of the 23rd, three and a half days before, when she had run out of the mist in the Denmark Strait to find the German battleship also dangerously close.

As the *Norfolk* again sheered away to open the range, she sighted the two British battleships in the distance and was able to give them a visual link with the enemy. It showed Admiral Tovey that he was steering too much to the northward and he adjusted the course of his battleships accordingly. They were roughly in line abreast, a little short of a mile apart and were rolling considerably with the sea on the quarter. For Captain Dalrymple-Hamilton in the *Rodney* it was a family as well as a professional occasion, for his only son was a Midshipman on board the *King George V*.

At 8:43 a.m., the battleships sighted the narrow grey shape of a ship nearly end-on and about twelve miles almost ahead. It was the *Bismarck*. At last she was in sight. It was nearly a week since Sir John Tovey had first heard of her being in the fiord near Bergen; and during the long and anxious days that had followed she had seemed almost too slippery and elusive ever to be caught. But there she was now in front of him, cornered in the end. However, though she had been lamed and overtaken, none of her exceedingly sharp teeth had yet been drawn. There was the prospect of a sharp fight.

At 8:47 a.m., the *Rodney*'s 16-in. guns opened the battle. Just as the salvo was due to fall, the *King George V*'s guns flashed out and both the British battleships were in action. The *Bismarck* had not yet replied and she remained silent for another two minutes. Then she, too, joined in. "Time of flight fifty-five seconds," announced the Fleet Gunnery Officer on the Admiral's bridge in the *King George V*, as the *Bismarck*'s guns went off, and he began to count out the seconds. But he was laughingly silenced by the Admiral, who said he preferred not to be given the exact moment when a 15-in. shell would hit him in the stomach. When the splashes went up, however, it was seen that it was the *Rodney* that was being fired at.

The *Bismarck*'s first salvo was a long way short. But it did not take her long to correct her aim, and her third salvo straddled the *Rodney* and nearly hit her. Having been given latitude to manoeuvre independently, Captain Dalrymple-Hamilton altered course to port and brought his A-arcs to bear. Since he was under fire and the enemy might start getting hits at any moment, it seemed time to develop his full gunpower in retaliation.

Across the way, the *King George V* was steaming straight for the enemy in conformity with Sir John Tovey's belief in an end-on approach. The value of this manoeuvre was not, however, about to be tested. The target ship was the *Rodney*, who had her broadside open, and the *King George V* remained unfired-at during the whole time she was pointing directly for the enemy. Since the *Rodney* was not part of the Home Fleet proper, Captain Dalrymple-Hamilton was unaware of Sir John's views about the end-on method of closing the range, or no doubt the *Rodney* would at this time have been steering a parallel course to the flagship. As it was, the *Rodney*'s early turn to port to open her A-arcs was subjecting the *Bismarck* to heavier gunfire than she herself could develop, and was also taking the two British battleships steadily farther apart.

The *Bismarck*'s salvoes were continuing to fall near the *Rodney*. But the latter, as well as returning the fire with all guns, was zigzagging to dodge the fall of shot, and no hits had yet come to her. At 8:54 a.m., the *Norfolk*, who was six or seven miles to the north-east of the British battleships, opened fire with her 8-in. guns at 20,000 yards. The battleships' range was already closer than that and was shortening rapidly; and at about this time the *Rodney* brought her secondary armament into action. The *Bismarck* was now under the concentrated fire of three ships, and her own gunnery efficiency was noticeably falling off. From being regular and well-placed, her fire was becoming more and more erratic, and the *Rodney* was no longer seriously worried by it. It became known later that the *Bismarck*'s main fire control position, the ship's gunnery brain, was hit and destroyed fairly early in the action, and it is possible that the marked deterioration in the volume and accuracy of her fire can be attributed to this cause. But the mass of shells now pouring in on her would have lowered her offensive power in any case.

Twelve minutes after the commencement of the battle, the *King George V* was in to 16,000 yards and Sir John Tovey thought it time to bring the flagship's full fire to bear. After a word up the voice-pipe to Captain Patterson to tell him what was coming, the Admiral made the signal for a course of south, nearly opposite to the very wobbly path the *Bismarck* was following. A minute before nine o'clock, the *King George V* began her swing to starboard towards the new course and her after turrets were soon in action. The *Rodney,* whose independent manoeuvrings had by now taken her out to nearly three miles from the flagship, turned south two or three minutes later. She may or may not have taken in the Admiral's signal, but was under the instruction to conform generally to his movements. The *Bismarck* continued her slow course towards the north-west, yawing considerably each side of the wind. Just before the *Rodney* turned, Captain Coppinger saw a heavy shell burst on the *Bismarck*'s forecastle, and gained the impression that one of her two foremost turrets had been put out of action. He was on the bridge with Captain Dalrymple-Hamilton, taking notes of the battle, and he made an entry to this effect.

Just after the turn, the *Bismarck* transferred her fire to the *King George V,* now the leading ship. But some of her guns were no longer firing and only an occasional shot or two fell close. On the British side, fire control had been difficult from the start. Against the dull, rainy horizon, the shell splashes did not show up at all clearly and it was hard to be sure of a straddle, more particularly with three ships mingling their salvoes round the one target. As the range decreased, the spotting of the fall of shot naturally became easier: but the turn to the southward introduced a new handicap. On that course, the resultant of the gale and the ship's speed gave a relative wind straight towards the *Bismarck.* Consequently, the clouds of brown cordite smoke that belched from the British gun muzzles at each salvo were hanging irritatingly in front of the firing ships, forming a semi-opaque screen between them and the enemy, to which the funnel gases added their quota. Fortunately, radar came to the rescue to some extent, but the fire control conditions were far from ideal.

A few minutes after the turn to the south, another British ship joined in the action from the eastward. This was the cruiser *Dorsetshire.* All night she had been coming up at her highest attainable speed, guided by the reports from the destroyers. She had, however, been obliged to turn into the wind about 2 a.m. and heavy seas had been steadily knocking her speed down, first to 25 knots, then to 20. Dawn came without her having sighted anything; but at 8:23 a.m., to Captain Martin's intense relief, the *Cossack* was sighted to the westward and course was altered in her direction. Twenty-five minutes later, gunflashes were sighted almost ahead, and very shortly afterwards the *Bismarck* was seen twelve miles away, firing at something to the westward. At four minutes past nine, with the range at 20,000 yards, the *Dorsetshire* opened fire. But owing to the many shots already falling near the enemy, observation of fire was very difficult, and fire was checked after nine minutes.[5]

[5] A survivor picked up by the *Dorsetshire* is said to have told Captain Martin that it was one of the *Dorsetshire*'s shells which wrecked the *Bismarck*'s fire control position. In view of the heavy concentration of fire against the *Bismarck* and of the fact that

The run to the south by the *King George V* and *Rodney* went on for about a quarter of an hour, with the range nearly steady at 12,000 yards. Interference by cordite smoke, as already mentioned, was bad. The *King George V*'s 5.25-in. secondary armament guns came into action a few minutes after the turn, but as they made the cordite smokescreen worse still, they were ordered to cease fire two or three minutes later. During this period, ten torpedoes were fired at the enemy, six by the *Rodney* at 11,000 yards and four by the *Norfolk* at 16,000 yards. None was seen to hit, and indeed it would have been a great fluke if any had done so when fired from such ranges.

This action on opposite courses naturally made the enemy's bearing draw fairly rapidly aft, and Captain Dalrymple-Hamilton decided to turn the *Rodney* round to preserve the broadside bearing and head the enemy off. The fact that the enemy's fire was now on the *King George V* would enable the *Rodney* to make her turn without danger, and at 9:12 a.m. the wheel was put over for the new course. Once round, the *Rodney*'s full fire was again brought to bear at 8,500 yards, and she was thus able to cover the turn of the *King George V*, who came round some minutes after her.

Captain Dalrymple-Hamilton's decision to turn north on his own responsibility may seem to have been within the discretionary power allowed him to manoeuvre independently. But, in fact, it was something more than that. A stipulated condition of that power was that he must conform generally to the Admiral's movements. By no reasonable standard could he be said to be so conforming if he turned north while his Admiral was continuing to the southward. In fact, though he doubtless did not realize it at the time, Captain Dalrymple-Hamilton was reviving the famous example set 144 years before by one Commodore Nelson at

---

the survivors are most unlikely to have studied the battle observers' records, this statement can probably be explained by a prisoner's natural desire to ingratiate himself with his captors.

the battle of St. Vincent. Not since 1797 had a British battleship Captain turned out of the line of battle by his own decision until Captain Dalrymple-Hamilton did it on this occasion.

The *Rodney* was now the leading ship and, perhaps for that reason, the *Bismarck* made her again the target. Several of the enemy's shots fell very close, one being only a few yards from the starboard bow. In the *Rodney*'s torpedo flat, twenty feet below the waterline, the torpedo tubes' crew had been listening to the sounds of battle over their heads. They could feel the ship shiver each time the heavy guns roared out a salvo, and the sounds of the enemy's shells falling in the water near the ship were unmistakable. It was a bit lonely sitting down there inactive amid the death-dealing turmoil, and the torpedomen were envious of the guns' crews busy with their job of raising and ramming home the huge shells and pushing over the levers that sent the great breech blocks slamming to behind the cordite charges. It had therefore been very welcome when the torpedo flat got the order "action port" during the run south and for some time the torpedomen were hard at work loading and reloading the three-ton torpedoes into the tubes. Now after the turn, there were more thuds of enemy shells in the water, and one very loud metallic clang. The starboard tube had just been loaded, but the sluice valve door (between the tube and the sea) was found to be jammed and could not be opened. That one had been close.

The turn to the north by *Rodney* and *King George V* removed the nuisance of funnel and cordite smoke interference and enabled a good clear view at last to be obtained of the enemy ship. Both British ships were getting close, being in to 8,500 and 11,000 yards respectively, at which ranges details of the *Bismarck* were easily discernible through binoculars. Obvious signs of punishment were visible on board her. A fairly large fire was blazing amidships. Some of her guns seemed to have been silenced, and the others were firing only spasmodically. Her foremost turrets fired a salvo at 9:27, but shortly after that the *Norfolk*, who had placed herself almost ahead of the *Bismarck* for flank marking purposes, saw two of the forward 15-in. guns run down to maximum depression, as if a British hit had caused a failure of hydraulic power in the turret.

At lessening ranges, the two British battleships steamed north past the slowly moving enemy ship, pouring in a heavy fire from both main and secondary armament guns. At this relatively close distance hits on the upper works were easily seen. A large explosion occurred just abaft B turret (the upper of the two foremost turrets), which blew the back of the turret up over the bridge. Another and very spectacular hit blew away the 15-in. aloft Director, which toppled over the side. The *Rodney* fired another two torpedoes at 7,500 yards, but neither of them hit.

The unsteady crawl through the water to which the *Bismarck* had by now been reduced meant that the British battleships quickly overhauled and passed her, and soon the bearing had grown so far aft that the foremost guns were almost ceasing to bear. It would have been simpler to have shot the battle out on a more or less constant broadside bearing; but this could only be done by using approximately the same speed as the enemy. This was, however, much too low for safety in view of the probable presence of enemy submarines. The *Rodney,* therefore, began to zigzag close across the enemy's bows, firing sometimes at her starboard side, sometimes at her port and sometimes down the length of her hull. At the end of each of the *Rodney*'s zigzags, her foremost turrets would be on their extreme after bearing and firing close past the ship's bridge, where the blast was severely felt. On one occasion, it removed Captain Coppinger's steel helmet from his head with such force that it hit and knocked out a signalman standing some feet away. The former's notebook also flew out of his hand and disappeared, to be picked up later on the quarterdeck.

In order to keep well clear of the *Rodney,* the *King George V* had taken a broad sweep out and back on the enemy's beam. Moreover, she was by now (about 9:30 a.m.) suffering badly from the same complaint that had afflicted her sister ship the *Prince of Wales* in the earlier battle. Gunnery breakdowns were occurring with unpleasant frequency. Her three turrets were severally out of action from this cause for varying periods, one for as long as half an hour, while there were in addition several breakdowns at individual guns. There were times when her available firepower was down to 20 per cent of the maximum; a reduction which might, in other circumstances, have had disastrous consequences. Fortunately, the *Bismarck* had by now been pounded almost into silence. Her after turret was still firing occasionally, but the others were dumb. Her A turret guns were drooping dejectedly downwards towards the sea; those of B turret were pointing starkly into the air on a fixed bearing. At the very close ranges to which her enemies had approached, hits were smashing into her one after the other. The *Norfolk* had been firing away all the time, and just before 9:40 the *Dorsetshire* joined in again from the north-eastward, the *Rodney* becoming aware of her presence by some of her 8-in. shells falling close ahead.

By 10 a.m. the *Bismarck* was a silent, battered wreck. Her mast was down, her funnel had disappeared, her guns were pointing in all directions, and a cloud of black smoke was rising from the middle of the ship and blowing away with the wind. Inside, she was clearly a blazing inferno, for the bright glow of internal fires could be seen shining through numerous shell and splinter holes in her sides. Her men were deserting their guns, and parties of them could be seen running to and fro on the upper deck as the shells continued to rain in, and occasionally jumping over the side, to escape by watery death from the terror on board. Captain Patterson of *King George V* would have ceased fire earlier had he known of this, but the *Bismarck*'s port side was so often screened by a wall of shell splashes along her whole length that it was none too easy to notice what was happening on board her.

And her flag still flew. Ostensibly at least, she remained defiant. Though powerless and, like Sir Richard Grenville's *Revenge,* surrounded by enemies, she did not surrender: though under modern conditions the intention to surrender a ship is not too easy to indicate. Surrender or not, however, the British ships meant to sink her and as quickly as they could. At any moment, long-distance German aircraft might appear or torpedoes come streaking in from U-boats that were already quite amazingly late in arriving on the scene; while to add to the urgency there was the nagging anxiety of the acute fuel shortage. Both the *King George V* and *Rodney* should from this point of view alone have been on the way home hours ago, especially the former. There was absolutely not a moment to be lost in putting the *Bismarck* underwater. Sir John Tovey's impatience showed itself by a desire for point-blank range: "Get closer, get closer," he began to tell Captain Patterson, "I can't see enough hits."

It was indeed astonishing that the *Bismarck* was still afloat after the battering she had received. She had been pierced and rent time after time by heavy and light shells from two battleships and two cruisers. She had been torpedoed by the *Victorious*'s, and by the *Ark Royal*'s aircraft. The *Rodney* was now (10 a.m.) firing nine-gun broadsides at her from the 16-in. guns, the huge shells hitting her in threes and fours at a time. At 3,000 yards, the *Rodney* also fired her last two torpedoes, and one of them was seen to hit the *Bismarck* amidships.[6] The *Norfolk* had also fired her remaining four torpedoes from a range of 4,000 yards and believed she obtained at least one hit. But still the *Bismarck* floated.

The *Ark Royal*'s aircraft had one more attack they could make, after which all their torpedoes would have gone. Vice-Admiral Somerville had intended sending them off at dawn. But, as already mentioned, there was so much rain and low cloud about that he was afraid of their mistaking the target. Sir James had been steering north towards the supposed position of the enemy, of whose exact whereabouts he was none too sure. However, at 8:10 a.m., the *Maori* was sighted ahead and gave the *Bismarck*'s position as eleven miles nearly due north. At 0855, the distant boom of heavy gunfire was heard to the northward above the

[6] Said to be the only instance in history of one battleship torpedoing another.

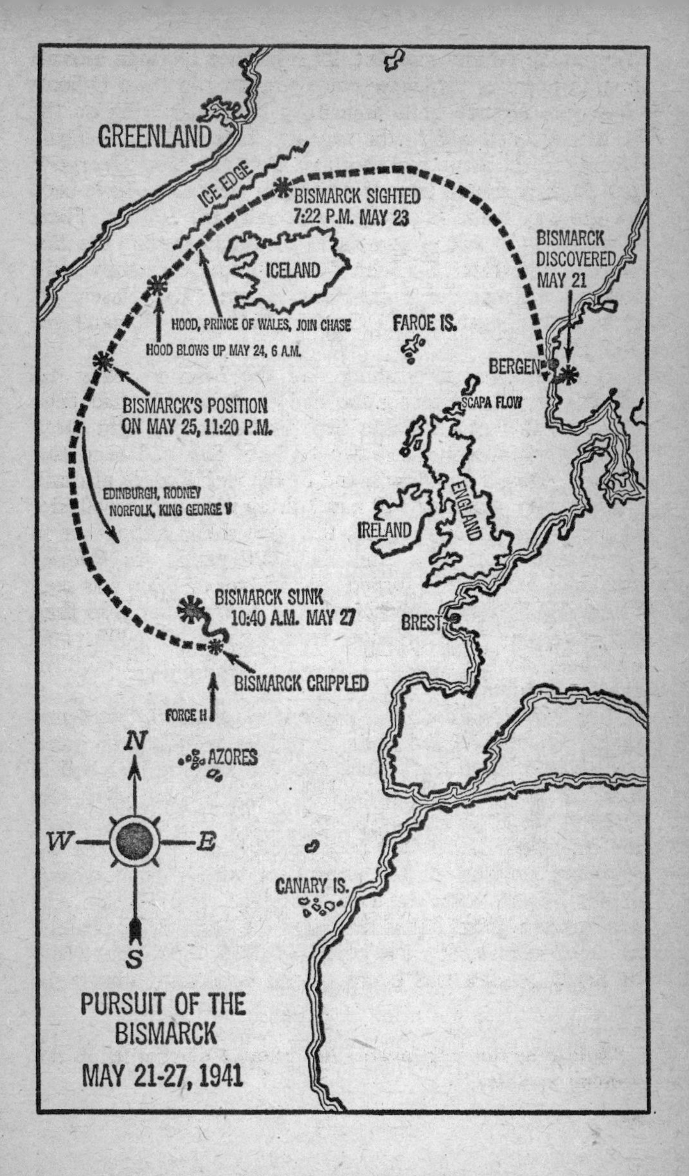

PURSUIT OF THE BISMARCK

MAY 21-27, 1941

noise of the wind, and Sir James thereupon decided to send off the striking force at once.

It was just as ticklish a job as on the day before, but the twelve Swordfish got safely away at 9:26 a.m. They formed up and went off to the northward; and just as they disappeared ahead, the clouds began to break and from the *Ark Royal* they spotted first one and then another Focke-Wulf.

The striking force soon found the *Bismarck*, but also realised that an attack on her would be very hazardous. She was being fired at from both sides by four ships, and many of their shots were going very wide. At the very close ranges too which the British ships had now got, the trajectories of their shells were almost flat. A very slight error in aim, which the rolling of the ships would facilitate, would therefore take the projectiles that just skimmed the upper works of the *Bismarck* to a distance of two or three thousand yards beyond her before they struck the water. The result was that shell splashes were going up hundreds of feet into the air a long way from the enemy, which would have been death to any aircraft that had flown into them. The aircraft therefore flew on towards the *King George V* to ask for gunfire to be ceased while they went down to the attack. But beyond having some anti-aircraft shells fired at them, they received no attention.[7]

Meanwhile, Sir John Tovey was feeling acute concern at the refusal of the *Bismarck* to sink. He had given her a hammering by gunfire that he had no conception any ship could stand. But there she was, still above water. If she could bear all that without going down, who could tell how much more she might not endure? And Sir John was already quite certain that he could not afford to spend any more time on firing at this ship. It was imperative that his force should start back. He had waited dangerously long, as it was; and every extra half-hour would make his return

[7] It is interesting to record that when Captain Patterson, who knew the mistake was being made, asked the officer responsible if he couldn't see the airmen waving at him, the officer replied he thought they were "Huns shaking their fists."

more hazardous. He looked at the burning hulk, lying deep and sluggish in the water, that had once been a fighting battleship. It was obvious to him that whether she sank now or sank later, she would never get back to harbour. At 10:15 a.m., he signalled to *Rodney* to form astern on a course of 027 degrees (about north-north-east). He was going home.

As Sir John steered away, he signalled that any ship with torpedoes was to close the *Bismarck* and torpedo her. As it happened, the *Dorsetshire* was the only ship in the immediate vicinity with any torpedoes left. Captain Martin, however, had not waited to be told, but was already using them. At 10:20, from about 3,500 yards, he fired two torpedoes at the *Bismarck*'s starboard side, one of which exploded right under the bridge. He then steered round to her port side and fired another torpedo from about 2,500 yards at 10:36. This torpedo also hit. The shattered leviathan, her colours still flying, silently heeled over to port, turned bottom up and disappeared beneath the waves. The time was 10:40. As she was turning over, Captain Martin received the Admiral's order to do what, in fact, he had already done. He at once made a signal to say that the *Bismarck* had sunk.

The great chase was over. The mighty *Bismarck* had been disposed of after a most gallant fight against superior force. All that was left of her were several hundred heads of swimming men, visible on the surface of the breaking seas. The *Dorsetshire* summoned the nearby *Maori* to help her pick up survivors. It was too rough to lower any boats, even had this been permissible. But lines were thrown out and jumping ladders let down the sides. Many of the men in the water were too exhausted to climb up them; but the *Dorsetshire* managed to haul eighty on board and the *Maori* thirty. Then came a lookout's report of a submarine periscope, and Captain Martin considered it high time to withdraw.

Duel in the Desert

The battle of the Atlantic went on—for the duration. Meanwhile, British land forces were engaging the enemy in North Africa. On September 13, 1940, the Italians under Marshal Graziani had crossed the Egyptian border, with six infantry divisions and eight battalions of tanks. Even before Italy's declaration of war in June, the Italians had been massing troops in Libya; they had their eyes on Egypt and the Suez, had built a wide highway across Libya to the Egyptian border, and turned their ports of Bengazi, Derna, Tobruk, Bardia and Sollum into supply depots for their forces.

With the French out of the war, Italy's fleet and air force made it painfully hard to supply British forces in the Mediterranean. To gain command in the Mediterranean, Britain would have to get reinforcements from her dominions—Australia, South Africa, India and New Zealand. This would take time. Fortunately, the Italians handed it to the British on a silver platter.

The Italian invasion was stopped cold at the border by light British forces, who had expected to fight a withdrawing action. The Italians' drive bogged down, at Sidi Barrani, before they could engage the main British forces at Mersa Matrûh—even these were considerably smaller than the Italian invading force. For three months the Italians dallied at Sidi, ostensibly waiting for more supplies from their depots—just some sixty miles away. Obviously the Italian army's heart wasn't in the effort—Mussolini had had to threaten Graziani with loss of command to get him to move into Egypt.

Now the British handily built up their forces at Mersa Matrûh to some 25,000 troops, and by December 15th, equipped with armor they'd previously lacked, drove the Italians back across the border, moving on into Libya and throwing encircling loops around the ports of Bardia and Tobruk. Nor did they stop there; by February 7th, Gen. Wavell's troops had pushed the Italians a full 500 miles along the North African coast to Tripolitania, capturing 130,000 prisoners, 400 tanks and 1,300 guns.

The British now needed time to consolidate their gains. The Italians would have been satisfied to hold a line at the border for the duration of the war. But the Axis command had passed over to the German Gen. Erwin Rommel. He could hardly wait to get a crack at the British. He mustered an attack by the end of March, and the British, who hadn't yet strengthened their defenses, were forced back to Bengazi, then to Tobruk, whose port facilities they decided to defend at all costs. Rommel simply bypassed Tobruk and the British had their backs against the Egyptian border.

The Germans had also been winning on the European mainland. By the end of May, 1941, they had occupied Yugoslavia, and ousted the British from Greece and Crete. Remnants of the British forces were brought to Egypt. Churchill urgently wanted an offensive to destroy Rommel's forces before the Germans could reinforce him. When he didn't get decisive action, Churchill transferred the desert command to Gen. Auchinleck who, during the autumn of 1941, gained back most of the area along the coast that Wavell had lost. Rommel, unlike the Italians before him, was retreating in good order. He built up his supplies, was reinforced by stronger air elements, and immediately struck back. By January, 1942, he had launched a drive that pushed the British back across Libya again, this time taking Tobruk along the way. On June 24th, Rommel crossed the Egyptian frontier and pushed onward; by the time he reached a position before El Alamein, his lines of communication were over-extended, and he couldn't mount the new attack he needed to break through to Cairo.

The desert war, about to enter its climactic phase, had become a conflict between fast-moving armored and motorized forces. As Churchill says, * "Tanks had replaced the cavalry of former wars . . . the fighting quality of the armored column, like that of a (naval) cruiser squadron, rather than the position where they met . . . was the decisive feature. Tank divisions or brigades . . . could form fronts in any direction so swiftly that the perils of being outflanked or taken in the rear or cut off had a greatly lessened significance. On the other hand, all depended from moment to moment upon fuel and ammunition and the supply of both was far more complicated for armored forces than for self-contained ships and squadrons at sea."

The desert fighting gave both sides a chance to perfect the art of

* *The Grand Alliance* by W. S. Churchill, pp. 557-558, published by Houghton Mifflin Co.

the hit and run raid, slicing clean through the porous defenses. During the autumn of 1942, counterattacks and raids flourished at El Alamein. A typical daredevil raid is reported in the following exploit behind Rommel's lines.

BEHIND ROMMEL'S LINES

by Capt. Douglas M. Smith
(as told to Cecil Carnes)

A British undercover man in Nazi-held Tobruk had reported to headquarters that the enemy had established an airfield outpost somewhere east of the town. He didn't know exactly where it was located, but he knew that every Saturday at dusk a fleet of supply trucks left Tobruk and headed for the outpost. So a party of our men, consisting of a captain, a sergeant and ten privates, volunteered to locate it and blow it to smithereens. They had about 500 miles to negotiate by truck, from our headquarters at Kabrit, Egypt, to the desert objective, and a patrol of Messerschmitts almost spoiled the party as it was stopped in a wadi for tea on the second day out. When the noise of their engines was heard, a camouflage net was hastily thrown over the truck and the men scattered. The enemy patrol, flying at only 1,000 feet, roared across the wadi and continued on. The truck must have looked like a pile of sand to the pilots.

It was a nerve-racking day. The fierce July sun drew out a man's juice, then boiled him in it. The heavily laden truck was stuck twice in patches of soft sand. The second time the churning wheels dug themselves in hub deep, requiring an hour of frantic shoveling to set them rolling again. A lone Nazi patrol plane, hunting for just such ground activity as this, caught them cold in an open, carpet-flat expanse. They spent a hideous hour beneath burlap camouflage mats, tormented by heat and thirst and flies, till the enemy pilot, wearied of describing aimless circles above a seemingly deserted area and droned away to the northwest.

Yet they made fair progress between delays, and did particularly well that night, by blundering onto a camel road from which the boulders had been removed. The succeeding day, too, was kind, so that the captain grunted with satisfaction as he checked their position that evening on his large-scale map.

"Barring an out-and-out catastrophe," he announced, sipping a steaming cup of tea, "we'll be near enough to our immediate goal by Saturday morning so we can cover up and sleep all day. That way we'll be fresh as daisies for the night's task."

The immediate goal was a curve some thirty miles east of Tobruk, along the coast road which was Rommel's main line of communication. It was known that at some point along the coast road, to the east of the town, the truck convoy customarily turned off into the desert. It was the raiding party's job to get into that convoy in the dark somehow —and this particular curve seemed the best place—and travel with it to the airfield outpost.

It worked out as the officer had hoped. At dusk on Saturday evening the truck was parked discreetly in a small deep ravine, out of sight of the coastal road, but not twenty yards from it. A sharp-eyed sentinel with the field glasses established himself on a bluff overlooking the road. An hour later, he came slithering down to announce he had spotted twelve sets of dimmed driving lights approaching in the distance.

"Every man to his place in the truck," said the officer, and waited till the order had been obeyed. "Now I'll let you in on the rest of our program. These trucks will be traveling, as usual, about a hundred yards apart. We will let eleven go by. Before Number Twelve comes in sight around the bend, we will cut into the road and fall in line."

"Mightn't it be better, sir, if we let all twelve go by and then fell in at the rear?" the sergeant asked.

"No," said the captain. "The men on the twelfth truck

will know they're the last in line. They'd probably be suspicious if another car turned up suddenly behind them. As it is, Number Eleven will think we're Number Twelve, and Number Twelve will think we're Number Eleven. Right? . . . When we reach the jerry camp, there are bound to be sentries at the entrance. We can't risk one of them noticing thirteen trucks, instead of the expected dozen. So, when we find ourselves getting close to the camp—and we're bound to see or hear some sign of it ahead—we break down in the middle of the road, blocking it. Jerry Number Twelve comes up, stops and asks what the trouble is. Well, we tell him—with knives. Then we park our truck beside the road, where it will be our rallying point for after the show. Privates Brewster and Guffey will stay with the car, ready to use the machine gun, if necessary, to cover our escape. Private Jones will take that gadget Captain Crumper prepared for us and proceed according to orders already given him." Captain Crumper was the explosives instructor at Kabrit. He had a fine, devilish sense of mischief.

"I think they're coming, sir," said Sam Barrett, the driver. His head was sticking out sidewise in the direction of the road. "I can hear somethin' that sounds like 'em."

"Right. Get your engine going, quietly. The noise they're making themselves will drown out ours. Be ready to start when I give the word. . . . You eight men in the back there, get down in the truck and pull the camouflage net over you. Every man check his equipment—canteen, iron ration, knife, revolver, bombs and two grenades. . . . That's Étienne Latour beside you at the rear, sergeant? Good. Better start chinning in German, you two—be in practice if you need it later. And if anything goes wrong, use your knives! One shot would give the show away."

"Here they are, sir!" whispered Barrett.

The dimmed driving lights of a truck swept into view around the curve, followed by another and another. Leaning forward to peer through the dark, the driver was studying the intervals between the units of the convoy as they flashed past the mouth of the wadi at an easy thirty-mile gait. He reported his findings with satisfaction. "Keeping a bit better than a hundred yards between 'em, sir."

"That's a break," muttered the captain. "Get ready, Sam!" He began counting aloud in a tense whisper: "Eight . . . nine . . . ten. . . . Here comes eleven. . . . Now!"

The truck shot out from the ravine as if the word had cut some invisible leash. A lurch or two, a few stiff jolts, and it took the highway smoothly, pointing east, some forty yards behind the jerry ahead and comfortably in advance of the one yet to round the curve.

"They're using no taillights!" exclaimed the captain. "Douse ours, quick!"

"Doused already, sir," was the reply from Sam Barrett. "I'd noticed it myself, sir."

"Good man! Now keep your fingers crossed for the next two or three minutes."

He crossed his own, blushing inwardly for his childish superstition. He kept his head turned, staring back at jerry No. 12, which had come out of the curve and was trailing by a scant fifty yards. The captain held his breath. What was the driver of No. 12 thinking? What had he thought when he straightened out from the curve and discovered himself so close to the truck ahead? Would he think No. 11 had fallen off the pace? Would he think he had been driving too fast himself? These Nazis were such methodical devils—would he speed up to investigate?

No. 12 was dropping back! His speed checked perceptibly till he was the required hundred meters to the rear. The captain's pent-up breath escaped in a long sigh of relief. He uncrossed his fingers and rubbed the palms of his hands on his trousers. He swallowed hard and was himself again.

"We'll be meeting Tobruk-bound trucks, I expect," the captain said. "Keep your eyes peeled."

They did presently meet a string of six empty lorries, coming head-on and presumably returning to their base from the German front for further supplies of men or matériel. They rattled past with a genial blinking of lights that Sam Barrett politely acknowledged with blinks of his own, and then the sergeant threw his voice over his shoulder cautiously, "Got a look at Number Twelve in their headlight glare, sir. Small open truck—not much of a load, I'd say—bit of canvas pulled over it. Two men on the front seat, sir."

Twenty minutes later there was an alarm that turned the captain colder than the night itself. It was three short blasts from the horn of No. 12.

The sergeant's voice was anxious as he reported, "Number Twelve put on speed a moment ago, sir. He's overhauling us fast. I think he meant that horn as a signal for us to stop!"

Another short, querulous blast from the German truck.

The captain forced himself to speak coolly, "We'd best pull up. Sergeant, this is your baby, I think. Let Latour do the talking. If a situation arises, meet it according to your best judgment. No more noise than necessary."

"We'll manage, sir," said the sergeant.

Their truck drew over to the side of the road and stopped. Twenty yards to the rear, the German did the same, and the man seated beside the driver jumped to the ground and came forward afoot. Outlined in the faint gleam of the truck lights behind him, his figure showed bulky and powerful.

The Nazi came within a yard of the truck. The sergeant and Étienne Latour sat motionless, their legs over the tailboard, their hands gripping their knives.

The German halted. He spoke, "Please, has anybody here got a match?"

"There isn't a bleedin' match in th' bunch except English," whispered Sam Barrett to the man next to him.

Étienne Latour, who had been born and raised in Alsace, replied in German. "I am sorry, my friend, but neither my comrade nor I has a match. However, here is a lighter which I will gladly lend you."

The captain moaned to himself. Latour's lighter was of French make.

Latour's voice went on serenely, "Please, you must be careful of it and give it back to me later, *hein?* I treasure it highly. It is a French lighter that I took from the body of a French major at Bir Hacheim." He hesitated, then added a detail with the delicate care of an artist. "I bayoneted him myself," he said.

The Nazi grunted his appreciation. "*So!* You were at Bir Hacheim? It must have been fun to stick those dirty French! I have heard they leave slime on one's bayonet instead of blood! Thank you, comrade; I will return your war trophy without fail." An impatient toot from truck No. 12 sped his departure. He called back gruffly. "*Auf wiedersehen!*"

"*Auf wiedersehen!*" said Étienne Latour.

"Get going, Sam," said the captain rather weakly. "Bear down on it, lad!" He was silent a minute or two while Barrett stepped on the gas, anxious to regain their ordained position before somebody came back to see where they were.

Twenty minutes more and the convoy swung sharply off the coast road to the south. The going was rougher, yet not too bad. It was obvious to the captain that the Germans had done a spot of roadwork. When they came to a steep wadi, the way down was cleared of rocks and the way up on the other side was surfaced with cord matting to afford traction.

He slid back the shield on his luminous wrist watch. It was eleven o'clock. He raised his glasses, and every time the truck mounted a rise he peered hopefully into the black distance. He didn't believe the jerries would go too deep into the desert just to establish a casual camp and airport, and he was right. At the end of an hour, the invisible track they were following topped a height and showed a cluster of pinpoint lights making a pale yellow circle in the blackness.

He announced the news quietly, without lowering his glasses, "That's it, Barrett. Half mile ahead."

"Yes, sir." Mindful of his officer, whose attention was distracted from the road, Barrett added, "Watch out, sir; we're just dipping into a wadi."

"Stop when you get to the bottom and park us across the road," the captain ordered, "as if we'd lost control and skidded, eh?"

The truck stopped with a jolt. A twist of Barrett's wrists

set the truck diagonally across the route, with one of two great rocks at each end.

Bumping and clattering, No. 12 came charging on. Barrett, standing alongside his truck and pretending it was disabled, swung the powerful beam of his flashlight straight into the faces of the two men on No. 12, thereby accomplishing three desirable results. It deepened the darkness in which the sergeant and Latour were lurking behind a rock; it blinded the two Germans, so that they halted their truck with a squealing of brakes; it startled and infuriated them, and angry men lose caution. Grumbling in gutturals, they jumped to the ground, one from each side of the cab. For luck, Sam Barrett gave them both another blinding flash from his torch.

They died quietly. The sergeant and Étienne Latour wiped and sheathed their knives, then hurriedly lugged their victims out of the roadway.

The captain began giving orders, "Tumble out, everybody! Into the jerries' truck! Make it nippy, men! . . . Barrett, get our truck parked fifty yards up the wadi; that will be our rallying point after the raid."

Latour, who was familiar with German truck controls, took the wheel and No. 12 took out after the convoy again.

"You know your mission," the captain went on. "Scatter, keep in the darkest areas as much as possible, set your fuses for thirty minutes, plant your bombs where you think they'll do the most damage. Bateson, Connolly and I will locate the airfield and fix the planes. . . . Jones, you're ready back there with Captain Crumper's gadget? We'll drop you off just before we reach the camp. Couple of minutes now."

No. 12 kept going at a rate which brought it up presently to its proper distance from No. 11. The trucks in the van of the convoy had already disappeared through a gap in what seemed a fence. Private Jones was the first to leave No. 12.

"Right-o, Jones! On your way, and good luck."

"Yes, sir. Good hunting, sir!" A thump and a metallic clunk from the tin container he was carrying announced Private Jones' contact with the desert. Since Brewster and

Guffey were back in the British truck with the machine gun, acting as rearguard and reserve, the party was now reduced to nine.

No. 12 lumbered through a broad gap in a triple fence of barbed wire. The sentries at each side were leaning idly on their rifles, looking at the vehicle incuriously. By the time No. 12 came into the parking space, the men of No. 11 were walking away from the dark bulk of their charge, heading for tobacco and coffee and beer.

A moment later, the driver shut off the engine and put out his headlights. Over his shoulder, the officer gave the order to jump out.

"I think I've spotted the airfield, sir," Bateson whispered. "Got a glimpse against the sky of a pole with what looks like a wind sleeve on it."

They slid through the night. Cautiously, they made a wide detour around the one building that showed signs of human life. A hum of voices came from it, and a paper-thin strip of light from an otherwise closely shuttered window. It was a cookhouse. They reached the airfield without incident and halted for a brief survey.

"Planes dispersed around the edges, of course," murmured the captain. "Connolly, you circle the field to the left. I will go this way. . . . Bateson, there's a group of buildings down at that end; pilots' quarters or repair shops, probably. Take care of them. When you've used up all your bombs, you two, don't hang around waiting for me. Leg it for our truck and hop aboard."

Left to himself, the captain swung to the right for his tour of the field. Presently he found what he was looking for—a wall of rubble and logs and rocks. Tucked behind it were nine planes—bombers and fighters. With typical attention to symmetry and neatness, the Germans had lined them up in threes, their wing tips almost touching. The captain placed one bomb in the center plane of each trio and went on his way rejoicing. He found two more revetments, but to his disappointment there were only three planes in the first and just one in the second. Still, that brought his total up to thirteen. If Connolly did as well, the night's bag would be something to shout about.

He tucked one of his two remaining bombs into the vitals of a small tractor which was probably used for odd jobs around the field. The other he placed under a tool shed. Then he turned and went back over the path by which he had come, moving in the same swift and stealthy fashion.

The officer was abreast of the cookhouse when it happened.

Out of the darkness near the building came a loud, harsh challenge in German, "Halt there! Who are you? Hands up! Quick, somebody! A light here! I've got—"

The shout ended on a gasp. But the alarm had been given. The cookhouse door was flung open and a dozen men boiled out. An arc light flashed on, illumining the whole area. It showed a thickset man on the ground, and another just yanking a dagger from the huddled body. The man with the knife headed for the nearest darkness, running like a frantic deer. Six or seven of the cookhouse contingent chased after him.

When beyond the circle of light, the captain whipped out his revolver and fired at the leading pursuer. The Nazi fell, rolling over and over. The men at his heels dropped in their tracks, flattening their bodies on the ground.

Lights were springing on everywhere. The post was a bedlam of shouting. Then, as the captain sprinted for the exit, from a point in the desert just beyond the southern boundary of the camp came an ear-splitting racket. The staccato explosions rose and fell convincingly, settled to a steady roar, then died away. No more than thirty seconds, just long enough for Private Jones to race away, elapsed between the revolver shot and the moment when Captain Crumper's special gadget went into action.

While the Germans were giving tongue to the south, the raiders made haste to escape to the east. The captain was about thirty yards from the gap in the barbed wire by which they had driven in. He remembered the two guards, and the lamp at one side which lighted the vicinity. He hugged the shadows and went slowly forward, revolver in hand. He stood still when the gap was in clear view. The light was still burning. That meant a nasty twenty-yard sprint in full view of anyone who happened to be around; the unattractive alternative was a try at breaking through or climbing the fences. Hardly practicable, with every passing second cutting into his margin of safety. The truck would not wait long, even for the party leader, nor would he want his men to risk their lives for a laggard. He must make a dash for it. Where the devil were those guards?

Abruptly, he saw them. One was stretched full length on the ground in the straight shadow of a fence post. Across the gap the other was doubled over the top strand of barbed wire, a monstrous human clothespin, his arms and legs dangling grotesquely. Guerrillas had passed that way. The captain put his head down and sprinted into the desert.

The wadi at last. The truck should be fifty yards to his right and a bit farther on. Rashly, he left the road and tried for a short cut. In half a minute he was lost. He stood, panting, a little more nervous than he cared to admit, even to himself. He looked about him and saw only darkness; he listened, and heard nothing. He drew in his breath sharply. Could the truck have gone?

Ears as keen as his own were listening too. Perhaps they had heard his stumbling step. Through the darkness, not at all from the direction he expected, came the softly whistled refrain of a barrack-room ditty then popular in the camp at Kabrit. He whistled it back, and his spirits revived. In a minute he was with his men, asking for reports.

"Three missing, sir," said the sergeant. "No use going back to look for them, sir. They copped it fair. I saw it. Four of us, including Sam Barrett, got twisted and came up against the wire. I found a hole and turned to call them. Then a light went on somewhere. There was a burst of machine-gun fire." The sergeant cleared his throat. "That's all, sir."

With Connolly at the wheel, the truck moved out of the wadi. The officer jumped out when the big car was safely over the sky line. He called his men and led the way back to the crest. "May as well see some of the show," he said, adding, "after all, we paid our admission."

They crouched, looking back in the direction of the Nazi camp. They were barely settled before the night split open in a crimson burst of flame that streamed to the heavens.

A crashing report almost deafened them, a concussion shivered the air, and even at that distance shook the ground beneath them.

"That's Number Twelve, the bus we rode in," said the sergeant. "The first half-hour bomb was planted in her."

With No. 12 still hurling destruction in every direction as lot after lot of ammunition exploded, a minor sheet of flame shot up to the left. Then the show really hit its stride and pyrotechnical effects came too fast and close together to be identified. There were two more major upheavals. One appeared to be a second truck of explosives possibly fired by burning debris from No. 12. The other was a thunderous fiery catclysm. The sergeant said he believed it was an ammunition dump he had mined.

A big stack of gasoline tins sent a great curtain of flame to the sky. By its light, the officer was able to get a clear view of the scene through his glasses. He ran over the score in his mind: twenty planes, an ammunition dump, two truckloads of ammunition and explosives, storehouses of food and miscellaneous supplies, a tractor, the gasoline dump, officers' quarters, a big barracks; he didn't try to estimate the number of smaller buildings and tents demolished. Against it he set the loss of three men killed in action, and the balance did not please him.

"They'll rebuild this camp," he said. "Now that we know the way here, I'd like to come back in a week or ten days and do a really good job."

They did just that, and blew it to pieces again without losing a man.

The Tide Turns

The El Alamein stalemate dragged on. In July, 1942, Churchill himself went to Cairo to relieve Gen. Auchinleck; he appointed Gen. Alexander as Commander of the Middle East Forces, and Gen. Montgomery as Commander of the 8th Army. October 23rd was picked as the jumping-off date against Rommel. The British 8th Army got major reinforcements. Two new divisions arrived from Britain, the armor grew to over 1,000 tanks—half of them Grants and Shermans furnished by the U.S.—and a powerful artillery concentration was put together.

The air force of fighters and bombers now totaled 1,200 planes, and the R.A.F. flew air strikes against troops, communications, convoys and airfields. The Royal Navy harassed Axis shipping, sinking more than 200,000 tons trying to reach Rommel.

The way the troops lived in the desert, waiting for the attack to develop, is described by Maj. H. P. Samwell, author of *An Infantry Officer with the Eighth Army.* He was then a lieutenant with the Argyll and Sutherland Highlanders, slated to lead his platoon in the attack on Rommel October 23rd. (Maj. Samwell was later killed in the Ardennes salient on January 12, 1945.) He wrote:

"Early in October we had taken over a sector in the front just above Alamein Station, a single railroad line which ran parallel to a road which was little more than a track. North of this line there was a further expanse of desert and then the main road to Mersa Matrûh, a modern tarred highway. On the far side of this were cliffs leading down to the long stretch of white sand bordering the sea.

"We had lived in boxes, i.e., large areas capable of holding a complete brigade boxed in on all sides by minefields with several recognizable exits. We were beginning to get used to the sun, but the flies were appalling. One couldn't raise a piece of bread and jam from plate to mouth without being covered with flies. They buzzed around one's head, eyes, mouth and ears. Every precaution was taken with food, latrines, etc., but it was difficult to stop men from throwing rubbish away or even not using latrines during the night, when they had to go anything up to fifteen times (from dysentery) and at night it was quite possible to get lost by moving just fifty yards from one's 'bivy,' so completely featureless was the desert. The training was dreadfully hard and monotonous and nearly all of us were feeling ill in varying degrees."

The task facing the 8th Army was to rip a hole in the German line. It was decided that a night engagement was preferable for the break-through, when a full moon would be up. A path through the mines had to be cleared before the infantry and armor could proceed.

On October 23rd, one thousand guns commenced firing on the German frontal positions. Sgt. J. K. Brown, a mortarman with the 8th Army, in an article that appeared in *The Saturday Evening Post* in 1943, describes the opening barrage:

"At 2140 hours a wide half moon of flashes rent the night sky to the zenith. An instant later the first ear-splitting crash of that perfectly co-ordinated fire order tumbled from the sky. Backward and forward the guns flickered and flashed as battery after battery opened fire. For twenty minutes the mighty artillery concentration roared and hammered a deafening chorus. The sound of thousands of shells falling on the enemy was like the sound of a hailstorm in a city of corrugated iron with the rumble of 10,000 drums. It was appalling."

Then the mortars joined in: "with a hiss and a cloud of sparks, the first salvo leaped from the mortar batteries in what was to be heaviest mortar barrage ever directed against any one position. At the same instant a regiment of heavy machine guns began to add their shrill clamor now to the almost indescribable uproar. Half a million rounds were to pour from the muzzles before cease fire. At 25 minutes to 2 the barrage lifted. The gun crews were exhausted and the barrels were so hot they burned through the thick gloves of the men who handled them.

"For minutes after the barrage ceased there was silence—complete silence. Then of a sudden a weird thin cry rose out of the ground ahead of us. It was the shout of the charging infantrymen. Slowly the sound grew in volume until it was something no longer human. I felt my hair bristle as I listened.

"Scores of bright illuminating flares began to dance along the enemy lines and machine guns raked the minefields and forward slopes of the long ridge. The action was taking place ahead of me and I could see nothing; but presently wounded men, some walking, some on stretchers, began to drift past us. Prisoners came in, and the first accounts of the action with them."

ATTACK AT EL ALAMEIN

by Maj. H. P. Samwell

It was part of the battle plan that Rommel should be made to expect that the main attack would come in the south across the ground recently fought over in his own attack. In order to strengthen that belief the whole division and many others were first moved south, where we camped in an area which had been made to look as obviously as possible like a concentration area. Dummy trucks and tanks were scattered about, and large numbers of real trucks and armoured cars were concentrated here. The German reconnoitring planes duly came over and reported these concentrations; then on the night of the 22nd-23rd October we quietly moved back north and took up positions already dug for us just behind the front. Strict orders were given that there was to be no movement after dawn, and for a whole day we had to lie cramped in temporary slit trenches waiting for night. We could not even move out to relieve nature, and one can imagine the discomfort we suffered.

The tension was almost unbearable and the day dragged terribly. I spent the time going over and over again the plan of attack, memorising codes and studying the over-printed map which showed all the enemy positions from the air. Oddly enough, though keyed up, I did not feel any fear at this time, rather a feeling of being completely impersonal, as if I were waiting as a spectator for a great event in which I was not going to take any active part.

After dark there was tremendous activity: last-minute visits by commanders and minor adjustments in plans. And

This selection is condensed from two chapters of the author's *An Infantry Officer with the Eighth Army.*

then a hot meal was brought up. Most of us were too excited to eat much, but I felt better after I had had some hot soup. About 9 p.m. we moved forward and took up our positions on the start line—a taped line stretching across the open desert just in front of the forward positions. It was deathly still and a full moon lighted the bleak sand as if it were day. Suddenly the silence was broken by the crash of a single gun, and the next moment a mighty roar rent the air and the ground shook under us as salvo after salvo crashed out from hundreds of guns. Shells whined over our heads in a continuous stream, and soon we saw the enemy line lit up by bright flashes. One or two fires broke out and the ground became clearer than ever. It seemed a long time before the enemy started to reply, but finally they did so, weakly at first, then gradually growing in strength. I could imagine the German gunners having just settled in for another quiet night's sleep, tumbling out of their bivies bewildered and still half asleep. Some of them would never reach their guns, and others would arrive to find their guns blown sky high.

Still I felt the same impersonal air of a spectator. Both sides were concentrating on each other's gun-sites, and no shells landed anywhere near us. Time passed and the firing continued, sometimes dying down only to start again with increased intensity; then suddenly I noticed a difference—our shells were now passing very close over our heads and bursting, it seemed to me, only a couple of hundred yards ahead. It was the signal to prepare to advance; our guns were now shelling the enemy's forward positions. I looked at my watch and saw there was still three minutes to go. I felt ice cool, and remember feeling very grateful that I was. Oddly enough I don't remember the actual start—one moment I was lying on my stomach on the open rocky desert, the next I was walking steadily as if out for an evening stroll, on the right of a long line of men in extended order. To the right I could dimly see the tall thin figure of the major commanding the other forward company. He had a megaphone, and was shouting down the line, "Keep up there on the left—straighten up the line." I turned to my batman, who was walking beside me, and told him to run along the line and tell the sergeant in charge of the left-hand platoon to keep his direction from the right.

I suddenly discovered that I was still carrying my ash stick. I had meant to leave it at the rear Company H.Q. with the C.Q.M.S. and exchange it for a rifle. I smiled to myself to think I was walking straight towards the enemy armed only with a .38 pistol and nine rounds of ammunition. Well, it was too late to do anything about it now, but I expected that someone would soon be hit and I could take his. I began to wonder, still quite impersonally, who it would be; perhaps myself! in which case I wouldn't need a rifle. Then I heard a new sound above the roar of the guns and the explosion of shells. The sharp rat-tat-tat of Breda and Spandau machine-guns—streams of tracer bullets whined diagonally across our front, not more than twenty yards ahead. We must be getting near the first enemy positions. I asked the pace-checker on my right how many paces we had done. He grinned and said he had lost count; then crump-crump-crump! a new sharper note. This was something that affected us—mortar shells were landing right among us. I heard a man on my left say, "Oh, God!" and I saw him stagger and fall. The major was shouting again. I couldn't hear what he said, but his company seemed to be already at grips with the enemy. At that moment I saw a single strand of wire ahead about breast high. I took a running jump at it and just cleared it. My sergeant, coming behind, started to climb over it, and immediately there was a blinding flash and a blast of air struck me on the back of the neck. I never saw that sergeant again. I remember wondering what instinct had made me jump that wire. Strange? I hadn't been thinking of booby-traps. We had broken into a run now—why, I don't know. Nobody had given any order. A corporal on my left was firing his Bren gun from the hip. I wondered if he was really firing at anything. Then suddenly I saw a head and shoulders protruding from a hole in the ground. I had already passed it and had to turn half round. I fired my pistol three times, and then ran on to catch up the line.

The line had broken up into blobs of men all struggling together; my faithful batman was still trotting along beside me. I wondered if he had been with me while I was shooting. My runner had disappeared, though; and then I saw some men in a trench ahead of me. They were standing up with their hands above their heads screaming something that sounded like "Mardray." I remember thinking how dirty and ill-fitting their uniforms were, and smiled at myself for bothering about that at this time. To my left and behind me some of the N.C.O.s were rounding up prisoners and kicking them into some sort of formation. I waved my pistol at the men in front with their hands up to sign them to join the others. In front of me a terrified Italian was running round and round with his hands above his head screaming at the top of his voice. The men I had signalled started to come out. Suddenly I heard a shout of "Watch out!" and the next moment something hard hit the toe of my boot and bounced off. There was a blinding explosion, and I staggered back holding my arm over my eyes instinctively. Was I wounded? I looked down rather expecting to see blood pouring out, but there was nothing—a tremendous feeling of relief. I was unhurt. I looked for the sergeant who had been beside me; he had come up to take the place of the one who had fallen. At first I couldn't see him, and then I saw him lying sprawled out on his back groaning. His leg was just a tangled mess. I realised all at once what had happened: one of the enemy in the trench had thrown a grenade at me as he came out with his hands up. It had bounced off my boot as the sergeant shouted his warning, and had exploded beside him. I suddenly felt furious; an absolute uncontrollable temper surged up inside me. I swore and cursed at the enemy now crouching in the corner of the trench; then I fired at them at point-blank range—one, two, three, and then click! I had forgotten to reload. I flung my pistol away in disgust and grabbed a rifle—the sergeant's, I think—and rushed in. I believe two of the enemy were sprawled on the ground at the bottom of the square trench. I bayoneted two more and then came out again. I was quite cool now, and I started looking for my pistol, and thinking to myself there will be hell to pay with the quartermaster if I can't account for it. The firing had died down and groups of men were collecting round me rather vaguely; just then a man shouted and fired a single round. I afterwards learnt that one of the enemy in the trench had heaved himself up and was just going to fire into my back when my man saw him and shot him first.

Our orders were to consolidate for fifteen minutes before moving on. I suddenly wondered what had happened to Company Headquarters and my company commander. He and I were the only two officers, commander and second-in-command. We had agreed that he should bring up Company H.Q. and the reserve platoon behind, while I led the forward platoons. I started to walk back, and at that moment the strange lull was abruptly ended by four shells exploding all round me. One covered me in sand, but I wasn't hurt; I found the company commander sitting on the ground trying to get through to Battalion H.Q. on the wireless. I gave him a quick report, but he was only half listening, still trying to get through. The commanding officer appeared from nowhere and asked him how things were going; the company commander replied and then turned to me. I told them we had taken the position and the men were lying resting and watching a few yards in front of the position. The commanding officer said, "Good work," and disappeared. The company commander said, "My God, you have left some pretty sights behind you; what was it like? I haven't fired a shot yet." I was quite surprised that he had seen the result of our fight, for I hadn't realised that we had been still advancing while fighting and had thought that the only positions had been those I had just left in front. I asked him to give me the reserve platoon and I would detail the right forward platoon to drop into reserve. There were very few of them left. He agreed, and I went forward again.

The stretcher-bearers were at work carrying the wounded to the battalion line of advance between the two forward companies. I remember reorganising the forward platoons, but again don't remember actually starting forward; I just found myself on the move. I heard the other company's piper starting to play just before we had bumped the enemy, and I wondered what had happened to our piper. I sent my new runner back to ask for him, but he never arrived, and the runner didn't return either. Afterwards I learnt he was wounded on the way.

All this time shells were landing among us, but suddenly there was a new danger: we were walking into our own barrage; shells were screaming above our heads and landing just in front of us. The platoon commander of the left platoon of the other company came across to me just at that moment and remarked, "We're going too fast; those are our shells, aren't they?" I agreed, and he went over to the major, his company commander, and warned him. At first the latter wouldn't agree to stop, but at that moment more shells of our own guns landed just in front and we felt the blast. I went across and persuaded him that we were ahead of time. We agreed to stop.

I pulled my men back a few yards to get completely out of the danger zone, and sent word back to my company commander asking him to come up closer. There was only supposed to be fifty yards between forward platoons and Company H.Q. and I couldn't see him. The runner reported that he couldn't find either the company commander or Company H.Q. or the reserve platoon. While my attention was on this, the other company had decided to advance again as the barrage had lifted. I didn't see them go and they failed to warn me. I found myself out in the "blue" alone with about forty men. I went over to the left flank to find out what had happened to the regiment that was supposed to be there. They weren't there, and I learnt afterwards that they never got past the first minefield.

My first feelings on realising that the company on my right had carried on without me was one of intense irritation, but when I discovered there was no one on my left either, my anger turned to fear. For the first time that night I was afraid; a nauseating wave of terror went right through me as I realised I was quite alone with the remains of two platoons; my company commander and Company H.Q. had disappeared together with the wireless; the "pilot" officer must have gone with the other company (we were sharing him). Instinct told me that I had gone too far to the left. All this time we had been steadily advancing again, and I started to swing to the right. I was still scared stiff, not at the shells that were exploding round us, but at the thought of being all alone, cut off from the battalion and even my Company H.Q. I was to find—and so was the battalion later—that the failure of the unit on my left to keep up was to cost us dearly. We came to another enemy position; they surrendered without fighting, and we didn't waste time mopping up. I was so anxious to make contact with someone again. It appeared that many of the enemy at this position scuttled down the trenches to the left and remained in the gap where the unit on my left should have been, until we had passed, and then filtered back and shot up the reserve companies and Battalion H.Q. who were coming up behind. I was to be blamed for not finishing them off, but if I had attempted to chase them right across a battalion front I should have been hopelessly lost, while at the same time failing to secure my own objective.

I was still feeling terribly afraid and lonely when I heard a shout behind, and up came a platoon of the reserve company under the second-in-command, and with them was the remains of my own Company H.Q. What a wave of relief swept over me! Immediately the fear vanished. I had someone to discuss the position with. It appeared that a shell landed right among my Company H.Q. just after I had left it, badly wounding the company commander and laying out the signals; however, the reserve company's platoon had a wireless with them, so we were all right. The platoon commander told me I was still too far to the left, and we wheeled half-right. Soon we came to another enemy position, which we recognised as our final objective. The enemy put up a half-hearted fight here, but soon gave in; but most of them escaped to the left again, and again I didn't consider it advisable to chase them with the few men I had left. We advanced a further 300 yards and then started to dig in. There was still no sign of the other company, but I was convinced I was in the right place. I got through to Battalion H.Q. by wireless and reported myself in position. The officer who had joined me went off to reconnoitre, and returned shortly to say that the other forward company was already dug in 200 yards on our right.

I felt elated by this news. It was almost dawn before we were finally dug in. We were left completely unmolested by the enemy, and our own and their artillery had stopped firing. Apart from the occasional sounds of small-arms fire well to our right, everything was peaceful. After stand-to I posted sentries, and leaving my company sergeant-major in charge settled into a trench with the two signallers of the reserve company's platoon and went to sleep. The officer commanding the reserve platoon dug in near me.

I was wakened at 8:30 a.m. by my batman with some "breakfast"—half a tin of bully, two biscuits, and a mug of water. I made out reports of casualties, and then, crouching down gingerly, made my way towards the position which had been pointed out to me as Battalion H.Q. Gradually, as there was no sign of firing, I became more daring, and ended by walking normally up to the trench which the commanding officer and adjutant were sharing. It was very small, and their legs were all mixed up together. Just at that moment a tank away on the right started firing, and the shells whistled unpleasantly close by over my head. I hastily jumped into the trench, squatting precariously on the combined legs of the two occupants. I told the commanding officer the main events of the previous night and gave him the casualties, which were high. The adjutant offered me a swig of rum, and after he had pointed out where the ammunition dump was, I started back to the company, passing through the other forward company on the way and stopping a moment to compare notes. There was no sign of the enemy, though I was to learn later that they were less than 300 yards away.

About mid-day on Sunday, 25th October, the commanding officer called a conference; it was obvious to all that our position was precarious so long as the left flank remained exposed. It was decided that one reserve company should stride across the mouth of this gap and capture the original objective of the unit which had still failed to put in an appearance, thus bottling up an enemy element still left in the gap, and at the same time making contact with the unit which had gained its objective on the far side.

The attack was to be made early in the afternoon, but was cancelled at the last moment in favour of a three-company night attack timed for 10 p.m. that night. We returned to our company areas, and at this time the major who had led the company on my right was wounded by shrapnel. The loss of officers was already serious; the two original forward companies had two officers between them—myself and one captain transferred from the right reserve company. This company had a company commander and one subaltern left; the fourth company had been split up. One platoon, the one that had joined me the previous night under the second-in-command, was still with me; the rest of the company which had been detailed to come up on the tanks had disappeared together with the tanks. I learnt later that they had been held up by an unexpectedly large and uncharted minefield. The total strength of the rifle companies available was not more than 150 all ranks. Our senior N.C.O. casualties had been heavy also.

We lay in our holes during the afternoon; there was desultory shelling and mortar fire; some tanks came up, and, moving forward to a rise in the ground ahead of us, lined up as if for a review, and we were further depressed by the sight of one after the other being potted off like the sitting ducks they were. In the late afternoon, while we were dozing in our holes, the enemy mortar fire suddenly grew in intensity and shells exploded all round us. At first I thought it was a prelude to the expected counter-attack, but soon we were amazed to see a company of another battalion advancing in extended line diagonally across our front, parallel to the main enemy positions. As they came level with us the enemy opened up with machine-guns to support their mortars, and bullets hissed angrily over our heads as we crouched in our holes, occasionally peeping gingerly over the top to watch this extraordinary and unexpected performance. I was to learn later that our own H.Q. were as mystified as we were. Two or three men of this advancing force fell close to our positions, and we crawled out to pull them into our holes. When they had advanced about two hundred yards beyond us, they went to earth and burrowed themselves in. We never saw them again, and I never discovered how they came to be there.

The rest of the day passed uneventfully. At 9:30 p.m. we prepared to move to the start-line. Some rum had come up, but there was not enough for each man to get the regulation tablespoon swig. Most of the N.C.O.s and myself had to stand down. Just after we arrived at the start-line the two platoons of the missing company came up, and the platoon which had been with me left to rejoin its company. I had now only thirty-two men, a company sergeant-major, two corporals, and myself. I was in the centre with the two original reserve companies on each flank. It was brilliant moonlight and we must have been seen by the enemy before we started; also the last-minute arrival of the last company, and the other reserve company being on the start-line, caused a certain amount of noise and confusion, and before we started the enemy were firing at us.

We started to advance; this time we had no artillery support, for the object had been to surprise the enemy. An officer in a reconnoitring car had reported earlier that the position was only lightly held by frightened Italians who had tried to surrender to him, but as he was alone and under heavy shell-fire, he had been unable to stay to round them up. This was cheering news and we advanced confidently. We had only gone a few yards when streams of machine-gun tracer bullets whistled across our front, intersecting at a point about 100 yards directly ahead of us. The enemy were firing across our front on fixed lines; some mortars added to our discomfort, but we pressed on. It was a strange feeling approaching the first almost continuous stream of machine-gun tracer, knowing that the next step would take us into it; we crossed it with a few casualties, but looking to my flanks I discovered I was again alone, and the fear of the night before returned with the same sickening intensity. We could hear sounds of heavy firing and shouting on our left, and I guessed that the left-hand company had run into some enemy positions. There was no sign at all from the right-hand company.

We continued to advance, and then ahead I saw barbed wire: breaking into a trot we jumped over and started to rush the positions we now saw clearly ahead. We saw German helmets, and I cursed that reconnoitring officer for his misleading information. A machine-gun opened up not more than fifteen yards half left from me; I saw the tracer bullets coming straight for me and I could clearly see the heads and shoulders of the three men manning the gun. The next second I felt a violent blow on my right thigh. I spun completely round and, recovering my balance, carried on; after going a dozen paces my leg suddenly collapsed under me and I fell forward. The men following, mistaking my involuntary action for intention, followed suit, and we lay there, about a dozen of us, not more than twenty yards from the enemy with bullets whistling over our heads. Although I found I couldn't get up, I felt no pain, and raising myself on one arm I shouted for them to rush in at the bayonet point. They did not respond at once; I think they were waiting for me to get up, and there were no N.C.O.s left. Then a corporal from the reserve section doubled up to me and asked what was happening. Almost incoherent with anger at the delay which was making our chances of taking the position less likely every moment, for the enemy were bound to realise soon how few there were of us, I shouted "Get in," and for the first time I remember I swore at my men. The company sergeant-major came up at that moment, and at the same time something little short of a miracle happened. The enemy shouted to us, and we saw that they had their hands up. The men jumped up and rushed in, and I dragged myself after them.

As I drew level with the machine-gun post three Germans jumped out and ran off as hard as they could. I had my pistol in my hand (I must have dropped my rifle when I fell). I fired four times, and saw one pitch forward on his face. The men then returned for me and carried me into a deep dug-out and laid me on a bunk beside other wounded. The blankets were still warm from the bodies of the Germans who had been sleeping there. There was a tin of cold coffee on the floor, and a stretcher-bearer gave me a drink.

The company sergeant-major came in and reported that they had rounded up prisoners, including one officer. I asked him to help me out so that I could supervise the defence and interview the officer prisoner. I knew I must get some information at once, for we were in a dangerous position. At first the German wouldn't talk and I had to use a little persuasion. Finally I learnt that they were an Austrian unit with German officers and that they had been rushed up to relieve the Italians that evening after dusk; so the reconnoitring officer's report was true after all.

Just then I saw some of our own men and recognised the company sergeant-major of the right-hand company. He was going off at an angle beyond the position. I shouted to him to come over, but he shouted something I couldn't hear and carried on; then I heard shouting on my left, and the left-hand company came rushing in. I shouted for an officer, for I wanted to hand over quickly as I was feeling very faint. A subaltern came over and rather indignantly asked me what I wanted, saying I was keeping him back from the fighting. I answered rather irritably that the fighting was all over and I wanted him to take over the defence for the inevitable counter-attack which I was expecting any moment. He still answered aggressively, "Why the hell can't you do it? I have my own platoon to look after." The German officer was still standing by, and I felt furious that he should hear this stupid squabbling and prayed he couldn't understand English. I answered angrily, "I order you to take over at once. I am wounded." He said, "Oh! Sorry, I didn't realise." He went off and I lay down again, but I wasn't happy in this dug-out. I felt too closed in and wanted to know what was happening, and if we were to be overrun in the expected counter-attack I wanted a chance to defend myself. I called to my batman, and he helped me out and dug me a shallow hole on the perimeter of a slight rise. He brought me a Bren gun and told me that the company commander of the left company was organising all-round defence and there was no need to worry. I felt much happier with the gun and fired a few rounds to make sure it was O.K. There was a good deal of movement going on on my right, but I couldn't see anything. I heard what I thought was a carrier, and shortly after an N.C.O., who had gone out to reconnoitre on his own initiative, came back to report that there were two enemy anti-tank guns about 300 yards out, and he thought they were preparing to fire on us. I told him to pass on this information to the left-hand company commander who was now in charge: he did so and returned shortly to say with disgust, "He isn't taking any action." I was puzzled, but I knew this company commander was an excellent officer and so presumed there was some reason.

The counter-attack didn't materialise, and later on I got two men to carry me farther into the perimeter, where they prepared a deep trench for me. Shortly after a wounded German was brought in. I got the men to bring him up to my trench and started to question him. He answered very listlessly; told me he was an Austrian, he was too old for active fighting, and that the officers were all Germans and they didn't get on with them. He kept asking when the doctor would be coming. The original plan was for Battalion H.Q. to move forward after us and come up when we had taken the position, so I told him quite cheerfully that we would both be safely in hospital before dawn. This cheered him up a lot, and he said he was glad he was out of it all. He told me he was a machine-gunner and pointed to the post where I had seen the three men running out, and I remembered I had shot one. I asked him where he was wounded, and he said, "In the back." This struck me as a coincidence; perhaps he was the very man that shot me and perhaps I had shot him, and now we were talking together like polite strangers in a railway carriage.

At this moment the enemy, who had obviously heard that we had captured the position, started mortaring us. It was deadly accurate and most uncomfortable. A trench nearby, with some light casualties in it, got a direct hit. The Austrian dragged himself into the other half of my trench; I didn't stop him. We lay in silence together for a long time, and I think I dozed off; at any rate I suddenly realised he was speaking to me again. *"Wann kommt der Arzt?"* he almost whined. I answered rather impatiently, "Oh, he'll be here soon." Then he said something I couldn't understand, but he pointed at my drill shorts, and I realised that they were soaked in blood. He stretched across, obviously in considerable pain, and I tried to stop him, but he insisted. Apparently the bullet had gone through the fleshy part of the thigh, coming out at the other side, and when the stretcher-bearer had hastily bandaged me he had placed the field dressing on the place where the bullet had entered, whereas of course it was bleeding from the place of exit. With great difficulty the Austrian bandaged it again, using his own field dressing. I felt guilty for having spoken so abruptly to him, and when he had finished I did my best to dress his wound. It was a bullet wound right between the shoulder-blades, and the bullet was still in. It was hardly bleeding at all and there was little I could do. I gave him my haversack as a pillow and he was pathetically grateful. I asked him if he was married, and he immediately started to fumble in his tunic pocket and brought out the inevitable family photo. He had been detailed to a machine-gun crew that afternoon and had only been in position two hours before we arrived. He had never fired a machine gun before that night. I talked feverishly, struggling to remember my German. I don't think he understood half I said, but I had to talk to keep my mind off realities; then I saw he was asleep. I relaxed, and suddenly I felt very tired.

The dawn was just breaking, and I thought to myself, "Well, I am excused stand-to this morning." I must have slept for three hours. I had dreadful dreams. When I woke up, the sun was glaring down on me in its full intensity. It was very silent. I was perspiring all over. My mouth was horribly dry and had a dreadful taste. I felt for my water-bottle; I remembered I had unstrapped it to give the Austrian a drink. It was only half full, but I knew I had my reserve bottle in my haversack under the Austrian's head. Then in horror I remembered that I had taken it out the night before while in the dug-out to give a wounded man a drink. Had I put it back? I couldn't remember. It was a pity to disturb the Austrian when he was sleeping so peacefully; but was he sleeping? I looked at him again; his skin was all drawn in and he was deathly white. Had he died in the night? I stretched over and felt his pulse; it was beating weakly. He stirred and murmured, *"Wann kommt der Arzt?"* I replied, *"Bald,"* and he sighed and went to sleep again. I carefully pulled the haversack from under his head and substituted my army pullover which I had taken off.

He stirred, but didn't wake up. I feverishly opened the haversack—my worst fears were realised! I had left my reserve bottle in the dug-out. I shook my issue bottle; it was less than half full. I drank very slowly, and then, filling my mouth, washed it out, spitting the water back into my bottle. I didn't feel like eating; I had a packet of hard biscuits and my emergency ration.

It was quiet, and I raised myself to the level of the trench and looked over. I could see two helmets protruding from a trench about thirty yards away. I called out, realising for the first time how painful my wound was now. Someone came doubling over to me after the second shout; it was my batman. I asked him what was happening. Why hadn't the doctor and Battalion H.Q. come? Had he any water? He left me his bottle, and said he would collect my reserve one after he had gone over to the company commander to find out what was happening.

Mortar shells started landing all around me. The Germans were watching our every movement, and had jumped to the conclusion that my trench was the H.Q. Twice I was covered in sand, and once a red-hot piece of metal landed on my chest. The Austrian stirred uneasily and woke up. He started to raise himself by placing his hands over the edge of the trench. There was an ear-splitting explosion. At first I thought our trench had been blown in. I looked carefully over the side; there was a huge crater less than five yards from the Austrian's end of the trench. Then I looked at the Austrian; he was lying half propped up against the trench looking curiously at the remains of his left hand; it had been partially blown away. I was nearly sick, but hastily tore my shirt and bound it tightly round the stump. He thanked me weakly and closed his eyes. His breathing was heavy and laboured; the poor devil was dying. I thought of his wife and children, of how damned stupid the whole thing was. First, he shoots me, then I shoot him, then we talk together as friends and share a trench where he is further wounded by his own side. Why were we fighting each other? Did it make sense? Then I thought of the massacres in Poland, France, Belgium. Yes, I suppose it was necessary. "*Wann kommt der Arzt?*" he interrupted my thoughts. Mechanically I replied, *"Bald!"* Almost petulantly he murmured, *"Bald! Bald! immer bald."* It was no use explaining to him that we were cut off and the doctor wouldn't be coming; he would certainly be dead in a few hours, and I, too, probably, if this shelling went on. As I moved back to my own end of the trench a bullet whistled past my head. That damned sniper was still watching. Our guns opened up now; the shells landed right among us. I hoped the wireless was still working, and the company commander would get through in time. Another salvo—just beyond us this time. I wondered how it would all end. I didn't really care much now.

The day dragged on; the shooting had died down, but it suddenly broke out again, but this time it was the sharp crack of tank guns. I appeared to be almost under their muzzles. A tank rumbled into view: one of ours—I shouted, but it was hopeless. The next moment it went partially over a trench in which some wounded, our own and Germans, were lying. I sank back into the trench. A little later an armoured car came up. I shouted, and this time the officer inside heard me. He got out and doubled over to me. I shouted a warning to him about the sniper; he reached me and lay down beside my trench. He was amazed to find us there; they had no idea we were there. Apparently we were in the middle of a tank battle. I told him we had a lot of wounded; could he do anything to get us out. He said he would report it at once on his return to his H.Q.

It was now early evening. The Austrian was lying peaceful, still breathing, but blood was oozing out of his mouth. I think I slept again; I was getting light-headed. I finished the second water-bottle; my thirst was more painful than the wound. I still had my batman's half-full bottle, but I couldn't use that; he would want it. Another two hours passed, and then suddenly I realised there were people round the trench. I can't remember how many, but the company commander was there and a doctor, not our own. He was wearing a forage-cap, and I thought what a risk he was taking. He was very cool and cheery. "Hold out your arm," he said, and he injected me with morphia. I asked him to give some to the Austrian. He stabbed him, but he scarcely stirred, and murmured, "*Der Arzt ist gekommen.*"

The doctor asked where the others were, and I pointed out the trenches I knew and called for my batman to guide him. Never have I seen such cool disregard for personal safety as that man showed. I don't know who he was; he strolled from trench to trench, completely ignoring the bullets and mortar shells which were hotting up again, his forage-cap stuck at a cheeky angle. Finally he returned to my trench unscathed. They held a hasty conference; I couldn't follow much, but I gathered that they were going to try and get the wounded out after dark. The Germans concentrated their mortars with increasing fury on my trench and the little party, which broke up hastily. I had an uncomfortable ten minutes, but I wasn't really caring at this stage. I had such a wonderful peaceful feeling. I must have fallen asleep again; for the next thing I remember, it was quite dark and men were carrying away the Austrian, who was apparently still alive. They came back for me, and pushed me on to the front of a 15-cwt. truck.

Soon we started off, bumping across the rough ground; one or two of the men inside groaned. I felt quite peaceful and had no pain. From time to time I had a feeling of anxiety in case I was going to be cheated out of my hospital bed at the last moment by a mine or a shell, but on the whole I was quite content to leave it to the driver.

We soon arrived at an advanced dressing station. I had another injection here, but after a quick glance at my bandage they left the wound alone. The last I saw of my Austrian he was lying on a raised stretcher having a blood transfusion. I wonder if he lived. I still have his papers.

I was placed in an ambulance, which was sheer luxury after the bumping of the truck, and soon we arrived at a big New Zealand casualty clearing station. They were frantically busy here, and when I assured them that I wasn't bleeding they just put another label round my neck and packed me back into another ambulance. From this I was transferred to a hospital train, and eventually landed at a South African base hospital in Egypt.

The End in Africa

El Alamein was a real breakthrough; now the 8th Army was to push Rommel all the way back to Tunisia. And, on November 8th, 1942, the Americans landed with elements of the 1st Army at Casablanca, Oran and Algiers. The common goal of the American and British forces, homing in from east and west, was to push the Germans out of Tunisia, move across the Mediterranean to Sicily, and, once a base of operations had been established, invade Mussolini's Italy.

Long argument and discussion had gone into this plan. The Americans wanted a bridgehead in 1942 in France, somewhere on the Cherbourg peninsula. The British argued for the invasion in Africa and the development of a thrust up from the south against Hitler's flank. The British maintained that, because of the terrible losses of shipping in the Atlantic (losses were again high because of the enormous increase in shipments to Britain from the U.S.), any bridgehead in France could not now be properly supplied and protected against German counterattacks. The Russians had also pressed the Allies to develop a second front, to take some of the German divisions off their backs, and the Americans believed the Russians might not hold out beyond 1942 unless a second front in Europe were established.

Agreement was finally reached only after intervention by Churchill and Roosevelt; Gen. Eisenhower was given command of the North African invasion.

By the end of December, 1942, the British 8th Army had thrust 1,200 miles across North Africa toward Tripoli. But Hitler had in the meantime reinforced Rommel in Tunisia, and this was to delay the Allies' victory by several months. In mid-February, 1943, the Germans had fourteen divisions on the spot, many of them flown in by air, the British and American ships having pretty well buttoned up the Mediterranean by this time. Rommel counterattacked the Americans in the vicinity of the Kasserine Pass, and stalled the American drive for a few days. However, it was only a matter of time before the Germans were pinned down in Tunis and Cape Bon. The remaining German troops were slowly chewed up. The U.S. 2nd Corps broke through and captured Bizerte on May 7th, and on the same day the British 1st Army took Tunis. On May 13th, 1943, the North African Campaign was declared over.

The Germans had suffered a loss of 250,000 prisoners, more than a thousand guns, many tanks and thousands of motor vehicles. Later that month, Churchill visited Roosevelt in Washington, and addressed the Congress. He announced that the Axis had lost almost a million men in North Africa, about two and a half million tons of shipping had been sunk, and nearly eight thousand aircraft destroyed. It was now time for the Allies to turn their combined efforts against Italy.

Attack by Air

But the Allies were already carrying the attack to the heart of Europe—by air. The aim was to destroy the German war industries, knock down the Luftwaffe (which by now had become a defensive unit), and reduce the land defenses facing the British across the Channel. The R.A.F. conducted their raids at night, preferring area-saturation bombing; the Americans flew their missions of Flying Fortresses during the day, bombing their targets as accurately as their instruments and daylight observation allowed. Losses were murderous in late 1942 and early 1943. Heavy damage was being visited on German war industry, but it was obvious that bombing missions in daylight needed fighter protection. The trouble was that, at this time, we had no fighters of long enough range to protect the bombers to the target and back.

Both air forces pounded aircraft factories, a job in which the bomber crews had a great stake. Successful raids could help cripple aircraft production, meaning fewer replacements for the Luftwaffe's air defense squadrons in the following months. When the Germans began to disperse their assembly plants, the Allies followed them tenaciously, continuing to do serious damage.

From November, 1943, through the following March, Berlin was heavily bombed. The second raid on the city, November 22nd, saw 2,300 tons of bombs delivered in one of the greatest raids of the war. Another 1,400 tons were delivered on the 23rd, and, on the 26th, another thousand tons. The Allies were bent on shattering the hub of the German government, and striking at civilian morale.

Through the spring of 1944 even more attention was paid to all elements of German air power; the date of the invasion of France had been set for the following June, and it was essential that the Luftwaffe be crushed so the Allies could hold complete air supremacy. The Allies offered battle at any time to German pursuit planes. A shuttle system was worked out so that on long raids British and American bombers could land at Italian bases, and now industrial cities such as Regensburg and Wiener Neustadt were in reach. Winter weather always caused difficulties for large-scale bombing, but when the weather began to clear in February, heavier raids than ever were launched on German industrial centers. Such fierce attacks meant heavy casualties. But the German air force was crippled—their aircraft production could no longer keep pace with their losses.

The following description of one of the raids on Regensburg is written by Lt. Col. Beirne Lay, Jr., American pilot of a day-bombing B-17 Flying Fortress.

RAID ON REGENSBURG

by Lt. Col. Beirne Lay, Jr.

In the briefing room, the intelligence officer of the bombardment group pulled a cloth screen away from a huge wall map. Each of the 240 sleepy-eyed combat-crew members in the crowded room leaned forward. There were low whistles. I felt a sting of anticipation as I stared at the red string on the map that stretched from our base in England to a pin point deep in Southern Germany, then south across the Alps, through the Brenner Pass to the coast of Italy, then past Corsica and Sardinia and south over the Mediterranean to a desert airdrome in North Africa. You could have heard an oxygen mask drop.

"Your primary," said the intelligence officer, "is Regensburg. Your aiming point is the center of the Messerschmitt One Hundred and Nine G aircraft-and-engine-assembly shops. This is the most vital target we've ever gone after. If you destroy it, you destroy thirty per cent of the Luftwaffe's single-engine-fighter production. You fellows know what that means to you personally."

There were a few hollow laughs.

After the briefing, I climbed aboard a jeep bound for the operations office to check up on my Fortress assignment. The stars were dimly visible through the chilly mist that covered our blacked-out bomber station, but the weather forecast for a deep penetration over the Continent was good. In the office, I looked at the crew sheet, where the line-up of the lead, low and high squadrons of the group is plotted for each mission. I was listed for a copilot's seat. While I stood there, and on the chance suggestion of one of the squadron commanders who was looking over the list, the operations officer erased my name and shifted me to the high squadron as copilot in the crew of a steady Irishman named Lieutenant Murphy, with whom I had flown before. Neither of us knew it, but that operations officer saved my life right there with a piece of rubber on the end of a pencil.

At 5:30 a.m., fifteen minutes before taxi time, a jeep drove around the five-mile perimeter track in the semi-darkness, pausing at each dispersal point long enough to notify the waiting crews that poor local visibility would postpone the take-off for an hour and a half. I was sitting with Murphy and the rest of our crew near the Piccadilly Lily. She looked sinister and complacent, squatting on her fat tires with scarcely a hole in her skin to show for the twelve raids behind her. The postponement tightened, rather than relaxed, the tension. Once more I checked over my life vest, oxygen mask and parachute, not perfunctorily, but the way you check something you're going to have to use. I made sure my escape kit was pinned securely in the knee pocket of my flying suit, where it couldn't fall out in a scramble to abandon ship. I slid a hunting knife between my shoe and my flying boot as I looked again through my extra equipment for this mission: water canteen, mess kit, blankets and English pounds for use in the Algerian desert, where we would sleep on the ground and might be on our own from a forced landing.

Murphy restlessly gave the Piccadilly Lily another once-over, inspecting ammunition belts, bomb bay, tires and oxygen pressure at each crew station. Especially the oxygen. It's human fuel, as important as gasoline, up where we operate. Gunners field-stripped their .50-calibers again and oiled the bolts. Our top-turret gunner lay in the grass with his head on his parachute, feigning sleep, sweating out his thirteenth start.

We shared a common knowledge which grimly enhanced the normal excitement before a mission. Of the approximately 150 Fortresses who were hitting Regensburg, our group was the last and lowest, at a base altitude of 17,000 feet. That's well within the range of accuracy for heavy flak. Our course would take us over plenty of it. It was a cinch also that our group would be the softest touch for the enemy fighters, being last man through the gantlet. Furthermore, the Piccadilly Lily was leading the last three ships of the high squadron—the tip of the tail end of the whole shebang. We didn't relish it much. Who wants a Purple Heart?

The minute hand of my wrist watch dragged. I caught myself thinking about the day, exactly one year ago, on August 17, 1942, when I watched a pitifully small force of twelve B-17's take off on the first raid of the 8th Air Force to make a shallow penetration against Rouen, France. On that day it was our maximum effort. Today, on our first anniversary, we were putting thirty times that number of heavies into the air—half the force on Regensburg and half the force on Schweinfurt, both situated inside the interior of the German Reich. For a year and a half, as a staff officer, I had watched the 8th Air Force grow under Maj. Gen. Ira C. Eaker. That's a long time to watch from behind a desk. Only ten days ago I had asked for and received orders to combat duty. Those ten days had been full of the swift action of participating in four combat missions and checking out for the first time as a four-engine pilot.

Now I knew that it can be easier to be shot at than telephoned at. That staff officers at an Air Force headquarters are the unstrung heroes of this war. And yet I found myself reminiscing just a little affectionately about that desk, wondering if there wasn't a touch of suicide in store for our group. One thing was sure: Headquarters had dreamed up the biggest air operation to date to celebrate its birthday in the biggest league of aerial warfare.

At 7:30 we broke out of the cloud tops into the glare of the rising sun. Beneath our B-17 lay English fields, still blanketed in the thick mist from which we had just emerged. We continued to climb slowly, our broad wings shouldering a heavy load of incendiary bombs in the belly and a burden of fuel in the main and wing-tip Tokyo tanks that would keep the Fortress afloat in the thin upper altitudes eleven hours.

From my copilot's seat on the right-hand side, I watched the white surface of the overcast, where B-17's in clusters of six to the squadron were puncturing the cloud deck all about us, rising clear of the mist with their glass noses slanted upward for the long climb to base altitude. We tacked on to one of these clutches of six. Now the sky over England was heavy with the weight of thousands of tons of bombs, fuel and men being lifted four miles straight up on a giant aerial hoist to the western terminus of a 20,000-foot elevated highway that led east to Regensburg. At intervals I saw the arc of a sputtering red, green or yellow flare being fired from the cabin roof of a group leader's airplane to identify the lead squadron to the high and low squadrons of each group. Assembly takes longer when you come up through an overcast.

For nearly an hour, still over southern England, we climbed, nursing the straining Cyclone engines in a 300-foot-per-minute ascent, forming three squadrons gradually into compact group stagger formations—low squadron down to the left and high squadron up to the right of the lead squadron—groups assembling into looser combat wings of two to three groups each along the combat-wing assembly line, homing over predetermined points with radio compass, and finally cruising along the air-division assembly line to allow the combat wings to fall into place in trail behind Col. Curtis E. Le May in the lead group of the air division.

Formed at last, each flanking group in position 1,000 feet above or below its lead group, our fifteen-mile parade moved east toward Lowestoft, point of departure from the friendly coast, unwieldy, but dangerous to fool with. From my perch in the high squadron in the last element of the whole procession, the air division looked like huge anvil-shaped swarms of locusts—not on dress parade, like the bombers of the Luftwaffe that died like flies over Britain in 1940, but deployed to uncover every gun and permit maneuverability. Our formation was basically that worked out for the Air Corps by Brig. Gen. Hugh Knerr twenty years ago with eighty-five-mile-an-hour bombers, plus refinements devised by Colonel Le May from experience in the European theater.

The English Channel and the North Sea glittered bright in the clear visibility as we left the bulge of East Anglia behind us. Up ahead we knew that we were already registering on the German RDF screen, and that the sector controllers of the Luftwaffe's fighter belt in Western Europe were busy alerting their *Staffeln* of Focke-Wulfs and Messerschmitts. I stole a last look back at cloud-covered England, where I could see a dozen spare B-17's, who had accompanied us to fill in for any abortives from mechanical failure in the hard climb, gliding disappointedly home to base.

I fastened my oxygen mask a little tighter and looked at the little ball in a glass tube on the instrument panel that indicates proper oxygen flow. It was moving up and down, like a visual heartbeat, as I breathed, registering normal.

Already the gunners were searching. Occasionally the ship shivered as guns were tested with short bursts. I could see puffs of blue smoke from the group close ahead and 1,000 feet above us, as each gunner satisfied himself that he had lead poisoning at his trigger tips. The coast of Holland appeared in sharp black outline. I drew in a deep breath of oxygen.

A few miles in front of us were German boys in single-seaters who were probably going to react to us in the same way our boys would react, emotionally, if German bombers were heading for the Pratt & Whitney engine factory at Hartford or the Liberator plant at Willow Run. In the making was a death struggle between the unstoppable object and the immovable defense, every possible defense at the disposal of the Reich, for this was a deadly penetration to a hitherto inaccessible and critically important arsenal of the *Vaterland.*

At 10:08 we crossed the coast of Holland, south of The Hague, with our group of Fortresses tucked in tightly and within handy supporting distance of the group above us, at 18,000 feet. But our long, loose-linked column looked too long, and the gaps between combat wings too wide. As I squinted into the sun, gauging the distance to the barely visible specks of the lead group, I had a recurrence of that sinking feeling before the take-off—the lonesome foreboding that might come to the last man about to run a gantlet lined with spiked clubs. The premonition was well founded.

At 10:17, near Woensdrecht, I saw the first flak blossom out in our vicinity, light and inaccurate. A few minutes later, at approximately 10:25, a gunner called, "Fighters at two o'clock low." I saw them, climbing above the horizon ahead of us to the right—a pair of them. For a moment I hoped they were P-47 Thunderbolts from the fighter escort that was supposed to be in our vicinity, but I didn't hope long. The two FW-190's turned and whizzed through the formation ahead of us in a frontal attack, nicking two B-17's in the wings and breaking away in half rolls right over our group. By craning my neck up and back, I glimpsed one of them through the roof glass in the cabin, flashing past at a 600-mile-an-hour rate of closure, his yellow nose smoking and small pieces flying off near the wing root. The guns of our group were in action. The pungent smell of burnt cordite filled the cockpit and the B-17 trembled to the recoil of nose and ball-turret guns. Smoke immediately trailed from the hit B-17's, but they held their stations.

Here was early fighter reaction. The members of the crew sensed trouble. There was something desperate about the way those two fighters came in fast right out of their climb, without any preliminaries. Apparently, our own fighters were busy somewhere farther up the procession. The interphone was active for a few seconds with brief admonitions: "Lead 'em more." . . . "Short bursts." . . . "Don't throw rounds away." . . . "Bombardier to left waist gunner, don't yell. Talk slow."

Three minutes later the gunners reported fighters climbing up from all around the clock, singly and in pairs, both FW-190's and Me-109-G's. The fighters I could see on my side looked like too many for sound health. No friendly Thunderbolts were visible. From now on we were in mortal danger. My mouth dried up and my buttocks pulled together. A co-ordinated attack began, with the head-on fighters coming in from slightly above, the nine and three o'clock attackers approaching from about level and the rear attackers from slightly below. The guns from every B-17 in our group and the group ahead were firing simultaneously, lashing the sky with ropes of orange tracers to match the chain-puff bursts squirting from the 20-mm. cannon muzzles in the wings of the jerry single-seaters.

I noted with alarm that a lot of our fire was falling astern of the target—particularly from our hand-held nose and waist guns. Nevertheless, both sides got hurt in this clash, with the entire second element of three B-17's from our low squadron and one B-17 from the group ahead falling out of formation on fire, with crews bailing out, and several fighters heading for the deck in flames or with their pilots lingering behind under the dirty yellow canopies that distinguished some of their parachutes from ours. Our twenty-four-year-old group leader, flying only his third combat mission, pulled us up even closer to the preceding group for mutual support.

As we swung slightly outside with our squadron, in mild evasive action, I got a good look at that gap in the low squadron where three B-17's had been. Suddenly I bit my lip hard. The lead ship of that element had pulled out on fire and exploded before anyone bailed out. It was the ship to which I had been originally assigned.

I glanced over at Murphy. It was cold in the cockpit, but sweat was running from his forehead and over his oxygen mask from the exertion of holding his element in tight formation and the strain of the warnings that hummed over the interphone and what he could see out of the corners of his eyes. He caught my glance and turned the controls over to me for a while. It was an enormous relief to concentrate on flying instead of sitting there watching fighters aiming between your eyes. Somehow, the attacks from the rear, although I could see them through my ears via the interphone, didn't bother me. I guess it was because there was a slab of armor plate behind my back and I couldn't watch them, anyway.

I knew that we were in a lively fight. Every alarm bell in my brain and heart was ringing a high-pitched warning. But my nerves were steady and my brain working. The fear was unpleasant, but it was bearable. I knew that I was going to die, and so were a lot of others. What I didn't know was that the real fight, the *Anschluss* of Luftwaffe 20-mm. cannon shells, hadn't really begun. The largest and most savage fighter resistance of any war in history was rising to stop us at any cost, and our group was the most vulnerable target.

A few minutes later we absorbed the first wave of a hailstorm of individual fighter attacks that were to engulf us clear to the target in such a blizzard of bullets and shells that a chronological account is difficult. It was at 10:41, over Eupen, that I looked out the window after a minute's lull, and saw two whole squadrons, twelve Me-109's and eleven FW-190's climbing parallel to us as though they were on a steep escalator. The first squadron had reached our level and was pulling ahead to turn into us. The second was not far behind. Several thousand feet below us were many more fighters, their noses cocked up in a maximum climb. Over the interphone came reports of an equal number of enemy aircraft deploying on the other side of the formation.

For the first time I noticed an Me-110 sitting out of range on our level out to the right. He was to stay with us all the way to the target, apparently radioing our position and weak spots to fresh *Staffeln* waiting farther down the road.

At the sight of all these fighters, I had the distinct feeling of being trapped—that the Hun had been tipped off or at least had guessed our destination and was set for us. We were already through the German fighter belt. Obviously, they had moved a lot of squadrons back in a fluid defense in depth, and they must have been saving up some outfits for the inner defense that we didn't know about. The life expectancy of our group seemed definitely limited, since it had already appeared that the fighters, instead of wasting fuel trying to overhaul the preceding groups, were glad to take a cut at us.

Swinging their yellow noses around in a wide U-turn, the twelve-ship squadron of Me-109's came in from twelve to two o'clock in pairs. The main event was on. I fought an impulse to close my eyes, and overcame it.

A shining silver rectangle of metal sailed past over our right wing. I recognized it as a main-exit door. Seconds later, a black lump came hurtling through the formation, barely missing several propellers. It was a man, clasping his knees to his head, revolving like a diver in a triple somersault, shooting by us so close that I saw a piece of paper blow out of his leather jacket. He was evidently making a delayed jump, for I didn't see his parachute open.

A B-17 turned gradually out of the formation to the right, maintaining altitude. In a split second it completely vanished in a brilliant explosion, from which the only remains were four balls of fire, the fuel tanks, which were quickly consumed as they fell earthward.

I saw blue, red, yellow and aluminum-colored fighters. Their tactics were running fairly true to form, with frontal attacks hitting the low squadron and rear attackers going for the lead and high squadrons. Some of the jerries shot at us with rockets, and an attempt at air-to-air bombing was made with little black time-fuse sticks, dropped from above, which exploded in small gray puffs off to one side of the formation. Several of the FW's did some nice deflection shooting on side attacks from 500 yards at the high group, then raked the low group on the breakaway at closer range with their noses cocked in a side slip, to keep the formation in their sights longer in the turn. External fuel tanks were visible under the bellies or wings of at least two squadrons, shedding uncomfortable light on the mystery of their ability to tail us so far from their bases.

The manner of the assaults indicated that the pilots knew where we were going and were inspired with a fanatical determination to stop us before we got there. Many pressed attacks home to 250 yards or less, or bolted right through the formation wide out, firing long twenty-second bursts, often presenting point-blank targets on the breakaway. Some committed the fatal error of pulling up instead of going down and out. More experienced pilots came in on frontal attacks with a noticeably slower rate of closure, apparently throttled back, obtaining greater accuracy. But no tactics could halt the close-knit juggernauts of our Fortresses, nor save the single-seaters from paying a terrible price.

Our airplane was endangered by various debris. Emergency hatches, exit doors, prematurely opened parachutes, bodies and assorted fragments of B-17's and Hun fighters breezed past us in the slip stream.

I watched two fighters explode not far beneath, disappear in sheets of orange flame; B-17's dropping out in every stage of distress, from engines on fire to control shot away; friendly and enemy parachutes floating down, and, on the green carpet far below us, funeral pyres of smoke from fallen fighters, marking our trail.

On we flew through the cluttered wake of a desperate air battle, where disintegrating aircraft were commonplace and the white dots of sixty parachutes in the air at one time were hardly worth a second look. The spectacle registering on my eyes became so fantastic that my brain turned numb to the actuality of the death and destruction all around us. Had it not been for the squeezing in my stomach, which was trying to purge, I might easily have been watching an animated cartoon in a movie theater.

The minutes dragged on into an hour. And still the fighters came. Our gunners called coolly and briefly to one another, dividing up their targets, fighting for their lives with every round of ammunition—and our lives, and the formation. The tail gunner called that he was out of ammunition. We sent another belt back to him. Here was a new hazard. We might run out of .50-caliber slugs before we reached the target.

I looked to both sides of us. Our two wing men were gone. So was the element in front of us—all three ships. We moved up into position behind the lead element of the high squadron. I looked out again on my side and saw a cripple, with one prop feathered, struggle up behind our right wing with his bad engine funneling smoke into the slip stream. He dropped back. Now our tail gunner had a clear view. There were no more B-17's behind us. We were the last man.

I took the controls for a while. The first thing I saw when Murphy resumed flying was a B-17 turning slowly out to the right, its cockpit a mass of flames. The copilot crawled out of his window, held on with one hand, reached back for his parachute, buckled it on, let go and was whisked back into the horizontal stabilizer of the tail. I believe the impact killed him. His parachute didn't open.

I looked forward and almost ducked as I watched the tail gunner of a B-17 ahead of us take a bead right on our windshield and cut loose with a stream of tracers that missed us by a few feet as he fired on a fighter attacking us from six o'clock low. I almost ducked again when our own top-turret gunner's twin muzzles pounded away a foot above my head in the full forward position, giving a realistic imitation of cannon shells exploding in the cockpit, while I gave an even better imitation of a man jumping six inches out of his seat.

Still no letup. The fighters queued up like a bread line and let us have it. Each second of time had a cannon shell in it. The strain of being a clay duck in the wrong end of that aerial shooting gallery became almost intolerable. Our Piccadilly Lily shook steadily with the fire of its .50's, and the air inside was wispy with smoke. I checked the engine instruments for the thousandth time. Normal. No injured crew members yet. Maybe we'd get to that target, even with our reduced fire power. Seven Fortresses from our group had already gone down and many of the rest of us were badly shot up and short-handed because of wounded crew members.

Almost disinterestedly I observed a B-17 pull out from the group preceding us and drop back to a position about 200 feet from our right wing tip. His right Tokyo tanks were on fire, and had been for a half hour. Now the smoke was thicker. Flames were licking through the blackened skin of the wing. While the pilot held her steady, I saw four crew members drop out the bomb bay and execute delayed jumps. Another bailed from the nose, opened his parachute prematurely and nearly fouled the tail. Another went out the left-waist-gun opening, delaying his opening for a safe interval. The tail gunner dropped out of his hatch, apparently pulling the ripcord before he was clear of the ship. His parachute opened instantaneously, barely missing the tail, and jerked him so hard that both his shoes came off. He hung limp in the harness, whereas the others had shown immediate signs of life, shifting around in their harness. The Fortress then dropped back in a medium spiral and I did not see the pilots leave. I saw the ship, though, just before it trailed from view, belly to the sky, its wing a solid sheet of yellow flame.

Now that we had been under constant attack for more than an hour, it appeared certain that our group was faced with extinction. The sky was still mottled with rising fighters. Target time was thirty-five minutes away. I doubt if a man in the group visualized the possibility of our getting much farther without 100 per cent loss. Gunners were becoming exhausted and nerve-tortured from the nagging strain—the strain that sends gunners and pilots to the rest home. We had been aiming point for what looked like most of the Luftwaffe. It looked as though we might find the rest of it primed for us at the target.

At this hopeless point, a young squadron commander down in the low squadron was living through his finest hour. His squadron had lost its second element of three ships early in the fight, south of Antwerp, yet he had consistently maintained his vulnerable and exposed position in the formation rigidly in order to keep the guns of his three remaining ships well uncovered to protect the belly of the formation. Now, nearing the target, battle damage was catching up with him fast. A 20-mm. cannon shell penetrated the right side of his airplane and exploded beneath him, damaging the electrical system and cutting the top-turret gunner in the leg. A second 20-mm. entered the radio compartment, killing the radio operator, who bled to death with his legs severed above the knees. A third 20-mm. shell entered the left side of the nose, tearing out a section about two feet square, tore away the right-hand-nose-gun installations and injured the bombardier in the head and shoulder. A fourth 20-mm. shell penetrated the right wing into the fuselage system, releasing fluid all over the cockpit. A fifth 20-mm. shell punctured the cabin roof and severed the rudder cables to one side of the rudder. A sixth 20-mm. shell exploded in the No. 3 engine, destroying all controls to the engine. The engine caught fire and lost its power, but eventually I saw the fire go out.

Confronted with structural damage, partial loss of control, fire in the air and serious injuries to personnel, and faced with fresh waves of fighters still rising to the attack, this commander was justified in abandoning ship. His crew, some of them comparatively inexperienced youngsters, were preparing to bail out. The copilot pleaded repeatedly with him to bail out. His reply at this critical juncture was blunt. His words were heard over the interphone and had a magical effect on the crew. They stuck to their guns. The B-17 kept on.

Near the initial point, at 11:50, one hour and a half after the first of at least 200 individual fighter attacks, the pressure eased off, although hostiles were still in the vicinity. A curious sensation came over me. I was still alive. It was possible to think of the target. Of North Africa. Of returning to England. Almost idly, I watched a crippled B-17 pull over to the curb and drop its wheels and open its bomb bay, jettisoning its bombs. Three Me-109's circled it closely, but held their fire while the crew bailed out. I remembered now that a little while back I had seen other Hun fighters hold their fire, even when being shot at by a B-17 from which the crew were bailing. But I doubt if sportsmanship had anything to do with it. They hoped to get a B-17 down fairly intact.

And then our weary, battered column, short twenty-four bombers, but still holding the close formation that had brought the remainder through by sheer air discipline and gunnery, turned in to the target. I knew that our bombardiers were grim as death while they synchronized their sights on the great Me-109 shops lying below us in a curve of the winding blue Danube, close to the outskirts of Regensburg. Our B-17 gave a slight lift and a red light went out on the instrument panel. Our bombs were away. We turned from the target toward the snow-capped Alps. I looked back and saw a beautiful sight—a rectangular pillar of smoke rising from the Me-109 plant. Only one burst was over and into the town. Even from this great height I could see that we had smeared the objective. The price? Cheap. 200 airmen.

A few more fighters pecked at us on the way to the Alps and a couple of smoking B-17's glided down toward the safety of Switzerland, about forty miles distant. A town in the Brenner Pass tossed up a lone burst of futile flak. Flak? There had been lots of flak in the past two hours, but only now did I recall having seen it, a sort of side issue to the fighters. Colonel Le May, who had taken excellent care of us all the way, circled the air division over a large lake to give the cripples, some flying on three engines and many trailing smoke, a chance to rejoin the family. We approached the Mediterranean in a gradual descent, conserving fuel. Out over the water we flew at low altitude, unmolested by fighters from Sardinia or Corsica, waiting through the long hot afternoon hours for the first sight of the North African coast line. The prospect of ditching, out of gasoline, and the sight of other B-17's falling into the drink seemed trivial matters after the vicious nightmare of the long trial across southern Germany. We had walked through a high valley of the shadow of death, not expecting to see another sunset, and now I could fear no evil.

With red lights showing on all our fuel tanks, we landed at our designated base in the desert, after eleven hours in the air. I slept on the ground near the wing and, waking occasionally, stared up at the stars. My radio headset was back in the ship. And yet I could hear the deep chords of great music.

Into Italy

The prospect of an Italian campaign heated up the arguments between British and American High Commands all over again. The Americans still wanted to invade France across the English Channel, and as early as possible. The British now argued for an immediate attack upon Italy—a momentum had been developed by the victories in North Africa which ought to be sustained by an advance to the Italian mainland.

The British were intent on an Italian campaign partly because they had their eyes on the Balkans; Churchill felt this was the place to establish a common front with the Russians, and also foresaw the need for a foothold there in the post-war power struggle. And then there was the attractive possibility of knocking Italy out of the war, for it was thought that Italy had little stomach left for fighting.

But the Americans were convinced the main task was to defeat Germany—and the quicker the better. Any grand strategy not directly aimed at this goal didn't appeal to them.

What is interesting is that the Germans expected the Allies to invade Europe through the Balkans; not even the successful capture of Sicily changed their minds. They kept twice as many divisions in the Balkans as they had in Italy.

The original Allied strategy provided for the 8th Army to invade the toe of Italy, but in the middle of July, 1943, Mussolini's government was overthrown, and the Italians under Marshal Badoglio began to discuss an armistice with the Allies. The surrender of Italy was to remove more than thirty divisions of Italians which would have opposed the Allies in Italy. As it developed, the Italian people regarded the Allies more as liberators than enemies. This brought about a revision of the invasion plan. The 5th Army was created out of three American and three British divisions, for an assault landing in the Gulf of Salerno. On September 3rd, the British 8th Army invaded Italy at the toe, and six days later, on September 9th, the 5th Army landed on the Salerno beaches.

Rommel commanded eight divisions in northern Italy, and Kesselring, eight divisions south of Rome. The invasion of Salerno had been no surprise to the Germans; Kesselring had expected a landing there, and ironically a Panzer division was carrying out anti-invasion exercises at the very time the 5th Army hit the beaches. The issue was in doubt for almost a week. As Fred Majdalany puts it in his *The Battle of Cassino,* "With a semi-circle of high ground overlooking the beaches, the battlefield resembled half a saucer with Germans sitting on the rim." The battle turned against the Germans partly because of constant pressure from air strikes and naval bombardment.

The British 8th Army, landing two divisions in the south, now moved up alongside the 5th, and by October 1st, Naples was taken. Both armies now prepared themselves for the drive to Rome. But they were to pay a heavy toll first to the harshness of the terrain, and the Germans' skillful tactics in utilizing it. Italy was beautifully suited to the kind of punishing defensive tactics the Germans adopted. Down the middle of the Italian peninsula is a formation of mountains, their highest points in the center, with riblike slopes moving out to either side to the coasts. Because of these mountains, and the poor roads, the two Allied armies had no common front. Here in Italy the Allies had to fight an entirely different war than they had in North Africa. In the desert plains, the war was one of maneuver; in Italy, it was one of attrition. And the Allies never did commit enough men and supplies to hit the Germans with the solid punches necessary for a real knockout.

Kesselring set his line of defenses along the Garigliano and the Rapido rivers, through Cassino into the central mountains, and then to the River Sangro on the east coast; the Germans worked tirelessly on the Gustav Line, as it was called, while the 5th and 8th Armies worked their way up the peninsula. Seven divisions were moved over from the Balkans now, and reorganized into two armies under Kesselring. (Rommel, incidentally, had been transferred to a command in western Europe.) The Germans had twenty-five divisions to call on in Italy—the Allies, only eleven. Two Allied divisions previously available had been recalled to Great Britain for the forthcoming strike across the Channel.

About January 15th, 1944, the 5th Army arrived in front of Cassino, where they looked forward to rest, reorganization and replacements for the casualties suffered over the previous four months' campaign. But rest wasn't in store for them; a plan had been developed in the previous weeks for a landing at Anzio, some sixty miles back of the Gustav Line. One British and one American division were to land and establish a beachhead to pull some of the Germans off the defense line at

Cassino. Because landing craft to be used at Anzio had to be returned to Britain for the forthcoming invasion, and supplies had to be moved up along the coast by sea in these same landing craft, the date for the landing at Anzio had to be fixed as early as possible—late January.

Gen. Alexander had taken over command of the land armies in Italy (Eisenhower and Montgomery had been recalled to London to assist in planning for the invasion); he now ordered the 5th Army, under the American Gen. Mark Clark, to attack. This was to co-ordinate with the two Allied divisions expected to be moving out of the beachhead at Anzio. The Cassino attack ended in a disaster for the 36th American Division, and two days later the American 34th Division was thrown into action. At the end of ten days' fighting, the 34th had won a bridgehead on one of the many hills in the Cassino area, but it was clear to the men doing the fighting that little progress was going to be made until the big hill overlooking the town of Cassino, on which the Benedictine monastery stood, was either taken or successfully bypassed. In the meantime, the French had put two of their divisions into action to the right of Cassino, and gained some ground after gallant fighting. But in the second week of February the whole operation ground to a halt. Both American divisions had lost more than 2,000 casualties apiece, and worse, the Anzio beachhead had now become a liability rather than an investment. While 70,000 men had been landed, the Germans were about to throw several fresh divisions against them in a counterattack. Without time for proper regrouping and a closer study of the Cassino problem, the Allied Command was forced to commit the troops to a second attack almost immediately. Gen. Alexander moved over several divisions from the 8th Army, which had slugged their way up the east coast of Italy. The news from Anzio grew worse. By February 15th, the second battle of Cassino had to be launched. Majdalany, who was at Cassino in the British army and who has written an account of the whole operation, says, "Wilson [the Allied commander] urged Alexander, Alexander urged Clark, Clark urged Freyberg, and Freyberg urged his two divisions to attack immediately."

THE BATTLE FOR CASSINO

by Fred Majdalany

No event of the war caused more heated and lingering controversy than the bombing, on February 15, 1944, of the Abbey of Monte Cassino.

It is possible to understand the bitterness and bewilderment of the Cassinese monks themselves. The cloister is not the place in which a detailed grasp of military practicalities can be expected to flourish.

One can discount the naïve foolishness of the uninformed —like the English newspaper correspondent who spent a few hours at Monte Cassino after the war, and then published the complacent view that the bombing was "vandalism" and the verdict on those who ordered it must be "guilty but insane."

It is more than a little surprising, however, that those who have emotionally wanted to believe that the bombing was a criminal act should have been fortified in their judgments by, of all people, the army commander who ordered it, General Mark Clark.

In his personal memoir *Calculated Risk,* General Clark wrote:

> I say that the bombing of the abbey . . . was a mistake, and I say it with full knowledge of the controversy that has raged round this episode . . . Not only was the bombing of the abbey an unnecessary psychological mistake in the propaganda field but it was a tactical military mistake of the first magnitude. It only made the job more difficult, more costly in terms of men, machines, and time.

This might be read as an admission of error, but in the pages that follow, Clark, who gave the order for the bombing, disclaims responsibility for it. If Clark had confined himself to a military reappraisal of the bombing, there could have been no objection to his being as outspoken as he liked. In fact, he ignores the special circumstances, conditions, and pressures prevailing at the time. He ignores the important psychological impact of the Monastery. He ignores the hard fact that two Commonwealth divisions were now being required to tackle a task that had just knocked the heart out of two American divisions. He makes little attempt to re-create the context in which the difficult decision had to be taken. He merely devotes himself to an angry apologia—disclaiming responsibility for an order which he himself gave, and blaming it on his subordinate commander General Freyberg.

It is unusual, to say the least, for an army commander to repudiate his own actions by blaming a subordinate for forcing them on him.

The great red herring that has been drawn across the bombing has been the relating of it to the question whether or not the Monastery was actually occupied by the Germans. It was afterwards reasonably well established that it was not. But this could not be known at the time. And in any case the question is irrelevant.

The simple inescapable fact is that the building was an integral part of a physical feature that was not only occupied but to a high degree fortified. The fortified mountain and the building at its summit were in military terms a single piece of ground.

Ground is the raw material of the soldier, as weapons are his tools. Ground is the factor which more than any other eventually controls the shape of a battle. Like pigment to the artist and clay to the potter, ground is the material which the soldier must study, cherish, understand, and adapt to his purposes. This is the basis of all military tactics.

A mountain is one kind of ground. A mountain crowned by a building is another. If the building happens to be inordinately strong, the ground is something else again. To the soldier the mountain and the building are not separate things but together comprise a whole. Ground is indivisible. The mountain and the building are one and must be considered as one. Their relationship may be likened to that between a coconut shy and a tray of china set in its midst. It would be foolish to tell someone to aim as hard as he likes at the coconuts but on no account to hit the china.

The piece of ground called Monte Cassino comprised a 1,700-foot mountain with rocky sides; a zigzag shelf of roadway twisting for five miles up one face of it, and providing both shelter and mobility for tanks and guns; and, at the summit, a building, more than two hundred yards long, with the thickness, strength, design, and structure of a powerful fortress.

Occupation of a piece of high ground like Monte Cassino can take two forms. It can be garrisoned with soldiers. Or it can be occupied by one soldier equipped with binoculars and a wireless set through which he can accurately direct the fire of guns on to any point of the landscape within his view. There is absolutely no limit to the number of guns that can be so directed by one man. A trained observer is therefore an even more potent defensive garrison than a battalion of soldiers.

It follows from this that any high ground likely to be used by the enemy as an observatory is an automatic target for attack by the other side. The attacker must use everything in his power to make this observation point untenable until such time as he can deprive the enemy of it by seizing it himself. Thus the pattern of advance of a modern army is from one line of good observation to the next.

The relationship between the summit of Monte Cassino and the important main route which it commands is so exceptional that it invariably impresses military men as the finest observation post they have ever seen.

To observe from the summit of this particular mountain, a man might set himself up comfortably (and because of its thick walls, more safely) inside the building. Alternatively he might (to get a wider view) install himself in a trench outside it, with a telephone link to an orderly stationed securely inside the building. If an observation point is of exceptional quality—as is the case with Monte Cassino—there are likely to be a number of separate observation posts set up by the different artillery formations and headquarters who will want to use it. A prominent peak of this kind may well become a mass of observation posts providing eyes for the many different departments of the army it is serving. Along the razorback of Monte Trocchio, for instance, where the Allied armies had their main view of the Cassino front, there were at one time more than a hundred observation posts.

The key to the German defense of the area for convenience called Cassino—though it comprised a combination of river line, mountain mass, and fortified town—was not the garrison, nor was it the prepared system of fortifications, formidable though both were—but the superlative observation which enabled such good use to be made of them.

> From the vantage point of the Monastery the enemy can watch and bring down fire on every movement on the roads or open country in the plain below [reported Freyberg to the New Zealand government].

> At New Zealand Divisional H.Q. [wrote Kippenberger] we felt certain that the monastery was at least the enemy's main observation post. It was so perfectly situated for the purpose that no army could have refrained from using it.

> This famous building [recorded Alexander in his final report on the campaign] had hitherto been deliberately spared, to our great disadvantage, but it was an integral part of the German defensive system, *mainly from the superb observation it afforded.*

The italics are mine.

Observation was the overriding issue at Cassino, not the relatively unimportant question whether the Abbey was occupied. And allied to the question of observation—in fact a corollary of it—was the psychological impact of this altogether exceptional observatory.

Because of the extraordinary extent to which the summit of Monte Cassino dominated the valleys; because of the painful constancy with which men were picked off by accurately observed gunfire whenever they were forced to move in daylight within its seemingly inescapable view; because of the obsessive theatrical manner in which it towered over the scene, searching every inch of it, the building set upon that summit had become the embodiment of resistance and its tangible symbol.

Everybody has experienced the sensation, when walking alone past a house, that invisible eyes were watching from a darkened interior. Hostile eyes can be sensed without being seen, and the soldier develops an exceptional awareness of this. Monte Cassino projected this feeling over an entire valley, and the feeling was being substantiated all the time by gunfire that could only have been so accurate and so swiftly opportunist through being directed by quite exceptionally positioned observers. Even in peacetime, Monte Cassino overwhelms even the least imaginative visitor gazing up at it from below. In the cold desolation of winter and the fatiguing travail of unresolved battle, the spell of its monstrous eminence was complete and haunting.

This was the psychological crux of the matter. To the soldiers dying at its feet, the Monastery had itself become in a sense the enemy.

Only the generals on the spot could be fully aware of this. It was their responsibility to order men to die attempting a task about which no one could feel optimistic. Theirs in the end are the only opinions which count.

This was the equally balanced, reasoned summary of General Kippenberger.

> Opinion at New Zealand Corps H.Q. and New Zealand Divisional H.Q. as to whether the abbey was occupied was divided. Personally, I thought the point immaterial. If not occupied today it might be tomorrow and it did not appear that it would be difficult for the enemy to bring reserves into it during the progress of an attack, or for troops to take shelter there if driven from positions outside.

> It was impossible to ask troops to storm a hill surmounted by an intact building such as this, capable of sheltering several hundred infantry in perfect security from shellfire and ready at the critical moment to emerge and counter-attack.
>
> I was in touch with our own troops and they were very definitely of the opinion that the Abbey must be destroyed before anyone was asked to storm the hill.

It is difficult to see how Freyberg could have come to any other decision than that the Monastery must be destroyed whether occupied or not.

But since so much has been made of the question of occupation, it is worth examining the evidence available at the time to the Allied commanders, and it will be seen that there was a considerable doubt about this.

During the conference at which the Second U.S. Corps handed over to the Second New Zealand Corps, General Butler, deputy commander of the U.S. 34th Division (who made the first attacks on the Monastery feature) said:

> I don't know but I don't believe the enemy is in the convent. All the fire has been from the slopes of the hill below the wall.

During the same conference a senior intelligence officer said:

> With reference to the Abbey, we have had statements from our own observers who believe they have seen observing instruments in the windows. We have had statements from civilians both for and against. Some have said that Germans are living there but this is not supported by others. It is very difficult to say whether it is being put to any military purpose this time.

Questioned further, the officer estimated that the Germans had a battalion-plus on top of the hill.

According to the official history of the U.S. Army Air Forces in World War II, the American Generals Eaker and Devers "flew over the Abbey in a Piper Cub at a height of less than 200 feet and Eaker states flatly that he saw a radio aerial on the Abbey and enemy soldiers moving in and out of the building."

There is one possibility, though it cannot be supported by evidence, which I think worth noting. Civilian refugees were lodged in the Monastery corridor being temporarily used as a rabbitry for the breeding of rabbits for food. This gave access to the open kitchen garden on the western, that is the German, side of the Abbey walls.

Anyone with experience of the more human side of front-line soldiering knows that no soldiers—lonely, uncomfortable, in danger, and bored—can be entirely restrained from making contact with any civilians within reach, either to exchange pleasantries with a woman or to barter cigarettes for eggs.

We know that three weeks before the bombing the military police guard was removed from the main entrance. For three weeks German soldiers were within a hundred yards or less of the kitchen garden to which the refugees had access. It can never be proved that some of them did not make contact with these civilians for one purpose or another, and that they were not seen doing so—thus giving rise to the reports that reached the Allies that German troops were in the Abbey: and perhaps explaining how it was that Generals Eaker and Devers were convinced during their flight over the Abbey that they had seen German soldiers moving about within its precincts.

Such unofficial excursions to a building which their Higher Command had formally placed out of bounds could easily have been accomplished without the monk's knowledge. The soldiers would merely have to wait until the sound of plainsong indicated that Abbot Diamare's small remnant community were safely inside the depths of the building at their devotions.

Finally, Sir D'Arcy Osborne, British Minister to the Vatican, had formally asked the Cardinal Secretary of State for an assurance that the Germans were not using the Abbey for military purposes. Sir D'Arcy's personal diary kept at the time shows that he received no reply until the evening of February 14 (the eve of the bombing) and then only a vague statement denying, on the authority of the German Embassy and German military authorities, that there were any considerable ("*grössere*") concentrations of German troops in the "immediate vicinity" of the Abbey. This was the only communication from the Vatican and it was hardly one on which action could be taken.

There remains the argument that a building becomes even more defendable after it has been destroyed. General von Senger, writing of the battle after the war, had this to say:

> As anyone who has had experience in street fighting —as at Stalingrad or Cassino—is aware . . . houses must be demolished in order to be converted from mouse-traps into bastions of defence.

This may be true as a general rule, but it is not necessarily so in the case of a building with walls ten feet thick, and the structural characteristics of a fortress. Nor had this consideration been overlooked by the New Zealand Command. They had discussed it thoroughly and had concluded that while the building would continue to be useful to the enemy after destruction, it would be more valuable intact. I again quote Kippenberger:

> Undamaged it was a perfect shelter but with its narrow windows and level profiles an unsatisfactory fighting position. Smashed by bombing it was a jagged heap of broken masonry and debris open to effective fire from guns, mortars and strafing planes as well as being a death trap if bombed again. On the whole I thought it would be more useful to the Germans if we left it unbombed.

It will be seen, therefore, that it was only after long and earnest deliberation, and after every aspect of the matter had been most thoroughly discussed, that General Freyberg reluctantly came to the conclusion that the destruction of the Monastery, by the only means powerful enough to have any effect on it, was tactically and psychologically necessary.

It may be added that General Clark was not in the closest touch with the Cassino front at this time. He was necessarily preoccupied with the bigger problem of Anzio—the crisis center where a German counteroffensive was known to be due very shortly. His opposition to the bombing—of which he has since made so much—was mostly expressed at second hand through his Chief of Staff. He was not, like Freyberg, continuously on the spot. So that it became necessary for General Alexander, as Army Group Commander, to influence the situation by stating unequivocally that he had complete faith in Freyberg's judgment.

And so, after days of doubt—the situation not being helped by the public airing of the pros and cons by the British and American press for the benefit of Goebbels and other interested parties—the decision was made. And General Clark gave the order for the bombing which he afterwards so bitterly repudiated.

If all the factors are considered dispassionately there can be little doubt that it was the only possible decision. The tragedy was that once the decision had been made, the matter became an Air Force responsibility. The Air Force, working alone without reference to the Army, projected it as a separate operation without co-ordinating it with the ground attack which was the only reason for its happening at all. The Air Force went ahead and carried out the bombing before the Indian division could possibly be ready to make the attack it was intended to support.

So the bombing, when it happened, expended its fury in a vacuum, tragically and wastefully. It achieved nothing, it helped nobody.

From the Air Force point of view the timing of the bombing depended mainly on the weather and on operational requirements elsewhere. A forecast of twenty-four hours of good weather was the first stipulation.

This operation was something new. For the first time the heaviest bombers of the Strategic Air Force were to operate with the Mediums in close support of infantry. Hitherto this had been the function of the Mediums only. These aircraft, based on forward airfields and bombing from a relatively low level, were the ones whose job it was to attack at short notice targets designated by the forward troops. The Mediums of the tactical air force were in effect another form of artillery under army control. The forward troops could indicate a target and the bombers would be over it within a short time.

The introduction of heavy bombers into an infantry battle created new problems. The operation had to be mounted from many airfields scattered through southern Italy, Sicily, and North Africa. Many of the aircraft would have to travel a long way to the objective. The Flying Fortresses bombed from very high altitudes, and it was something new for them to be asked to attack a pinpoint target. Sustained good weather was therefore more than usual a factor in timing the operation.

The second factor—requirements elsewhere—meant, of course, Anzio. The combined air forces could not make a maximum effort at Cassino and Anzio simultaneously. It had to be one or the other. Anzio was at this time the major anxiety. The new German counteroffensive was expected to go in there not later than February 16. (In the event, this forecast proved to be correct.) Cassino had to be disposed of before then.

It was inevitable in the circumstances that the timing of the bombing should have been a matter for the Air Commanders to decide. But this does not excuse the lack of liaison between the air and army. At the same time there seems to have been a failure on the part of General Freyberg to appreciate the difficulty the Indian division was experiencing in getting ready to make their attack. Otherwise he must have requested that the bombing be delayed until they were ready to take advantage of it.

"Ask of me anything but time," Napoleon once said. It is common to most operations that the subordinate commanders protest that they have insufficient time. It is the duty of senior commanders to treat such protests with some reserve. In this case Freyberg, himself under extreme pressure from above, appears to have carried skepticism too far.

The difficulties of the Indians were not being exaggerated. There were some extraordinary hazards attending the relief of the Americans by the Indians' assault battalion—the shortage of mule transport; the loss of their entire reserve of grenades and mortar ammunition; the laborious process of trickling the division across the Rapido valley—the false no-man's-land—to the remote and separate battleground in the mountaintops; the insufficiency of mules; the necessity to manhandle stores and supplies up the final stretches of the precipitous tracks; the limitation on daylight movement owing to the positions being overlooked; the impossibility of reconnaissance of the ground over which attacks were to be made; the constant casualties from shellfire, including the shells of Allied guns that had not yet mastered the intricacy of this isolated salient that, in relation to the gun lines, was *behind* the German positions.

There was the question of the all-important Point 593, the peak adjacent to the Monastery. The Americans had claimed that they held it, and it was not until the Indian division arrived to take it over that they found that the Germans still held this key piece of ground, and that it would have to be cleared before the attack on the Monastery could go in. This does not appear to have been understood at New Zealand Corps H.Q. which continued to show 593 in its Intelligence Summaries as held by the Allies.

An illuminating comment on this situation is that of General Kippenberger who, writing long after the event about the difficulties of his opposite number Brigadier Dimoline, had this to say:

> Poor Dimoline was having a dreadful time getting his division into position. I never really appreciated the difficulties until I went over the ground after the war. He got me to make an appointment for us both with General Freyberg, as he thought his task was impossible and his difficulties not fully realized. The General refused to see us together: he told me he was not going to have any soviet of divisional commanders.

So Dimoline protested that he needed more time; Freyberg insisted that he could not have any; and the United

States Army Air Force waited with one eye on the meteorologists and the other on Anzio. On February 14, after a great storm which raged throughout the 13th, the experts promised a twenty-four hour period of clear weather. The bombing was accordingly ordered for nine-thirty the following morning, the 15th.

In the early afternoon of February 14, the monks were preparing to take to his last resting place Dom Eusebio who had died the previous day of the unidentified epidemic[1] which had broken out among the refugees in the Abbey. Still in his monk's habit, he lay in one of the underground passages where the others had taken turns to maintain a twenty-four hour vigil over his body. Now they were ready to consign him to one of the improvised coffins which he himself had been constructing in the carpenter's shop for those refugees who had died of the same disease.

As the monks prayed for the last time over the body of Dom Eusebio a group of refugees rushed up to them in high excitement. They brought with them leaflets that had just been dropped by an American aircraft. The leaflets, addressed to "Italian Friends" and signed "The Fifth Army" bore this message:

> We have until now been careful to avoid bombarding Monte Cassino. The Germans have taken advantage of this. The battle is now closing in more and more around the sacred precincts. Against our will we are now obliged to direct our weapons against the Monastery itself. We warn you so that you may save yourselves. Leave the Monastery at once. This warning is urgent. It is given for your good.

At once there was a great commotion. Alarm quickly spread among the refugees scattered in pockets throughout the vast building. They began to stream in to where the Abbot stood, reading and rereading the leaflet. The best thing, the Abbot said, would be to find a German officer and see if it could be arranged for the Abbey to be evacuated.

[1] Subsequently diagnosed as paratyphoid fever.

Three young men volunteered to leave the safety of the Abbey walls and make a dash for one of the German posts not many yards away. This meant showing themselves in the open. They set off, but before they had traveled very far they were frightened by the shellfire and turned back. Panic broke out afresh, and while the Abbot deliberated, and the monks and the refugees argued about what should be done, the Sacrist and half a dozen helpers quietly lifted Dom Eusebio into his coffin, and bore him off along the corridors and staircases to the Chapel of St. Anne where he was laid to rest in the central grave of the presbytery.

By the time the burial party had returned, the refugees were barely controllable, still demanding from the Abbot a magical solution. One monk suggested a mass exodus under a white flag, but another opposed this with grim stories of massacres he said had taken place in similar circumstances. Another argued in favor of staying and making the best of it. Before long the uncertainty had prompted one of the men to start a rumor that the monks were in league with the Germans, and that the leaflet was a trick concocted between them to get the Abbey cleared of the refugees—whose relationship with the monks was always inclined to be strained. In desperation the Abbot ruled that it was everyone for himself. They could make a run for it or stay—whichever they preferred. Another effort would be made to get in touch with the Germans after dark.

Shortly after nightfall two men did succeed in making contact with the German armored car troop which patrolled the road up to the monastery entrance during the hours of darkness. They said that the Abbot wished to speak to an officer and were told that this could not be arranged before five o'clock the following morning. Then two representatives of the Abbot—but not more than two—could come along to their headquarters. So they resigned themselves to a night of fear and uncertainty, and from time to time, unable to bear the suspense, the refugees would shout from the rabbitry to the nearby German posts, which were within earshot—but the soldiers did not reply. At five o'clock, just as the Abbot's secretary and the man chosen to accompany him were leaving the building, the officer they were to try to locate turned up. He was introduced to the Abbot and shown the leaflet.

The Abbot suggested that it would be convenient if he and the monks could be allowed to make for the Allied lines, and the refugees were removed to the German rear. There was a wistful irony in the old man's suggestion that his own small group and the refugees should move in opposite directions, and also, perhaps, in the choice of directions he proposed.

The officer, a lieutenant, said that there could be no question of anyone being allowed to walk to the Allied lines. He pointed out that it would be a risky business leaving the Monastery at all, and they would have to take full responsibility for any move decided upon. He added, however, that during the night he had discussed the situation of the Monastery with his commanding officer, and the latter had arranged for one of the paths leading down to Highway Six to be opened to the refugees from midnight until 5 a.m. the following morning, February 16.

The Abbot protested that it might be too late then. The officer said that this was the best he could do and after being taken, at his request, into the cathedral for a few moments, he left. It was still half an hour before daylight. Those civilians who were at hand dispersed to the various passages and corners that had become their temporary homes. The monks repaired to their small subterranean chapel in the *torretta,* the oldest part of the building, the one link with St. Benedict's original abbey, and there they prepared to start the day's devotions which in winter begin at five-thirty.

Tuesday, February 15, 1944, began, like any other day, with the celebration of Matins and Lauds.

The morning of Tuesday February 15 was cold, but the sky was clearer than it had been for many days. In that part of their refuge which they had turned into a temporary chapel, the Abbot and the monks were addressing themselves as usual to the succession of holy offices which make up the Benedictine day: to that rhythm of prayer and psalmody and meditation precisely laid down for them fourteen centuries before by their founder.

It had begun, after the departure of the German officer, with that part of the Divine Office that ended with Lauds. At eight-thirty they recited together the psalms and prayers prescribed for *prime* and the first of the Little Hours, *terce*. And then, as it happened to be the week of the Feast of St. Scholastica—St. Benedict's sister, whose bones lay alongside her brother's in the great tomb below the high altar of the cathedral of Monte Cassino—they celebrated the conventual mass appropriate to this particular saint.

Not long afterwards they went to the Abbot's room for the second and third of the Little Hours, and then they returned to their temporary chapel. They had improvised an altar there, and on it they had set the little Madonna of De Matteis which normally rested on the tomb of St. Benedict in the cathedral. Kneeling before this altar, and chanting antiphonally, they invoked the blessing of the Madonna.

It was a little after nine-thirty and they had just sung the words "Beseech Christ on our behalf" when the first of a succession of great explosions sent a shudder through the thick abbey walls and great gusts of thunder echoed along the vast stone passageways, giving continuity to the crashes so that they were no longer a succession of explosions but a single great cataclysmic roar.

To these men whose lives had been passed in near-silence; whose scant conversation was in a low voice; whose meals were taken in silence; whose habitation was a mountaintop that was the apotheosis of tranquillity; whose most violent acquaintance with sound was the Gregorian chant of the Divine Office, the bombing was, apart from anything else, an overwhelmingly terrifying baptism of sheer noise beyond anything they could conceivably have imagined. They huddled together in a corner on their knees, numb with terror. Automatically the eighty-year-old Abbot gave them absolution. Automatically they composed themselves for death.

The explosions seemed incessant. A great haze of dust and smoke was discernible through the narrow window, and great yellow flashes as the bombs crashed about the building, dispassionately destroying. All the time the thunder of the explosions echoed and re-echoed along the vaulted corridors and stone passageways, adding immeasurably to the noise.

After the first few minutes of petrifying shock there was a diversion, marked by that quality of melodrama which was never long absent from Cassino. A breathless figure, covered in dust, appeared suddenly at the side of the praying monks. He was gesticulating like a man demented, but he uttered no sound. It was the deaf-mute servant. In the sign language of the deaf-and-dumb, heightened by terror into almost maniacal convulsions, he was trying to tell them that the cathedral had gone. It had been one of the first parts of the Abbey to receive a direct hit. A bomb had passed through the frescoed dome.

The bombardment continued throughout the morning, and though only about ten per cent of the heavy bombers succeeded in hitting the Abbey, this was enough to wreck the interior.

Inside the cathedral the pipes of the celebrated Catarinozzi organ, which had cost 10,000 ducats, were shredded like paper foil; the high altar, incorporating parts of an original attributed to Michelangelo, subsided into a mound of rubble about the tomb of St. Benedict; the wooden stalls of the choir, a masterpiece of the Neapolitan carvers who have no equals in this work, were reduced to a tangle of splinters. Fragments of marble inlay were scattered everywhere like outsize confetti.

One by one the five cloistered courtyards were shattered into dumps to contain the rubble of the elegant cloisters and the solid buildings which had formerly surrounded them.

The entrance cloister was a series of broken stumps and a heap of debris that was knee-deep. The Cloister of the Priors, around which the boys' college had formed a square, had been totally submerged by the collapsed college, and nearly one hundred refugees were buried under the ruins. The Bramante Cloister, the one unquestionable architectural masterpiece of Monte Cassino, no longer existed.

This cloister had been built round three sides of the central courtyard. Along the top of its arches ran the celebrated gallery known as the Loggia del Paradiso—and from the fourth side rose a magnificent stone stairway, sixty feet wide, leading up to yet another cloister, the Cloister of the Benefactors, decorated with the marble statues of seventeen popes and kings who had befriended the Monastery. This cloister led to the cathedral. In the center of the courtyard, too, was a cistern, decorated with a handsome pillared fountainhead.

By noon the central courtyard was unrecognizable. The cloisters were like broken teeth. The great flight of steps had vanished. The portico above the cistern had been leveled to the ground leaving only a gaping hole filled with water that was now colored red.

Once during the morning, when there seemed to be a lull in the bombardment, the Abbot left his shelter to inspect the damage. He found that most of the upper stories of the Abbey had gone and that all that remained of the cathedral was its shell, wide open to the sky. He heard the groans of refugees buried under the ruins of the Priors' Cloister, and found that nothing could be done to rescue them. He saw other refugees making a dash for the open, and about a hundred got away during this interlude. And he was accosted by the three peasant families, who from the earliest days of what might be termed the siege had been allowed to stay on in the Abbey. They asked if they might now go down to the monks' refuge, and the Abbot gave them permission to do so. Then the sound of aircraft was heard again, and everyone hastily returned to his shelter.

The monks were safe in their chapel, and the lay brothers, it turned out, had been able to make themselves comfortable and secure in the bakery. Meanwhile the Sacrist had made a hazardous journey through the rubble and the half-collapsed walls to bring the Holy Sacrament from another chapel so that the monks could celebrate Communion.

The bombardment reopened. It was now the turn of the medium bombers. They dropped smaller bombs, but they dropped them more accurately. The Mediums attacked from a low level in tight little formations of twelve, and their bombs fell in a compact carpet. Once again the Abbot, those monks who were still with him, and the three peasant families who had attached themselves to him, prepared for the worst. Soon an explosion more powerful than any they had yet experienced seemed to tear the heart out of the crumbling abbey. A great wave of debris thundered about the refuge, blocking the entrance to it, but the thick walls held.

To Allied observers, watching the bombing with a sense of uncomfortable awe, it did not for a long time seem as effective as they had expected.

Christopher Buckley, the British war correspondent, noted:

> As the sun brightened and climbed up the sky I could detect little modification in the monastery's outline as each successive smoke cloud cleared away. Here and there one noted an ugly fissure in the walls, here and there a window seemed unnaturally enlarged. The roof was beginning to look curiously jagged and uneven . . . but essentially the building was still standing after four hours of pounding from the air.
>
> Just before two o'clock in the afternoon a formation of Mitchells (Mediums) passed over. They dipped slightly. A moment later a bright flame, such as a giant might have produced by striking titanic matches on the mountain-side, spurted swiftly upwards at half-a-dozen points. Then a pillar of smoke five hundred feet high broke upwards into the blue. For nearly five minutes it hung around the building, thinning gradually upwards into strange, evil-looking arabesques such as Aubrey Beardsley at his most decadent might have designed.
>
> Then the column paled and melted. The Abbey became visible again. Its whole outline had changed. The west wall had totally collapsed . . .

The Mediums, operating in tight formation, had administered the *coup de grâce,* and this had been the explosion more powerful than any that had gone before, the one that had blocked the entrance to the monks' refuge.

(The wall, though breached, had not been split from top to bottom, as it had seemed to Buckley watching from a hillside five miles away. The lower part, the battlemented base, ten feet thick, was still intact. The Abbey had been wrecked but there was still no easy way in for any soldiers who succeeded in storming their way up the slopes of the mountain.)

During the afternoon the Abbot and those with him dug their way out of the refuge they had been using, and made for the chapels under the largely intact *torretta,* which now seemed the safest place left. There they did what they could to help the injured. A little food was located and distributed. But there was no water. With the arrival of darkness, and periodical collapses of walls and ceilings—not to mention the artillery fire that was by this time following up the work of the bombers—a new kind of terror set in. Should they attempt to get away at once, risking the shells? Or should they wait for the German officer to whom they had spoken in the morning?

At eight o'clock this same lieutenant arrived at the Abbey. But it was not, as they had hoped, to guide them to the escape route that had been promised early that morning.

The lieutenant had come to say that Hitler, at the request of the Pope, was asking the Allies for a truce so that the monks and the civilian refugees might leave Monte Cassino. They would be taken away in German army transport, but owing to the state of the road, would have to make their way to the transport on foot. Kesselring would ask for a truce that night. If the Allies failed to grant it the responsibility for the fate of the monks and the refugees would be theirs.

The Abbot was then asked to sign a statement to the effect that there had been no German soldiers in the Monastery before or during the attack. The statement was already prepared:

> I certify to be the truth that inside the enclosure of the sacred monastery of Cassino there never were any German soldiers; that there were for a certain period only three military police for the sole purpose of en-

forcing respect for the neutral zone which was established around the monastery, but they were withdrawn about twenty days ago.

Monte Cassino *(Signed)* GREGORIO DIAMARE
February 15, 1944 Abbot-Bishop of Monte Cassino.
DIEBER
Lieutenant.

On the altar of the Chapel of the Pietà, his black habit still white with the clinging dust, the eighty-year-old Abbot signed the document and the officer left. Although his feelings were by no means pro-Allied at this moment, the Abbot and the remaining monks had little doubt that the statement about the request for a truce meant nothing. There is an innocent pathos in the way one of them expressed his doubts: "The truce did not take place. It is indeed doubtful whether the request for it was ever even put forward, and whether it was not a case of deception." But at this extreme time they needed some sort of hope to cling to, and the mention of a truce, however skeptically they felt about it, provided them with it. It was this hope of a truce that helped them to face the long twelve-hour night in darkness that was penetrated only by the flash of bursting shells, the moans of the wounded, and the fearful rumble whenever some further part of the ruins collapsed.

As they composed themselves to await the morrow there was one result of that day that affected the monks more profoundly than any other. In a devastation that had spared no part of the extensive monastery buildings, except those below ground, the cell used by St. Benedict himself, and preserved through the ages, had unaccountably escaped. They would have been filled with even greater wonder had they known (what was discovered many months later after the war had passed on) that during the afternoon a large-caliber artillery shell had landed within a foot of the saint's tomb, but had failed to explode.

So it happened that in all this destruction the cell where Benedict lived in his lifetime and the tomb in which his remains had rested during the fourteen hundred years since his death were the only places to escape injury.

That night the Air Command announced flatly that 142 B-17 Fortress bombers and 112 Mediums had by nightfall dropped 576 tons of bombs on Monte Cassino. The Monastery buildings had been wrecked and breaches made in the outer walls, but because of the great thickness of these walls the bombs had not breached them from top to bottom.

On this same Tuesday morning, February 15, the foremost troops of the 4th Indian Division were facing their third day in the uncomfortable mountain salient. The conditions were unlike anything they had previously experienced. Only a shallow jagged hump separated their forward posts from those of the Germans seventy yards away. The whole of this isolated private front line was overlooked from enemy-held heights on three sides, which made daylight movement out of the question. It had been difficult enough to relieve the Americans in the first place, and since taking over two nights before, it had been even more difficult to bring up the supplies they would need for the major attack they were being pressed to launch almost immediately. Living conditions were not improved by the presence of over a hundred unburied—and unreachable—bodies scattered about the area.

The best way to visualize this salient, cutting into the heart of the German mountain positions, is to imagine a rocky, uneven ridge roughly in the shape of a boomerang and a thousand yards long. From the British side the boomerang curved away to the left, the Royal Sussex being astride the near end, the Germans occupying most of the rest of it, and Monastery Hill being just beyond the far end. At the "elbow" of the boomerang was the dome-shaped mountain known on the map as Point 593. The Germans manned its forward slopes in strength.

The boomerang-shaped ridge, which the Americans had called Snakeshead, provided an approach to the Monastery, but blocking the way was the natural obstacle of Point 593. The sides of the ridge sloped away sharply, at times precipitously, and the only alternative to an advance along the ridge (taking 593 en route) was to cut directly across the open "elbow" to Monastery Hill, giving Point 593 in the middle a wide berth. This, however, would entail crossing a chaos of slopes, gullies, ravines, boulders, gorse thickets, and shattered walls where shells had churned up the terracing. On the whole the approach along Snakeshead seemed the lesser of the two evils, but first Point 593 would have to be captured.

Two basic (as well as a score of minor) difficulties influenced the projected operation over this unpromising ground. The first was supply. Everything, including water, had to be brought seven miles across the valley on mules by an oblique route, and then manhandled for the last few hundred yards up the final steep paths to the forward positions. This supply route took five hours to cover, was constantly shelled so that only a proportion of the mules actually got through on most nights. The wounded had to endure the same long and hazardous journey in the opposite direction.

The second basic difficulty was that the ground itself—this tangle of rocky ledges, slopes, ravines, boulders, narrow ridges, and gorse thickets—was such that only a few troops could be deployed on it at a time. To adapt itself to these conditions, the Division's plan had been to establish one of its three brigades (the 7th) in the forward area as a firm base and assault force, and to feed battalions of a second brigade (the 5th) into the 7th as required. The 7th Brigade would therefore act as a funnel not only for its own jug of water, as it were, but also for that of the 5th Brigade. The third brigade of the division, the 11th, would be used as a corps of porters, carriers, and laborers to keep the other two supplied.

By Tuesday morning the 7th Brigade were just beginning to become acclimatized to their spearpoint position. The 1st Royal Sussex were astride Snakeshead Ridge, seventy yards from the Germans, a thousand yards from the Monastery. The 4th/16th Punjabis were echeloned down the slope to their left. The 1st/2nd Gurkhas were in reserve a few hundred yards behind.

To the Royal Sussex, who were the point of the spear, the focal point of the landscape was, of course, the cream-colored Abbey on which they looked slightly downward from this height. But what worried them more was the rocky dome of Point 593 rising up immediately to their front. While everyone else could talk of nothing but the Monastery, the Royal Sussex were doing their best to make it clear that Point 593 would have to be captured first. No 593, no Monte Cassino. At the headquarters of the Second New Zealand Corps across the valley this had not been fully appreciated. Thus it was that the 4th Indian Division, now gloomily aware of all the local difficulties, was thinking in terms of a preliminary clearance of Point 593, to be followed by an attack on the Monastery: while Second New Zealand Corps, constantly being urged to get a move on, was visualizing an immediate direct attack on the Monastery as soon as the bombing had taken place.

While the officers were preoccupied with these problems on that Tuesday morning there was nothing for the soldiers to do but to make themselves as tolerably comfortable as they could in the circumstances. They would try to sleep, or read, or even shave if they had saved the dregs of their tea—for when water had to be brought seven miles by mule it had also to be severely rationed. They would clean their weapons, but not themselves. They would smoke, if they had not run out of cigarettes, for ammunition had to take precedence over comforts while mules were still in short supply. They would write letters. They would stare at the Monastery.

When, shortly after nine-thirty, the formation of Fortresses passed high overhead, no one paid any attention. Except when the weather was bad, Fortresses were always flying over—so high that they were only just visible—to those regular assignments: marshaling yards, railway bridges, communications centers, that to the soldier seemed always so remote and useless. Then the bombs began to drop on the Monastery and some of them quite a distance from it and a few of the soldiers were wounded by flying rock splinters before they had quite grasped what was happening.

As the first salvo crashed down, Colonel Glennie, C.O. of the Royal Sussex, picked up his telephone and called his brigade headquarters, but before he had time to speak the voice at the other end said: "We didn't know either!" No one had remembered to tell the ground troops primarily concerned that the bombing, which they had been warned to expect on the 16th, had been brought forward a day. "They told the monks," remarked Colonel Glennie, "and they told the enemy, but they didn't tell us!" Of this curious lapse perhaps it may be said that army-air co-operation was still in its adolescence, if not its infancy, and that this was yet another occasion when a number of lessons were learned the hard way.

For the soldiers, the bombing was a spectacular diversion in the monotony of the front-line day—albeit a nerve-racking one, for many of the bombs fell close to their positions and caused several more casualties. For the officers it was the background to a day of feverish planning, for it wasn't long before the order came through that, however unexpected the advancing of the date of the bombing, however unready they might think they were, an attack must be made that night. The preliminary clearance of Point 593 must be disposed of immediately. The Royal Sussex must deal with it that night.

The factors were brutally simple. The nearest German posts were 70 yards away: too close for the British battalion to employ direct artillery support. The peak of 593 was only another 100 yards farther on. The ground was rock hard, and littered with loose stones, making silent approach virtually impossible. There had been no time to build up a picture of exact enemy dispositions through patrolling and continuous observation. This was a battle that would be settled by grenade, bayonet, mortar, and light machine gun, and the unfortunate Sussex would now have bitter cause to regret the loss of their mortar and grenade reserves on the journey forward when the two lorries carrying them plunged off the road. (In passing, one may wonder why the Divisional Staff failed to make good this loss.)

This must have been one of the few battlefields of the second world war which reproduced the close conditions of

1914-18. The Flanders phrase is entirely applicable. What the Royal Sussex had to do was to go "over the top."

In view of their limited knowledge of both the ground and enemy dispositions the Sussex decided to make their first attack with one company only. That night, about the time that Abbot Diamare, propping himself against the altar of the Chapel of the Pietà, was signing the document declaring that there had been no German soldiers in the Monastery, a company of the Sussex, 3 officers and 63 men strong, moved stealthily forward astride Snakeshead Ridge toward Point 593 at the "elbow" of the boomerang.

They moved in normal formation of two platoons abreast, the third following behind in reserve. They moved very slowly. On this ground there was a danger at every step of a stone being dislodged and rattling against another: and in these high places sounds of this kind were audible a long way away. On this ground, too, it was fatally easy to turn an ankle, or stumble. It was especially easy for a man laden with something heavy, such as a Bren gun. With every single step there was a danger of breaking the silence that was essential to their approach—with an alert enemy a bare seventy yards away.

The leading troops had advanced no more than fifty yards when they came under a withering fire of machine gun and grenade. They went to ground. They wriggled across the sharp, stony ground from one position to another, trying to work round to the flanks. Time after time individuals and groups made a new effort to find a way round, a way closer to an objective that was so near and yet so inaccessible. But the steep ground defeated them. And their grenades began to run short, though the Germans, sending them over in showers from their positions up the slope, had unlimited quantities. To help them out grenades were collected from the other companies of the battalion and passed forward, but long before dawn these too had been used up.

If they had remained in the open after daybreak they would have been wiped out to a man. Before first light they were therefore ordered to withdraw. February 15, a calamitous day for Monte Cassino, had not spared the Royal Sussex either. Of the 3 officers and 63 men who had undertaken this exploratory trial of strength against a preliminary objective, 2 officers and 32 men had been killed or wounded no more than fifty yards from their start-point. It was a foretaste of things to come.

During the morning the Sussex were ordered to try again that night, using the whole battalion. At the same time it was learned that the counteroffensive against the Anzio beachhead had started, as expected, a few hours before.

The Germans had massed four infantry divisions on a 4,000-yard front and were making an all-out effort to cut through the heart of the beachhead to Anzio, eight miles away. This was their biggest offensive operation of the campaign. It was supported by 452 guns. Following up the infantry divisions and their supporting tanks ready to exploit their success were two Panzer divisions, each reinforced by a battalion of the newest and heaviest tanks, the Tiger and Panther.

There was no doubt at all where the Allied Air Forces were going to be needed for the next few days. Everything that could fly would be wanted at Anzio. Cassino could look for no help from the air for a few days. The bombing offensive that had started the day before with the destruction of the Monastery had to end with it.

Poor Abbot Diamare and his reduced party of monks and refugees could not know this, however, and they spent a forlorn day in the Abbey ruins waiting in vain for the Germans who had promised to return and help them get away.

By now the party was reduced to about forty. Most of the able-bodied survivors of the bombing had got away during the night or at dawn. There remained the three dogged peasant families who never left the Abbot's side now; some children—three of them badly injured—who had been deserted by their parents; a number of other injured including an old woman whose feet had been blown off; about half a dozen able-bodied men, and a few of the lay brothers. Only two monks remained. One, as we saw, died in the epidemic. Two others were killed in the bombing.

Apart from one brief visit from fighter bombers during the day, there was no air activity, but there was a great deal of artillery fire. Quite early in the day the Abbot decided that he could expect no further help from the Germans and that he must organize the evacuation himself. He decided that first light the following morning would be the best time, as he had noticed that there was generally a lull in the fighting then. Once again he and the monks had to resign themselves to another long night in the ruins.

There were two small comforts in a day of otherwise unrelieved fear and hopelessness. One of the lay brothers managed to rescue a breviary from the rubble: it enabled the Abbot and the monks to celebrate the divine offices as usual. The other, and more earthly comfort was the discovery that a small water tank was undamaged in the ruins of the kitchen.

The first thing the Sussex C.O. did when he was ordered to attack 593 again that night was to send a strongly worded SOS for grenades. The company battle of the night before had confirmed that grenades more than anything else were what were wanted for this close-quarter fighting among the rocks. Then he planned his attack.

B Company, reinforced by a platoon of A Company, were to be the main effort company: they were to attack 593 from the left and take it. Simultaneously the depleted A Company were to make a diversionary effort on the right, to distract the German defenses. When B Company were on the hill, they were to send up a light signal, whereupon D Company, fresh and carrying as much ammunition as they could, were to rush through, relieve B on the newly captured height and immediately prepare to repel the inevitable counterattack. C Company, the one halved in strength by the battle of the previous night, would remain in reserve.

With the objective beginning only seventy yards away, it was not possible to have it shelled in advance.

The shortage of ammunition for the mortars was solved by salvaging the bombs (of a different caliber from the British) left behind by the Americans. These could be fired through some captured German and Italian mortars which the Sussex had brought back from North Africa as souvenirs.

No one was happy about the operation. The trial of strength the previous night had shown how strongly defended 593 was. The impossibility of prior reconnaissance made night movement over this broken and difficult ground a dangerous gamble. Ammunition was still far from adequate—it would take many nights to build up the necessary stocks. But Anzio was facing its gravest crisis and the Cassino attack had to go in. It would be something if the all-important grenades arrived in time. For the Royal Sussex it was a day of tension.

The attack was ordered for 2300, because that was the earliest time by which the mule train bringing the grenades could arrive. By 2300 the mules had not arrived. The supply route had been heavily shelled that night, and many mules had been lost. The attack was postponed for half an hour. By 2330 the mules had still not arrived, and the attack was postponed for another half hour. A few minutes later the mules did arrive, but owing to losses on the way through the shelling, they brought only half the number of grenades required.

The attack at last started, calamitously, at midnight. As we have seen there could be no direct artillery support on an objective so close to the attackers. Instead the task of the artillery was to neutralize the adjacent peaks, especially Point 575, 800 yards to the right of 593. From the point of view of the guns—firing from the far side of the valley, 1,500 feet below the altitude of these hills—the ridge along which the Sussex had to advance was a crest only slightly below that of Point 575. To hit the latter, it was necessary for the shells to skim the top of Snakeshead by a few feet, and gunnery as precise as this allowed no margin for error. The tiniest fraction of a variation in elevation and the shells would hit the top of Snakeshead instead of Point 575, 800 yards away.

This is precisely what happened. As the two leading companies, closely followed by Battalion Headquarters and the Reserve Company, formed up on the start-line of the attack, the artillery opened fire on Point 575. But several shells failed to clear Snakeshead, and burst among the leading companies and Battalion Headquarters. It is axiomatic that the most demoralizing beginning to any operation is for the attacking force to be shelled on its start-line. It is not less disturbing if the shells happen to be from its own guns. Only one company—the one that was to take over and consolidate the hill if it was captured—escaped.

After a hurried reorganization the attack went in according to plan. As on the previous night fifty yards were covered before the advancing troops ran into a withering fire. The reinforced main effort company worked round by the left, as they had been ordered, while the smaller company set about creating their diversionary display of fireworks on the right. This company at once ran into trouble. Just in time they stopped on the edge of a forty-foot precipice not indicated on the map. There was no way round by the right, so they edged leftward, and then found themselves faced with a crevice fifteen feet deep and twenty feet across. There was nothing they could do except go to ground and give fire support.

Meanwhile the main effort company on the left, thanks to a number of individual feats of valor which destroyed some of the German machine-gun nests, did succeed in forcing their way on to the main part of the feature. But the Germans, defending ruthlessly, could not be dislodged from well-prepared positions in which they were determined to stay. A hand-to-hand battle then raged, and in the confusion a number of the Sussex pushing through to the rear of the objective went beyond it, and fell down another of the small precipices in which the area abounds. They were wounded and taken prisoner. Another party, driving through to the rear of the peak, unluckily ran into a more numerous party of German reinforcements on their way in. As on the previous night it turned into a grenade battle, but while the Germans were sending them over in showers, the British battalion soon began to run out. After about two hours of this, the right-hand company had had all their officers killed or wounded, and the reserve company went to reinforce them. On the left the main effort force was rapidly running out of ammunition, and all of their officers had been wounded.

The one fresh company—the one that had been intended to exploit the captured position—was sent in as a last resort, but they came up against the deep crevice that had halted the right-hand company, and at the same time they were caught in a murderous cross fire.

The attack had failed and there was nothing for it but to withdraw the remnants of the four companies to the point from which they had started.

Out of 12 officers and 250 men that had taken part in the attack, 10 officers and 130 men were killed, wounded or taken prisoner. In the two nights, therefore, the Sussex casualties had been 12 out of 15 officers, 162 out of 313 men. In two nights a fine battalion that had fought since the earliest days of the war, and which had never previously failed to take its objective, had been cut to pieces.

The casualties speak for themselves. The battalion could not have tried harder or more gallantly. It wasn't their fault that they had to attack before they were ready. With the supply line what it was—the night was barely long enough for the mule trains to make the round journey of fourteen miles—they had no chance to build up their ammunition stocks to the level required.

At dawn on Thursday (by which time Tuesday's bombing seemed an age ago), while the commanding officer of the Royal Sussex was reorganizing the remains of four powerful companies into three small ones; while General von Mackensen's Fourteenth Army, after a nonstop attack which had driven a mile and a half into the Anzio beachhead, was approaching the climax of its tremendous onslaught; Abbot Diamare, summoning up the last reserves of his strength, prepared for the final stage of his long ordeal.

He called the surviving monks and refugees together by the entrance arch of the Abbey (above which the inscription PAX was still intact) and gave sacramental absolution to each one of them. Then, taking hold of a large wooden crucifix, he led the way through the rubble on to one of the bridle paths leading westward through the mountains. Before the party of forty left there was a last distressing decision to be taken. Three small children, a sister and two brothers, had been found in the ruins. All three were injured. Their mother had been killed in the bombing and their father had since abandoned them. It was clear that the girl and one of the brothers had a very short time to live. When an attempt was made to lift them they screamed with pain, and it was thought kinder to leave them. To have carried them up and down steep mountain paths would have only made their last moments more painful. The other brother was less badly hurt, he was only paralyzed in both legs. A lay brother hoisted him onto his shoulders. A ladder was found which could be used as a stretcher for the old woman whose feet had been blown off, and two of the very few survivors who were not either sick or wounded carried her at the rear of the column.

Progress was slow and painful, the paths being steep and rough. But the Abbot, supported by the monks and lay brothers, insisted on holding up the heavy crucifix as they stumbled down the mountainside. Whenever they came to a German post the Abbot asked for permission to pass, saying that he was abandoning the Monastery with the consent of the German High Command. For the most part (one of the monks recorded) the soldiers just stared openmouthed at this strange company and said absolutely nothing. Inevitably the little column straggled and after a time there were shouts from the rear. The men carrying the ladder bearing the woman who had lost her feet shouted that they could not keep up, the track was too steep and too difficult. Those in front shouted back encouragement. There was not much farther to go, they must keep up. After they had been walking for some time they came to a level piece of ground and the Abbot called a halt so that they could rest a little, and to give the stragglers a chance to catch up. It was discovered then that the two men who had been carrying the old woman had given up some way back and abandoned her. They were too exhausted to carry on, they said. The column moved off again and after a time they came to a cottage in which the Germans had established a medical post. There the injured were given some attention, but when the Abbot asked to be put in touch with a headquarters he was told that the telephone line was cut. The Germans said it would be better for the party to keep moving until they were farther to the rear. They would receive help there. They pointed out a suitable path and suggested that it would be safer (there was a certain amount of shelling) if they moved off at intervals in small groups.

This was arranged and one by one the groups moved off. The last to leave were to be the Abbot and the Sacrist. For the time being these two rested inside the cottage as the Abbot was by this time close to collapse. While they were there a messenger arrived to say that an urgent search for the Abbot had been instituted and all forward units had been warned to look out for him. As soon as he had reported back that the Abbot was found, a further message was sent to the medical post ordering them to look after him until he could be picked up. The ambulance arrived during the afternoon.

The German corps commander, General von Senger, has described the end of the story:

> I had the Abbot picked up there by car and brought to my Headquarters . . . I lodged the venerable old priest, who was accompanied by a solitary monk companion, for one night.
>
> While the Abbot was my guest I received orders from the German High Command to induce him to make a radio statement regarding the attitude of the German troops and their respect for the neutrality of the Monastery. I decided to comply, as the destruction of the Monastery was an event of historic importance in which my personal honour as a soldier and as a Christian was involved. After a conversation with his companion the Abbot agreed, and we conducted a dialogue into the microphone which went even further than I had intended, complaining of the deplorable ruin and destruction of many valuable and irreparable works of art. After the broadcast I had him taken by car to Rome, appointing an officer to

deliver him safely to Sant' Anselmo, where he informed me he wished to go. Sant' Anselmo on the Aventino is the centre of the Benedictine Order . . .

My plan to convey the Abbot safely to Sant' Anselmo was thwarted. On the road to Rome the car was waylaid by agents of Goebbels, the Propaganda Minister. Goebbels had no intention of missing this excellent piece of propaganda and according to the methods of the Fuehrer Principle meant to act with complete disregard of what others might do in the same line. The frightened old priest was accordingly brought to a radio station, kept waiting a long time without food, and finally induced to make another statement as prescribed by the radio columnists . . .

But this was not sufficient. Hitler's most stupid and most arrogant henchman, the Foreign Minister, also wanted his share of the cake. The statement which he required was shaped upon distinctly political propaganda lines. The unfortunate old priest at last broke down, refused to make any more statements, and asked to be released, as he now understood that he was no longer a protected guest but a prisoner.

War exacts its wages indiscriminately. In the mosaic of suffering and endurance created by the battle of Cassino, Gregorio Diamare, eighty-year-old Abbot-Bishop of Monte Cassino, has an honorable place. So, it may be thought, has the old peasant woman with the severed feet, whom they carried part of the way to safety on a ladder and then left to die alone on the cold mountainside. For it was her fate to be a battle casualty without even knowing what the battle was about.

That evening, the German propagandists having completed their work, the Tenth Army was able to make some small adjustments in its dispositions on and around the summit of Monastery Hill by establishing posts in the Abbey ruins.

For the 4th Indian Division and the New Zealanders it was a day of urgency. Both divisions were at last ready to make the concerted attack originally designed to follow the bombing. That night the Indians would attack not with one battalion, but with three.

At midnight the 4th/6th Rajputana Rifles would pass through the Royal Sussex and attempt to storm Point 593. If they succeeded where the Sussex had failed, the depleted Sussex would then follow up the success, and sweep along the ridge to Point 444 at the far end of the "boomerang."

At 0215, with the help of the moon which would then be rising, two battalions of Gurkhas, the 1st/2nd and 1st/9th, starting from the left of the Sussex would sweep across the slopes and ravines in a direct assault on the Monastery. It was an appalling route that they had to cover, but the Gurkhas, born and bred in the foothills of the Himalaya, were the most expert mountain fighters in the Commonwealth armies. If anyone could negotiate the impossible mountain terrain, the Gurkhas could. Two entire reserve battalions of the division were organized into carrying parties to provide the necessary replenishments of ammunition and other essentials.

While the Indians projected themselves at these mountain strongholds, the 28th (Maori) Battalion of the New Zealand division was to advance from the direction of Monte Trocchio along the railway causeway and take Cassino Station.

The New Zealanders had not had the same difficulty as the Indians in getting into position, but like the Indians they had found themselves on ground where few troops could be deployed at a time. Owing to the flooded state of the valley, the causeway was the only usable line of approach.

On the heels of the Maoris would follow a company of sappers to remove mines, deal with the demolitions that the Germans had left behind to make the causeway impossible for transport, and to erect Bailey bridges over two waterways—a canal and the Rapido—which lay between the start-point and the station. The success of the operation depended on the sappers making the route fit for transport by dawn, so that tanks and anti-tank guns could join the Maoris on the objective by daylight. Massed behind Trocchio, ready to exploit the Maoris' success, was the rest of the Division supported by 180 tanks of the U.S. 1st Armored Division.

The Maoris had a special place in the New Zealand division. They were cheerful ebullient men, with a keen sense of humor, and a natural fighting spirit: great soldiers in the assault and pursuit. Temperamentally, they were the "wild Irish" of the New Zealand division. The advance started soon after dark to give the engineers as long a period of darkness as possible in which to complete their vital bridging and repairs to the route. In the closing stages of the advance the Maoris came up against minefields and barbed wire, and they were continuously mortared. But they fought their way through, and shortly after midnight they had stormed into the sheds and buildings of the Station, and triumphantly taken possession of them—and also of a number of prisoners.

Meanwhile, two thousand feet above them in the mountains—just faintly discernible from the Station in the dark—the Rajputana Rifles edged along Snakeshead Ridge toward Point 593. But, as on the previous two nights, within an hour or so the battalion was pinned down by impenetrable fire as it crouched at the base, and on the lower slopes, of the rock. They tried everything they knew to work their way round the boulders and ledges, and more than one small party succeeded in reaching the summit, but they were invariably killed or wounded. It developed into the same story as on the two preceding nights: successive small individual efforts that made no progress but always cost a few more lives. By two in the morning one company commander had been killed, two of the other three wounded.

While the Rajputs fought it out on 593, the 1st/9th Gurkhas, only 300 yards to their left, set off on the rough direct route to the Monastery, about 1,000 yards away. Their preliminary objective was Point 444 at the end of the "boomerang." Almost immediately they came under heavy cross fire from 593 and points on their left, and their efforts to deal with these positions brought them up on the left of the Rajputs, but neither battalion could make any headway. The stronghold of 593, supported by the neighboring high points, was well able to take care of both.

The second Gurkha battalion, the 1st/2nd, then moved off, but some way further to the left, with a direct approach to the Monastery via Point 450. As they worked their way down to the steep ravine which was the final obstacle—the ravine at the bottom of the northern slope of Monastery Hill—they approached a belt of what looked like scrub. It stood out in a landscape that had been bereft of so much of its vegetation by shellfire. They remembered noting it on their air photographs, on which it showed up as a long, prominent shadow. As the leading platoons approached it, a shower of grenades came down on them from the higher ground behind, and swiftly they dashed forward to take cover in this patch of scrub.

There was a series of staccato explosions. The scrub was not scrub at all, but a thicket of strong thorn, breast-high. It had been laced with barbed wire, and was thickly sown with interconnected anti-personnel mines set to explode when any of the trip wires, cunningly placed across all approaches, was touched.

As the leading platoons dashed into what they took to be cover, half of them were blown up by mines, those that weren't were mowed down by the rows of machine guns a little way to the rear, which had only to pour their fire into the cries and flashes and the silhouettes grotesquely lighted up on the thorn and barbed wire every time a mine went off. The colonel, shot through the stomach, was among those who fell wounded at this place. Despite this setback, the follow-up companies tried to press on with the attack, but a line of machine guns across the full width of Monastery Hill presented a curtain of fire through which they could not break, though they did not stop trying. The Monastery was only four hundred yards away, but they were four hundred of the longest yards in the world.

The full story of these deadly night battles can never be known, because too many of its authors died writing it. Undersupplied, without sufficient time to prepare, these few fought a lonely battle in the mountains and no one in the rest of the army had any idea of what they were facing. They had nothing to sustain them except that potent imponderable, their regimental identity. It mattered to the

Rajputana Rifles that they were Rajputana Rifles: it mattered to the Royal Sussex that they were Royal Sussex. In the end it was probably this alone that enabled them to keep on. His mother in a village near Katmandu would never know about her stretcher-bearer son making sixteen

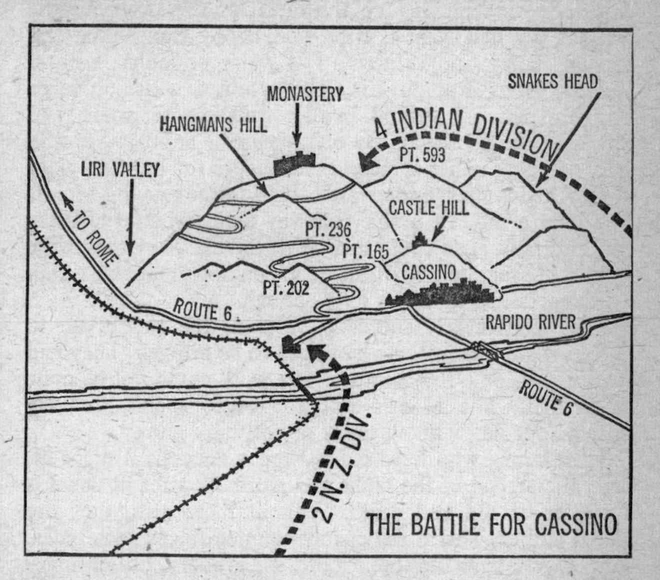

THE BATTLE FOR CASSINO

journeys across this inferno until, as he raised his last load, he fell dead with a burst of tracer in his back. Like the English officer who lay dead at his side, he had done what he had done not only because it was his job as a soldier, but because over and above that he was conscious of being a Gurkha Rifleman.

By first light on Friday the situation on Snakeshead was exactly as it had been the morning before, except that there were three battalions instead of one pinned down among the boulders of this nameless three acres of mountain. Once again there was nothing for it but to withdraw the survivors before daylight.

By first light in the area of Cassino Station, the New Zealand sappers had almost completed the night's work. They had lifted scores of mines, despite the additional time-wasting labor of having to dispose of the blown-up railway line. (It could otherwise not be known whether the mine detectors were picking up the metal of the mines or the line.) They had cleared wire, and booby traps; they had thrown Bailey bridges across two water obstacles, a canal and the River Rapido; they had spanned with rubble or bridging material several smaller gaps the Germans had blown in the causeway. By one means or another—and in spite of being under shell and mortar fire for half the night—they had managed to create behind the advancing Maoris well over a mile of usable roadway along which the tanks and anti-tank guns could race at daybreak. Now they were working desperately to finish by the end of the night, which for sappers can never be long enough.

They very nearly succeeded. But as the sky began to lighten there was just one more gap to be bridged. They had been beaten by a few minutes. The work could not be done in daylight. The Maoris would have to spend the long twelve-hour day without tanks or anti-tank guns.

To infantry who have carried out a successful night attack, the arrival of the tanks and anti-tank guns at dawn is a matter of life and death. Without these aids, they are naked and exposed if the enemy counterattacks with tanks. They would have the support of their artillery, but ordinary artillery can do little from long range against armor. Tanks have to be tackled with the armor-piercing shells of anti-tank guns firing from close range in the infantry area.

Like the Indian division nearly two thousand feet above them, the Maoris had had severe casualties: 128 of them had been killed or wounded. But by dawn they were well established and dug in. The station buildings provided plenty of cover and also room for maneuver. They cheerfully accepted the order to hang on, in splendid isolation, until the next period of darkness, twelve long hours away.

At daybreak of this same day, Friday, the German Fourteenth Army, now two and half miles into the heart of the Anzio beachhead, committed its armored reserves, an indication that this day was to prove the climax of the counteroffensive. Lowering black clouds there warned the hard-pressed American and British beachhead divisions that they could expect no help from the air forces that day. The Germans had also introduced a new weapon, the "Goliath," a small tank filled with explosives which was directed by remote radio control into the Allied positions, and then exploded.

In Rome a citizen recorded in her diary:

> All Rome is thickly placarded today with posters showing photographs of the ruins of Monte Cassino with monks and refugee civilians, and reproductions of handwritten signed statements by the Abbot and his administrator. This is certainly a trump card in the German propaganda game.

It was an uneasy morning all around for the Allied commanders.

In the mountains the Indian division made a melancholy count of the night's losses. The Rajputana Rifles had lost 196 officers and men including all their company commanders. The Gurkha battalion so many of whom had been crucified on the thorn and barbed wire of that mined thicket had lost 7 British officers including their colonel, 4 Gurkha officers, and 138 N.C.O.'s and men. The other Gurkha battalion had lost 96 of all ranks. In three nights four crack regular battalions had been cut to pieces, without a chance to do anything but die well. Nothing whatever had been gained.

Its crest only a hundred yards away, Point 593, the intermediate rocky eminence they had hoped to dispose of with a preliminary clearing operation, had proved to be a major fortification in its own right—thanks partly to the fragment of an old fort which provided its forward slope with a steel heart, but also to the skill and tenacity of first-class soldiers who knew how to make the best use of it; and to the closely co-ordinated fire of the adjacent German-held peaks. If you attacked one, six others could come to its rescue with machine-gun and mortar fire.

Everything now depended on the Maoris. Could they hold on to the Station for a whole day without the means of dealing with tanks, if tanks should be sent against them? If they could, the battle could be saved. As we have seen, the Station area—a thousand yards from the town and half that distance from the corner where Highway Six swung round Monastery Hill into the Liri Valley—not only provided a means of bypassing the core of the Cassino defenses, but made a jumping-off point for an armored break into the valley. It all depended now on the Maoris.

At daybreak General Kippenberger went forward to visit them. He found them cheerful and confident. They are the kind of soldiers who thrive on success. Their leading companies were well dug in, and they had good cover from the buildings, for the Italians construct their stone buildings well, even in railway stations and yards.

The chief difficulty was Monastery Hill, its southeastern corner a mere five hundred yards away, towering over the Station area so overwhelmingly that it made a man feel puny and helpless just to look up at it. There were tanks and artillery pieces at all the key points of that corkscrew road which cut across the face of the mountain, and many eyes to direct their fire. To be in the Station so near to the base of Monte Cassino was like being stared at hugely and malignantly. But the position must be held. If they could only hang on till nightfall, the engineers could hurry along the causeway, deal with the last gap, and the whole weight of the division could then pile up behind the Maoris.

When he had seen the position for himself from a forward viewpoint, General Kippenberger decided to cut off the Station from the view of the Monastery by laying a smokescreen and keeping it going all day. There was no difficulty about making the screen, the gunners said, but to keep it going all day would require many more shells than they had available. The artillery do not normally lay much smoke—it is generally left to the mortars—and the standard proportion of smoke shells at the gun sites is small. Where were the nearest reserves, Kippenberger asked. In Naples, seventy miles away. Then someone must go to Naples and get some. The Service Corps rose to the occasion. A column of lorries was sent off to bring back the necessary quantity of shells (to keep the screen going all day would require about 30,000) and within a few minutes the Maoris were relieved to find themselves screened from Monastery Hill by a thick artificial fog.

There was nothing for it now but to wait. The hours passed slowly. By ten there had been no counterattack. By midday there had been no counterattack. One o'clock, and no counterattack—but reports from the Maoris that they were being mortared. Two o'clock. Only four hours to dusk. The lorries were back from Naples, and the gunners were thickening up the screen confident that they could now keep it going indefinitely.

But soon after three, the ominous grating of tanks was heard in the Station. A few minutes later German infantry and tanks, skillfully using the New Zealand smokescreen to disguise the direction of their approach, burst through it into the Station area from two sides. Unluckily the men manning the bazookas were early casualties. The Maoris had nothing to pit against the tanks. There was a short sharp fight; the New Zealanders lost a number of prisoners: a few more were killed or wounded; the remainder were pulled back. The smokescreen had proved a two-edged weapon. But without it few of the forward troops would have survived the day.

The sweating gunners, who in relays had been pumping smoke shells into their guns without respite for more than eight hours, stood down exhausted. The battle was over. The single net gain on both divisional fronts was a bridge over the Rapido.

Viewed from a distance, the second battle of Cassino may be thought—especially after the world-wide commotion which preceded and followed the bombing—to have been something of an anticlimax. In the mountains a company attack on Tuesday night, a battalion attack on Wednesday, and a three-battalion attack on Thursday—all unsuccessful. In the valley, an attack by a single battalion, also unsuccessful.

Commentators at the time and since have been inclined

to dismiss the failure as a simple case of attacking in driblets instead of strength. The criticism is not valid. Ground and weather were the factors which determined the number of troops that could be used in this battle. We have seen already how these factors controlled the Indian division's operations. In the valley, though the New Zealand division did not have the same difficulty over the supply line, ground and weather imposed the same limitation on deployment. The valley was waterlogged, and the only feasible approach to the Station objective was along the railway and on a two-company front.

It must also be realized that there are two ways in which the might of a division can be used. It can attack with several battalions on a wide front, in which case its action is that of a scythe. Or it may initially use a small force on a narrow front, in the hope of making a penetration which can be followed up by the rest of its battalions piled up behind. In that case the action is that of a chisel, with a large number of hammer blows ready to force it through in a series of sharp thrusts. The ground and the weather made the second method the only possible one in this battle, and the New Zealanders nearly succeeded.

It was subsequently known that the Germans had been extremely alarmed by the capture of the Station. They did not expect their counterattack to succeed, as is shown by the following conversation between Kesselring and Vietinghoff on the night of the 18th:

> V: We have succeeded after hard fighting in retaking Cassino Station.
> K: Heartiest congratulations.
> V: I didn't think we would do it.
> K: Neither did I.

Had the New Zealand sappers been able to bridge the final gap on the causeway, and make it possible for tanks to come up on the objective, it seems likely that it would have been held.

The second battle of Cassino was notable, also, for two other things.

It showed how, in the most mechanized war in history, conditions of ground and weather could arise in which machines were useless, and the battle had to be fought out between small forces of infantry with rifle, machine-gun and grenade. An army that could call on six hundred tanks, eight hundred artillery pieces, five hundred airplanes, and sixty or seventy thousand vehicles of all shapes and sizes found itself dependent on the humble pack mule. In the mountains above Cassino in February a mule was worth half a dozen tanks.

The other lesson was that when Army and Air Force are working together there must be unity of command and the closest co-ordination of plans. Retrospectively this may seem too obvious to be worth mentioning. The plain fact is that in the last year but one of the war it was a problem that had still to be solved.

Out of Anzio

Four major attacks were necessary before the final breakthrough was made at Cassino. The 8th Army was brought over to work with the 5th, on a twenty-mile front. In the meantime, the 5th Army's Anzio forces were increased to six divisions. On May 11th, 1944, the last offensive opened in front of Cassino, and finally on May 18th, Mt. Cassino fell to the Polish Corps. The Germans were suddenly in full retreat, and Alexander gave the signal for the attack from the Anzio beachhead. The Allies waited for victory for weeks; if the Anzio force could break out of the beachhead and cut off the Germans' retreat, they would be in a position to destroy the German 10th Army utterly.

ANZIO TO ROME

by Eric Sevareid

The Allied armies waited, contesting now with time. Only the airplanes moved in their formations, preparing the earth behind the enemy lines. The belated spring arrived; the peasants were plowing up the soft, black soil; the snowline moved high on the mountains of frustration, and the roads to the front were arrows of beige-colored dust. Shawled Italian women trudged barefoot, carrying great baskets on their heads; their faces were stolid until a truckload of Italian men in remnants of uniform would pass

This selection is condensed from the author's *Not So Wild a Dream.*

on the road, and then the women would show their white teeth as they shouted greetings. The gathering engines caused dust to settle upon new acres of peace and permanence, stippled with white crosses. These acres contained the bodies of the first conquerors from the New World ever to invade this much violated land. They lay as dead as Visigoth or Saracen, and in the afternoon the broken arches of the ancient aqueduct shadowed these acres with unaltered precision.

Behind the Allied fronts the earth trembled in the night under the tread of silent convoys. Whole armies switched positions unnoticed by the enemy; the Americans on the central front moved down to the Tyrrhenian Sea; the French faced impossible peaks to our right; the British and the Poles looked at Cassino and the Liri Valley. Each prong of the steel rake was imbedded in position; very soon the signal would be given, and the rake would move northward up the length of the peninsula, furrowing the earth, heaping the mangled houses and bodies together as it moved. It was May. Everywhere the fields were delicately tinted with flowers.

The Allied commander-in-chief invoked the name of God; the German commander invoked the name of Adolf Hitler. The moon was high and full and impartially illuminated both sides of the front, blessing and betraying both defender and attacker. It lighted the way for the men who crawled on their bellies up the Italian drawbridge toward Fortress Europa; it exposed them to Europe's jailers, touching with iridescence coat buckle, water bottle, gun shaft, and wide young eyes. From Cassino to the sea on the central front the soft spring earth shuddered and heaved in grunting convulsions; the venerable olive trees burst their trunks, bent beneath the blasts of air, and then, half erect, exhibited to the moon their leafless limbs, thin and naked as the arms of an obscene hag.

The first blow for the freeing of Europe had fallen in the night, and in the first hour personal friends lay wounded and dead. Two divisions of young Americans who had never before seen combat moved forward over the rolling hills at which they had stared for weeks until they knew each tree and stone in this small area of fate, which to them had become all the planet, its beginning and its end. Within twenty-four hours they were veteran soldiers. By the next dawn, fear was a secondary impulse, and they moved like automata, their limbs stiff with chill, their nostrils black with grime, their beards one day dirtier. They smelled the clover and the dead in alternation and were aware of neither.

It seemed to me that I had been living with the war since that month of September five years before; while the faces, the instruments, the talk were all familiar now, still the moving picture of the fight was new to me, for always before I had known only stalemate or retreat. This was victorious attack, and the spectacle was not at all as the military writers had pictured it. Troops did not "sweep ahead," "wave after wave," tanks did not "charge" the enemy, divisions did not "plunge" nor "pour" at or into anything. It was far more the slow, deliberate behavior of a surveying party than the agitation of a football team. One never saw masses of men assaulting the enemy. What one observed, in apparently unrelated patches, was small, loose bodies of men moving down narrow defiles or over steep inclines, going methodically from position to position between long halts, and the only continuous factor was the roaring and crackling of the big guns. One felt baffled at first by the unreality of it all. Unseen groups of men were fighting other men that they rarely saw. They located the enemy by the abstractions of mathematics, an imagined science; they reported the enemy through radio waves that no man could visualize; and they destroyed him most frequently with projectiles no eye could follow. When the target became quiet, that particular fight would be over and they moved ahead to something else. Never were there masses of men in olive drab locked in photogenic combat with masses of men in field gray. It was slow, spasmodic movement from one patch of silence to another.

The men were real, and the results one saw all around were shockingly real. There is an atmosphere at the front, a heightened feeling which can never be transmitted nor described. Until one becomes drugged with exhaustion, every scene is a vivid masterpiece of painting. The tree and the ditch ahead are all the trees and ditches of creation, informed with the distillation of sacred *tree*ness and *ditch*ness. Each common odor goes down to the final nerve endings; each turn of the road is stamped indelibly upon the brain; every unexplored house is bursting with portent; every casual word and gesture bears vibrant meaning; those who live are incredibly alive, and the others are stupefyingly dead. Obscure villages which were meaningless names on the map —Minturno, Castelforte, Santa Maria Infante—soon acquire the significance of one's native town, each street and each corner the custodian of intimate, imperishable acquaintance.

A young German soldier lay sprawled just inside a sagging doorway, his hobnailed boots sticking into the street. Two American soldiers were resting and smoking cigarettes a few feet away, paying the body no attention. "Oh, him?" one of them said in response to a question. "Son of a bitch kept lagging behind the others when we brought them in. We got tired of hurrying him up all the time." Thus casually was deliberate murder announced by boys who a year before had taken no lives but those of squirrel or pheasant. I found that I was not shocked nor indignant; I was merely a little surprised. As weeks went by and this experience was repeated many times, I ceased even to be surprised—only, I could never again bring myself to write or speak with indignation of the Germans' violation of the "rules of warfare."

Not a single tree in the ravine had retained its leaves; it was exactly as though a cyclone had just swept through. We sat down on the gray earth with a young captain from West Point named Aileo. He had had six hours' sleep in the last seventy-two, but he merely relaxed in the sun, closing his eyes and smiling to himself as our great shells chortled over sounding like locomotives at high speed. An indolent cook handed us hot, fresh cherry turnovers with a wink, as if to say: "All the comforts of home." The shells were sending up sudden plumes from an enemy-held castle on the next ridge. No one watched it; everybody was already bored with battle. A young corporal trudged by, lugging his personal equipment and a book. The captain asked: "Corporal, are you happy in the service?" "Yes, sir," said the corporal. "Why?" "Because I found a room to sleep in tonight," the boy replied. Then he looked at the volume he carried, *The Return of the Native*. "Only thing bothering me right now is that character here they call the Reddleman. That guy keeps coming in and out of the story, and he confuses me." Puddles of dust advanced up the road, and a lieutenant with a smug and happy look on his face emerged, leading a dozen German prisoners walking with their fingers locked behind their necks. They were exhausted and without expression. Between victorious youth and defeated youth no manner of human transaction occurred.

Battles were large or small; points at issue were vital or of minor consequence; but always and everywhere procedure and pattern were monotonously the same. German guns betrayed their presence. We called our planes to bomb them, and we concentrated our own artillery, too numerous to be opposed, and they shelled the German guns. Thereupon the infantry flowed slowly ahead. At each strong point or village there were always a few snipers to be blasted out, always mines which exploded a number of vehicles, always booby traps which filled a few rooms with smoke and mortal cries. Bulldozers would clear the rubble, engineers would fill the craters, the medical troops would set up their aid stations, a few half-starved Italian families would be rooted out of evil-smelling cellars, and while silent men hoisted limp bodies into trucks the news would go out to the world that the place was "liberated." This is the way it was, day after day, town after town, as the enemy moved back and the line of corrosion moved northward across the peninsula leaving an ever-growing area of stately Italy in blackened ruins which were final beyond despair.

Columns of infantry emerged from side paths and with a censor—a Minnesota classmate, Arthur Burck, who voluntarily went to the front to see the events he had to judge with the blue pencil—I stepped into line to take part in the occupation of Scauri on the coast. They were bearded and unwashed, and they walked very slowly (the headlines said

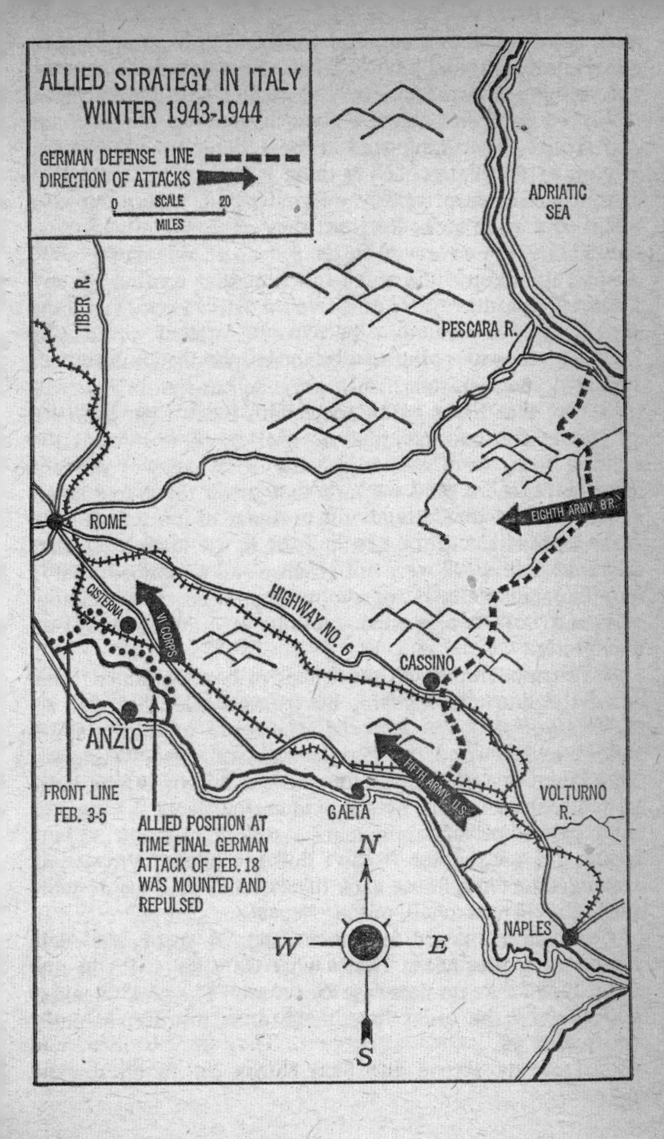

ALLIED STRATEGY IN ITALY
WINTER 1943-1944
GERMAN DEFENSE LINE
DIRECTION OF ATTACKS
0 SCALE 20
MILES
ADRIATIC SEA
TIBER R.
PESCARA R.
ROME
EIGHTH ARMY BR.
CISTERNA
VI CORPS
HIGHWAY NO. 6
CASSINO
ANZIO
FIFTH ARMY U.S.
GAETA
VOLTURNO R.
FRONT LINE FEB. 3-5
ALLIED POSITION AT TIME FINAL GERMAN ATTACK OF FEB. 18 WAS MOUNTED AND REPULSED
N
W
E
S
NAPLES

they were "racing" along the coast), carrying their packs and clusters of bright yellow hand grenades at their belts. They would fight before they slept again, and only those two things were on their minds. You noticed that their bodies were relaxed, but their faces were not. If you grinned at a man, he grinned back at once. I realized suddenly that in a way these men were happier now than during the long months of waiting. At long last they were doing what they had trained themselves to do, and if death was closer now, so was climax and the end to their bestial routine. A boy walking toward his life's crisis would call: "Hey, Mac, how about puttin' my name in the paper?" Another would ask: "When's the war going to end, correspondent?" Another: "What's going on, fella? They never tell us nuthin'." I realized, too, that I was happy to be with them; that, however officers at the rear regarded a reporter, these men at the fighting front were glad to see me. They knew I did not have to be there, and perhaps that made them one small degree less afraid. Certainly the presence of journalists gave them some slight lifting of the heart in the knowledge that they and their work were not obscure and unnoticed, that if they became victims, somebody somewhere would know why and how it happened. Nothing is quite so awful as anonymity.

A German sniper, no more than a boy, stumbled back down the line under guard, his trousers widely ripped so that his buttocks were exposed. There was muttering as he passed, and I wondered that he was still alive. While we talked with a young lieutenant who was still breathing hard from a reconnaissance by armored car out from the town, a pink-cheeked private approached and hesitantly said: "Lieutenant, sir, pardon me. I can't find my officer. We've got some civilians in a house back there. What shall we do with them, sir?" The excited, puffing lieutenant snapped out: "If you can spare a guard send them back. If you can't, why, shoot 'em in the back. That's what we always did in my outfit. Don't take no nonsense from 'em." The pink-cheeked boy received the order to commit mass murder, saluted, and trotted off.

The sea lay serene and blue before us. In an orange

orchard the birds were singing, and between the thunderous claps from the big guns one could hear their sweet, untroubled notes. Two jeeps halted beside me. One contained General Clark and his aides; the other contained the army photographer who always accompanied the General. Clark said: "Sevareid, aren't you a bit off limits here?" I had the impression he was slightly disgruntled at seeing a reporter at the point of advance before *he* had reached it. He drove slowly on between the two lines of infantry, leaning out now and then to call encouragement and praise to a soldier who would be startled, then draw himself up and walk more stiffly for a few moments. It was good behavior for a general; it was a help. Just outside the town, the General's party halted, and we overtook them on foot. No one could proceed farther on the road without being shot. While Clark looked at a map and pointed toward the hill where the "fire fight" was in furious progress, his photographer scrambled about to snap the pictures. They were always taken of the General's left profile. I noticed that, although an ordinary soldier risked a fine for not wearing his helmet in a combat area, the General was wearing his little overseas cap. When the pictures were finished and he had seen what he wished, he shook hands all around, mounted his jeep, and turned back toward the pacified area. Then he replaced the overseas cap with his steel helmet.

Newly routed civilians, now homeless like the others, with no idea of where they would next sleep or eat, with all their future lives an uncertainty, trudged back from the fighting zone. A dust-covered girl clung desperately to a heavy, squirming burlap sack. The pig inside was squealing faintly. Tears made streaks down the girl's face. No one moved to help her; the thought did not occur to me any more than to the others. There was too much misery, so much that no one could possibly feel sorrow or compassion. We strolled back through the town and came upon a group of filthy, white-faced Italians standing before a ruined house. One merely noted that they had not been shot, after all. The children were the color of paste and looked more dead than alive. The men gestured as we approached, pleaded for food, and showed us how they had eaten grass and roots while they huddled in the cellar. They were in stocking feet, the Germans, they said, having confiscated their shoes.

A few miles up the hills, I knew, the French, who advanced so rapidly that the communiqués could not keep up with them, were taking their towns, running up their flags, talking loudly, and sending up organized cheers. My countrymen around me here were a different kind of conqueror. It was quiet in the town now, and they stood about, a bit awkwardly, wondering what to do. A youngster with fuzz on his chin uttered a low whistle before a tank which was standing foolishly on its nose. One, who looked like a farm boy with great red hands, surveyed a perforated resort hotel. "Ah'll take a room with a southern exposure," he drawled. Conquerors? They had no sense of conquering a country; they were just after the Germans and had to walk over this particular piece of the earth's surface to get at them. Liberators? The Italians were merely harmless creatures who sometimes got in the way. The New World had returned to the Old. America was now in the world. The American Century, perhaps. This was the way it looked.

Allied army authorities nearly always told the journalists everything. It was a wise method. We did our work more intelligently and reduced to a minimum the errors that embarrassed both generals and reporters. But it also entailed certain risks for the generals. If we were told and asked to publicize the fact that General Alexander was making all decisions, this helped to glorify him, but it also left him no easy way out if the decisions brought poor results. If we were told, as we were, that the whole object of the campaign was to "destroy the German armies in Italy," with Rome a secondary objective, that only complete destruction of the enemy here would aid the coming second front in France, and that merely pushing the Germans back would amount to failure of the Italian mission—then the issue was irrevocably stated, and the commanders would be judged by their own statements and standards.

The night before the assault out from the [Anzio] beachhead was to begin, we were ushered into the illuminated caves, and they told us all their plans. It was the custom of assembled correspondents to rise when a general entered in recognition of his rank. It had always been a voluntary gesture on our part, but in this headquarters the ceremony followed a different pattern. As we sat in the rows of benches, a beefy staff colonel would rush in and bellow: " 'Tenshun!" We were always startled and a little resentful, but we would rise. Just as we got to our feet, General Clark would stride in, cut the air laterally with his palm, and call: "Sit down, gentlemen!" in a tone which indicated that this was all a mistake, we were all men of parts together, and that he was embarrassed by his colonel's unjustified command. We frequently wondered if they rehearsed it beforehand—it went off with such dramatic flourish.

The German radio often called Anzio "a prison camp where the inmates feed themselves." If that is what it was, this would be the greatest jail break in history. We had overwhelming superiority in men, vehicles, guns, tanks, and planes, and we needed them, for the Germans held the arc of hills and we must assault them directly. As Clark outlined the plan, the main impetus of our attack would be straight north to take Cisterna, continue on to cut Highway Six at Valmontone, carry on farther in a straight line to cut other roadways, and thus bottle up the main body of the German army from the Cassino front, which the British and others were pushing back up the Liri Valley. Thus the greater mass of the enemy in Italy would be eliminated at once, Rome could be taken almost at leisure, and the Germans would have to pour immense forces into northern Italy to hold that valuable industrial region—thus aiding the second front—or give up Italy altogether. The attack would begin at dawn. We would be allowed by the censors to say very little about its aims, of course, but it would be all right, the press officers told us, to say that General Clark was in personal command.

At dawn, I stood on a slight rise in the flat prairie among the tents of a field aid station attached to the First Armored Division. It was chill and cloudy. There were daisies and flowering thistle at our feet, and as we looked at our watches we could hear the meadow larks singing. A veil of fog partly obscured the German hills. At 5:45 the gun flares spurted in clusters from the left, then far to the right, then all around us they sounded, and the earth began a faint trembling. Shells passed over our heads, and our jackets flipped from concussion. The planes began to arrive. Through a break in the clouds we saw their tight formations, the fighter bombers wheeling and darting and disappearing in the curtain dividing the two armies. Around us now sleepy men crawled from their holes in the ditches and grubbed for cigarettes with stiff and dirty hands. They were waiting for the first violated bodies to be passed back into their care. The tanks came clanking up the highway, moving very slowly and well apart, their radio antennae nodding behind like the drooping pennants of armored horse and knight, jolting slowly to take the field. In and out of their ranks courier jeeps scuttled like agitated beetles. The barrage slackened off; it was 6:30, and we knew that up ahead the infantry was moving into battle. It was now irrevocable; the men had been "committed." Now one could only wait and hope; if any prayed he did it unnoticed. We slid down into a ditch and drank coffee with the medics. One man read and reread an old American newspaper that lay on a sandbag. The black headline said "Joan Sobs on Stand," and the story had a Hollywood dateline. Another man studied and restudied a single page in a book on photography. Nothing portentous was said. One remarked: "They can hear this in Rome, maybe." A shell screamed too close overhead, and we slid deeper into the ditch. A lad grinned at us and said: "Are you noivous in the soivice?"

An ambulance jolted off the highway into our camp. The man with the book, who had not yet turned the page, carefully marked his place and got up. Others, with artfully pretended boredom, followed slowly. The soldier lay unmoving on the grass floor of the tent, staring at the roof. Blood was seeping rapidly through the bandage on his head. His helmet lay on the grass beside his litter, the steel bent back from the hole the shell fragment had caused. I bent down to the boy to say: "You're going to be all right." There was only the faintest flicker in his staring eyes; he said nothing. Two men entered, supporting a German prisoner who hopped on one leg. He sat on a chair and smiled as they bandaged his leg, then nodded briskly and hopped out again into the waiting ambulance. Everyone talked now. The man sterilizing instruments began to whistle. Another ambulance bumped into camp. The familiar routine of war and systematized suffering was well under way.

On the exposed tableland one felt unnaturally large and vulnerable, if not expendable. My jeep driver said: "On this road if you smile Jerry can tell if you have brushed your teeth."

I could never quite reason out the reactions of soldiers to danger. Men seemed to behave in two completely opposed ways. If somebody related a dramatic occurrence in which he had figured, part of his audience would react by saying something like this: "Aw hell, that ain't nothing like what happened to me on the Volturno. Why, lemme tell you, we was . . ." Those were the men to whom nothing was quite real except as it involved themselves. The other part of the audience would have a feeling of wonder and awe at the story, even though they themselves had had experiences equally astonishing, if not more so. They were the men for whom anything that happened to themselves was not quite real or valid, who could never come to think of themselves as actors in this performance, as the very persons everybody was writing and thinking about. If such men were stationed in the rear, no matter what their tasks, they thought of those at the front as the ones who were really in danger. Those like them at the front line thought of those out on patrol, and as likely as not when they were out on patrol they thought of those immobilized farther back as the men really in danger. As someone else has pointed out, it was the same with the air force. Men on the ground thought of those in the air as "the ones." Those in the air thought of the wounded, and the wounded thought of the dead.

The offensive was going well; after thirty-six hours we had taken more than a thousand prisoners, and the key town of Cisterna seemed certain to fall. But our attention was now fixed on the progress of the Americans from the southern front who had passed Terracina and were moving rapidly up the coast for an inevitable juncture with the Anzio forces. When they met, the beachhead would no longer be a beachhead, and all the allied armies in Italy would have overland connection. In the late night of May 24 I wrote a broadcast script saying that in a matter of hours there would be only one front in Italy. I fell asleep on the floor while awaiting the broadcast time. I awakened because someone was shaking my shoulder. General Clark's Press Colonel was standing over me, shining his torch in my face. "Eric, old boy, I'm sorry to wake you up. I just wondered if you wouldn't do me a favor and change that script to read: 'There will be one *Fifth Army* front in Italy.' "

The join-up had caught everyone by surprise, and even General Clark, who got there as fast as anyone else, had to re-enact the greeting for the photographers. The Germans had pulled out of the low marshlands along the coast, and the troops from the southern front had simply driven overland without opposition. At a small bridge that was blown, Captain Ben Souza of Honolulu encountered Lieutenant Francis Buckley of Philadelphia strolling up the road. "Where the hell do you think you're going?" the former demanded. Buckley replied: "I've come to make contact with the Anzio forces." Souza said: "Well, you've made it."

The Fifth Army publicity machine promptly issued a statement saying that Anzio was now justified and broadly implying that the commanders responsible for the landing there had been right all along, always knew they were, and that, in fact, the whole operation proved the wisdom of the high command whose subtle methods were frequently misunderstood by grosser minds. If any correspondents sent off the statement I did not observe them.

Military commentators in London and New York were enthusiastically saying that day that "up to a hundred thousand Germans" were trapped in the coastal lowlands by the juncture. I drove that afternoon down to Naples for an overnight stay and it was clear that the Germans had escaped through the hills. We had captured a few dozen. The net result was that the Allies now had a connected front, shipping could be diverted elsewhere, and the advancing southern troops found great stores waiting for them at Anzio. It was all very dramatic, and it seemed like a great victory; in truth, we had merely extricated ourselves from our own stupid mistake, committed when we landed on those beaches in January.

Something happened now to change the whole strategy of the Fifth Army offensive. We learned that the impetus of the drive had been radically switched. Although we had taken Cisterna and were interdicting Highway Six with a constant rain of shells, we were abandoning the officially stated strategy of continuing north to cut the remaining German escape roads, the move designed to bottle up their main forces. We were now to turn west with our spearheads and try to drive to the left and right of the Alban Hills, straight for Rome. What had happened? Was the Eighth Army coming too slowly up the valley to effect a mass capture of the enemy? Or had orders arrived from some higher authority to get Rome without delay? It seemed to some of us that, in view of Alexander's declaration that the aim of the campaign was the destruction of the enemy in Italy, this was a serious mistake. In a broadcast script I wrote: "There is a question whether the two aims [of getting Rome and of destroying the enemy] are compatible or mutually exclusive." The censors cut this line out. But General Clark, who saw each morning all press and radio copy of significance, reacted strongly to my suggestion. Before all the correspondents he referred to "a broadcast" that suggested that we might be able to capture the bulk of the Germans. "That is sheer nonsense," he asserted with vigor, and with his pointer he indicated various side roads to the north by which, he said, the Germans could easily escape. No amateur could prove otherwise. (Almost nothing can be proved or disproved in the realm of strategy and tactics, for "military science" is not a science at all, but only a rude kind of art.) Yet such a capture had been our unquestioned aim. Now the General spoke in a manner that seemed to deny that the idea had ever entered his head. Some of us remained puzzled and skeptical. What had happened that we must now rush straight for Rome?

On Memorial Day the white crosses in what was probably

the largest American cemetery in the war at that time were shimmering in the hot morning sun. Detachments from every division assembled with their banners. Thick smoke from our concealment screen drifted across one edge of the field, and one could hear the sound of our guns and the motors of the ambulance planes which lifted away toward Naples every few minutes, bearing the injured. On this day each white cross bore a small American flag fastened above the name plate and the number. A crowd of shirt-sleeved Italian laborers stood by the great mounds of fresh earth where the unfilled graves were ready. The unfilled graves were so neatly aligned, and there were so many of them, waiting. The General spoke of the glorious achievements of the fighting men and the imminent freeing of the first European capital from tyranny. The corps chaplain (the Baptist who kept a neat file of clippings about himself and always had a new story of his exploits for the reporters) announced over the loud speaker that the men who lay dead before us had died in the cause of "true religion." When orators and formations had marched away, I came upon six new bodies stretched in the sun behind the canvas curtains at the field's edge. The burial sergeant was a West Virginia schoolteacher who begged me not to write a story about what he was doing in the war. One of his assistants said: "You get used to it after a while." The sergeant answered: "That isn't true—I never get used to it." He looked at the bodies and went on: "With a thousand, it would be just a problem of sanitation. With six, it seems like a tragedy."

One saw so many dead each day, so many bleeding bodies. I realized that I was becoming a little obsessed with the tragedy of these youngsters, tending to write about death more and more. Sometimes in the long, lovely evenings when we sat by the sea, the old feelings about the death of youth which I had experienced as a college boy began to steal back, unnerving and frightening me. It would not do; one had to shake off these moods. But it was becoming harder and harder to escape them. I realized now with a start that the sight of a dead German boy did not affect me, while the sight of a dead American did. Did this reaction come from the deep-seated national feelings which go back to childhood, or was it due to simple propinquity? I was unsure.

Even to noncombatants in the field like myself the Germans were not quite real any more as human beings, such is the mental derangement of war. Their bodies did not affect me. But when a colleague showed me some letters, written in a girlish scrawl, which he had taken from a dead German boy, I was moved. I saved the letters, which in part went as follows:

> Vienna, April 14. Dear Robert: First of all heartiest greetings. Since I don't hear from you I write you a few lines. I hope they will not be unwelcome. I sent an Easter card to your grandmother, and when she answered she enclosed your address with the hint that I should write to you. And now that I have time, I write, as you see. How do you like the army? I would like to see you as a soldier. How are your girls? Do they write to you often? I want to close now with the heartiest regards. Best regards from Mother.—Feli.

The letters became bolder, more intimate:

> Vienna, May 1. Dear Robert: I received your dear letter on the 22nd of last month with great joy. . . . I'm enclosing some writing paper to make sure that you write me more. Maybe I'll take a ride to your grandmother this week. Say, dear Robert, what do you mean by telling me that she is not the only one who loves me? I can't imagine who has the courage to love me. I'm sorry that the army doesn't agree with you. . . . I feel sorry for the poor girl you broke off with. Don't you think she feels hurt? Well, what do I care? . . . I close for today with heartiest regards.—Your Feli.

> Vienna, May 7. Dearest Robert: . . . Your grandmother worries very much about you. Please write cheerful letters to her. She worries very much about

you and more so when you write her that the going is bad.—Your Feli.
P.S. A stolen kiss.

The attack toward Rome slowed to a stop, embarrassing for the generals and deadly for the fighting men. It was the bitter situation so familiar in the Italian campaign: the enemy was holding the high ground—in this case the Alban Hills, the last breastworks defending Rome. Clark had sent the First Armored across the flat ground between the hills and the sea. Every vehicle was easily spotted in the enemy's gun sights and within ten minutes we lost twenty-five tanks. The other divisions could get nowhere in the vineyards, which were dominated by the hill city of Velletri, key to the German defense. Hitherto the summer campaign had been a straightaway, bludgeoning business of hammering frontally with our great superior weight of shells and bombs. I, at least, had never seen anything subtle or unorthodox attempted at any time. Unorthodox ideas are generally frowned upon in military commands, and, to be sure, they are usually not worth the risk when one has overwhelming superiority in everything. But the proposal of Major General Fred Walker of the Thirty-sixth Division was accepted. He drew two regiments from in front of Velletri, circled them around to the right in darkness, and started them climbing the two-thousand-foot height *behind* Velletri. It was a gamble. If the Germans could close their lines again, these men would be lost. If not, the final defenses of the Eternal City were breached.

With that brave and tender-hearted photographer-writer, Carl Mydans of *Life,* I set out to witness this seemingly impossible feat. By noon we had found the advance C.P. of the division, which now consisted of several bearded officers squatting under a railroad trestle studying a map. General Walker gave me a curt nod and continued pacing back and forth under the trestle. He was a solemn, self-contained man, and this was the first time I had ever observed him in a state of perturbation. A good friend, Lieutenant Colonel Hal Reese, smiled benignly at me as he drew a map with his cane in the dirt to indicate the route we would have to follow in order to mount the hill—"if you get past the snipers." I had bunked with Reese in the LST that brought his division to the beach.

A husky young major with a full pack hitchhiked a ride with us. He was John Collings of Detroit, who had just come from the Pacific and was seeking his new battalion, somewhere up the mountain. We left the highway, bumped across the rail tracks, and thumped our tortuous way up a newly cut trail among cornstalks and vineyards. Only a jeep could do this, but there were sharp descents and sudden upthrusts where we thought the jeep would go over on its back. It was very silent. The sun filtered down through the thick trees. A lone sentry stepped out. "Watch for the snipers, sir," he said to Collings. Freddie looked back from the steering wheel, a question on his face. He had orders, as did all the press drivers, to go only as far as he himself considered safe, regardless of what the correspondent passengers requested. With a casual gesture that somehow held the impact of drama, Collings flipped out his pistol, held it cocked in his hand, and, keeping his eyes steadily upon the trees ahead, remarked: "Go ahead, driver. Snipers aren't so bad." A machine gun began to sound near by, like corn popping in a deep kettle. The jeep trudged over ruts and roots, and a party of approaching peasant women carrying great water bottles through which the sun's rays filtered, squeezed against the trees to let us pass. They were one of the invariable signs of fighting just ahead.

We emerged again upon the highway. Three soldiers rested in a ditch. "You're visible to the enemy next couple hundred yards," they told us. Implied was: "We are alive by the grace of God; you may die in the next few minutes." The tone was the tone of men saying that it looked like rain. This is the way it was, nearly always, among men in the regions of death. The jeep darted the next stretch and was halted by a soldier who seemed no more than a boy in his teens, the artless, helpless type which ought never to be taken into any army. His eyes were unnaturally large, and his hands were twisting a towel, rapidly, senselessly. "Do you know where the aid station is, sir?" he asked through trembling lips. We thought it was just ahead. "Are you hit?"

"No, sir, it's my nerves, I guess." We left him. Though he was a casualty, as surely as any man with a bullet in his head, he could be condemned for desertion.

Another quarter-mile and we could go no farther on the highway. Velletri was invisible, but lay only another thousand yards to the west. Machine guns were sounding again, and it was certain death to proceed. Here now was the cut-off, a narrow "jeepable" trail, mounting sharply between high banks. Freddie would have continued with us, but he had nothing to gain by getting the "story," and it was foolish to risk another man. He stayed at this point with the jeep, which was a mistake. We began hiking upward in the hot sun; we rounded a bend and there were *tanks* chugging up, their massive breadth plugging the whole road cut, scraping down dirt and stones from the banks. Scrambling around the tanks, we found the ubiquitous bulldozer, simply carving the trail into a road, roaring and rearing its ponderous way at a forty-degree angle upward. This was all madly impossible, and yet it was being done.

The men themselves, bearded, silent with fatigue, swung their shovels through the loose dirt and pitched it over the banks. A rifle snapped very close at hand, and we heard the sigh of the bullet this time. A trained soldier is generally more afraid of snipers than of artillery; I found I had the reverse reaction. Heavy shell fire was unnerving to me after a while, and I could hardly bear the sense of helplessness and exposure if it were coming in while I was in a vehicle. Rifle fire, though it might be directed right at me, left me completely calm; and it was reassuring to be standing on my own feet, able to take cover by a simple muscular reflex. Perhaps most amateurs are this way; they react to noise and concussion rather than to the missiles themselves.

A couple more bullets whistled overhead and a party of shovelers stood upright. "Oh-oh," one said. Mechanically, as though they had done it a thousand times, two of them let their shovels fall, slipped their carbines from their backs, and crawled over the bank, disappearing in the direction of the sniper. Now a jeep with the Red Cross marking tilted precariously down the trail. Strapped across the hood was a stretcher with a man upon it. His head was almost covered with bandages, only the eyes, nose, and lips exposed. The lips held a cigarette. When Carl pointed his camera, the boy turned his head toward the lens and, in an unforgettable voice tinged with irony, asked: "Do you want me to *smile?*"

We found ourselves with a rifle company, men I had last visited in the fields before Velletri. They had detrucked in the night, then made a ten-mile hike around Velletri and gone straight up the hill, carrying their heavy mortar shells in their bare hands, clutching them to their stomachs. The weighty metal boxes of rifle ammunition they had strapped to their backs, and they had climbed all night, silently, like Indians, forbidden by Walker to have a cartridge in the chamber of their rifles. He would permit no firing, to avoid alerting the Germans. Only a grenade could be used, if absolutely necessary, for the Germans would easily mistake that for a mortar shell and remain ignorant of its origin. (The Germans were ignorant enough—later we learned that they believed that two companies, not two regiments, had made the infiltration.)

In a sun-speckled grove the men lay sprawled on their backs, oblivious to the traffic's dust or the spasmodic machine-gun fire so close at hand, catching any moment that fortune provided for precious sleep. A soldier walked past, going downhill. He held up his hand to show bandages covering what remained of his thumb. "How's that for a cheap Purple Heart?" he said. No one cared for the medal; what he was saying was: "I'll never have to fight, sleep in mud, and be frightened again." One witness muttered: "He's got the war made." "Lucky bastard," said another. Battalion headquarters was a farmhouse. Inside, three young officers sat at ease around the kitchen table while the farm wife served them wine. One of the men had flown from Cairo with me. We drank and discussed Cairo cafés, like two casual acquaintances in a smoking car. Outside the door lay a dead German sniper wearing American army boots. A Texas lieutenant jerked his thumb toward the body. "That guy shot two of our medics. He made us sore." The German had violated the "rules of war"—or rather, he had outraged his youthful opponents. When they captured him, they instructed him to turn and run for it. He ran and fell with thirteen tommy-gun bullets in his square body.

We debated whether to try to reach the summit. The way seemed clear, but it was growing late, and we must reach Anzio before dark. In any case, the mountain position was safely established; everything was in order. We said goodbye to Collings and started down. (Two months later Mydans met Collings in Rome and learned that the major had pulled away from the farmhouse in a jeep with four other men. They proceeded upwards a quarter-mile and received a burst of German machine-gun fire. Collings alone survived.)

On the highway, we found Freddie crouched in the ditch, clutching his rifle. Machine-gun bullets had just been whispering around his ears. We wrenched the jeep around and departed at full speed, hanging to our helmets.

In the night the Germans tried a counterattack and failed. Our men clung to the heights and fired remorselessly upon the desperate enemy within Velletri. In the morning General Walker, his tanks, and his men rushed the town, entering upon the highway. Lieutenant Colonel Hal Reese insisted upon walking ahead of the tanks; a shell burst killed him at once. When he was informed, Walker averted his face and said: "I asked him not to go ahead like that. I asked him not to." Why did Reese, who was not a professional soldier, who had everything to live for, who understood prudent behavior, act in this rash manner? I do not know. I do not know what lay behind his serene and gentlemanly countenance. But in his notebook they found that he had written: "I got through the last war all right, but I will not survive this one." It is my impression of men who have lost many comrades and who feel no escape for themselves, that they not only take risks in a fatalistic manner—they welcome them. They seek death.

Rome must now fall. Generals Alexander and Clark would soon receive the key to the city, but surely it was General Walker who turned the key. From him they were really receiving it.

Perhaps it is true that we love best those to whom we

give and dislike those who give to us. We were never told the reason, but a few weeks later General Walker, whose love for his division was returned in his men's respect for him, who was at the height of his brilliant combat career, was relieved of his command and sent back to the States.

In the morning again we drove around the eastern slopes of the lovely green hills, past mutilated Valmontone (another old city we had shot up to no purpose in our reckless way, for the bridges and skirting roadway were all that we required), and as we progressed it began to dawn upon us that the German defenses were falling apart so fast that we would be into Rome within hours. The air was charged with excitement, with savage triumph and obscene defeat. German vehicles were smouldering at every bend of the road, and dead Germans lay sprawled beside them, their faces thickening with the dust sprayed over them by the ceaseless wheels that passed within inches of the mortifying flesh. Shells were screaming over in both directions, but in the general frenzy not even the civilians paid them much notice. By wrecked gasoline stations, in the front yards of decapitated homes, flushed Americans were shoving newly taken prisoners into line, jerking out the contents of their pockets and jabbing those who hesitated with the butt ends of their rifles. A child was vigorously kicking a dead German officer, until a young woman shoved the child aside and dragged off the man's boots. Infantry of the Third Division were arriving in trucks, and their general, "Iron Mike" O'Daniel, jumped from his jeep before it had stopped and in stentorian voice shouted the orders for their detrucking and deployment. One of our tank destroyers ahead burst into flames, and shells began falling nearer. American officers, throwing themselves down and clutching their helmets, shouted questions at one another about how the race for Rome was progressing. While Mydans remained with his camera—he spent a frightening night under bombs—I turned back to Anzio, impelled by the realization that things were now moving faster than anyone had expected and that somehow the press installation, the censors, and the radio transmitters must be uprooted at once and taken to the front lines, or the story of the fall, the whole impact of the "psychological and political victory" that Rome was to be, would surely be delayed and half ruined. In the wrecked villages to the immediate rear, medical aides were pulling our wounded from their ambulances, shabby civilians were gathering in the rubble-strewn public squares, all looking toward the capital city, and standing beside their ruined parents the children, in their innocence of tragedy and death, were clapping their small and grimy hands as we passed them by.

I was black with a thick covering of grime and dust when I reached the press villa on the now silent beach. I was exhausted by the hectic journey and by sheer nervous excitement, and my hands were trembling when I tried to eat at the mess. It appeared that no orders whatsoever had been given for uprooting the transmitters—indeed nobody there seemed quite aware of what was happening; and I fear that I transgressed the limits of dignity in urging immediate action. But nothing could move until morning. At midnight I did my last broadcast from Anzio and was up again with the others before dawn. Nearly all the other correspondents had vanished in the night toward the front, and it appeared that I would have to guide the slow caravan with Vaughn Thomas of the BBC, since no others knew the detours. We moved with agonizing slowness, and I was certain that I would miss the entry into the city. Near Valmontone the transmitter van behind us hesitated at a crossroads, and I ran back a couple of hundred yards to direct them. Returning to the jeep was one of the most horrible experiences of my life. Perhaps it was that the breeze shifted or died; I do not know. But I walked into a veritable lake of stench. There was not a body in sight; the bodies must have been dragged into the brush just off the road, but the hot sun was directly on them. I had smelled the sharp, sweet, gaseous odor of death before, but nothing like this. It inflamed the nostrils, and I could even taste it in my mouth. Each breath drew it in deeply. I began to choke, and water streamed from my eyes. I started to run blindly up the road, which made me breathe more heavily. All my insides were convulsed, and I felt vomit in my throat. I was almost in a fainting condition when I reached the jeep, and I stayed sick for hours afterwards. The sight of death is nothing like its smell.

The army had not yet crossed the city limits; German antitank guns were interdicting the highway, delaying us, while the enemy hurriedly pushed the bulk of his troops out of Rome by the northern gates. A few hundred yards from the city limits we turned off into a group of workers' apartment buildings, while an army captain named Wickham, who was something of a technical genius, threw up the antennae in an open field. It was Sunday noon. Rome was just ahead, yet all the city proper was obscured in haze and smoke. Guns and shells sounded loudly near us, and from somewhere in the city came the dull sound of explosions—evidence, we thought, that the Germans were blowing the bridges on the Tiber. We hiked up the road and crouched beside cement ramparts along the trolley line, as far as one could go. There was a curious feeling in the air: a combined spirit of battle and of holiday. Reporters sat typing with their machines balanced on their knees. A dying German lay groaning in the hot sun on a cement driveway by a villa while a group of civilians silently watched him. An old man held a cup of water to his lips with one hand and stroked his hair with the other. People hung out of every window and gathered before every gate. The girls and children tossed flowers at the two lines of slowly walking American soldiers, and bouquets were now displayed on the turrets of our tanks.

Rome was falling, and all the world was waiting and watching. It was a day of climax and portent, a day for history. I sat before the microphone at a portable table while shells passed over and the concussion whipped my papers. I could say nothing of consequence. I could only say that Rome was falling and that we were all tired and happy. In a thousand editorial columns, on a thousand public platforms, men far from the scene would utter the big thoughts about this. Here, none among us seemed to have anything to say.

(Up the highway a short distance, a conversation was going on, which was not then publicly recorded, but which also, perhaps, merits a footnote in the history of the war and of the personalities who directed it. Brigadier General Robert Frederick, the young and capable commander of the special "commando" regiment of Americans and Canadians, was watching the progress of his men who led the assault. A jeep drew up, and Major General Keyes, corps commander, descended. "General Frederick," he asked, "what's holding you up here?" Frederick replied: "The Germans, sir." Keyes then asked: "How long will it take you to get across the city limits?" Frederick answered: "The rest of the day. There are a couple of SP guns up there." "That will not do. General Clark must be across the city limits by four o'clock." Frederick asked: "Why?" The corps commander answered: "Because he has to have a photograph taken." Frederick looked at Keyes steadily for a long moment and said: "Tell the General to give me an hour." The guns were silenced, the General and his faithful photographer arrived, and the pictures were taken of the conqueror within his conquered city.)

Early in the morning the big entry by troops and correspondents was made. Many great cities were liberated after Rome, and the spectacle was nearly always the same. But to me this entry was a new thing, and I found myself having to hold tight to my emotions. Everyone was out on the street, thousands upon thousands from the outlying areas walking toward the center of the city. A vast, murmurous sound of human voices flooded everywhere and rose in joyous crescendo at every large avenue we crossed. There was a gladness in all eyes, and now and then, as when a German sniper in his green-daubed cape was marched out of the Colosseum, remembrance of hate contorted the faces, even the young children uttered savage cries, and the fists that had held bundles of flowers were doubled in anger. The Piazza di Venezia was jammed with a monstrous crowd, and our jeep proceeded at a snail's pace, while flowers rained upon our heads, men grabbed and kissed our hands, old women burst into tears, and girls and boys wanted to climb up beside us. One tried to remember that they had been our recent enemy, that they were happy because the war was over for them as much as because we had driven out the Germans, that noncombatants such as I had no right to this adulation. But one tried in vain. I felt wonderfully good, generous, and important. I was a representative of strength, decency, and success, and it was impossible at this moment to recollect that Germans or Fascists had also once received this same outpouring of gratitude.

In the *Stampa Estera* building the correspondents were typing madly, shouting for censors, and demanding to know how the copy was to be transmitted to London and New York. Everything was in confusion. All the elaborate army plans for joint broadcasts to the world, to give dramatic effect to the great "psychological victory," had apparently broken down. The press reporters were in a frenzied state of fury. Then the chief public relations officer burst into the room to announce that General Clark would hold a press conference at the Campidoglio building immediately.

The General was lounging against the balustrade that overlooked the square when we hurried up the outside stairway. There was a jam of people around him, and already the news-reel men were grinding away, photographing the lean, smiling victor against the appropriate background of the great city spread out below. General Truscott arrived, then General Keyes. They worked their way to Clark's side and regarded the mob of reporters and photographers with a questioning look in their eyes. General Juin of the French Corps hastened up the steps and also looked at us with an expression of bewilderment. Clark shook hands with them and in a modest drawl said to us: "Well, gentlemen, I didn't really expect to have a press conference here—I just called a little meeting with my corps commanders to discuss the situation. However, I'll be glad to answer your questions. This is a great day for the Fifth Army." That was the immortal remark of Rome's modern-day conqueror. It was not, apparently, a great day for the world, for the Allies, for all the suffering people who had desperately looked toward the time of peace. It was a great day for the Fifth Army. (Men of the Eighth Army, whose sector did not happen to include Rome but without whose efforts this day could not have occurred, did not soon forget the remark.) Then Clark spread a map on the balustrade, and with the whole mob pressing close proceeded to point out something or other to his commanders. The cameras ground, the corps commanders, red with embarrassment, looked back and forth from us to the map. We pushed down the steps.

Up to Overlord

The Americans had entered Rome on June 4th, 1944, by the end of the day the city was fully taken. Alexander now had twenty-eight divisions in Italy, hard on the heels of the retreating Germans. But great disappointment was in the cards for Alexander. At the Teheran Conference the previous year, it had been decided that an invasion of southern France, labeled Anvil, was needed to effect a pincers with the Normandy invasion against the German forces in France. On June 6th, the Allies landed on the Normandy beaches and the eyes of the world turned to the invasion efforts there. The American general staff insisted that Anvil now be carried out. The objections of Alexander and the field commanders in Italy, who fought the decision, were overruled; Alexander was deprived of seven of his divisions, three American and four French, for Anvil.

The battle for Italy was to be a bitter, frustrating engagement to the end, but the campaign had, and would continue to have, important effects upon the main target, Germany. One of the chief strategic goals was to subdue the German Luftwaffe. Airfields were now available in Italy to raid the Rumanian oilfields, and heretofore unreachable targets in Germany and the Axis satellites. Furthermore, the Allies in Italy were holding down twice as many German divisions as they themselves had committed, at the very time the Germans on the Russian front were in need of reinforcement.

Meanwhile the plans for the invasion of France, Operation Overlord, had been shaped, refined and elaborated on from conference to conference among the Allied leaders. In the beginning, the initial assault was to provide for three seaborne divisions and two airborne brigades, with two more divisions to follow right behind. Churchill, however, argued throughout 1943 to enlarge the strength of the assault by twenty-five per cent. To support the increase, additional landing craft would have to be provided. They were available only if withdrawn from U.S. Pacific operations, and the American Naval Commander, Admiral King, fought against this.

Depending upon whether one consults the American or the British view, the arguments that hammered out the final invasion strategy range from good logic to national prejudice.

The Americans were deeply involved in the Pacific campaign, and planning for both theaters created an inevitable conflict. And the Americans still kept up the initial drive and optimism of the early days of war mobilization. Result: a policy of immediate attack, without waiting for reinforcement from the Pacific.

The British wanted to be certain that the German army would give way at the Atlantic Wall; they still recalled the stalemate and bloodletting in the trench lines of World War I. They had also been mobilized for war since 1939. And had already seen three land operations thrown off the continent. Result: a policy of caution, of not moving until overwhelming power had been built up.

This conflict was resolved at the top level, by Montgomery and Eisenhower. Gen. Eisenhower had been appointed the Supreme Commander-in-Chief on December 6, 1944, with Field Marshal Montgomery to command all ground operations. When they met in London later that month, both men saw the need to strengthen the invasion forces. The plans for Overlord now moved forward in earnest.

Just where on the long European coast the Allies would invade worried the German High Command. Hitler was already fighting on two fronts, soon to be three. His armies were being chewed up and pushed back in Russia. The Italian front held down twenty-one divisions. The long western coastline that was once the symbol of Hitler's victories was now a liability to German strategy. Behind the Atlantic Wall, the Germans finally decided to keep a central reserve of troops in France, which could be quickly shifted to any point along the coast once the invasion point was known. While this was sound strategy, Hitler sapped it by constantly draining the reserve for the Russian front.

In the spring of 1944, Von Rundstedt, the German Commander-in-Chief in the west, had fifty divisions spread along the coast, to be increased to sixty by June 6th. He expected the Allies to make a successful landing and breach the Atlantic Wall, but he hoped to be able to mount a strong enough counterattack immediately after D-Day, by maneuvering the central reserve force, to drive the Allies back into the sea. Partly because of this strategy, Von Rundstedt hadn't paid much attention to the condition of the Atlantic Wall. Rommel, who, under Von Rundstedt, commanded the German armies in Holland, Belgium and France to the Loire River, inherited the job of strengthening the Wall in 1944. He soon found the defenses in poor shape.

Rommel foresaw the Allied superiority in the air, and realized the Germans therefore wouldn't be able to deploy their mobile reserves in time for the counterattack. And so he set to work strengthening the fortifications all along the coast under his command. The beaches were heavily mined, many kinds of underwater obstacles were planted, and new pillboxes were constructed, with guns set to rake the beaches with enfilading fire.

The Allied plans for Overlord, as now revised, provided for an air drop of three airborne divisions, and five divisions to assault from the sea, with two more divisions to follow up. This meant increasing the beachhead area to approximately fifty miles, increasing the aircraft operational support, and supplying the previously mentioned landing craft, plus adding a U.S. naval task force to help escort the enlarged convoys and bombard the beaches. The lessons learned from other landing operations were put to use in Overlord. The British, from their bitter experiences at Dieppe and Norway, knew that pre-assault air and naval bombardment wouldn't necessarily knock out the Germans long enough to enable the troops to reach the beaches safely.

Small support ships were devised to increase firepower close in to the beaches, providing covering fire as troops spread out and took up positions on shore. Batteries of rocket and mortars were mounted on small boats. The infantry was to be followed immediately by heavier artillery anti-tank guns, and then by tanks themselves to give stronger support to the men moving up the beaches.

There were also special tanks designed—flail tanks to beat through the mine fields, DD tanks which could swim ashore under their own power, and flame-throwing tanks to subdue stubborn pillboxes.

A further innovation was the creation of two artificial harbors, to be constructed in England and floated across to the French coast. Until the port of Cherbourg could be captured, they would receive the supplies that would pour across to the continent.

The Allies hoped to land eight divisions on D-Day, another two on D-plus one; by D-plus four, they hoped to have fifteen divisions ashore. The Russians had agreed to launch an offensive to coincide with the landings, and pressure was to be increased against the Germans on the Italian front.

It was enormously important that the Germans discover neither the exact landing areas for the invasion nor the date it was to be launched. Unusual security measures were taken to restrict travel in the United Kingdom, and two weeks before the invasion the troop assembly camps and embarkation ports were sealed off from all civilians. The Allies outdid themselves to mislead the Germans and to camouflage invasion preparations. The British had conceived of Operation Fortitude, a plan to suggest to the Germans that the invasion would occur at Pas de Calais, a section of the French coast north of the real landing area. The Pas de Calais was the point of shortest distance between France and England. The British hoped that if the Germans swallowed the bait they might also be led to consider the landings in Normandy a diversionary tactic, and *still* expect major landings in the Pas de Calais area.

To make a convincing show of it, divisions to land after D-Day were assembled in England in an area opposite the Pas de Calais; fake landing craft were assembled in ports near by, dummy gliders were staked out on fields—all the signs of a huge staging area were exposed. The British also released dozens of messages, orders and signals all designed to be guided along into the hands of known enemy agents. And finally, right up until D-Day, bombing was twice as heavy as usual in the areas immediately behind the Pas de Calais.

On the eve of the invasion, Operation Fortitude really came into its own. Through use of aircraft and small ships of the Royal Navy, the impression of "big ship echoes" was produced on enemy radar (according to Wilmot in his *The Struggle for Europe*) while bombers created the effect of huge air armadas, again on radar, by dropping quantities of metalized paper in front of Pas de Calais. Every tactic suggesting a realistic invasion was pursued.

In fact, Von Rundstedt had already persuaded himself that the invasion would be at the Pas de Calais; it was closest to England, and he knew the British Spitfire's range was severely limited and, in providing proper air cover, would be most effective here. (Operation Fortitude seems to have accomplished everything and more than the Allies hoped for; on D-plus ten the Germans were still expecting a major attack from the fake divisions in the staging area across from the Pas de Calais.)

Air force strategy raised a new argument in the Allied staff. Through the winter of 1944, with the combined air forces of Britain and the U.S. hammering German industry, the air commanders still believed that bombing raids alone could bring Germany to her knees—if only enough sorties could be flown. But Overlord's planners wanted rail traffic in France paralyzed to keep the Germans from maneuvering for anti-invasion counterattacks. The airmen would have to shift their attention to this job. Finally, the air forces came around and, beginning in March, rail lines, depots, and traffic centers were strafed and bombed. By D-Day rail traffic throughout France had been reduced by seventy per cent. The immediate effect of this was to keep reinforcements from reaching the Atlantic Wall.

The invasion plans in their last details were made irrevocable in early May. Gen. Montgomery was to lead and command the land forces. His aim was to secure the beachheads, and send armored columns probing inland as fast and as far as possible, to offset the expected counterattacks from Rommel's Panzer divisions. Montgomery had guessed that Rommel would try to throw the Allies off the beaches at once, to try to produce another Dunkirk, and this Montgomery had to prevent at all costs.

The landings, after long rehearsals, were to be carried out by the following forces:

Three airborne divisions would be dropped on the evening of D-Day, the 6th British Division into the Orne Valley, and the 82nd and 101st American Airborne Divisions on the Cotentin Peninsula. Their objectives were to strike at the beach defenses from the rear, and secure the flanks of the bridgehead: the Americans, the right flank to the south; the British, the left flank to the north.

On D-Day itself, the 1st U.S. Army under Gen. Omar Bradley was to land on two beaches, at two separate invasion points: Utah Beach, and Omaha Beach on the left. The 2nd British Army, under the command of Gen. M. C. Dempsey, was to land between Bayeaux and Caen on three beaches: Gold Beach, Juno Beach (to be assaulted by the Canadians), and Sword Beach.

In early May, June 5th had been set as D-Day, but only after the most comprehensive research into weather, problems of tide, circumstances of German reinforcements, availability of all naval support and landing craft, etc. The month of May provided perfect invasion weather, and the Germans, it is now known, expected the invasion almost daily. The Allies were not yet ready.

On the weekend preceding June 5th, a storm brewed up in the Atlantic off Great Britain that would affect the Channel waters, and this forestalled plans for the 5th. Some naval elements had already been started across the Channel early on the morning of the 5th, and had to be called back—several convoys were more than halfway to France before the signal reached them to return. Soldiers already committed to the invasion ships had to be kept aboard as their ships pitched and tossed at anchor—some men had been aboard for three and four days. They couldn't be taken off the ships; their places in the invasion camps had already been filled by the divisions slated to follow them after the beachhead was established.

At the Allied headquarters, there was to be a brief period of comparative calm on the evening of the 5th, although the weather outlook was still not good. Any postponement beyond June 6th would involve a delay of at least two weeks before another attempt could be made; Eisenhower decided late on Monday morning the 6th to give the signal again, and the invasion ships headed out into the storm-tossed Channel. Even though the weather was to clear later on, there were still high winds and waves. Some of the smaller landing craft had to return to port. By mid-afternoon of June 6th, there were more than 3,500 ships in the Channel, of which more than 500 were warships to escort the convoys and lay on the first bombardment.

The waters off the Normandy coast first had to be swept of mines, and the minesweepers worked in the last few hours of daylight, surprisingly without interference from the Germans. Operation Fortitude was now producing some effect, but the Germans were simply not alert. The Luftwaffe flew only one reconnaissance mission, and that was too far north to spot the invasion fleet while at sea; the Luftwaffe was grounded by the bad weather, and what was left of the German navy kept inside the harbors. Rommel himself was on his way to Berchtesgaden where he hoped to get Hitler to agree to move a Panzer division into the St. Lô area where, ironically, the Americans were to drop their airborne divisions later that night.

The minesweepers and underwater demolition teams had done their work. After dark had closed in, the three airborne divisions filed into their planes and gliders, every paratrooper armed to the teeth. Just before midnight, 1,100 air transports filled with British and American troops headed for their drop points behind the Atlantic Wall.

The following account of the drop is taken from the regimental history of the 501st Parachutists of the 101st Airborne Division, as set down by Capt. Laurence Critchell.

AIR DROP ON NORMANDY

by Capt. Laurence Critchell

The night of June 6th was sullen and rainy. Fitful gusts of wind rocked the planes. Twilight was late in England at that time of year and, though the planes did not take off until 10:21—in military time 2221—a desolate blue light still showed behind the storm clouds. The C-47s climbed to their formations and straightened out, at two thousand feet, to head for France. Within the cabins we sat with darkened faces and stared out at the lampless countryside far below. Those of us who had taken the round, pink seasick pills felt drowsy. The wild excitement characterizing the scenes at the field prior to the takeoff had subsided, and no one talked very much. In the planes ridden by the Catholic and Protestant chaplains, the men said short prayers, bowing their blackened heads where they sat. Forward, by the pilot's compartment, were equipment bundles waiting to be kicked out the open door; on racks under the planes, like bombs, were more.

Over the English Channel a familiar and tranquil moon came out. Looking down to the indigo water, we could realize for the first time the stupendous effort of which we were a part. As far as the eye could see on the rough surface of the Channel, extending from beneath the plane to either wing-tip and dissolving into the far-off murk, were the ships of the Allied invasion. The thought crossed many of our minds that, down in each one of those tiny fragments, were men like ourselves, sitting in darkness and waiting dry-mouthed for the unknown. And suddenly it seemed as though we could see the whole great, sprawling, disconnected plan, which had begun at the induction centers ("Did they ask you about the paratroops?"), coming together into a single arrow of assault. And we were the tip.

The man who is going into combat does not feel much different from the man who is going to make his first parachute jump. What lies ahead of him is too unfamiliar to be frightening. He may realize that his heart is beating a little faster than normal, that the skin of his face is hot and his hands are cold. Otherwise he feels all right. But all his faculties are keyed up to abnormal alertness. And if the inner nervousness has not made him drowsy—which is one effect of tension on the system—he is acutely aware not only of himself, his physical presence in the plane or ship, but also of everything around him. From the moment he leaves the security of the rear to go forward he lives completely in the present.

The weather was clear across the Channel. By the time the planes began to encounter scattered clouds near the French coast, most of us were asleep. We were awakened by an unfamiliar sound, like the close-by popping of an outboard motor. Looking out the celluloid windows, we could see what it was: we were being fired at. The tracer bullets were speckling up into the sky in streams, thousands of them. Curiously enough, they were all colors—red, green, yellow, blue. It seemed unreal; it gave the darkness a nightmarish quality, like a multicolored blast furnace.

For all of us, pilots and soldiers alike, this was our first instant under fire. Nobody stopped to analyze his feelings. But if we felt anything at all it was surprise—surprise that anybody actually hated us enough to want to kill us. It was a feeling that tightened us in around ourselves painfully. And if the reader is interested in knowing what causes the gulf between a civilian and a veteran soldier, it is simply the difference between a man who has lived all his life in a reasonably friendly world, compared to the one who has existed where other people are literally trying to spill his brains on the earth.

The machine-gun bullets turned on Sergeant Rice's plane. They appeared out of the darkness below as little colored specks and whizzed past at the same instant. The popping noise sounded, oddly, as though it were close underneath the plane. It was not a loud noise, but it was distinct above the roar of the motors.

At the shouted order we shuffled to our feet. Hooking up, we checked our equipment. The familiar rote of parachute school was reassuring. But then we had to wait, pressed close against each other in silence. And we were having a hard time keeping on our feet. Almost at the first shots from below, the inexperienced pilots—men who later were to take us through enemy anti-aircraft fire as nervelessly as on a bomb run—had begun evasive action. This was contrary to orders. Their formations loosened up. A cloud bank near the Merderet scattered them still further. Sergeant Rice's plane dipped and turned, sometimes rising a hundred feet in a second or two, buckling the men's legs under the pressure.

All this had taken only a few moments. Now there was a new sound in the sky—the noise of explosions. The distant ones made an odd, enveloping *wop,* like a sound curling in on itself; close by, they had the concussion of dynamite. A noise like the rattling of chains beat against the walls of the plane; it was expended shrapnel. Nothing had prepared us for the surprising discovery that flak made noise. A glare lit up the sky. Rice saw a plane on fire as it dipped down below him, curling off on one wing. One—two—three dark figures hurtled out of it; then flames enveloped the cabin. In his mind's eye he saw the men shriveling up inside—maybe Suarez, maybe Colonel Johnson . . .

He wanted to get out of the plane . . .

A red light glowed over the door. There were more explosions. All semblance of formation had been lost. In the steady popping of the machine-gun bullets, the *wham wham wham* of the 20-mm. tracer shells and the explosions of the 88-mm. flak, the sharp arrow of the invasion seemed hopelessly blunted. One or two pilots slammed the doors of their compartments and circled back for England; they had had enough. But for the most part the planes blundered on. Men got sick and vomited on the floor; shrapnel tore up through the greasy pools or through the seats they had quitted. In the planes carrying loads of high explosives known as Composition C-2, the men held their breaths, waiting to find out what it would feel like to be blown to pieces.

"Take it easy, boys!" yelled Lieutenant Jansen at the door of Rice's plane. "It'll be all over in a minute!"

Fifty-caliber machine-gun bullets tore through the wings like the chattering of gravel. Rice's plane was much too high. Everything was going wrong.

Over the door, like a signal of relief, the green light went on.

How the hell did the pilots know where they were?

A K ration bundle lay in front of Lieutenant Jansen. He kicked it out the door. That was the last they ever saw of it. The second bundle weighed three hundred pounds. Before he and the crew chief could get rid of it, sixty seconds had passed. In that time the plane, going too fast anyway, had traveled almost two miles. What none of the men realized was that those chance sixty seconds were taking them—as in Colonel Johnson's plane, where a similar delay occurred—to La Barquette.

The anxious men dove out. Rice was wearing too much equipment; his left arm caught in the door. For three seconds he hung outside in the hundred-mile-an-hour wind. When he was torn free, the metal edge of the door scraped his skin almost to the flesh, taking with it his hundred-and-fifty-dollar wrist watch. He scarcely felt it. But his body position was so bad that the opening of the parachute almost knocked him unconscious. Dazed, he floated down. The only sounds were the sharp cracking of bullets that struck the edge of his nylon canopy. One arm was almost useless; with the other he slipped to earth as fast as he could. It was dark. He lay still on the ground for a moment. Machine-gun bullets firing to his right were thirty and forty feet in the air. He could hear the explosions of mortars and the sounds of planes going away, going back to England . . .

The pilots were hopelessly confused. The area had looked right that was all. How could anybody be sure of anything in all this confusion? But it would work out. It had to work out . . .

All over the Cotentin Peninsula the parachutists were coming down that way. Out in the English Channel the great armada of ships moved steadily towards set destinations—beaches later called Utah and Red Leg and Omaha, where hundreds of infantrymen died in the bleak daybreak. But that was four hours away. Meanwhile, we had no encouragement, no assurance, even, that the seaborne invasion would actually take place. And we were scattered. Where we had expected to land in selected drop zones, to assemble as complete battalions, each man found himself virtually alone.

A prize military secret—the dim locator lights on the equipment bundles—was quickly rendered useless; the German machine gunners fired on the lights. Later they booby-trapped the abandoned bundles. The biggest secret of them all—the pathfinder radar devices, the operators of which were dropped in Normandy half an hour before the first wave of planes—also turned out poorly: the operators were unable, as a rule, to reach their sets. All over Normandy, that night, the long prepared plans and the careful strategy were going awry.

Small groups of men worked their way across country, collecting more men as they went. Privates or sergeants or colonels led them—whoever kept his wits. Staff Sergeant Clarence J. Tyrrel of Georgia, who had been dropped twenty miles beyond his objective, gathered enough men to act as a tactical unit and on his way back through the darkness destroyed two light tanks. Lieutenant Colonel George Griswold and Captain Eldia Hare collected another group of men and brought them to the division command post at Hiesville, knocking off a horse-drawn German ammunition train enroute. But some of the groups were so small and so thoroughly lost that they fought for days before they learned that the invasion had really taken place.

This scattered fighting in the darkness seemed useless at the time. In effect, however, it worked out all right. The German soldiers had been accustomed to a pattern of formal war, with front lines, outposts and command posts. They found themselves fighting all around the clock. They themselves had developed vertical envelopment at Crete and Holland, but counter-offensive had evidently not occurred to them. There was nothing in their books to prepare them for situations where fire came from one direction one moment and from another the next. War waged by small independent groups of soldiers without leaders or without strategy was inconceivable. It was not war; it was chaos. How were such men controlled?

The Americans were not controlled. They just killed Germans.

Colonel Johnson was near Sergeant Rice when he landed. A dark building suggested one way of finding out where he was. But he left it alone—it was a German command post—and worked his way along the ditches in the general direction of the south, killing his first German when an enemy soldier opened up at him with a machine pistol. He was looking for La Barquette. He crawled for half an hour before he met anyone. Then he encountered a small group from one of the other battalions. None of the men knew where he was.

Tom Rice, meanwhile, had done all right. He and a small number of men moved into the apparently deserted village of Addeville. Finding no Germans there, the platoon leader, Lieutenant Rafferty, set up a temporary command post. Addeville had not been an objective. Everybody knew it. But just then they were not thinking about the plans that had been laid out for them in the sanity of England. They considered themselves lucky to hold what they had.

General Eisenhower, listening to the first word of the seaborne landings early next morning, had no idea of what had really happened to his airborne troops. But neither, as a matter of fact, had his airborne troops.

Across the Channel

The 101st Airborne Division got down out of the air with comparative safety, but then their troubles began. Because of heavy anti-aircraft fire and the bad weather, the troops were dispersed over such a wide area that out of more than 6,000 men, less than half had been brought together by the evening of D-plus one. They captured many of their objectives but they, like the 82nd Airborne, had trouble organizing enough men to achieve all they had been assigned to do.

On the eastern flank, the 6th British Airborne Division was to land near Caen and hold that flank against an expected counterattack from Panzer divisions in the area. Compared to the Americans, the British had a more successful drop, accomplishing most of their objectives by the time of the sea landings later that day.

Even the airborne operations hit the Germans with an element of surprise. Most of their radar warning system had been knocked out by bombing, and what was left was taken in by the deceptions of Operation Fortitude. Reports that did come in to German headquarters only helped to compound confusion. The Germans knew nothing of the invasion fleet's approach until it had gotten close enough to launch landing boats, and even then they were sure this wasn't the "real" invasion. They still held themselves in readiness for the Pas de Calais thrust. By early morning, part of the German Command had asked permission to move some armor in against the Normandy landings, but Hitler advised them to wait until the main direction of the invasion could be determined in the coming daylight hours. The late Chester Wilmot, Australian correspondent, describes what happened on Utah and Omaha beaches.

ASSAULT FROM THE SEA

by Chester Wilmot

A rising, surging sea carried the invasion fleet uneasily into the night. To the men whose destiny lay beyond the black horizon, the voyage seemed lonely and interminable. Cold, stinging spray swept the decks, but it was better there than it was below, where the pitching and throbbing of the ships was magnified and the humid air reeked of sickness. Nausea accentuated the natural anxiety of expectation. They did not imagine that the enemy was ignorant of their approach and his failure to respond seemed to many not only surprising but sinister. The sense of anticlimax added to their qualms, and they were slow to draw reassurance from the German inactivity.

Because the voyage was uneventful, it took on an air of unreality, which still prevailed at 2 a.m. when Naval Force "U" (Rear-Admiral D. P. Moon, U.S.N.) began assembling undisturbed in its transport area off the Cotentin, 12 miles north-east of Utah sector. Aboard its ships, nearly a thousand all told, were 30,000 men and 3,500 vehicles due to be landed that day on this beach alone.

Good fortune smoothed their way. The E-boats, which had been ordered out from Cherbourg to patrol the Bay of the Seine, turned back "on account of the bad weather" without making contact. The twin islands of St. Marcouf, lying athwart the line of approach, were found to be undefended. The coastal batteries were silent, for their radar was being jammed. Moreover, during the night they had been severely hammered by R.A.F. Lancasters and at first light they came under fresh onslaught from air and sea. At 5:20 a.m. 300 medium bombers of the Ninth U.S. Air Force flew in below the clouds to strike at these guns again and at strongpoints on Utah beach, which was already shuddering under shellfire from two battleships, two cruisers and a dozen destroyers. The accuracy of this double bombardment was evident as the assault craft, carrying two battalions of the 4th U.S. Infantry Division, drove in-shore leaving great white wakes on the dark-green sea. Even then there was little response from the coastal artillery and the beach defences were subdued by drenching fire from the "mosquito fleet," which moved in behind and on the flanks of the assault craft to rake the shore with rockets, flak-guns and howitzers.

In the vanguard of the invasion were two squadrons of DD tanks. These were to have been launched four miles off-shore, but because they were delayed by the weather, the LCTs carried them more than two miles closer before setting them to swim. By then they were under the lee of the Peninsula, which gave them considerable protection from the wind that was lashing the beaches farther east, and 28 out of 32 "DDs" got safely ashore. At least a dozen of them touched down with the first wave of infantry at 6:30 a.m. and began firing from the shallows as the men leapt from their landing-craft.[1]

With the tide still well out, most of the craft came to rest short of the belt of obstacles set up for their destruction and the troops had nearly 500 yards to run before they reached the long, low line of dunes. From these there came not the expected torrent of fire, but fitful and erratic spurts, for the defenders were numbed by the bombardment which still rang in their ears. They were slow to realise that it had switched to targets on the flanks and those Germans who did come up to man their weapons found their fire answered at once by tanks on the water's edge.

[1] The authors of *Utah Beach to Cherbourg,* a campaign study prepared by the Historical Division of the U.S. Army, say (at p. 44) that "the 32 DD tanks played little part in the assault" and that they "beached approximately 15 minutes after the first assault wave." This view is supported neither by the commander of the leading American regiment (Col. J. A. Van Fleet), nor by the reports of prisoners.

Although Rommel had given warning that the Allies would employ "water-proofed and submersible tanks," his troops do not seem to have taken his admonition seriously, for the appearance of the "DDs" unquestionably came as a shock to them. They had thought that they would turn their guns against soft human targets advancing unprotected over open beach, but now the Americans were covered by fire from armour which had come up out of the sea. Nothing in war is more unnerving than the unexpected. Surprise gave the DD tanks an influence far beyond their fire-power, striking terror in the hearts of the Germans and adding confidence to the resolution with which the Americans swept ashore. By 9 a.m. the leading regiment and the tanks had broken the crust of the Atlantic Wall on a two-mile front between the sea and the coastal lagoon.

In this they were aided by a mistake which proved no misfortune. Owing to the early swamping of two control vessels, a slight error was made in navigation, with the result that the assault battalions were landed nearly a mile south of the prescribed beach. This brought them to a sector where a single battalion of doubtful quality was manning defences less formidable than those the Americans would have encountered farther north. The Germans had presumed that the double belt of inundations in this extreme corner of the Peninsula would effectively discourage any attempt at landing or at least render nugatory whatever foothold might be gained there.

In the wake of the assault waves came naval demolition units and special squads of army engineers to blow and bulldoze clear lanes through the beach obstacles, thus preparing the way for the rapid and early landing of the rest of the 4th Division. This clearing operation was doubly hazardous, for most of the obstacles were mined and the foreshore came under increasingly heavy shellfire from long-range guns now able to operate without the aid of radar. Nevertheless, adequate gaps were cleared by the time the main body of the follow-up regiment began landing at 10 a.m. The infantry moved quickly through the shellfire and swung north along the dunes to attack the sector where the landing should have been made. There they

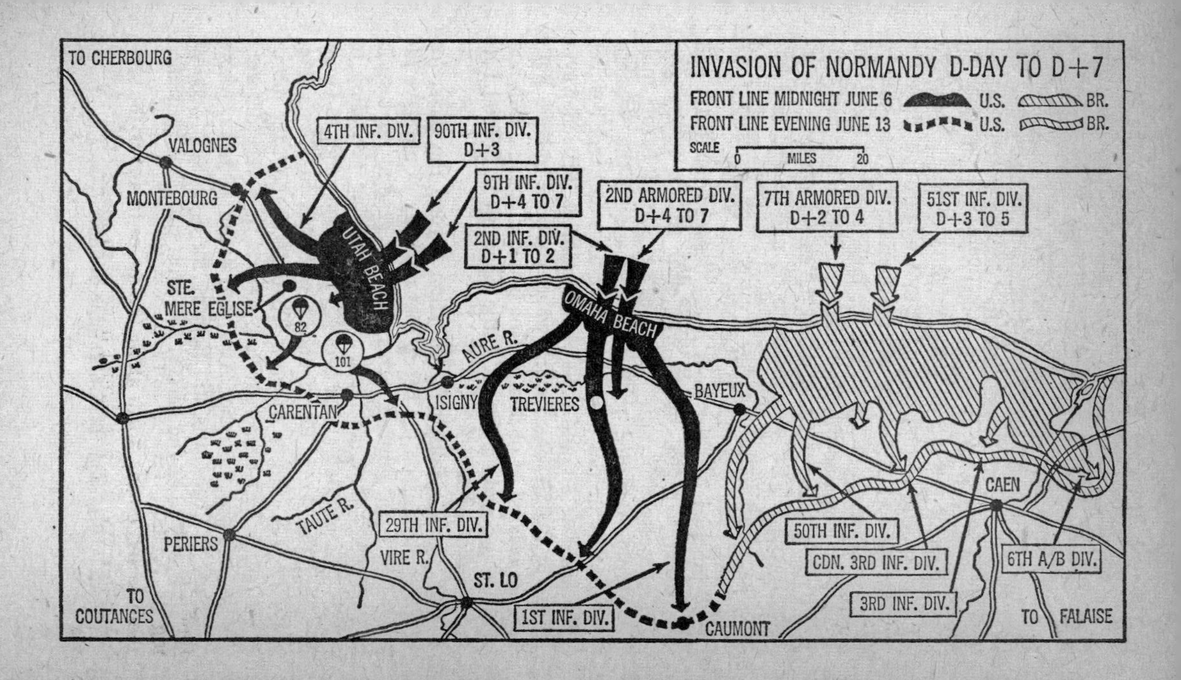
INVASION OF NORMANDY D-DAY TO D+7
FRONT LINE MIDNIGHT JUNE 6 U.S. BR.
FRONT LINE EVENING JUNE 13 U.S. BR.
SCALE
0 MILES 20
TO CHERBOURG
VALOGNES
MONTEBOURG
STE. MERE EGLISE
4TH INF. DIV.
90TH INF. DIV. D+3
9TH INF. DIV. D+4 TO 7
2ND INF. DIV. D+1 TO 2
2ND ARMORED DIV. D+4 TO 7
7TH ARMORED DIV. D+2 TO 4
51ST INF. DIV. D+3 TO 5
UTAH BEACH
OMAHA BEACH
82
101
AURE R.
ISIGNY
TREVIERES
BAYEUX
CARENTAN
TAUTE R.
29TH INF. DIV.
VIRE R.
PERIERS
ST. LO
1ST INF. DIV.
CAUMONT
50TH INF. DIV.
CDN. 3RD INF. DIV.
3RD INF. DIV.
6TH A/B DIV.
CAEN
TO COUTANCES
TO FALAISE

encountered determined opposition, and they were not able to reach the guns, which continued their harassing fire in spite of counter-battery bombardment by the Navy.

This enemy shelling did not seriously delay the landing and unloading, and a stream of men, tanks, guns and vehicles came in to consolidate the division's hold on the coastal strip and to strengthen its westward advance. In the middle of the morning the infantry set out across the causeways with amphibious tanks moving through the water in close support. A few enemy positions on the far shore of the lagoon were still active, but the tanks subdued them and by 1 p.m. the seaborne and airborne forces had met. Already the parachutists had seized the exits from four causeways, while a fifth was found to be undefended and unmined even though it linked the beach with the main road leading straight through to the Merderet Valley.

No junction had yet been made between the 101st and the 82nd Divisions, but it was clear that a strong grip had been established on the Peninsula. Shortly before midday, Moon signalled to Kirk, commanding the Western Task Force, "Initial waves made landings on exact beaches after accurate air and naval bombardment. Fifteen waves landed by 0945B.[2] Succeeding waves continue to land. Both beaches cleared of obstacles. Roads under construction and vehicles proceeding inland. Little opposition. Coastal batteries under control."

This signal idealised the situation beyond the facts, for no one who was on the beach that morning would have reported in such glowing terms. But the general impression it conveyed—that the battle was developing according to plan—was justified and it brought profound relief to Omar Bradley, the Army Commander, who was in Kirk's flagship, the U.S. cruiser *Augusta*. There throughout the morning Bradley had been receiving reports of a very different character from the other American sector, Omaha, where Gerow's V Corps was still fighting for a foothold against what proved to be the fiercest and most sustained resistance of the day.

[2] That is, 9:45 a.m. British Double Summer Time.

Omaha was a concave beach four miles long and dominated at either end by cliffs which rose almost sheer for more than 100 feet. Between these two bluffs the gently curving strand sloped up to a cultivated plateau which reached a height of 150 feet half a mile inland and commanded the whole foreshore. The escarpment of this plateau was indented at four points where small watercourses had cut their way to the sea and these narrow valleys provided the only exits for vehicles. On the beach itself the tidal flat, some 300 yards deep, was firm sand, but it ended in a bank of heavy, smooth shingle which sloped up rather sharply.

On the western third of Omaha this shingle ran up to a sea-wall and a paved road, beyond which the escarpment soon rose at a steep angle. On the rest of the beach the shingle bank was backed by sand dunes which were impassable by vehicles, as was the shingle in many places. On the far side of this line of dunes was a broad stretch of sand which was marshy and tufted with coarse grass at the entrances to the valleys. Here the rough slope was less steep, but it could not be negotiated even by tracked vehicles except in a few places. Apart from the paved road under the lee of the western bluff, the routes running inland were little more than cart tracks and all led through thickly-wooded cuttings into the stout stone villages of Vierville, St. Laurent and Colleville, which thus commanded every exit.

The inherent strength of this sector had been well exploited by the Germans in designing their defences. On the tidal flat there were three belts of obstacles; the beach above the shingle, and parts of the slope, were mined and wired; all the natural exits were blocked by mines and by either concrete obstructions or anti-tank ditches. The main strongpoints, consisting of entrenchments, pillboxes and bunkers equipped with machine-guns, anti-tank guns and light artillery, were concentrated on the bluffs at either end of the beach and at the mouths of the four valleys. There the fire positions were terraced up the slopes on either side and were echeloned inland, so that they were almost impregnable against head-on assault. From these the Germans could cover most of the beach with direct and flanking fire.

Between the exit valleys, however, the defences were less formidable. There were trenches and weapon pits along the crest of the escarpment and some minefields on the plateau, but the Germans relied on their reserves in the string of coastal villages to cut short any penetration between the main strongholds. These villages formed a second defensive chain and three miles inland the flooded valley of the River Aure provided a further barrier which the Americans would have to force in order to avoid being contained in the narrow coastal belt.

This stretch of beach, thus fortified, was hardly inviting, but it was the only part of the entire 20 miles between the mouth of the Vire and Arromanches, north-east of Bayeux, where a landing could be made in strength. Elsewhere in this zone sheer cliffs or outcrops of rock off-shore provided natural protection and allowed the Germans to concentrate on the defense of Omaha.

When the American plan was made it was thought that this four-mile sector was manned by little more than a battalion of the 716th Division, which was then holding 45 miles of coastline from the Orne to the Vire. This was an indifferent formation, containing many foreign conscripts and equipped only for a static role, but a mobile division of good quality, the 352nd, was known to be in close reserve around St. Lô. In May British Intelligence had come to suspect that this division had moved up to strengthen the coastal crust by taking over the western half of the Orne-Vire sector, but the evidence of that move was slender and the Americans were disinclined to accept it. When some confirmation was received early in June, it was too late to pass the warning on to the assault troops who were already embarking. Consequently, they went into action believing that though Omaha was strongly fortified it was not particularly heavily garrisoned.

The plan provided for the 1st U.S. Division (Major-General C. R. Huebner) to assault with two Regimental Combat Teams, each of three battalions, supported by two battalions of DD tanks and two special brigades of engineers. On the right the 116th Regiment (attached from the 29th Division) was to land between Vierville and St. Laurent, and on the left the 16th Regiment, between St. Laurent and Colleville. For the assault both these regiments were to be under Huebner's command, but once a foothold had been gained, the 29th Division (Major-General C. H. Gerhardt) was to take over the western sector and clear the area between the coast and the Aure as far as Isigny. Meantime, the 1st Division would swing east to link up with Second British Army at Port-en-Bessin and drive south to secure a bridgehead over the Aure, east of Trévières. It was hoped—a little ambitiously perhaps—that by nightfall V U.S. Corps might have a beachhead 16 miles wide and five to six miles deep, but it was realised that whether or not this "phase-line" could be reached depended primarily on the whereabouts of the 352nd Division.

Soon after 3 a.m. Naval Force "O" (Rear-Admiral J. L. Hall, Jr., U.S.N.) began lowering the assault-craft from their "mother-ships" into a rough and unfriendly sea twelve miles off-shore. Several craft were swamped within a few minutes of touching the water; others were kept afloat only by strenuous bailing by troops who used their steel helmets as buckets. None but the most hardened stomachs were unmoved by the pitching and tossing and men became weak from sickness long before they began the run-in. Perhaps the most unpleasant experience was that suffered by a boatload of the 116th Infantry. "Major Dallas's command party," says the regimental account, "made their start under inauspicious circumstances. In lowering the boats from the davits of H.M.S. *Empire Javelin,* the command boat became stuck for 30 minutes directly under the outlet of the ship's 'heads' and could go neither up nor down. During this half-hour the ship's company made the most of an opportunity that Englishmen have sought since 1776."

The rough seas had more serious consequences in the case of the DD tanks. One battalion decided not to attempt any launchings; the other put 29 tanks into the water, but some sank like stones as soon as they left the LCTs, others were swamped on the run-in and only two reached the shore. The weather was the primary factor in this disaster, but the casualties might not have been so severe if the tanks had not been launched so far out (they were set to swim nearly four miles) and if the training and maintenance had been more thorough. But whatever the reason, the plan to land the DD tanks ahead of the infantry miscarried, and the men themselves approached the shore under the gravest disadvantages. As one report says, "Men who had been chilled by their wetting, cramped by immobility in the small and fully-loaded craft and weakened by sea-sickness were not in the best condition for strenuous action on landing." [3]

While the assault battalions were heading for the shore, warships and aircraft began the bombardment of the coast defences. Owing to low cloud, visibility was poor when the shelling began and after a few minutes the dust and smoke made it almost impossible to pinpoint targets on shore. The task of the bombers thus became extremely difficult and, fearful of hitting their own troops, they left a good safety margin. This was unquestionably wise, but it meant that most of the bombs fell behind, not upon, the beach defences. In addition, many rocket-firing craft, confused by the smoke and over-anxious about the coastal guns, loosed their salvos well out of range and the in-coming troops had the mortification of seeing most of the projectiles burst in the water short of the beach.

Batteries and strong points were still active when the bombardment lifted, and the assault craft came under heavy shelling and mortaring over the last half-mile before they touched down on a beach almost unscarred by friendly bomb or shell. The severest fire came from the bluff which commanded the western end of the beach and from the Vierville exit, directly in front of which the 1st Battalion of the 116th Regiment was due to land in column of companies.

[3] *Omaha Beachhead,* p. 38. This authoritative account of the landing, prepared by the U.S. War Department's Historical Division, is admirably frank and comprehensive.

At 6:30 a.m., as the leading company approached this beach, known by the code-name Dog Green,[4] one of its six craft foundered and another was sunk by a direct hit, but the rest went on till they ran aground on a sandbar several hundred yards short of the sea-wall. The ramps went down and the men leapt into water which was waist to shoulder deep. Then, says the battalion's own story: [5]

> As if this were the signal for which the enemy had waited, all boats came under criss-cross machine-gun fire. . . . As the first men jumped, they crumpled and flopped into the water. Then order was lost. It seemed to the men that the only way to get ashore was to dive head first in and swim clear of the fire that was striking the boats. But, as they hit the water, their heavy equipment dragged them down and soon they were struggling to keep afloat. Some were hit in the water and wounded. Some drowned then and there. . . . But some moved safely through the bullet-fire to the sand and then, finding they could not hold there, went back into the water and used it as cover, only their heads sticking out. Those who survived kept moving forward with the tide, sheltering at times behind under-water obstacles and in this way they finally made their landings.
>
> Within ten minutes of the ramps being lowered, A Company had become inert, leaderless and almost incapable of action. Every officer and sergeant had been killed or wounded. . . . It had become a struggle for survival and rescue. The men in the water pushed

[4] Between the Vire and the Orne the Normandy coast was divided by the planners into beach sectors labelled alphabetically from the West. The three sectors of Omaha—D, E and F—were known from their lettering as Dog, Easy and Fox, and sub-sectors were designated by colours. Thus the 116th Regiment landed on Dog Green, Dog White, Dog Red and Easy Green; 16th Regiment on Easy Red and Fox Green.

[5] This account was prepared by the U.S. War Department's Historical Division after close interrogation of the survivors.

wounded men ashore ahead of them, and those who had reached the sands crawled back into the water pulling others to land to save them from drowning, in many cases only to see the rescued men wounded again or to be hit themselves. Within 20 minutes of striking the beach A Company had ceased to be an assault company and had become a forlorn little rescue party bent upon survival and the saving of lives.

The vanguard of the assault on this flank of Omaha was still at the water's edge when the next company came in 25 minutes after H-Hour. Several boatloads, which landed on Dog Green, the same sector as the first wave, were riddled on the water's edge, but the others, carried farther east and farther inshore by the tide, touched down on a less heavily defended stretch of beach which was enveloped in smoke. This shielded them as they dashed for cover of the sea-wall and from there two groups, each less than twenty strong, struggled through the wire and minefields and up the ridge to Vierville, 700 yards inland, not stopping to deal with the fortifications but infiltrating between them as best they could.

Because of the drag of the wind and tide, all six boats of the following company came in east of the Dog Green death-trap, and moved across the foreshore and up the slope with less than a dozen casualties, for they found an unmined gap between the strongpoints which guarded the natural exits. Before 10 a.m. this company and part of 5th Ranger Battalion, which landed behind it, had joined the two earlier groups in Vierville, just in time to beat off a sharp counter-attack. There some 200 men stopped a thrust which would have carried through to the beach, where the remnants of the 1st Battalion lay almost helpless in their foxholes, lacking the support of armour or heavy weapons.

A mile to the east, the other two battalions of the 116th Regiment, landing in succession on either side of the Les Moulins exit, met less opposition on the beach, because the Germans were blinded by smoke from grass and buildings on the crest set afire by the naval bombardment. This unintentional smoke screen saved many lives, but it caused great confusion. Most companies came in farther east than had been planned and "officers, knowing they were to the left of their landing areas, were uncertain as to their course of action, and this hesitation prevented any chance of immediate assault action." [6] They were slow in rallying, slower still in advancing up the slope, since they tended to move in single file through the minefields, and those who did reach the crest soon lost cohesion and direction, for there the smoke was so thick that the troops had to put on their gas-masks.

There was little progress until someone discovered, east of Les Moulins, a sector where the minefields had been detonated by the bombardment, opening the way for elements of both battalions to infiltrate towards St. Laurent before the enemy closed the gap with shellfire. This accentuated the congestion on the beach, for supporting weapons and transport had begun to land before the engineers had cleared any exits and before the infantry had subdued the strongpoints which raked the foreshore with fire. Wrecked landing-craft, burning vehicles, exploding ammunition and intermittent shelling added to the confusion, making it extremely difficult for commanders to organise the scattered and bewildered groups who had taken shelter under the sea-wall or the shingle bank, and impossible for the follow-up regiment to come in as planned at 9:30 a.m.

Meantime, the counterpart of this battle had developed along the eastern half of Omaha, where two battalions of the 16th Regiment had landed at half-past six. Here, too, the bombardment had missed the beach defences and the assault craft were dragged by the run of the wind and tide half a mile and more to the east of their appointed stations. The whole assault side-slipped with most unfortunate results. On Easy Red, where the enemy fire at first was relatively light, barely 100 men were set down during the first half-hour, but the best part of three companies made their landfall on Fox Green directly beneath the unscathed guns of formidable strong points which covered the exit leading to Colleville. The terrible story of Dog Green was repeated.

[6] *Omaha Beachhead,* p. 47.

On Easy Red, where the 2nd Battalion should have landed, the first meagre assault forces were pinned to the beach until "a lieutenant and a wounded sergeant of divisional engineers stood up under fire and walked over to inspect the wire obstacles just beyond the embankment. The lieutenant came back and, hands on hips, looked down disgustedly at the men lying behind the shingle bank. 'Are you going to lay there and get killed, or get up and do something about it?' Nobody stirred, so the sergeant and the officer got the materials and blew the wire." [7] This courageous gesture rallied the men and the lieutenant led them to the top of the ridge in single file along a narrow pathway which was under fire and sown with anti-personnel mines. By that route, this platoon, followed by another company, got within striking distance of the strongpoints which had turned this sector into a slaughter-ground. One by one these were silenced but the hazard of the minefields remained. One false step and a man lost a foot or a leg, if not his life. The wounded lay where they fell, afraid to move lest they might set off another mine, and the men in the shuffling line stepped over them. Shells dropped close but none dared to go to ground, for every yard was lethal. When the reserve battalion tried to find its own pathway, the minefield claimed 47 victims in the leading company, but some 300 men finally got through and headed for Colleville. The gap thus opened became a funnel for movement off Easy Red during the rest of the morning, but that movement was slow and perilous.

On the extreme left, however, the 16th's other assault battalion was able to make reasonable progress, in spite of early mishaps which might have proved disastrous. Rough sea and bad navigation delayed the landing. Several craft were swamped, or sunk by direct hits, one assault company was an hour and a half late and the other came in half a mile too far to the east. This, in fact, proved an advantage, since the men were able to organise under the lee of the cliffs and, instead of trying, as intended, to force the strongly-guarded exit from Fox Green, they found their

[7] *Omaha Beachhead,* p. 58.

way up a steep but ill-defended gully farther east. The rest of the battalion followed and opened a clear breach in the defences with the aid of fire from destroyers and small craft operating close in on the flank. Here by 9:30 a.m. the Americans were moving slowly but steadily east along the cliff-top towards Port-en-Bessin, where they were due to link up with the British.

Elsewhere on Omaha, however, the situation was still extremely grave. By half-past nine, according to the After-Action Report of V U.S. Corps, the assault units "were disorganised, had suffered heavy casualties and were handicapped by losses of valuable equipment. . . . They were pinned down along the beach by intense enemy fire. . . . Personnel and equipment were being piled ashore on Easy Red, Easy Green and Dog Red sectors where congested groups afforded good targets for the enemy. The engineers had not been able to clear sufficiently large gaps through the minefields with the result that companies attempting to move through them off the beach suffered considerable casualties. . . . Action in this early period was that of small, often isolated groups—a squad, a section or a platoon without much co-ordination. Attempts were made to organise units but . . . the beaches were too confused to permit it."

In this confusion the forces already ashore were powerless to break the deadlock, and the men, tanks and guns which were so urgently required could not be landed because the engineers had not been able to clear the underwater obstacles or the general wreckage on the foreshore. Even those tanks and vehicles which had been landed were still immobilised on the narrow strip of sand between the rising tide and the shingle bank through which as yet no gaps had been cleared. The assault regiments were clinging to barely a hundred yards of beach. A few small parties, which were to reach Vierville, St. Laurent and Colleville, had made minor penetrations, but these had been partially closed behind them by enemy fire. The Atlantic Wall was holding firm, and the Americans now knew that the Omaha sector was held by units of both the 352nd and the 716th Divisions.

In May, during the general strengthening of Normandy following Hitler's intuitive inspiration and Rommel's policy of strengthening the coastal crust, the 352nd Division had moved up to garrison the Bayeux-Isigny sector. There it took under command the regiment of the 716th which was holding this extensive front, and proceeded to nose in three of its own six battalions to defend Omaha and another likely beach at Arromanches on the British front. This left three battalions of the 352nd in close reserve behind Omaha and by chance one of these was carrying out an exercise on that stretch of coast on June 5th-6th.

There were thus eight battalions in the area between Bayeux and Isigny, where the Americans had expected to find four, and the defences had some depth, provided moreover by troops of fair quality, equipped for something more than a static role. This meant that when the bombardment miscarried and the amphibious armour failed to arrive, the Americans entered an unequal struggle with every advantage of weather, position and armament against them. The presence of the 352nd Division in and close behind the beach made it a matter of the most vital consequence to break through the coastal defences before they could be further reinforced.

This was the prospect at 9:50 a.m. when a signal from the troops ashore told Huebner, "There are too many vehicles on the beach; send combat troops. 30 LCTs waiting off-shore; cannot come in because of shelling. Troops dug in on beaches, still under heavy fire."

Huebner acted promptly. He called on the Navy to engage German batteries and strongpoints regardless of the danger of hitting his own troops, and he ordered the 18th Regiment to land at once on Easy Red. Of that regiment, however, only one battalion was loaded in craft which could make what amounted to an assault landing. The others had to be transhipped from their LCIs into small craft, and it was early afternoon before they were ready to go ashore.

By that time, the situation had been improved by the landing of one battalion on Easy Red and another on Easy Green. Both battalions found the beaches still under fire, but they curbed it by capturing several pillboxes. In the attack upon these they were supported by DD tanks, which had been landed dry-shod, and by sustained and accurate shelling from destroyers standing only a thousand yards off-shore.

At noon a report from Easy Green said, "Fire support excellent. Germans leaving positions and surrendering." A few minutes later came another report, from Easy Red, "Troops previously pinned down on Easy and Fox now advancing inland."

Even more important, by this time the last enemy strongpoints at the main exit from Easy Red had been reduced and engineers had begun clearing the minefields. Thus after a six-hour battle the defences began to crumble and the foreshore was gradually freed of small arms fire, but the shelling of the beach continued, in spite of counter-battery bombardment by warships and fighter-bombers. There were still no exits for vehicles; most of the passages through the minefields were little more than single-file tracks; and the enemy was opposing most strenuously any attempt to deepen the penetration. The first crisis had passed, but the battle was by no means won.

In the early afternoon movement off the beach was limited and sluggish and the enemy had time to re-form his front roughly along the line of the road that ran through Colleville and St. Laurent. Within an hour and a half of landing part of the 18th Regiment, by a very remarkable effort, reached the northern edge of Colleville, a mile inland, where several weakened companies of the 16th Regiment were waging a house-to-house battle. But the enemy, too, had been reinforced and throughout the afternoon the Americans could do no more than hold on and hope that additional support in men and weapons would get through from the beach.

Unfortunately, movement inland was delayed, primarily because of the psychological supremacy of German mines over the American engineers and infantrymen. Even when the minefields were no longer under direct fire, the engineers were tardy in tackling them and the infantry were so ill-schooled in the art of "de-lousing" mines that they preferred to pick a dangerous passage through them rather than set boldly about the task of clearance. In mid-afternoon, for instance, one battalion was led slowly and painfully in single file up the ridge, stepping over the wounded who lay on the mined path. By resolute action the way could have been cleared in half the time it took to pass the battalion man by man along it. Yet no one would grasp the nettle.

It was 2 p.m. before the engineers succeeded in clearing any exit track. Another two hours elapsed before tanks and vehicles began moving off the beach, and then full use could not be made of the exit because of shelling. Late in the afternoon this became so severe that Huebner's third regiment did not finish landing until after seven o'clock and two battalions of artillery were even further delayed. Thus the infantry who had battled inland were left without adequate supporting fire until some time after 7 p.m., when a few tanks and tank destroyers came to their aid as the fight for the coastal villages hung in the balance.

Even the possibilities of direct air support could not be fully exploited, mainly because so many of the leading companies and battalions had lost their radio sets in struggling ashore. No one in the H.Q. ships knew where the front line was, the troops on the ground were far too busy to put out visual signals, and the smoke and dust which overhung the beachhead made accurate identification of targets impossible. This obscurity also handicapped the warships, but their bombardment was the most effective aid the infantry received.

It was only at the end of the long day that the Americans forced the line of the coastal road, and this success was principally due to the unquenchable spirit and drive of the 1st Division. On the right the units of the 29th Division, fighting their first battle, made little progress after taking Vierville and reaching St. Laurent in the morning. In the face of aggressive German probing, it was all Gerhardt's troops could do to hold a beachhead 1,200 yards deep, for only two of his infantry regiments and one artillery battalion were landed during the day, and that battalion lost all but one of its 12 guns. At dark the situation was still confused and St. Laurent was not completely clear. The American grip on this stretch of Omaha was by no means secure, and there was considerable anxiety about the danger of a counter-attack against the tired and weakened battalions during the night. The opportunity was there and the Germans could exploit it—if they were to commit their reserves in the right place.

For eight hours after the airborne assault began, the H.Q. of the German 84th Corps (Marcks) was handicapped by lack of reliable information. Reports of the main paratroop and glider landings were reasonably prompt and accurate, but the jamming of coastal radar prevented the enemy from gaining any indication of the strength and dispositions of the forces at sea until after daylight, and by that time the coast defences were under fire from aircraft and warships. Although this bombardment did not cause serious damage to the defences on Omaha, it did disrupt communications, especially in the Cotentin area. The start of the naval shelling was duly reported by 84th Corps to Seventh Army at 6 a.m., but Marcks received no word of the seaborne landings until two hours later, and it was nearly 11 o'clock before he learned that troops were landing from the sea on the Cotentin. This news, which came only from the German Navy, could not be confirmed, and at 11:45 a.m. 84th Corps signalled, "Regarding East coast [of Cotentin] no reports available since at the moment communications are severed." [8]

In the meantime, the news from the Omaha sector, though scanty, was encouraging. At 9:25 a.m. Marck's H.Q. reported, "The forward positions in the area of 352nd Division have been penetrated but the situation is not so critical as in the area of 716th Division," i.e. between Bayeux and Caen, and it was for this sector that he requested immediate counter-action by panzer divisions. This policy seemed justified when at 1:35 p.m. it was stated by the Chief of Staff of the 352nd that "the Division has thrown

[8] This, and the other messages that follow, are taken from the Telephone Log of Seventh German Army H.Q.

the invaders back into the sea; only near Colleville is there, in his opinion, a counter-attack still in progress." On the strength of this news Seventh Army informed Rommel's H.Q. that "the situation in the area of 352nd Division is now restored." There was no contrary report from this division until 6 p.m. and in the meantime all armoured reserves had been directed against the British with the object of preventing the fall of Caen. None were sent to the area west of Bayeux.

In any case the reinforcements which Marcks could have thrown into the Omaha battle were not as great as Allied Intelligence had feared they might be. Around St. Lô there was only a mobile brigade, and its mobility was limited to the skill of its members as cyclists, for it had no motorised troop transport. Nevertheless, if it had intervened at Omaha during the afternoon the consequences might have been serious, but at midday it was ordered to counter-attack the British east of Bayeux. Thus the only reserves which could be employed against Omaha that day were three battalions of the 352nd, deployed in close reserve between Bayeux and Isigny. Before dawn in response to the airborne landings on the Cotentin two of these battalions were ordered to move west "to establish and maintain the link through Carentan." One had started moving before Marcks learned of the Omaha assault and the other, which had been stationed around Bayeux, was drawn into battle with the British. This left only a single battalion in position to reinforce the Omaha defences, and it was pitted against the American right flank at Vierville and St. Laurent. It was here that the Germans should have made their counter-stroke during the night with the battalion which had started for Carentan and been recalled, but they made the fatal mistake of looking over their shoulders at a landing which was not and could not have been any real threat.

Soon after seven o'clock that morning three companies of Rangers (the American counterpart of British Commandos) had landed three miles west of Omaha at the base of Pointe du Hoe, an almost sheer cliff 100 feet high. Their primary task was to silence a powerful coastal battery capable of firing upon both Utah and Omaha beaches. The cliffs appeared to be unassailable, but the Rangers shot grappling hooks and rope ladders to the top with rocket charges and scaled the heights under covering fire from two destroyers. This fire drove the Germans into their dug-outs and the Rangers met little opposition as they moved to the battery position. They found it so cratered by bombs and shells that it looked like the face of the moon; the casemates were wrecked, and the guns had gone.

Patrols were sent inland and after going half a mile two men found the missing battery, camouflaged and intact. There were stacks of ammunition on the ground, the guns were ready to fire on Utah, but there was no sign of the crews or of any recent firing. The battery was put out of action with explosive charges, but the mystery of the silent and deserted guns on Pointe du Hoe remains unsolved. Whatever the reason, the most dangerous battery in the American assault area was never used and was exposed to destruction by a two-man patrol!

As the day wore on the small Ranger force, numbering 130 men, drew increasing attention from the enemy. There were two counter-attacks in the afternoon and three more after dark, when the Germans pitted against the Rangers the reserves which should have been used for an attack against the western and most vulnerable sector of the Omaha beachhead.

There was no such diversion to aid the 1st Division in the slogging battle which carried it across the Colleville-St. Laurent road in the last few hours before dark. The recovery Huebner's men had made since the middle of the morning was extraordinary. It had seemed then that the leading regiment was broken and beaten, but at the critical moment its survivors had responded to the intrepid leadership of its commander, Colonel G. A. Taylor, who became famous that morning for the rallying cry, "Two kinds of people are staying on this beach, the dead and those who are going to die—now let's get the hell out of here."

In that spirit the first small parties had made the break and the follow-up regiment had exploited this slender advantage with a thrust to Colleville and beyond, which ended by cracking the second German position. This village was the keystone of the defence once the coastal fortifications had begun to yield. At dark some Germans were still holding out in Colleville, but they were so hard pressed by infantry and tanks that the village had lost its tactical significance. Maintaining the pressure south and east so long as the light lasted, the 1st Division's own regiments extended their beachhead to an average depth of a mile to a mile and a half on a four-mile front by the end of the day. It was a slender enough footing, but it was held by men who had been ashore before in North Africa and in Sicily, and who could not be dismayed even by the most desperate situation. Had this sector of Omaha been assigned to troops less experienced, less resolute or less ably commanded, the assault might never have penetrated beyond the beaches.

The near-disaster which befell the Americans at Omaha was in some degree due to the weather, which led to the miscarriage of the preliminary bombardment and the mislanding of the assault units, but the sea off Omaha was hardly, if at all, more hostile than it was on the more exposed British beaches farther east. In so far as they suffered more severely from the rough sea, this was chiefly due to the fact that the U.S. Navy, concerned about the fire of coastal batteries, insisted upon lowering the assault craft as much as twelve miles off-shore, whereas the British "lowering areas" were less than eight miles out. The longer passage not only added to the strain upon the assault infantry but greatly increased the danger of swamping and of faulty navigation. The leading assault craft had to start their run-in while it was still dark, and were excessively and unwarrantably exposed to the vagaries of wind and tide. On the other beaches very few mislandings were made on D-Day, but on Omaha less than half the companies in the assault battalions were landed within 800 yards of their appointed sectors. The U.S. Navy's unwillingness to take advice from Ramsay was the start of the trouble.[9]

[9] In his public comment on this Ramsay was tactfully restrained, for in his *Dispatch* (paragraph 40) he was content to say: "The

So far as operations on shore are concerned, it is suggested by the War Department's historians that "the principal cause of the difficulties of V Corps on D-Day was the unexpected strength of the enemy on the assault beaches." [10] This is only a partial explanation, for there were grave defects inherent in the American plan. The first of these was the fruit of the American predilection for direct assault. The plan for Omaha was a tactical application of the head-on strategy which Marshall had so consistently advocated in pressing the case for cross-Channel invasion. The Americans knew that the main enemy fortifications covered the natural exits, and yet they deliberately planned to make their heaviest landings directly in front of these strongpoints with the object of taking them by storm. They scorned the lessons of earlier amphibious operations, which had shown the wisdom of landing between the beach strongpoints, not opposite them, infiltrating and assaulting them from the flank and rear. The plan for Dog sector was typical. Dog Green and Dog Red were each known to be covered by powerful "exit" strongpoints. Between those Dog White was comparatively weakly defended. The American intention, however, was to land four companies in succession on each of the former during the first hour and only two companies on the latter where prospects of success were greatest. The results might have been anticipated. Two companies of the 2nd Rangers landed according to plan opposite the Vierville exit on Dog Green; only 62 men out of 132 reached the sea-wall. But 450 men of the 5th Rangers landing at the same time on Dog White between the strongpoints "got across the beach and up the sea-wall with the loss of only 5 or 6 men." [11]

There might have been some justification for the policy of direct assault if the Americans had accepted Montgomery's plan for landing armour *en masse* at the start of the

---

longer passage inshore for the assault craft of the Western Task Force appeared to add appreciably to their difficulties."

[10] *Omaha Beachhead,* pp. 109-10.

[11] *Omaha Beachhead,* p. 53.

attack, and for using the specialised equipment of Hobart's 79th Armoured Division to deal with the fortifications and the underwater obstacles. When Montgomery first saw this equipment he ordered Hobart to make one-third of it available to the Americans, and set himself to interest Eisenhower and Bradley in its revolutionary employment. Hobart's account of the reaction of the three generals is illuminating.[12]

"Montgomery," he says, "was most inquisitive. After thorough tests and searching questions he said in effect: 'I'll have this and this and this; but I don't want that or that.' Eisenhower was equally enthusiastic but not so discriminating. His response was, 'We'll take everything you can give us.' Bradley appeared to be interested but, when asked what he wanted, replied, 'I'll have to consult my staff.' "

Bradley and his staff eventually accepted the "DDs" but did not take up the offer of "Crabs," "Crocodiles," "AVREs" and the rest of Hobart's menagerie.[13] Their official reason was that there was no time to train American crews to handle the Churchill tanks in which most of the special British equipment was installed, but their fundamental scepticism about its value was shown when they rejected even the "Crabs" which offered few training difficulties, since the "flail" device was fitted to the standard American Sherman tank.

The terrible consequences of this short-sightedness were only too apparent on Omaha on D-Day. The failure of the bombardment and the non-appearance of the DD tanks left the infantry at the mercy of the strongpoints which they were required to take by storm. Where tanks were available, landed direct from LCTs, they proved invaluable, but they were too few and too dispersed, and they found great

[12] This account was given to me by General Hobart on November 10th, 1946.

[13] "Crabs" were "flail-tanks" and "Crocodiles" were flame-throwing tanks. "AVRE" stood for "Armoured Vehicle, Royal Engineers," "AVREs" were used in demolishing fortifications and surmounting obstacles.

difficulty in manœuvring because of the congestion of vehicles on the foreshore.

This congestion was chiefly due to the absence of specialised armour capable of dealing with the natural obstacles and fixed defences. The British had learned from the Dieppe Raid that engineers cannot consistently perform under fire the deliberate tasks required of them unless they are given armoured protection. No such protection was available on Omaha. Apart from lightly armoured bulldozers the Americans had no mechanised equipment for dealing with the obstructions and fortifications. They were expected by their commanders to attack pillboxes with pole-charges and man-pack flame-throwers, to clear barbed wire entanglements and concrete walls with explosives manually placed and to lift mines by hand, all under fire. That they often failed is not surprising. Throughout the morning tanks, guns and vehicles were immobilised at the water's edge because the engineers could not clear gaps in the shingle bank, a comparatively minor obstacle. Throughout the afternoon, infantry were compelled to move across the beach in single file because the sappers had no mechanical means of dealing with mines and hand-clearance was too slow. At the Vierville exit the last strongpoints were reduced by 2 p.m., but it was another eight hours before the mines and obstructions had been cleared, for they had to be cleared by hand.

At dark only this road and one other were open for vehicles, and the full sweep of the beach was still under fire from artillery and mortars. The corps beachhead was six miles wide and less than two miles deep at the point of greatest penetration, and there was a grave shortage of tanks, anti-tank guns and of artillery generally. Most of the battalions were seriously weakened, for the day's fighting had cost 3,000 casualties. In short, although the Americans were ashore, they held an area barely large enough to be called a foothold, and were in no condition to withstand any large-scale counter-attack with armour during the next two critical days. But whether or not the Germans would, or could, develop such an attack depended on the course of events on the front of Dempsey's Second British Army.

Off the Beaches

The British assault on their three beaches was a larger operation than the Americans'. Three British divisions were landed, their chief objective being Caen, the Germans' main base for the defense of Normandy. The British met fierce resistance on the beaches, but flailing tanks were employed to knock out mine fields and flame-throwing tanks to reduce pillboxes. The British were also lucky to have longer naval bombardments; their jumping-off time for the beaches was scheduled later than the Americans' because of tide conditions, and the Royal Navy had four times as long to smash at the German coastal batteries. And their landings were only seven to eight miles offshore, which, as we have seen, shortened the tortuous ride to the beaches.

At the end of D-Day the British had captured Bayeux, one of the two principal objectives, but they had not taken Caen. (They would not occupy it for a month.) Montgomery knew the Germans would hurl their heaviest counterattacks against him, because Caen guarded the road to Paris, and the Germans believed Paris was the Allies' prime objective.

The day's best success went to the 3rd Canadian Division, supported by the 2nd Canadian Armored Brigade, which pushed farther inland than any other division in the Normandy landings. They almost reached Caen, but lacked enough support, and their unloading on the beaches had been delayed. The 21st Panzer Division prevented the capture of Caen; it was firmly lodged between the 3rd Canadian Division and the 3rd British Division between Caen and the coast. Here the German coastal defenses were still intact. But Rommel was unable to move enough reserves to reinforce the 21st Panzer—he lacked air superiority, and the German High Command had lost the initiative by wavering in the early hours of the invasion. When the 12th SS Division was finally sent to help on D-plus one, it was badly strafed; by the time it reached Caen there was not enough fuel for an immediate counterattack.

The Luftwaffe was nowhere to be seen on the coast during the daylight hours of D-Day or D-plus one—an astonishing lapse. What was even more amazing, on D-Day only about 120 fighter planes were available to the Luftwaffe on the Channel front. Against this the Allies had more than 5,000 fighters available in Britain. The Allies had air supremacy throughout the day, and the invasion fleet steamed across the Channel without the slightest interference through D-Day and D-plus one.

The Allies hadn't reached all their objectives, but there was reason for cautious optimism. Neither the two American beachheads nor the British beachhead had been able to consolidate with each other, but they were established, and only major counterattacks could dislodge them.

In all, the Allies, had lost fewer than 2,500 men killed; while there were many more casualties, the blood-letting feared by the peoples of the United Nations was not to take place on the beaches.

Then the German counterattacks finally materialized; they were successfully beaten off during the next few days, but there was fighting of the most stubborn kind in all sectors. As the Allies held firm, they knew the decision lay in whether they could beat the Germans in the build-up of supplies and reinforcements.

The Americans' first objective was to seal off the Cotentin Peninsula and then free the port of Cherbourg at its tip, giving the invasion a real port of supply; if the Germans had committed more of their heavy armored units here, the offensive would have been in real trouble. But the Germans still held back divisions to the north of the British beachhead, expecting another landing, and they continued to throw the majority of their armor at Montgomery.

Hitler and the German High Command believed the Allies were only feinting at the Cotentin Peninsula, to make the Germans swing their main forces in that direction; the Allies would then follow up with a second landing of even greater force, driving into France farther to the north. The Germans were still without effective reconnaissance, and they were suffering serious difficulties in all their troop movements.

The over-all SHAEF strategy was this: the 1st U.S. Army, once it had cleaned out the Cotentin Peninsula, was to capture Cherbourg to the west and drive for St. Lô to the east; the British 2nd Army would protect the Americans' flank and keep pressure on the German armored divisions, so they wouldn't be sent south. Bradley's first efforts to move on St. Lô brought the American infantry and tanks into the

Bocage country, where the hedgerows turned out to be Hitler's best allies—dirt banks, with thorn-bushes growing on top, that lined the small lanes and roads in Normandy. This natural defense was so rugged that heavy tanks could operate only on the roads. Bradley decided that his troops would have to have special help. Until his tanks were equipped with new cutting devices, not much progress was to be made, other than cleaning up the Cotentin Peninsula. Here Gen. J. Lawton Collins, commanding the 7th U.S. Corps, fought up the peninsula. Actually the Bocage was at its worst on the peninsula; it is interesting to note that hedgerows held fewer terrors for Collins, who had commanded infantry on Guadalcanal, than they did for some of the other generals. Collins's men moved up the peninsula in quick jabs, with the infantry having little fire support other than rifles, mortars and bazookas.

The fall of Cherbourg was official on June 26th, 1944. The port would not be in working order for some time, but the fate of the German divisions left in the peninsula had been sealed when Eisenhower ordered two American airborne divisions dropped to cut off their escape to the east.

The Americans could now ready the drive on St. Lô, while the British held the main German offensive power around the Caen sector.

Alan Moorehead's description of the St. Lô breakout follows.

BREAKOUT AT ST. LÔ

by Alan Moorehead

Towards the end of July nearly a million American and British troops were either ashore in Normandy, or about to come ashore. The bridgehead was stretched like a drum. Even though a completely new system of roads and ports had been built, the traffic blocks sometimes extended for ten or fifteen miles. We were approaching the crisis of the campaign, the crucial moment for the whole of western Europe. Montgomery remained Allied commander in the field, working from a headquarters near Bayeux, midway between the American and the British armies.

Rommel lay on a hospital bed fighting for his own life. The long personal struggle between him and Montgomery was over. Allied fighters, little knowing what they were doing, had swooped on the German commander's car near Lisieux. Rommel was sitting in the front seat beside the driver, and the smashed corner of the windscreen had splintered against his temple. A chemist from the neighboring French village looked at the unconscious figure on the road, and said he could do nothing. After that Rommel lay for a long time in the field hospital without regaining consciousness. At last, when he had sufficiently recovered to be removed to Paris, it was seen that it would be months at least before he could return to active command, and indeed his death followed soon afterwards in Germany. His place was taken by Von Kluge, a Nazi.[1]

Everywhere the Allies were moving into position for the great battle: the Americans at St. Lô, the British towards Pincon and the southwest of Caen. It is quite true to say that the bulk of the German armor and some of their best divisions were spaced round Caen, opposite the British; it is quite untrue to suggest that because of this the Americans had no serious opposition at St. Lô. Both armies had immense battles to fight; the British a static battle, the Americans a breakout battle. In neither sector were the opening stages particularly brilliant; many mistakes were made. These errors were followed by a most memorable stroke of arms, when the American First and Third Armies fanned out through Brittany and western France; and still another

[1] July 4th until July 17th (the date of Rommel's injury): There were constant upheavals inside the enemy command. On the 4th Rommel told Hauser there was an express order from Hitler he "must not withdraw an inch." Hauser replied the enemy had already broken through. "In that case," Rommel answered, "the enemy will be in St. Germain tomorrow." It is interesting to see the steady disintegration of Rommel's morale right up to the moment of his wounding; it is almost as if he knew that both he and his army were doomed.

extraordinary feat when the British took up the running and headed straight for Belgium. These vast and fast pursuits took the headlines. Being easily explicable operations, and in themselves the proof of victory, they engaged the public's attention, and no doubt will remain longest in everyone's mind. In actual fact, they were no more than the intelligent and courageous exploitation of a *fait-accompli.* The real decisive issues were fought out on the bridgehead perimeter, and later round the Falaise pocket. It was here in Normandy that the German army was defeated, and in military history the battles of St. Lô and Caen will take precedence over the subsequent rush to the Rhine.

It was already late in July when Montgomery decided to try and smash the German hinge at Caen. Caen, though occupied by the Allies, was still under fire. We now wanted to push beyond the town, and run out over the flatter wheatfields of the Falaise plain, which was said to be excellent tank country. All this time Caen had been in the position of the hinge of a door which stretched out westward towards St. Lô. The plan was for the Americans to keep pushing the door open until General Patton and his fresh Third Army could slip round the corner at Avranches, and over-run Brittany. At the same time the British were to try and unseat the door at its hinge. Then, when the whole structure was wobbling, the Americans would run round behind the open door and pin against the British such Germans as were left on the spot.

General Dempsey, the commander of the combined British and Canadian forces, now had three full armored divisions—the Seventh, the Eleventh and the Guards—plus several independent armored brigades. He decided to move these in secret to the extreme eastern part of the bridgehead. Bridges were to be thrown up at night across the Orne Canal north of Caen. The armor, some five or six hundred tanks, would then cross and charge due south through the German lines in the general direction of Falaise. Some three divisions of infantry would follow to consolidate. The bombers would prepare the way for the tanks.

At this moment the whole question of the use of heavy

four-engined bombers was in debate. One school believed that they should be used exclusively for the strategical bombing of Germany; the other school argued that every available weapon should be thrown into this Normandy crisis. The latter school won. We were committed to the use of a new and immensely powerful weapon in circumstances for which the personnel had had no proper training. When you fly over a battlefield you can very rarely see where the front-line runs. For the most part, nothing shows on the ground except a few indeterminate puffs of smoke. Since all the Normandy countryside looked alike it was extremely difficult to pin-point targets. And now the four-engined bombers were asked to bomb not clearly defined targets like towns and bridges but the open countryside where, unseen to the crews, the Germans were hiding. Furthermore, they were asked to bomb targets within a thousand yards or less of our own troops. There had already been a series of mistakes. British and Americans alike had been hit by their own bombs.

By the time Dempsey came to make his tank drive there had been some advance in technique. It was now at last accepted that you do not necessarily hit armies in the field by knocking down towns, and you do frequently retard your own advance because of the craters and the piles of debris. And so this time it was resolved that we should bomb in "strips." The four-engined planes would lay a path of bombs along either side of the projected tank run. This was designed to silence the anti-tank guns and infantry on the flanks. Then the lighter machines would scatter non-cratering anti-personnel bombs along the central strip, where the tanks had to travel. In addition, as soon as the tanks started their run the artillery would commence a creeping barrage. The shells would fall just ahead of the oncoming tanks, and the barrage would advance about the same rate—five miles an hour. In other words, the armor would go into action surrounded by a wall of our own explosive. It was a plan that depended on perfect timing. It went wrong. The bombs failed to silence the German gunners. The gunners simply stayed underground until the bombing was over, and then they emerged and opened up at very close range on the hundreds of vehicles deployed across the plain. Two hundred British tanks were lost within a few hours. A number of villages were destroyed by the Lancasters, but the Germans were sheltering outside. And now the enemy rushed his Panthers and Tigers with their superior guns to the front. Only three bridges had been laid across the Orne canal; blockages quickly occurred. The Luftwaffe managed to catch a number of replacement crews while they were sheltering for the night. And so the advance faltered and stopped after a few miles.

We tried again a few days later, using new devices. Pink smoke was put up to blind the enemy to our movements. Searchlights were shone against the clouds at night to give the effect of moonlight. Colored lights were fired into the enemy lines to direct our bombers. All these maneuvers were countered by one means or another. The enemy, for instance, quickly seized on the idea of firing colored guiding lights into *our* lines as soon as aircraft appeared.

It was decided to bomb still more closely to our own infantry, and then we really began to take casualties. It was impossible to strike the targets accurately. I watched one great salvo fall five or six miles inside our own lines. It wiped out a headquarters and caused hundreds of Canadian casualties. Exactly the same thing was happening on the American sector at the opening of the battle of St. Lô. The army was growing distinctly nervous about its own air force, and although much more good than harm was done by the bombing the effect upon morale was becoming serious. A senior American general had been killed, and in the forward platoons the soldiers became just as apprehensive about the bombing as the Germans were. There is always something particularly unnerving about being hit by your own side.

Fortunately the need for heavy, close-support bombing vanished soon after this, and subsequently the technique was greatly improved. One brilliant exception all through had been the British Typhoon rocket planes. They had by now developed such accuracy that they were diving upon single tanks and even if they did not get one-hundred-per-cent results, they often succeeded in scaring the crews into hiding.

All through this period, too, our artillery was increasing

and increasing until it reached fantastic proportions. It was an unsettling thing to drive anywhere near the front. Hundreds of guns would suddenly erupt out of the bushes on either side of the road, and the blast would make your eardrums ache for hours on end. In numbers of tanks also we had immense superiority. Provided the crews had been saved, it was no great tragedy to find a hundred wrecked Shermans lying about the fields; one knew that another couple of hundred had just been put ashore. The whole plan was to keep attacking, never to let the enemy rest; to bomb him all the way to the Seine, to shell him all night, to submit him to infantry rushes day after day. We now had overwhelming fire-power, and at the end of July it was in continuous operation for a hundred miles along the front.[2]

[2] Conditions in the enemy lines were going in just the opposite direction: towards disintegration. At the end of June German coastal commanders were complaining "the fire of enemy naval guns is unimaginable." On July 5th there was much discussion at German headquarters about the possibility of new Allied sea and air landings. On the same day Seventh Army headquarters was reporting that all their counter-attacks were "suffocated" by the Allied air force. The Chief of Staff added: "Our ground forces will be simply slaughtered if it goes on." July 7th: General Jodl, back at supreme headquarters, told Rundstedt that he "could not" put up to Hitler proposals for new withdrawals. But on July 15th the Germans were describing the battle as "one tremendous blood bath." Appeal after appeal went out for more fuel, more tanks, more aircraft, more men; and above all, permission to withdraw.

Hitler followed the battle very closely, village by village, unit by unit. His occasional direct orders were treated with the utmost reverence even by such seasoned professionals as Rundstedt. "The Führer says"—that was enough to make every German soldier spring to obey. All through this period one has a picture of Hitler, tormented, harassed and blindly angry as the appalling news kept coming in. Even his closest advisers like Jodl were balking at the job of acquainting him with the worst disasters. Possibly there were moments when Hitler was not sane. In the midst of his passionate megalomania one can conceive the bitter per-

There was little enough to show on the map. Villages were won and lost by the dozen, and still the front-line did not move. All the way down the Odon river to Pincon and thence to St. Lô the German line bulged under an intolerable weight, and still somehow it was patched up and kept together. When prisoners were taken they came out of the line with gray lined faces, suffering not so much from wounds as from shock. Their pocket diaries told the story of the gradual crumbling of the will under persistent fire. The belt of destruction thickened and lengthened every day, until all the area of the perimeter began to assume that beaten, worn-out appearance of the French battlefields in the last war. Great stretches of forest were uprooted. One after another the villages went down into dust. Hundreds of bulldozers struggled to keep pace with the wreckage of the bombing. It did not matter in what direction you turned; within an hour's run by jeep from the beaches you found yourself involved in a battle, and the incessant aching noise of gunfire never ceased. One began to marvel at the German endurance. Somewhere surely the line had to break.

It broke at last at St. Lô. General Bradley, who controlled the American armies under Montgomery, was rapidly developing into one of the ablest field commanders of the war. At St. Lô he was determined to force the issue one way or another. Old friends like the American Ninth Division were being cut to pieces, but still he persisted. On July 24th St. Lô collapsed, a heap of ruins. Patton raced through the gap. He was round the corner at Avranches, a bloodhound in full cry. Aircraft patrolled ahead of the armored columns. At the slightest opposition the tanks and armored cars raced round, attacked on the flanks and pressed on. Prisoners who were completely bewildered began to come in by the thousand.[3]

---

sonal struggle in trying to force down his mind to the humiliating facts. And the final bitter awakening must have come when the attempt was made upon his life by his own people in the middle of July.

[3] July 31st: The German Seventh Army headquarters informed the High Command, "The left flank has collapsed."

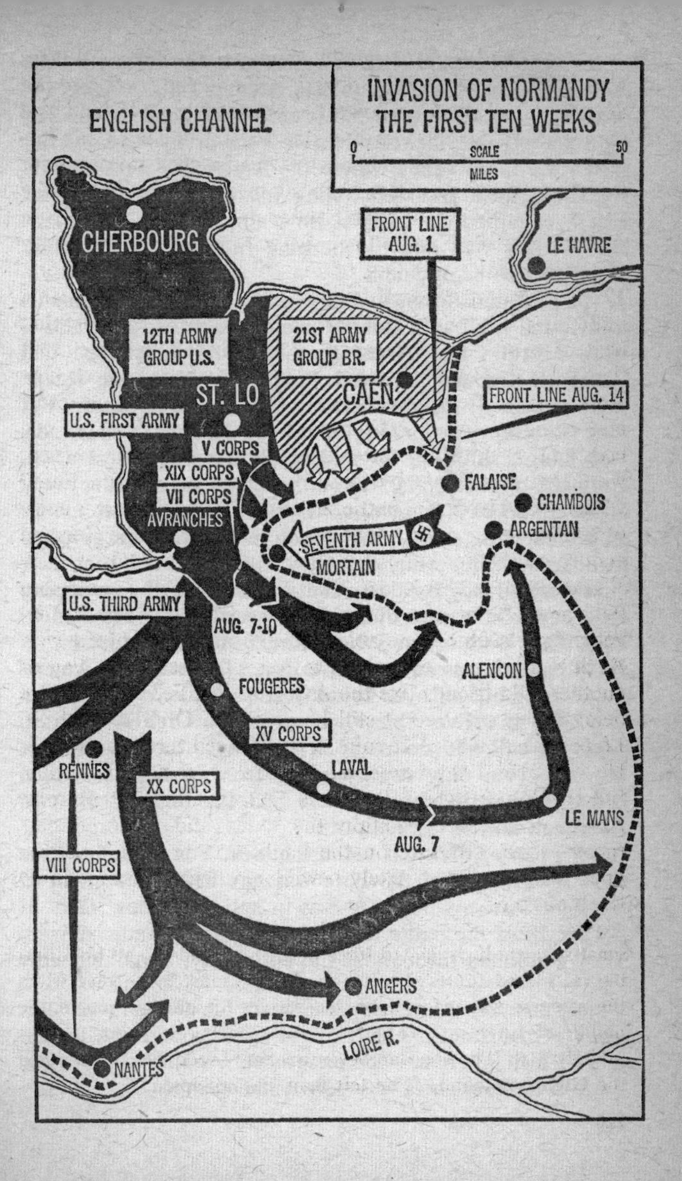

INVASION OF NORMANDY
THE FIRST TEN WEEKS
0
SCALE
50
MILES
ENGLISH CHANNEL
CHERBOURG
LE HAVRE
FRONT LINE AUG. 1
12TH ARMY GROUP U.S.
21ST ARMY GROUP BR.
ST. LO
CAEN
FRONT LINE AUG. 14
U.S. FIRST ARMY
V CORPS
XIX CORPS
VII CORPS
AVRANCHES
FALAISE
CHAMBOIS
ARGENTAN
SEVENTH ARMY
MORTAIN
U.S. THIRD ARMY
AUG. 7-10
FOUGERES
ALENCON
XV CORPS
RENNES
LAVAL
XX CORPS
LE MANS
AUG. 7
VIII CORPS
ANGERS
LOIRE R.
NANTES

And now the whole line began to give way. Bit by bit the door was pushed wide open. On August 7th the British at last surged up to the crest of Mount Pincon, and for the first time since D-Day looked down over the bridgehead and out across the Loire valley, where the Americans were already beginning their great encircling movement. Village after village collapsed on the Falaise plain, and the Canadians battled their way into the burning ruins of Falaise itself. The trap was being laid.

The German Seventh Army and all its reinforcements now found itself in a rough rectangle bounded by Falaise, Vire, Mortain and Argentan. Since the Americans had passed right round the south of their position, one escape route remained: the area between Falaise and Argentan. But they were not yet thinking of retreat. Rommel's successor, Von Kluge, sitting in his underground headquarters at St. Germain, outside Paris, was on the telephone to Hitler every night. And always he received the same order: Resist. Counter-attack. No retreat. It did not matter that corps commanders were reporting that they could not hold, that their lines were already breaking, that the chances of re-grouping on a better line were diminishing every day. They had to hold. They were ordered to a counter-attack at Mortain.

On paper it was an attractive idea. Here were the Americans strung out all over Brittany and the Loire valley on a very thin line. Everything had to pass through Avranches, since we still had no ports in Brittany. The Germans at Mortain were only twenty miles from Avranches. Once break through to the sea there and the bulk of the two American armies were cut off.[4]

Two panzer divisions led the attack. For a while things were locally critical. If there was any deficiency at all in the American equipment it was in anti-tank guns. Then at the height of the battle the rocket-firing Typhoons arrived. They continued throughout the entire day, remaining only

[4] July 31st: Von Kluge's appreciation of the position was: "The whole western front has been ripped open. Avranches is the anchor of Brittany, It must be recaptured." And he himself came down to the battle area to supervise the operation.

long enough on the ground between trips to reload. Nearly a hundred German tanks were destroyed. Their entire striking front was broken up, and the attack turned abruptly into defeat. Whatever Hitler ordered now, only one course remained for the Seventh Army: retreat. But could they retreat?

A revolutionary change had overtaken the situation while the Germans were wasting time round Mortain. Rennes had fallen. So had Laval and Le Mans, Angers and Tours on the Loire. Orléans was falling. So was Chartres. Paris itself was in immediate danger. The Americans raced on and on through the unguarded south. Their tanks roared through one city after another, leaving behind great empty stretches of road, great regions of open countryside; and still they kept on. It had the effect of an octopus laying tentacle on tentacle round a victim, and now the grip began to tighten. Everywhere the French Resistance was rising. Little groups of maquis ambushed the German garrisons along the path of the American advance. Snipers were surprised, road blocks cleared, mines torn up. It became unnecessary for us to occupy the country we took; the French were doing that for us.

In Brittany the scattered remnants of the enemy army gathered themselves into the coastal fortresses, chiefly at St. Malo, Dinard, Brest, St. Nazaire and Lorient. Here at least they could stand aside from the general route and take refuge behind concrete and minefields. The German policy of denying us the ports was started in good earnest. A series of sieges began, and this was later to develop into the only coherent line of action the Germans were able to adopt to the west of the Rhine valley. For the moment, however, the battle for the ports was secondary, just as the fall of Paris was secondary. Everything was focused upon that Homeric scene round Falaise where the German armies in the west were about to fall headlong into one of the greatest military defeats in history.

Even those of us who were visiting different sectors of the front every day were unable to grasp the enormity of the thing that was happening. All we knew was that somewhere to the south of Falaise, in an ever-dwindling pocket of rolling countryside, there was a horde of broken and bewildered men, the survivors of some thirty or forty divisions. And now they were being killed and captured and maimed at the rate of several thousand every day.

It had been a dull and indifferent summer. Since D-Day we had never been able to rely on the weather for two days at a time. But now the sun shone out day after day. The trampled corn turned brilliant yellow. The dust rose up with the smoke of the explosions. And through this hot August sun the Allied aircraft streamed down on to the trapped German armies with such a blitz of bombing as western Europe had never seen. No German convoy could take the roads in safety before nightfall. But now in their extremity they were forced out into the open, and the carnage along the roads was horrible. Unable to stay where they were, unable to go into hiding, little groups of enemy began feeling their way blindly towards the east. They used side-roads. They traveled as much as they could by night. It made no difference. Sooner or later they found the forests on fire around them, and Allied troops cutting in from the flanks. The pressure on the western end of the pocket became unbearable. Conde and Tinchebray fell, and with them all the villages of the upper Orne.

The Germans now abandoned all pretense of keeping up a continuous or coherent line. Their regular units lost all identity. Little battle groups were formed, given a sector and told to look after themselves as best they could. In one day alone we captured men belonging to thirty different German formations. As the refugees streamed back they were grabbed at the mouth of the pocket, re-formed, and put into the crumpling line. Cooks and signalers were fighting side by side with gunless gunners and grounded airmen. Tank fitters became infantry, along with butchers and staff officers and road menders. Then presently, towards the concluding stages, the battle groups lost contact with one another. In a blind instinct for self-preservation the Germans were either surrendering or deserting in little companies, in the hope of reaching the Seine on foot. There were no drugs for their wounded; no time to bury their dead. One after another their field hospitals were over-run.

The time when half or even a third of the diminishing army could retreat had long since disappeared. Nearly all their vehicles had been lost. The horse-drawn traffic was utterly disorganized. Those who had struggled back to the Seine came under a new and still fiercer blitz from the air on the river itself. Barges and ferries were shot up in scores. The bridges were already down.[5]

A little group of surviving German generals met in the forest of Chambois for a conference. What should they do? General surrender? One last effort to get the best of their men away? They took a vote, and by a narrow margin decided on the latter course. Foreign troops, raw and second-rate troops, wounded men and men who had got themselves isolated—all these were abandoned. The surviving panzers and SS troops climbed on to what was left of their tanks and vehicles and headed northeast for the Seine. Already the British and American armies had locked the gate. But this last desperate column determined to smash it open again for a few hours; for just sufficient time to enable them to get away. They struck through a village called Trun, outside Falaise. A Polish division in the Canadian army took the first blow. Then for the next thirty-six hours all this sector of the battlefield disappeared under continuous smoke and explosion. Broken staccato reports came out of the arena. A few German tanks were getting through. Canadian reinforcements were rushed in. There was a final headlong onslaught round the hamlet of St. Lambert. I do not think I can do better than to describe the scene in the same words I used in a message to my newspaper at the time:

"If I were to be allowed just one more dispatch from this front this would be it; not because the dispatch itself is important, but because we have begun to see the end of Germany here in this village of St. Lambert today.

"The best of Von Kluge's army came here *en masse* forty-eight hours ago. They converged upon the village to fight

[5] August 8th: The Seventh Army reported: "A break-through has occurred at Caen the like of which we have never seen." August 10th: The order at last came down from Hitler: "Disengage." In the opinion of the army staff it was already too late.

their way out; long caravans of horses and gun-carts, tanks and half-tracks, hospitals and workshops, artillery and infantry. It was the sort of panzer battle array that the Germans have used to terrorize Europe for four years. We knew no combination to stand against it.

"And now, here in the apple orchards and in the village streets one turns sick to see what has happened to them. They met the British and the Allied troops head on, and they were just obliterated. Until now I had no conception of what trained artillerymen and infantry can do, and certainly this is the most awful sight that has come my way since the war began.

"It begins in the back streets of St. Lambert, where the German columns first came in range of the British fire. The horses stampeded. Not half a dozen, but perhaps three hundred or more. They lashed down the fences and the hedges with their hooves, and dragged their carriages through the farmyards. Many galloped for the banks of the river Dives, and plunged headlong with all their trappings down the twelve-foot banks into the stream below, which at once turned red with blood. Those animals that did not drown under the dragging weight of their harness, or die in falling, kept plunging about among the broken gun-carriages, and trampled to death the Germans hiding under the bank. The drivers of the lorries panicked in the same way. As more and more shells kept ripping through the apple trees, they collided their vehicles one against the other, and with such force that some of the lighter cars were telescoped with their occupants inside.

"At some places for stretches of fifty yards vehicles, horses and men became jammed together in one struggling, shrieking mass. Engines and broken petrol tanks took fire, and the wounded pinned in the wreckage were suffocated, burned and lost. Those who were lucky enough to get out of the first collisions scrambled up the ditches and ran for cover across the open fields. They were picked off as they ran. One belt of shell fire fell on the Dives river bridge at the moment when two closely packed columns were converging upon it. Those vehicles and beasts and men on the center of the bridge were all pitchforked into space at once.

But so many fell that soon the wreckage piled up level with the bridge itself, and made a dam across the river.

"At the far entrance to the bridge, where a number of heavy guns were attempting a crossing, a blockage was caused and took fire. Those in front apparently tried to struggle back. Those behind, being utterly bewildered, tried to push on. And so the whole column was wedged immovably until it was reduced to flames.

"I suppose there were about a thousand German vehicles of every sort lying out in the fields behind. All these came under fire. The Germans made no attempt to man their guns. They either huddled beneath them, or ran blindly for the futile cover of the hedges.

"They ran in the direction of the fire, shouting that they had surrendered. They gave up in hundreds upon hundreds. There was no fight left in them any more, and now, here, you can see what is left by the battle in the warm midday sunlight. It is exactly like one of those crowded battle paintings of Waterloo or Borodino—except of course the wreckage is different. Every staff car—and I suppose I have seen a hundred—is packed with French loot and German equipment. There is a profusion of everything: field-glasses and typewriters, pistols and small arms by the hundred, cases of wine, truck-loads of food and medical stores, a vast mass of leather harness. Every car is full of clothing, and every officer seems to have possessed a pair of corsets to take home.

"If you want a car you walk up and take your pick—anything from a baby tourer to a volkswagen or a ten-ton half-track. The Tommies start them up and go off through the orchards. Two Russians in German uniform stand stupidly on the river bank, and they timidly hold out cigarettes to anyone who comes by. They stand in the middle of piled-up riches they never dreamed of before; purses crammed with notes that have fallen from dead men's bodies, radio sets and dumps of rich clothing looted from the French. I have just picked my way across the wreckage to the house on the far side of the orchard. It is full of Germans—Germans beaten and numbed into senselessness. Like animals, they seem to have no will of their own. They are all armed with machine-pistols and rifles, but no one takes the slightest notice of them. It would be absurd to think that they would fire, and nobody has time to take their arms from them and lead them into captivity.

"Over at the hospital it is far worse. The dead and the wounded lie together. Living or dead there is not much difference in the appearance of the men. Many hours ago life ceased to count for anything at all. The wounded keep dying, but quietly, so that one is not aware at any given moment of just how many are surviving. They are all jumbled on top of one another, and the stench makes it difficult for one to refrain from being sick. Outside a Canadian soldier is mercifully going round shooting wounded horses with a Luger pistol. It would be equally merciful if he did the same for some of these enemy patients who are beyond hope and too weak to cry any more. At any rate, I have just directed this mercy-killer down to the river, where there are about thirty horses wounded and unable to get up the steep banks. Long ago they stopped trying, and they stand patiently in the water waiting unconsciously to die.

"I do not know the limits of this battlefield, since I have been here only four hours. It stretches I know for about a mile up the Falaise road, because for a good part of that distance you see the line of many hundreds of German helmets flung away by the enemy at the moment of their surrender. A young Canadian lieutenant explains: 'They kept coming up the road in bursts every three minutes. We shot the leaders of each group and captured the others.'

"I have just selected a volkswagen to get me back to my billet. The back seat is piled with the belongings of the man who now lies dead by the front wheels. He had taken the precaution, I note, of procuring a civilian suit, which is always a good thing to use if you are going to desert.

"Well, there it is; there could be no reason in this ghastly scene. I say again I think I see the end of Germany here. This was their best in weapons and men, their strongest barrier before the Rhine. It has been brushed aside, shattered into bits. The beaten Wehrmacht is a pitiable thing."

To the Rhine

But over a third of the German 7th Army did get out of the Falaise Gap, partly because the Allies couldn't keep the noose tightly closed; the men escaped, but they were unable to save their equipment.

The Germans withdrew to the Seine, in a state of high disorganization, expecting the Americans to turn on Paris itself. But Patton's 3rd Army kept driving east, under orders to seize a bridgehead over the Seine southeast of Paris. Patton was stalled only by the insurrection in Paris. To help out the beleaguered French, the Allied High Command sent an American and a French division into Paris to help liberate the City of Light.

Paris was freed on the 25th of August, 1944, and Patton loaded up with gasoline; now his 3rd Army lashed out once more south of Paris, pounding for the German Saar; the 1st U.S. Army pointed for the Ardennes to the north; farther to the northwest the 1st Canadian Army and the 2nd British Army headed for Belgium, aiming to cut off the German 15th Army which held the V-rocket sites on the coast, and to open up another major port. A port in the north, to shorten the supply route for the thrust into Germany, was an essential. The American armies were being supplied from Cherbourg; by the end of summer the supply lines stretched out 400 miles. The British were supplied from Bayeux, some 250 miles away, and this would be lengthened as they drove on Belgium. The irony was, the supplies were ashore, but they couldn't be moved to the front fast enough to launch an Allied smash to the Rhine while the German armies were still reeling.

The supply problem fed a disagreement between Montgomery and Bradley over the strategy of mounting the knockout punch. Montgomery's idea was for the American and British forces to move out together north of Paris; the 1st and the 3rd Armies would then fan out toward the Ardennes, while the British and Canadian armies would free the Channel ports, move into Holland and then wheel to the east aiming a punch at the German Ruhr. He asked for forty divisions and a majority of the supplies during September to build up the knockout punch, and planned to attack on a short front. To get the forty divisions, the 1st U.S. Army would have to be placed under his command. The 3rd would proceed to the Meuse River and hold there to protect the flank of the northern operations.

Eisenhower showed some interest in this, but Bradley and Patton were thoroughly aroused. Patton, a restless and aggressive commander, had continued his drive, and he couldn't abide the idea of waging a defensive campaign, particularly after the success of the breakthrough at St. Lô. SHAEF had also laid down that American armies were to serve under American commanders only, once they were fully established in France.

To resolve the conflict, Eisenhower took over as commander of all the land armies, giving Montgomery part of what he wanted—the major share of supplies for the strike into Belgium and Holland, and the promise of some of the divisions from the 1st Army. This didn't really calm things between Montgomery and Bradley. Patton continued to press for supplies, particularly gasoline, so that he could keep pushing the Germans in front of the Meuse River.

On August 29th, Montgomery opened his attack toward Belgium. The British 2nd Army's armored columns drove north, pushing the Germans ahead of them, crossed the River Somme, captured the German 7th Army at Eberbach and entered Belgium on September 2nd. To the east, two American armored divisions also crossed the border on the same day. The British met little resistance on their way to Brussels, taking the city on September 3rd; the British 11th Armored Division pushed on to Antwerp, entering the city on September 4th. The German 15th Army was now cut off, isolated along the Channel coast (they could save themselves only by getting across the Scheldt estuary to the west of Antwerp.) Remnants of the 7th Army were being cut up, those not captured were being driven back against the Ardennes and the Meuse River to the south. Now the German Ruhr, the heart of the German steel industry, might be vulnerable to Montgomery. From the Ruhr, Berlin was only a jump away.

Montgomery now urged Eisenhower to put his strategy for the solid punch at the German Ruhr, and the outflanking of the Siegfried Line, into effect while the Germans were still staggering. Eisenhower, under pressure from Bradley and Patton, felt the Allies could still operate on a broader front; not only could Montgomery strike at the Ruhr, but Patton, too, could undertake limited offensives toward the Saar (particularly while Montgomery was held up at Antwerp flushing the Germans out of strong positions on the Scheldt estuary that blocked access to the port). Eisenhower was a leader who assessed all opinions, and tried to arrive at the best common denominator; he never took a strongly defined stand on the long-range strategy, never committed himself to one or the other of the opposing views, and so was buffeted between Bradley and Montgomery for the rest of the war.

Eisenhower decided to give Patton's 3rd Army half the supplies available, with a go-ahead to cross the Moselle River and force the Siegfried Line; Montgomery was to secure the approaches to Antwerp, then launch his attack across the Rhine River at the Ruhr. The U.S. 1st Army, now commanded by Gen. Courtney H. Hodges, was asked to cover Patton's northern flank while he pushed to the south, and to furnish flank support to Gen. Miles Dempsey's 2nd British Army to the north, preparing to strike across the Rhine. This was stretching his resources over an ever-widening front, a condition that would make for trouble later in December.

Meanwhile, Montgomery was given some assurance that his supplies would be built up for the impending British drive into Holland. This drive, labeled Operation Market Garden, was to begin September 17th with an airborne drop north of the jumping-off point of the British 2nd Army. This was to be the largest airborne operation ever undertaken; three divisions, 1st British Airborne, the 101st and 82nd American Airborne, were to form a corridor stretching fifty miles north to Arnhem. Holland would be split in half, and Montgomery would move his armored columns up the corridor. Strong resistance was expected from the Germans from *both* sides, for to the west they were still holding on to their V-2 rocket sites; if Montgomery could consolidate the corridor, the sites could no longer be supplied from Germany.

But the Arnhem operation met with only limited success. The attack was stalled cold by September 25th. Bad weather at the airfields in Britain prevented reinforcements from being dropped to the British 1st Airborne, holding the northern end of the corridor at Arnhem. In any case, the 1st Airborne hadn't been dropped close enough to the Arnhem bridges, which the Germans then used to reinforce their besieged elements down the corridor. Also, the British 43rd Division didn't move as fast up the corridor as planned. Wilmot says this failure was largely due to the conservative tactics of the British commanders. He maintains that if the British hadn't been so cautious about casualties, and if the Americans had committed larger supplies, concentrating on a smaller front, Montgomery could have succeeded at Arnhem; this would have put him in a position to persuade Eisenhower to give him what he needed to punch through to the Ruhr.

Instead, the British succeeded only in driving a narrow wedge into Holland; the approaches to Antwerp could now be taken without any counter-pressure from the Germans to the east. But the British had lost 6,000 casualties. Instead of being in a secure jump-off point for the push to the Ruhr, the British to the east of the corridor faced tough fighting, while the Canadians to the west had hard work to free the port of Antwerp.

The following selection is taken from Capt. Andrew Wilson's *Flame Thrower,* an account of war seen from one of the British Crocodile tanks, which were designed for flaming stubborn pillboxes and heavily entrenched positions in the kind of fighting that now engaged the British infantry.

FLAME THROWER

by Capt. Andrew Wilson

The three Crocodiles which Wilson inherited were called "Supreme," "Sublime" and "Superb."

"Supreme" was the troop leader's. The driver was a quiet, fatherly man, who went into battle as phlegmatically as if he were driving a bus. When he came out, he spent hours trying to straighten damaged headlamps and track guards. The co-driver was a cheeky Welshman called Randall, who, when he wasn't arguing with Wilson, was constantly at war with the gunner and the wireless-operator.

The squadron was sent to Winssen to the west of Nijmegen. At first the farm at Winssen looked forbidding. It stood on the edge of a cheerless marsh, and the rain and wind

This selection is condensed from the author's book *Flame Thrower.*

which blew across the polder beat hard on the flaking paint of the doors.

The front was all around. To the east was Germany; to the west a big enemy pocket which reached to the sea; to the north a desolate stretch of heavily-shelled ground called "the island."

Nijmegen was in the front line. In the streets were big smoke canisters, which were set alight whenever the enemy started shelling. The great steel bridge was guarded by Royal Engineers, who watched for mines which the Germans were floating down the river. Fire engines waited in the streets to put out fires which the shells started, and all the time the remaining civilians were going about their business.

One morning the squadron left on the road to 'sHertogenbosch. It was a fine day with a touch of autumn in the air. For a while they ran through the quiet countryside. Then they heard the sound of guns and turned off the road where a knocked-out Sherman stood facing an abandoned anti-tank gun.

The ground was held very thinly here. The squadron stopped by some cottages and a woman told them that the enemy came round in the night, foraging for bicycles.

The crews not on guard spent the night in a hayloft, and next morning the squadron joined up with a squadron of Cromwells from an armoured brigade, which had been probing the enemy's defences. They made a common harbour in two adjacent fields. Away to the east, across the flat countryside, you could see the broken spire of Rosmalen church, with an even round shell hole in what once was the belfry. The enemy had a look-out there.

Wilson met the Lancers' Sergeant-Major. "What's the form?"

The sergeant-major winked. "Watch haystacks," he said. "They've got a habit of changing position."

They were to attack Rosmalen next morning. In the afternoon Barber came back from an infantry battalion order group and told the troop leaders to go up and do a reconnaissance.

They found a lonely company dug in behind a hedge.

"O.K.," said the Company Commander. "Keep your heads down and follow me."

They crawled along a ditch, which struck out into no man's land. The mortars were crumping gently a little way down the line, and somewhere a Spandau zipped. Now and then, as they worked their way forward, a bird would fly up.

"There you are," said the Company Commander. "The village is in the trees. The red roof by the church is what we call the Rectory. There's some sort of anti-tank gun to the left, and a bit of a stream in the dead ground just before it. O.K.?"

"O.K.," said Wilson.

They crawled back faster than they came. The mortars were ranging on them, hitting the ditch and throwing up clods of earth.

Wilson fell asleep, wondering what kind of gun it was by the Rectory. He was sure that death, when it came, would be from an anti-tank gun. He saw in his mind's eye the muzzle of the gun as it moved behind the leaves of some bush or in a shadowy space between buildings. He had learned the aspect of every gun by heart. It had a certain advantage: it made him almost indifferent to shelling.

Someone pressed his shoulder and said, "Reveille." He looked at the luminous dial of his watch: it was four-fifteen. He put on his belt and beret and picked up his map-case.

The darkness was absolute. A breeze swept the harbour, cold and edged with rain. Around the vehicles the first shadowy figures were moving, opening up and stowing away the blankets. An hour to zero. At any moment now the five-fives would open up. He waited in the shelter of his tank.

At the fixed moment the sky to the rear was lit with a sheet of flame, and the earth shook gently beneath him. He stood listening. From high in the darkness came the long, fluttering thrum of the shells. He strained to look eastwards, away beyond the village where the enemy's support line ran.

Two, three, four seconds passed. He was aware of other figures round him, which had stopped whatever they were doing and were looking eastwards too. But all that came back was a deep, protracted rumbling of the ground.

"All right," he said. "Get mounted."

In the turret the operator was answering the netting call. Dunkley came up on the air, and then Sherrif, reporting their troops ready to move. A moment later a dozen long shapes came looming through the darkness and went clanking out of the harbour. It was the Lancers.

The squadron followed. They moved slowly. Sometimes there was the exhaust-glow of the tank in front to follow, and sometimes only a cloud of dust. Down below the gunner was asleep, his head lolling against Wilson's legs. He was a funny little country lad, and the others were always teasing him because he was so scruffy and tongue-tied. Wilson wondered if he dreamed down there, and if so, what. It was always the gunner who got out last when a tank brewed up.

Suddenly the Lancers stopped. It was the forming-up point.

Wilson and the co-driver dismounted and opened up the valves on the trailer. Outside the tank, away from the hum of the headphones, there was a world of noise and death. The enemy was shelling along the start-line, and every now and then something solid and heavy slammed through the air. You couldn't mistake an anti-tank gun. This one was firing blind, perhaps at the sound of the engines.

They re-mounted, and Wilson looked at his watch. He thought of the dials in the trailer, which would still be going up, showing the rising pressure of the nitrogen on the fuel tanks; he wondered about the gun again; and suddenly he remembered that they hadn't had breakfast.

Zero came.

"Driver advance."

Everything was blotted out except the few yards of grass and bushes in front of the tank, the place where he had to pass through the infantry. As the tank moved forward, he saw helmets where men crouched low in a trench, waiting for the order to get up and walk upright. Then there was just the pressure of his brow on the periscope pad, and ahead an open flatness, ending in a line of flickering explosions.

He tried to see which of the explosions was the gun; but it might have been any one of them. The shots went slamming through the air. It was still more than three-quarters dark.

"Hello, Oboe three . . ."

A Lancer troop moved up on his left, their Besas spitting tracer. They were going to shoot him in. He felt an intense comradeship with the long Cromwells. They and he were out ahead—the little black arrows on the war maps.

"Co-ax, five hundred, fire!"

His own gunner opened up, and the fumes blew back into the turret, sharp and choking, towards the ventilator fan.

"Just keep spraying, gunner."

They moved with infinite slowness. It seemed to be getting lighter, but really it was just the distance closing. The low black line of the trees emerged; the spire of the church, dim against the dawn.

"Get ready, flame-gunner—fire!"

The flame shot out, fell, broke, rolled along the ground.

"Left, sir. Left!"

Suddenly, from the side of the periscope, Wilson saw something flash against the armour of a Cromwell. The driver jerked the Crocodile towards a small, dark opening in the trees, and for one long moment the flame-gunner pumped in the fire.

They worked down the trees which masked the front of the village, pouring the fire into the darkness. Now and again there was the sound like men screaming, which Wilson had once heard in Normandy. When they reached the end of the trees, Wilson halted the troop and they stood off the target while the infantry went in.

Two minutes later Barber came on the air. "Our friends are held up," he said. "Go in and help them."

He led the Crocodiles into another opening in the trees, and everything went dark again. The front of his tank began to nose up a tall bank; it lifted slowly, reached the top and stood poised for a moment. All at once the bank gave way.

"She's slipping," shouted the driver. "I can't hold her."

One of the tracks started to race. The tank began to turn over, sliding a little, rolling on its side. Wilson thought: We shall be helpless, like an upside-down turtle. Next moment the tank slid off the bank and crashed into a dark space below.

His head must have struck the gun mechanism. When he came to, the tank was on its side. The seventy-five and the Besa were useless. The wireless was dead. All he could see was the red indicator lamp of the flame gun, which still glowed on the turret wall.

"Are you all right in front?"

The flame gunner answered, sounding dazed.

"Can you see anything?"

"Yes, a house."

"All right, flame it."

The flame shot out. Its sudden glow lit up the periscopes. He leant against the seventy-five ejector shields and tried to manipulate them, straining to see the enemy who must be coming in with their Bazookas. But the periscopes would move only a few degrees.

He directed the flame to the only other target he could find—a group of cottages, a little to the right, about a hundred yards away. The fire crashed in and ran through the buildings from end to end. It's always the same, he thought. Flame anything in sight and you're terrifying. Stop, and you're a sitting target for the Bazookas. But, fired continuously, the flame lasted only a few minutes.

All at once, the gun gave the snort which meant that the fuel tanks were empty.

"Take your guns and get out," he said.

They climbed out with their Sten guns, and made a small group round the Crocodile. He saw now that, coming over the bank, it had run onto the roof of a small house. The house had collapsed and the tank had fallen down among the rubble. The battle was going on all around.

"Wait here," he said. "I'll try to find the others."

He took a Sten and went through some bushes to the left, where there was firing. A few moments later he found himself in a sunken garden: it must have been the garden of the place they called the Rectory. There was an ornamental summerhouse in the middle, and a gate in the wall on the far side.

It seemed quite empty. Then he saw the German officer. He was standing ten yards away, with a pistol in his hand; and he saw Wilson at the same moment.

Wilson pressed the trigger of his Sten. He thought: It's the first time I've killed a man this way. But nothing happened. He tugged at the cocking handle. The Sten was jammed.

Slowly the German raised his pistol and fired. The bullets smacked dully into the bushes at Wilson's back. It seemed so stupid. He was struggling to get out his own pistol, which was caught in the lining of his pocket.

Then the German turned and ran. As he went through the gate, a Bren gun fired on the far side of the wall: he tilted sideways and fell in a little heap.

Wilson found the Bren and a corporal in charge of it.

"Have you seen the Crocodiles?"

"Frig, no," said the corporal. "But the place is lousy with Jerries." He was going in to clear the Rectory. His men were all-out. They'd been doubling in through the Spandau fire, and now he was urging them on again.

At last he got them to their feet. They ran across a lawn and the corporal threw a grenade through the door. As they went in, he shot left and right through every door with the big German Schmeiser he was carrying.

Wilson watched them, and then went off through the trees again, hoping to pick up track-marks or perhaps find Barber. At the foot of a big oak a German lay clutching his stomach. He was half moaning, half shrieking. As Wilson passed, the noise subsided to a sob, and he saw that the man was dying.

Beyond was a kind of garden shed, ripped open by a shell and full of smashed bicycles. There must have been twenty or thirty—tall Dutch bicycles, with pieces of German equipment tied to them. Then there was a trench with a pile of bodies. When Wilson crossed, he found the open ground.

He was facing the knocked-out Cromwell. The crew had tried to bale out. One, a boy of about nineteen, was lying on the ground with his head on his arm; he was smiling, as if asleep, and his brain had spilled out on his battledress.

Further on, Barber's Support tank was trying to pull a Crocodile out of the stream. Wilson ran over.

"What's happened?" said Barber.

Wilson told him. "Whose tank is this?" he asked.

"One of Sherrif's."

"Let me have it."

Just then the Support tank pulled the Crocodile free. The corporal tank commander handed over the headset, and Wilson took the Crocodile into the village.

He found the rest of the troop and told them to follow him. At the end of the village six or seven Cromwells were firing across the fields. He led the troop into position among some broken buildings.

The ground ahead was utterly flat, except for a single hedge, and away in the distance a row of haystacks. For a moment it was difficult to see what the Cromwells were firing at. Then, unexpectedly, the early morning sun broke through a cloud bank, lighting up the ground in clear detail.

Wilson ran his glasses over the pattern of greens and browns, which a moment before had been monochrome. Almost at once his eye caught something moving—a line of grey figures which doubled and paused and doubled again, moving across the front, left to right, towards the 'sHertogenbosch road.

"Co-ax, traverse right. Steady . . . on. Six hundred. Got them, gunner?"

The gunner spun his elevating wheel.

"On, sir."

"Fire!"

The Besa broke into a roar, hosing out tracer in a flat arc. The burst fell short but quickly moved up, cutting into the figures as they ran. Through his glasses Wilson saw some stumble and fall. The rest went to ground.

Then another group was running.

"Co-ax, stop. Up two hundred, left."

The gun began to hose them. Quickly the sergeant and corporal picked up the target. But the group went on, a man or two dropping at a time. Wilson saw now that they were making for one of the haystacks. Suddenly he remembered what the sergeant-major had said.

"Co-ax, stop. Seventy-five load A.P."

The operator opened the breech, ejected the high-explosive round which lay there, and threw in the long black armour-piercing shot.

"Seventy-five traverse right."

The turret swung right with a gentle whine from the traverse motor.

"Steady . . . on. Haystack eight hundred. Fire!"

There was the usual convulsion as the gun fired; the breech running back on recoil; a haze of flame and heat above the muzzle; the shot with its single red trace, spinning towards the target.

As it struck, there was a violent flash. The haystack burst into flame and poured out smoke—the thick black smoke which comes from fuel oil.

The operator threw in another round.

Suddenly the Lancers were firing A.P. too. Then, without warning, something big and square emerged from a haystack further along the line. It moved sedately from left to right, gradually gathering speed. Wilson brought over his gun, and twice the gunner fired at it. But it was no good. The thing disappeared in a sunken road.

He wirelessed back to the Lancers squadron commander, who was at the other end of the village.

"Hello Item Two, there's a Tiger just gone across our front, moving your way. Over."

"Hello, Item Two. Thanks for the tip. Out."

For the first time Wilson felt sure of himself in battle. More than that, he was elated. He'd led in the infantry, flamed an anti-tank gun, burned down half a dozen buildings which might or might not have held enemy, switched tanks, knocked out what was generally thought to have been a Mark IV in a haystack, and seen a Tiger long enough to fire at it.

"Well," said Barber. "Did you have a good time?"

"Fine," said Wilson.

The squadron was going back to refuel, and he went off to find his own crew. When he reached them, the fitters had arrived with the A.R.V. and were fixing tow-ropes to pull the Crocodile upright. The place was full of smoke from the burned cottages. Every now and then a mortar bomb fell, and they all dived under the A.R.V. for shelter.

Presently the mortaring slackened, and they made breakfast. There was a tin of bacon and some jam and biscuits. They ate happily and almost silently in a place where they could see no dead, knowing that the Crocodile would be out of action for a good many hours yet.

When they had finished, the gunner disappeared in the direction of the Rectory. A few minutes later he came back with a handful of black cigars.

"Have one, sir. They're out of a Jerry funk hole."

But Wilson shook his head. He pulled a crumpled Player's from his pocket and stood for a moment, listening to the sound of firing, which now came from far on the other side of the village.

"I'm going for a walk. If you want me, I'm up where the anti-tank gun was."

Ever since his first action in Normandy he'd been drawn by a fierce curiosity to see what happened where they'd flamed. Yet he'd never done so, because always they'd be switched from one place to another, and there was never a chance to explore the objective.

He walked down the front of the trees, where here and there the brushwood still smouldered among the blackened trunks. The burning away of the undergrowth had completely uncovered some trenches. He looked in the first and for the moment saw only a mass of charred fluff. He wondered what it was, until he remembered that the Germans were always lining their sleeping-places with looted bedding.

Then, as he was turning to go, he saw the arm. At first he thought it was the charred and shrivelled crook of a tree root; but when he looked closer, he made out the hump of the body it was attached to. A little way away was the shrivelled remains of a boot.

He went on to the next trench, and in that there was no concealing fluff. There were bodies which seemed to have been blown back by the force of the flame and lay in naked, blackened heaps. Others were caught in twisted poses, as if the flame had frozen them. Their clothes had burned away.

Only their helmets and boots remained, ridiculous and horrible.

He wanted to vomit. He'd vomited before at some sights. But now he couldn't.

Suddenly he heard someone behind him and he looked round with a start. It was Randall, his flame gunner. He must have come round from the opposite direction.

One didn't make favourites in a crew, but from the moment he'd taken over, Wilson had felt a special affection for Randall. With his constant cheekiness, his eternal arguments with the turret crew, he was utterly free from all false sentiment. He was a soldier because he had to be. He took no pride in killing.

"Come up and see what's by the gun," said Randall.

They went. The gun itself was crushed. One of the Cromwells or one of the other Crocodiles had run over it. A little to the side were the bodies of the crew. One of them had been caught by the flame as he ran away, splashed with the liquid which couldn't be shaken off. His helmet had fallen off and now he lay with black eyeballs, naked and charred and obscene.

There came from it all an enormous disgust, which couldn't be expressed, yet somehow one had to say something.

"We certainly did a proper job of it," said Randall.

About midday they had the Crocodile upright and joined the broken tracks. It was a makeshift job, because they had to break off some steel keepers which held the track pins in place.

On the way back to the refuelling point they met the rest of the squadron coming out.

"Catch us up when you're ready," shouted Barber.

As the column passed, Wilson saw his sergeant—Warner. Barber had put him with Sherrif's troop to replace a corporal who'd been killed in the village. Warner waved as he went by.

A little further on they had to let a scout car pass. As the car came level, it stopped, and the man in the commander's seat dismounted. It was Waddell.

He asked Wilson how the action had gone and where the

squadron was. Wilson told him. The C.O. looked at the Crocodile, scored with bullets and with all its track guards ripped away, and grinned.

"Fine," he said, and then with a curious finality: "Good luck." Next moment the scout car disappeared towards the squadron in a cloud of dust.

The refuelling-field was littered with piles of empty drums. Wilson took the Crocodile round the perimeter until he found his own drums, full and neatly stacked, together with five new nitrogen cylinders.

They started heaving the heavy drums to the top of the trailer and pouring in the four hundred gallons of white, treacly flame-fuel. While they were doing it, the fitter sergeant arrived.

"You're not taking her out again without those keepers fixed?" he said.

"They'll hold a bit longer."

Sergeant Pye shook his head. "I'll go back and get the welding kit."

"Too long," said Wilson. "There's a R.E.M.E. section down the road. Go and borrow theirs."

Pye went off in his half-track.

"What did you do that for?" said Randall. "We could have been here till tomorrow."

Wilson didn't answer. Even if he had wished to answer, he couldn't have explained what the sight of those bodies at Rosmalen meant—that either one threw up everything and made one's protest, or else one did everything more thoroughly and conscientiously than ever before, so that there was no time to think.

On the Border

At SHAEF headquarters the great Montgomery-Patton duel dragged on. During the fall months, Montgomery had pressed Eisenhower to hold back Patton in the south. Eisenhower, seeing that Montgomery couldn't be ready for his strike at the Ruhr until Antwerp could supply him (the port wasn't opened until November 27th), allowed Patton and Bradley to build up for a limited offensive; if Patton could reach the Rhine and threaten the Saar, a breakthrough might occur at a weak spot, or at least the Germans would have to commit reserves to the south rather than hold them in the north against Montgomery.

The 3rd Army struck across the Moselle River on November 8th, in the midst of rainy weather. The Germans gave ground but there was no real breakthrough, partly because the attack was launched on a thirty-mile front. They still had a long way to go before their backs were to the Siegfried Line, in the Saar.

North of the Saar the 1st and 9th U.S. Armies had been trying since September to smash through to Aachen, but they hadn't enough supplies to get very far, since Patton was now getting priority. And the Germans had had time to construct a solid defense line, from the Huertgen Forest all the way north of Geilenkirchen, where the 2nd British and the 9th U.S. Armies joined fronts. (According to Wilmot this was the most strongly defended area in the western front.) In the Huertgen Forest the 1st U.S. Army met some of their toughest fighting; with constantly bad weather, the American troops measured their gains in inches.

The following selection is taken from *Yank*, the famous Army weekly newspaper written by and for the American serviceman.

IN THE HUERTGEN FOREST

by Sgt. Mack Morriss

The firs are thick and there are 50 square miles of them standing dismal and dripping at the approaches to the Cologne plain. The bodies of the firs begin close to the ground so that each fir interlocks its body with another. At the height of a man standing there is a solid mass of dark, impenetrable green. But at the height of a man crawling there is room, and it is like a green cave, low-roofed and forbidding. And through this cave moved the Infantry, to emerge cold and exhausted when the forest of Huertgen came to a sudden end before Grosshau.

The Infantry, free from the claustrophobia of the forest, went on, but behind them they left their dead, and the forest will stink with deadness long after the last body is removed. The forest will bear the scars of our advance long after our scars have healed, and the Infantry has scars that will never heal.

For Huertgen was agony, and there was no glory in it except the glory of courageous men—the MP whose testicles were hit by shrapnel and who said, "Okay, doc, I can take it"; the man who walked forward, firing Tommy guns with both hands until an arm was blown off and then kept on firing the other Tommy gun until he disappeared in a mortar burst.

Foxholes were as miserable but they were covered, because tree bursts are deadly and every barrage was a deluge of fragmentation from the tops of the neat little firs. Carrying parties were burdened with supplies on the narrow trails. Rain was a constant but in Huertgen it was cold, and on the line there was constant attack and a stubborn enemy.

For 21 days the division beat its slow way forward, and there were two mornings out of those 21 when the order was to re-form and consolidate. Every other morning saw a jump-off advance, and the moment it stopped the Infantry dug in and buttoned up because the artillery and mortars searched for men without cover and maimed them.

There was counterattack, too, but in time the Infantry welcomed it because then and only then the German came out of his hole and was a visible target, and the maddened Infantry killed with grim satisfaction. But the Infantry advanced with its battle packs, and it dug in and buttoned up, and then the artillery raked the line so that there were many times when the Infantry's bed rolls could not be brought up to them.

Rolls were brought to a certain point, but the Infantry could not go back for them because to leave the shelter was insane. So the Infantry slept as it fought—if it slept at all—without blankets, and the nights were long and wet and cold.

But the artillery was going two ways. The division support fire thundered into the forest, and it was greater than the enemy fire coming in. A tired battalion commander spoke of our artillery. "It's the biggest consolation we have," he said. "No matter how much we're getting, we know the kraut is getting more." So the Infantry was not alone.

Tanks did the best they could when they could. In the beginning they shot up defended bunkers and dueled with machineguns in the narrow firebreaks, and they waddled into the open spaces so that the Infantry could walk in their tracks and feel the comfort of safety from mines. At the clearing before Grosshau they lunged forward, and some of them still dragged the foliage of the forest on their hulls when they were knocked out.

One crew abandoned their tank, leaving behind all their equipment in the urgency of the escape. But they took with them the mascot rooster they had picked up at St. Lô.

The advance through Huertgen was "like wading through the ocean," said S-3 at the regiment. "You walk in it all right, but water is all around you."

There were thickets in the forest where two battalion CPs had been in operation for three days, and physical contact between them had been routine. Thirteen Germans and two antitank guns were discovered between them. The CPs were 800 yards apart. "Four thousand yards from the German lines," said S-3, who had been one of the battalion commanders, "and we had to shoot krauts in our own front yard. Our IPW team got its own prisoners to interrogate. The engineers bridged the creek, and before they could finish their work they had 12 Germans sitting on a hill 200 yards away, directing artillery fire on them by radio." These things were part of Huertgen, a green monument to the Wehrmacht's defense and the First Army's power.

At that, the monument is a bitter thing, a shattered thing. The Germans had four lines of defense in the forest, and one by one those lines were beaten down and the advance continued. This was for the 4th Division alone. There were other divisions and other lines. And these MLRs were prepared magnificently.

Huertgen had its roads and firebreaks. The firebreaks were only wide enough to allow two jeeps to pass, and they were mined and interdicted by machinegun fire. In one break there was a teller mine every eight paces for three miles. In another there were more than 500 mines in the narrow break. One stretch of road held 300 teller mines, each one with a pull device in addition to the regular detonator. There were 400 antitank mines in a three-mile area.

Huertgen had its roads, and they were blocked. The German did well by his abatis, his roadblocks made from trees. Sometimes he felled 200 trees across the road, cutting them down so they interlocked as they fell. Then he mined and booby-trapped them. Finally he registered his artillery on them, and his mortars, and at the sound of men clearing them he opened fire.

The first two German MLRs were screened by barbed wire in concertina strands. The MLRs themselves were log-and-earth bunkers six feet underground and they were constructed carefully, and inside them were neat bunks built of forest wood, and the walls of the bunkers were paneled with wood. These sheltered the defenders. Outside the bunkers were the fighting positions.

The Infantry went through Huertgen's mud and its splintered forest growth and its mines and its high explosives, mile after mile, slowly and at great cost. But it went through, with an average of perhaps 600 yards gained each day.

The men threw ropes around the logs of the roadblocks and yanked the ropes to explode the mines and booby traps in the roadblock, and then they shoved the trees aside to clear the way. The engineers on their hands and knees probed the earth with No. 8 wire to find and uncover non-metallic shoe mines and box mines which the Germans had planted by the thousands. A wire or bayonet was shoved into the ground at an angle in the hope that it would touch the mines on their sides rather than on the tops, but they detonated at two or three pounds' pressure. Scattered on that ground there were little round mines no larger than an ointment box, but still large enough to blow off a man's foot.

At times, when there was a clearing, the engineers used another method to open a path. They looped primacord onto a rifle grenade and then fired the grenade. As it lobbed forward it carried with it a length of primacord, which was then touched off and exploded along the ground with enough force to set off or uncover any shoe mines or S mines hidden underground along its path. In other cases, when the area was known to be mined, it was subjected to an artillery concentration that blew up the mines by the force of the concussion. There could be no certainty that every mine was blown. The advance was costly; but the enemy suffered.

One regiment of the 4th Division claimed the destruction of five German regiments in meeting 19 days of constant attack. The German had been told the value of Huertgen and had been ordered to fight to the last as perhaps never before. He did, and it was hell on him. How the German met our assault was recorded in the brief diary of a medic who was later taken prisoner, and because it is always good for the Infantry to know what its enemy is thinking, the diary was published by the 4th Division. The medic refers to the Infantry as "Ami," colloquial for American. These are some excerpts:

It's Sunday. My God, today is Sunday. With dawn the edge of our forest received a barrage. The earth trembles. The concussion takes our breath. Two wounded are brought to my hole, one with both hands shot off. I am considering whether to cut off the rest of the arm. I'll leave it on. How brave these two are. I hope to God that all this is not in vain. To our left machineguns begin to clatter—and there comes Ami.

In broad waves you can see him across the field. Tanks all around him are firing wildly. Now the American artillery ceases and the tank guns are firing like mad. I can't stick my head out of the hole—finally here are three German assault guns. With a few shots we can see several tanks burning once again. Long smoke columns are rising toward heaven. The Infantry takes cover, and the attack slows down—it's stopped. It's unbelievable that with this handful of men we hold out against such attacks.

And now we go forward to counterattack. The captain is leading it himself. We can't go far though. Our people are dropping like tired flies. We have got to go back and leave the whole number of our dead and wounded. Slowly the artillery begins its monotonous song again—drumming, drumming, drumming without letup. If we only had the munitions and heavy weapons that the American has he would have gone to the devil a long time ago, but, as it is, there is only a silent holding out to the last man.

Our people are overtired. When Ami really attacks again he has got to break through. I can't believe this land can be held any longer. Many of our boys just run away and we can't find them and we have to hold out with a small group, but we are going to fight.

Then two days later came the final entry:

Last night was pretty bad. We hardly got any sleep, and in the morning the artillery is worse than ever. I can hardly stand it, and the planes are here again. Once more the quiet before the storm. Then suddenly tanks and then hordes of Amis are breaking out of the forest. Murderous fire meets him, but he doesn't even take cover any more. We shoot until the barrels sizzle, and finally he is stopped again.

We are glad to think that the worst is past when suddenly he breaks through on our left. Hand grenades are bursting, but we cannot hold them any longer. There are only five of us. We have got to go back. Already we can see brown figures through the trees. As they get to within 70 paces I turn around and walk away very calmly with my hands in my pockets. They are not even shooting at me, perhaps on account of the red cross on my back.

On the road to Grosshau we take up a new position. We can hear tanks come closer, but Ami won't follow through his gains anyway. He's too cowardly for that.

Perhaps this German who called the Infantry cowardly and then surrendered to it will never hear the story of one 4th Division soldier in Huertgen. He stepped on a mine and it blew off his foot. It was one of those wounds in which the arteries and veins are forced upward so they are in a manner sealed, and bleeding is not so profuse as it otherwise would be.

The man lay there, but he wasn't able to bandage his own wounds. The medics tried to reach him but were fired upon. One was hit, and the trees around the man were white with scars of the machinegun bullets that kept the medics away. Finally—after 70 hours—they managed to reach him.

He was still conscious, and for the medics it was a blessing that he was conscious; and for the man himself it was a blessing. For during the darkness the Germans had moved up to the wounded man. They took his field jacket from him, and his cigarettes. They booby-trapped him by setting a charge under his back so that whoever lifted him would die. So the wounded man, knowing this, lay quietly on the charge and told the men who came to help him what the Germans had done. They cut the wires of the booby trap and carried him away.

The green monument of Huertgen is a bitter thing.

Before the Bulge

During October, 1944, there were no large scale assaults by the Allies, and Hitler was able to strengthen his front. He believed that he still might inflict enough damage upon the British and Americans to bring about a stalemate and force them to negotiate peace. Immediately after Arnhem, Hitler and Jodl drew up a plan for an offensive through the Ardennes, designed to break through all the way to the Channel coast. Hitler's generals argued for a much smaller offensive, but he would not listen. The complete plans for the Ardennes attack were given to Von Rundstedt, labeled "Not to Be Altered." And as so often in the past, Hitler had accomplished the impossible—he had scraped up more reserves than his commanders or the Allies believed possible at the time; and his faith in the ability of his troops to hold their positions through the fall was sustained. If the Ardennes attack fell short of the coast, at least valuable supplies would be captured, particularly the oil dumps stocked at Liege. The German General Staff knew that such a grandiose offensive could do little more than expend and exhaust the build-up Hitler had achieved. But the Fuehrer had been right often enough, and still had enough personal magnetism to bend the generals to his will.

In the Allied Lines, no hint of what was to come disturbed the troops, who engaged in routine patrols. As the following wartime *Life Magazine* report shows, "routine" was hardly the word for it.

The italicized opening section and the footnotes are from Capt. Laurence Critchell's *Four Stars of Hell.*

THE INCREDIBLE PATROL

by Cpl. Russ Engel

The officer in charge of regimental intelligence was a youthful-looking, well-proportioned first lieutenant named Hugo Sims. Sims was married and came from Orangeburg, South Carolina, where he had been studying law before the war. He had a soft, slow, deliberate voice and a rather superior air, an air that sometimes annoyed other officers of the same grade. Nobody denied that Sims was competent, but everyone doubted whether he was as good as he thought he was.

Sims was worried. Since the lines had quieted down, his battalion patrols were doing poorly. A sense of injustice was evidently strong among the soldiers selected for the task: they felt they were risking their lives to no good purpose while their comrades slept safely in foxholes behind the line. So strong was this sense of injustice that some patrols went only as far as the German shore, rested for an hour or two in some place hidden from sight of our lines and then returned with a negative report.

Sims was in the dark concerning the nature of the German forces opposing the regiment on the other side of the river [Rhine]. For all he knew, the enemy was building up strength for an attack in force. If it came unexpectedly, the blame was his.

Turning these thoughts over in his mind one night, he conceived the idea of leading a classroom patrol into the enemy territory across the river: not an ordinary patrol—he expected ordinary patrols from the battalions. This should be a patrol that would shame the rest of the regiment. Studying one of the maps of the area, he thought of going inland five or six miles to the main Utrecht-Arnhem highway. There he could set up an observation post, stay hidden for twenty-four hours, report the traffic, take a few prisoners and return with them the following night.

He put the request in writing to Colonel Ewell. It came back with five letters scrawled across it: "O.K.—J.J.E."

Like a great many Southerners of old families, Sims had great self-assurance and a strong sense of what he thought the world ought to be. Given permission for the first time in his military career to devise an ambitious project entirely without supervision, he made preparations for what would be the perfect patrol.

From a group of aerial photographs he selected a house on the Arnhem-Utrecht highway, about six miles within the enemy lines. Plotting the coordinates of this house on the map, he could predetermine the azimuth line of march from the river.

The next step was to arrange for the British heavy guns to fire a single shell at regular intervals of time at a fixed and known point in the area. The explosions of these shells would give him a further check on the accuracy of his line of march. Finally, to deceive the enemy, he arranged for his own mortars to fire a flare half-hourly into the enemy lines. Flares were the usual indication that no patrols were out from lines firing them.

From S-4 he drew a 300 radio. From the regimental intelligence team and the prisoner of war interrogation group he got five volunteers: Private First Class Frederick J. Becker, Private Roland J. Wilbur, Private First Class Robert O. Nicholai, Corporal William R. Canfield and Master Sergeant Peter Frank. Frank spoke fluent German.

As such things usually happen, the rumor of this impossible patrol reached the soldiers of the regiment almost at once. Those who knew Sims, and especially those officers whose patrols had failed, grinned happily to themselves and settled down to watch the fun.—L. C.

The night of the patrol was very dark.

"All of us were a little nervous in the last few hours," testified Private First Class Frederick J. Becker of Atlantic, Ohio.[1] "We all had blacked-out our faces and we began to

[1] This interview, written by Corporal Russ Engel of the 101st

look as if we were really going on this deal instead of planning it. I was stuck with one of the musette bags with half the radio in it. One of the other boys was to carry the other half, and I was a little griped because I was stuck with the heaviest part. But the other boys had their jobs, too. They had demolition blocks for blowing the railroad we planned to cross on the return trip.

"Instead of the steel helmets we had been wearing for the last month or two, we wore our soft overseas hats. Each of us had our pockets full of extra ammunition plus grenades and honed knives. We were really going prepared. In addition to our regular weapons we all carried .45 pistols. Wilbur was the only one of us taking an M-1 rifle, the rest of us chose the Tommy gun for more firepower. We tried to talk him out of the M-1, but we knew it would be nice to have him along with it. Wilbur has the reputation of being pretty accurate with that gun and is famous for never shooting at a man unless he can aim dead center for the head. He doesn't miss.

"After a dress rehearsal in front of headquarters, where Lieutenant Sims checked over our equipment, we decided we were set. Now it was only a matter of waiting for darkness. We sat around for a while and then went in for some hot chow. The cooks seemed to know what was up, and the boys in the mess line gave us a few pats on the back. Lots of our buddies came up and wished us well and said they were sorry they couldn't go along. They really were, too. We all tried to act as if it meant nothing at all. After we washed our mess kits one of the cooks came up and gave each of us three K-ration chocolate bars and said when we came back he'd have a swell hot meal waiting. It was getting dark now and we all sat around the S-2 office getting fidgety."

Here Pvt. Roland J. Wilbur, the M-1 rifle expert, took

Airborne Division public relations office, and copyrighted by Time Inc., 1945, appeared in *Life* for January 15, 1945, entitled "The Incredible Patrol." It is reprinted here by courtesy of the publishers. The interview, as given to Corporal Engel, included all members of the patrol except Lieutenant Sims.—L.C.

over. He comes from Lansing, Michigan, where he used to work for Nash-Kelvinator. Now he almost looked like a soldier in one of their magazine ads, sitting there with a grim look on his face, cleaning the M-1 as he spoke.

"The S-2 office wasn't too far from the dike on the Neder Rijn. We took off about 7:39. We rechecked all our stuff and piled into two jeeps. In a few minutes we were up near the area where we planned to cross. We stopped and got out of the jeeps and began to wonder if the clothes we had on were enough to keep us warm. It was overcast and cold and it had begun to rain. We were wet before we had really gotten started. A couple of hundred yards away we ran into the group who had the boats ready to take us across.

"We were awfully careful about reaching the dike because a lot depended on those first few minutes. We knew that a couple of other patrols had been knocked off before they had gotten to the water. Our main hope was that the Jerries weren't on the alert because we were going over a little earlier than the other patrols. We started to go down towards the bank when a whisper from Lieutenant Sims halted us in our tracks. He thought he had heard a sound from the other side. After a couple of minutes of shaky waiting we decided to take a chance. Edging down to the bank, we came to the two rubber assault boats. Lieutenant Sims and two of the boys carefully slid into one and the rest of us crouched low at the bank and waited with our guns ready in case Jerry should open fire as they crossed. It seemed to take them hours to get across and we could hear every dip of the paddles in the water. We were certain they would be heard and the whole deal would be off, but they weren't. They made the opposite side and crouched low to wait for us.

"Finally we landed. Arrangements were made with the men with the boats so we could signal them by flashlight when we came back. They wondered if we had any idea when it would be and we told them that we hoped it wouldn't be until the next night. We hunched down and told the boatmen to be quiet going back. We could just barely see them as they hit the opposite shore."

Pfc. Robert O. Nicholai, a former member of the Merchant Marine who comes from Midlothian, Illinois, now broke into the story. He was given the Bronze Star for his part in the Normandy campaign and is the cocky member of the group.

"All of us started up the bank to the top of the dike, Lieutenant Sims in the lead. Nothing ahead looked like a Kraut, but there was something that we hadn't expected. A little way ahead there was a big pond directly across the route we had planned to take. We decided that it would be better to go around and change our route a little.

"We skirted the edge of the water but found we still had to do some wading in the dark. By the time we passed the pond our feet were slogging wet. Lieutenant Sims seemed to have on a pair of boots about ten sizes too large and they squished with every step he took. Someone said, 'Dammit, pick up your feet.'[2]

"Suddenly the first of our mortar flares lit up the sky and we were all flat on the ground. We cautiously looked around the countryside but there wasn't a Jerry in sight. It was now 8 p.m. and the flares were working just as we had planned. As soon as the flare died out we got up again. About 200 yards ahead we saw a light and a few shadows moving. We held a confab and decided that because we didn't want to take prisoners too early we would alter our course again. We bypassed the light and circled around to the right. Then we heard the unmistakable sound of Germans digging in for the night. It was the sound of folding shovels digging into the earth and the clunking noise they made as they were tapped on the ground to loosen the mud. We now turned left again and as we did someone stumbled into the brush in the darkness. Immediately we stood still as statues

[2] This entire account minimizes Lieutenant Sims. In point of fact, the patrol would never have taken place without his initiative. It would never have succeeded without his inventiveness, and most of the decisions mentioned in the narrative were his own. From the introductory remarks in the *Life* story, here omitted, it seems evident that none of the patrol members understood what part Sims had played.—L. C.

and waited. Then we heard the zip of a German flare going up. We hit the ground and froze as more of the flares lit up the countryside. To either side of us we could hear Germans moving around. Now and then one of them shouted to ask what the flares were for. They had heard something and had whole batches of flares ready to shoot off. Each time a flare burned out we crept forward between the two enemy groups. In a half hour, when our own flare next went up, we had covered less than 300 yards.

"Then we crossed a road and found ourselves within twenty yards of a lighted tent. I was all for going in and taking whoever was there a prisoner. I thought it might be a Jerry officer and a good bag but once again we decided that it was best to skirt the area. We went one way and then the other through the fields. Every time we heard activity we edged in the other direction."

Corporal William R. Canfield of Selman, Oklahoma, now interrupted the story. "I was a little to one side of the group and suddenly I heard someone blowing his nose. I moved over to the left and saw a group of Jerries stopped for a minute on the road. I asked Lieutenant Sims if I might capture them and take them along but he said not now. I was sure feeling cocky.

"A little later I heard Becker make a noise and as I glanced at him he began to pull himself out of a slit trench he had slipped into. I walked over to him and saw a big, fat Jerry snoring away in the hole. For a moment we thought he might waken and looked down ready to pounce on him if he made a noise. When he remained asleep we went on and joined the rest up ahead. Now we were in a wooded area and we had to be careful of every step. At a clearing in the woods we came to a small road and not ten yards away we saw a couple of Jerries walking down the road with something on their shoulders. Nicholai sneaked along the road and looked more closely. He came back and reported that they were carrying a mattress. A little farther down the road we saw them walk into a house with their mattress. We waited but they didn't come out so we figured they must have turned in for the night.

"Farther on we crossed the road and stumbled right into

an ammunition dump. Sergeant[3] Frank, the interpreter, went over to check the writing on the boxes. He found they were shells for a heavy 150-mm. infantry gun which Lieutenant Sims marked down in a little book he was carrying. He also marked the position of the ammo dump and the location of the mattress house. Just as we were starting to make a more thorough inspection around the ammo dump we heard the unmistakable sound of a German Schmeisser gun bolt being snapped back. In a second there came another. We stood rooted to the spot, afraid to breathe. The things seemed to come from just across the road. There wasn't much else for us to do but go sneaking back through the area of the sleeping men."

Sergeant Frank now pointed out that he hadn't been too scared when the bolt snapped back. He had a story all ready for the situation. Every time they came to a new emergency he would review in his mind a story that might work the patrol out of it. This time he was ready to raise hell with the Jerries for making so much noise with their machine-gun bolts. Frank continued:

"Now we cut straight across the fields for about two miles. Nicholai was getting hungry and he simply reached down and grabbed a handful of carrots from a vegetable patch and began to eat them. Soon we had enough of the fields and decided that we were deep enough in the enemy territory to brazen it out on the road. When we came to a good paved road we walked right down the middle of it. Just ahead we heard the clank and rumble of a Jerry horse-drawn vehicle. We crawled into the ditch along the road and waited for it to pass. In a couple of minutes we were on the road again.

"Farther on we checked our compass course and started off to the right. We hadn't gone more than twenty yards when I saw Becker throw his hands in the air.[4] Right in front of us was a huge German gun emplacement. The gun and pits for the ammunition were there but there didn't

[3] Later lieutenant.—L. C.

[4] This was the infantryman's hand signal for contact with the enemy.—L. C.

seem to be any Jerries. About a hundred yards farther on we came to a strange collection of silhouettes. We couldn't be sure what they were and kept on going until we made them out. It was a Jerry motor pool with all types of vehicles parked for the night. We were all for taking one of the cars but Lieutenant Sims again turned thumbs down. He pulled out his map and noted the exact location. Soon we were on the edge of the town of Wolfheeze and decided that it would be best to work around it. As it later turned out, this was a good thing. The place was lousy with SS troops.

"We skirted the town pretty closely and could even smell the smoke from stinking German cigarettes. We now crossed the railroad which we knew marked the two-thirds point on our trip. We were some distance behind the enemy lines and had the feeling we would be able to bluff our way out of almost any situation that might arise. The last three miles of rushing through the fields was pretty hard. The tall grass slowed us down but it also sheltered us from observation. Nicholai was in the lead, eating carrots again. When he heard the rush of a car going by he whispered to Sims that this must be the road we had crossed so much country to reach. Within a few hundred yards we came out on the road."[5]

Nicholai broke in again: "We all waited a few minutes at the side of the road while Lieutenant Sims brought out a map and checked our location. We were right behind a house that marked the exact spot where we had planned to hit the road. This was only luck[6] but it made us feel as if everything was going according to plan. Lieutenant Sims, looking over the house and the area, decided we might as well occupy the house for cover. We sneaked up carefully, listening for the slightest sound. Becker and Canfield now went through a window and a minute or so later came back to whisper that all was clear inside. But after a conference we decided that this was not so good after all. If Jerry were to see any activity around a house which he knew to

[5] The Arnhem-Utrecht highway.—L. C.

[6] A mild understatement.—L. C.

be empty he would become suspicious. Becker and Canfield climbed back out and we headed down on the road again. In front Sergeant Frank was carrying on a monolog with Becker in German. This was funny because Becker didn't understand a word of it. We all fell into the spirit of it, feeling we could fool any Germans who came along. Soon one of the boys was singing *Lili Marlene* and we all joined in.

"After about a mile of walking along the road without meeting a single German we came to a couple of houses. One of them had a Red Cross marking on the front. It was a small cross and the place hardly looked as if it were a hospital. At any rate it looked like the better of the two houses. As Sergeant Frank and myself edged close we could hear what sounded like snoring inside. We walked to the back door and found it open. In the front room of the house we found two Germans sleeping on piles of straw. They wore big shiny boots and I was sure they were officers. Sergeant Frank said they were cavalrymen. Leaving Frank on guard I went back outside and reported to Lieutenant Sims. He said we would take the men prisoner and stay at this house. I told Frank the plan and he began to shake the Germans. One of them finally began to rub his eyes. He stared at us and Frank kept telling him over and over that he was a prisoner. They just couldn't believe it."

After the dazed Germans had been thoroughly awakened they were questioned by Sergeant Frank. He got all the information he could from them and relayed it to Lieutenant Sims. Sims was now up in the attic setting up the radio with another man. In about ten minutes the men heard him saying into the radio, "This is Sims, Sims, Sims. We have two prisoners. We have two prisoners." They knew the radio was working and everyone felt swell. Soon Sims was sending information about the things he had noted along the way.

After questioning the prisoners Sergeant Frank told them to go back to sleep but they just sat up and stared. Frank asked them if they expected any more soldiers in the area. They said that another man was supposed to pick them up at about 5:30 in the morning.

After the radio had been set up everything was quiet until daybreak. The men took turns watching the road while the others tried to get a little sleep. At about 7 a.m., Nicholai reported the arrival of a young civilian at the front door. The civilian proved to be a boy of about sixteen in knee pants. He was both surprised and pleased to be taken captive by the "Tommies." The men took some time to explain to him that they were not Tommies but airborne GIs. When this had been taken care of, Sergeant Frank was allowed to go ahead with his questioning. The boy explained that the house belonged to some friends of his and he had just come over for some preserves. He knew the people had been evacuated and said they might not be back for some time.

The boy went on to say that his older brother, who was a member of the local underground, would also be along shortly. Almost immediately the brother was brought in by Nicholai. He was a slick-haired, effeminate young man and the patrol had doubts about him. He spoke a little English and produced papers to prove that he was a member of the Dutch underground. He began to tell the men about the various enemy installations in the area. He gave them artillery positions and unit numbers and all this was immediately relayed back over the radio.

In the following hour six more civilians were guests of the patrol. They all seemed to know that there was no one home and all wanted something from the house. They were told they would have to stay until after the patrol had left. The civilians were happy to see the men, but they didn't like the idea of having to stay. One of the captives, a very pretty Duch girl accompanied by what appeared to be her boy-friend, wouldn't take no for an answer. The men said she was not averse to using all of her charms to get out, either, but they were firm.

At noon the traffic on the road began to increase. Convoys of big trucks appeared to be heading from the Utrecht area toward Arnhem. The men observed all kinds of vehicles and guns. Presently an unsuspecting Jerry entered the courtyard for a drink of water. Opening the front door a little, one of the men pointed his Tommy gun at the German and commanded him to come in. The German came in laughing, apparently not quite convinced that the whole thing wasn't a joke. He turned out to be a mail orderly who had lost his way after taking mail to a near-by town. He seemed to be an intellectual type and was very philosophical about being captured.

Shortly afterwards the idea of food occurred to everyone in the house. The men in the patrol got out their K-ration chocolate and the civilians began to dig into the little bags they all carried. It began to look as if the civilians had been going on a picnic. They brought out bread and cheese and shared it with the Americans. An hour or so later the German who was supposed to meet the first two prisoners at 5:30 finally showed up with two horses and a cart. The men let him enter the courtyard and water the horses. Then they called out to him, "Put up your hands, you are a prisoner." He didn't seem to understand and it was necessary to repeat the order. Then he answered calmly, "I must feed my horses." Finally he raised one hand and came toward the house, muttering that it just couldn't be true. Now the civilians helped in the questioning, because the Germans were not too sure about the names of towns where their units were stationed.

Once the men watching from the windows were tempted to whistle at a passing car. It was driven by a pretty German WAC. The men said that the only thing that restrained them was the fact that their lives depended on it. Because everything had gone so smoothly the men were feeling pretty cocky. They wanted to capture a truck, a couple of staff cars with German WACs and drive back to Renkum.

Two more Germans entered the courtyard and were immediately taken prisoner. They were very sore, mainly because they had come along the road just to goldbrick away a little time. By this time a big fire had been built up in the front room where the prisoners were kept. The prisoners kept the fire going and the men argued to see who would stand guard in the warm room.

As darkness approached the men began to assemble their equipment. Becker was left on guard in the house with the prisoners and civilians while Lieutenant Sims and the others went out to look for a truck. The German mail orderly, who seemed the happiest to be captured, was chosen to help them. He agreed that as soon as Sergeant Frank told him, he would help stop the truck by shouting, *"Halt Kamerad!"* As they waited the German said to Frank, "I am happy because the war is over for us." Frank replied that it would all depend on the next few hours and that he would be able to say with more certainty the next day.

Becker reported that when the lieutenant and the others left the house the remaining prisoners looked a little scared. Finally one man came and asked Becker in pantomime if they would be shot. Becker told them that such things aren't done in the American Army. All of the Germans in the house wore the Iron Cross and had seen service against the Russians.

While the men were waiting along the road a whole German company passed on bicycles. As each German rode by he would shout, *"Guten Abend"* to the men along the road and they shouted back the same. One man stopped and asked Sergeant Frank if this were the right road to the next town. Rather than become engaged in conversation, Frank told him he didn't know.

Getting impatient after an hour and a half, the men decided they would stop the next truck that came along, no matter what kind it was. In the meantime a motorcyclist stopped by the road and went into the courtyard of the house. Nicholai rushed across the road and grabbed him. It developed that he was checking up on the absence of the other men. When Nicholai brought him across the road he saw the mail orderly and rushed up to shake his hand. They were old friends and had served together for years.

A few minutes later the men heard a truck coming down the road and told the two Germans to step out and shout, *"Halt Kamerad!"* When the truck came, all the men shouted at once and the truck stopped. It turned out to be a big five-tonner carrying 15 SS men. Nicholai jumped on the back and herded the Germans off, taking their weapons as they got down. They were all very surprised. At first the driver refused to leave his seat, but after a number of strong threats, namely shooting, he finally got off. He was a tall man and very cocky. When asked to put up his hands he said, "Who says so?" When he was told that he was a prisoner of war he looked astonished and said that it was impossible. As he spoke he put one hand up and with the other drew a pistol, but only to hide it in his pocket. Sergeant Frank took it away.

The driver was told to get back in the truck and pull it off the road. He seemed reluctant and Frank had to hold a gun against his ear while he started the motor. He seemed unable to keep the motor from stalling every few seconds and when he moved into the courtyard he had trouble turning. It was obvious that he was stalling for time. He kept looking at Frank and saying in German, "This can't happen to me." He told Frank he was on his way to meet the captain of his battalion. When he was told he was to drive the truck and the men to the Neder Rijn he said there wasn't enough gas. He was told that if that were true then he would be shot, so he said there was enough gas for twenty miles.

Now Becker and the prisoners in the house came out and piled into the truck with the SS men. The Americans spaced themselves around inside the truck so they could keep guard. Lieutenant Sims and Sergeant Frank sat in front with the driver. When they were on the road the truck stalled again. As the driver tried to start the motor an amphibious jeep pulled up and a tall SS officer began to bawl him out for blocking the road. Canfield was off the truck in an instant and had brought the officer inside. As it turned out, this was the captain the truck driver had been going to meet.

Again the sergeant concentrated on getting the driver to start the truck. He worked hard at stalling the motor and had to be threatened before he would drive at all. Finally he got the truck under way and they set out on the return route they had mapped out before the patrol. Every now and then the driver would get temperamental, folding his arms and saying, *"Hab' ich eine Wut!"* ("Am I mad!"). After a prod or two with the gun muzzle he would go back to safer driving. Farther along the road toward Arnhem he was told to turn off to the right. Shortly the truck came to a muddy place in the woods and bogged down hub-deep.

No amount of trying by the SS driver was able to move it. It was now 10 p.m. and the patrol decided they might as well try to make it back on foot.

Now the men regretted having so many prisoners. As they piled down from the truck the SS captain bolted to the side of the road in the darkness. In a flash he was in the woods. Nicholai shouted for him to stop and ran after. In a moment the others heard two shots and Nicholai's only two words of German, "*Hände hoch*, you son of a bitch!" followed by a great crashing in the underbrush. Becker also ran into the woods to see if he might help. Following the noise he found Nicholai and the captain. Nicholai was still shouting, "*Hände hoch*" and with every shout he would kick the captain in the seat of the pants. When they came back to the truck the captain was cowed and willing to go quietly.

Lining the Germans up in two columns, Sergeant Frank now gave them a little lecture. He said they could just as easily be shot as taken back and that all six Americans were risking their lives to get them back safely. He told them that if anyone tried to escape or made an unnecessary noise he would be shot immediately. Starting out again with the SS captain and Sergeant Frank in front, the column made its way along the road toward the river. As they walked the SS captain told Frank that it was useless to try to cross the Rijn with the prisoners. He said the Americans might as well turn over their guns because they would surely be caught by the Germans.

The captain also asked if he might have a cigarette. He was told he couldn't have one now, but that later he would have more and better cigarettes than there were in all of Germany. The captain said the Germans had nothing against the Americans and he couldn't see personally why the Germans and Americans didn't get together to fight the Russians and Japanese. We are both white races, he said. Sergeant Frank answered that the Russians were also white. Yes, replied the captain, but they are inferior. Finally the captain asked if it were not possible for them to rest a while, or at least to slow down. He was told that he had the misfortune to be a captive of American paratroopers, who just didn't walk any slower. Now as they walked along they constantly heard German voices.

Arriving at the railroad crossing the patrol decided finally that they didn't dare blow up the tracks with the two and a half minute fuse they carried. Reluctantly they crossed the tracks and ditched their demolition charges in bushes by the road. Along this last stretch of the road they passed countless houses with Germans inside.

When they came to the town of Renkum the patrol marched boldly down the center of the main street with a great clicking of German hobnailed shoes. It was obvious from the sound alone that they could be nothing but a group of marching Germans. They went through the town without incident and headed straight for the near-by dike. Everyone was feeling wonderfully light-headed. Arriving at the dike, they had marched right down to the water when they saw a squad of Germans at a river outpost. As they came close Sergeant Frank called out to them in German that there was nothing to worry about. When they stopped two of the men rushed over and told the Jerries to put up their hands. The column moved on, cleaning out two more posts along the river. The six-man patrol now had a total of 32 prisoners.

On the dike Lieutenant Sims gave the prearranged flashlight signal to the other side. Soon the answer came—three blinks. The SS captain,[7] his truck driver and one of the patrol were the first to get to the other side. Part of the patrol stayed behind to cover the crossing while the rest of the prisoners were ferried over. Finally the last three men touched the Allied side of the Rijn. The incredible patrol was over. Shortly afterwards the soldiers were awarded Silver Stars. Lieutenant Sims, who received the Distinguished Service Cross, had dinner with General Taylor and was promoted to captain. The story of the patrol went the rounds of the European Theater, and the battalion intelligence officers of the 501st Parachute Infantry tightened their belts and sighed.

[7] Who remarked: "I congratulate you. I didn't believe it was possible."—L. C.

In the Ardennes

The Germans were still building up for the attack in the Ardennes; the Allies were still weak on precisely that front. En route to a meeting with Montgomery in the first week of December, 1944, Eisenhower had passed through the Ardennes area, and made note of the thin support behind the main American lines. There were four divisions stretched along a front of twenty-five miles. As Gen. Bradley states in *A Soldier's Story,* Eisenhower discussed this with him but Bradley was torn by commitments to Patton in the Saar, and those to the 9th U.S. Army, soon to assault north of Aachen at the Roer River. There had been intelligence reports, in mid-December, indicating a shift of some German divisions from the north into the Ardennes area (Hitler had assembled twenty-eight divisions in the Ardennes with new supplies, tanks and assault guns; the Allied High Command had no inkling of anything this size). However, Bradley took a calculated risk that the Americans would be able to mount an attack of their own before the Germans had an opportunity to discover and exploit his weakness in the Ardennes. He was not to get away with it.

On December 16th, the Germans began an artillery barrage of over 2,000 guns; the infantry moved up close behind it, five Panzer divisions following on their heels. The Germans, without proper air reconnaissance or aerial bombardment support from the Luftwaffe, needed bad weather to launch the attack. The morning of the 16th was foggy and misty, and the American High Command, also deprived of air reconnaissance because of the weather, didn't immediately realize this was a major attack, even though division after division was being thrown at the American lines, penetrating in five different sectors. Bradley admits that he thought it a spoiling attack at first. His staff had simply not believed the Germans could assemble strong enough forces for such an assault. And part of the lack of immediate response at Bradley's headquarters can be charged to poor communications. The Germans had dressed some of their troops in captured American uniforms, to infiltrate the Allied lines to the rear and stir up confusion, with special attention to communications. The air forces were to be grounded right up to December 25th because of the weather, and the Germans could supply and reinforce their attacking divisions without interference. Gen. T. H. Middleton's VIII Corps, facing the Ardennes at the time of the breakthrough, had three infantry divisions—the 106th, sent to the front lines only four days before the German attack, the 4th and 28th Divisions, which had been badly hurt in the Huertgen Forest, and the 9th Armored Division. The Americans, even though cut off and surrounded, fought back courageously and tenaciously in islands of resistance. But by December 18th the Germans had achieved a major breakthrough, their troops and Panzer columns fanning out toward the Meuse River. But the Americans still maintained two salients in the area under attack. From the north, the St. Vith salient was a solid arm thrusting out at the Germans, manned by the 7th Armored Division under Gen. Hasbrouck. To the south was Bastogne, sitting astride several important roads, over which the German armor would have to move if they were to drive on to the west. Gen. Middleton issued orders to hold Bastogne, calling on the nearest reserves, including the 101st Airborne Division.

Many men of the 101st Airborne were on leave in Paris, and with both division commanders home in the U.S., the artillery commander, Brig. Gen. Anthony J. McAuliffe took over. The night of the 17th, via a huge truck convoy, the division set out for Bastogne.

Capt. Laurence Critchell, author of *Four Stars of Hell,* and the following account of the fight at Bastogne, says, "The truck convoy ride to the Ardennes was unforgettable. The division had usually gone into battle by air drop, but now jampacked in approximately 380 trucks it rolled along through a countryside pockmarked with excavations of World War I. The convoy traveled with lights on, a deliberate risk to gain time and speed. Up and down the shaven hills of northern France went the convoy, and wherever the road made a sharp turn, the vehicles could be seen for miles ahead and miles behind." The commanders, McAuliffe and his Cols. Ewell and Kinnard, had arrived in Bastogne ahead of most of the units and had been making reconnaissance to prepare for the expected Panzer divisions. When the division got to Bastogne, they met straggling groups of soldiers in retreat.

BASTOGNE

by Capt. Laurence Critchell

It was foggy and damp at six o'clock in the morning. The 1st Battalion had been selected to lead off on the push out the Longvilly road. The coatless men moved through the streets of Bastogne, sloshing in mud and dirty water. Between their double lines, on the road itself, heavy armor still was moving eastward, away from the oncoming enemy. It was a ludicrous sight to see a few of the airborne troops wave at the retreating armor—fire power much stronger than any of them could have. One paratrooper, still without a weapon, picked up a stick and, for the benefit of the demoralized columns, shook it in the direction of the enemy. Here and there unhelmeted men were wearing wool caps or were bareheaded. Few wore overcoats. But they pushed forward out of the town with a sense of confidence, and in a little while they were in the silent, foggy countryside.

Following the 1st Battalion as it moved out of Bastogne was B Battery of the 81st Anti-Aircraft with eight 57-mm. guns. Behind that unit in turn—considerably behind it, as a matter of fact—were the 2nd and 3rd Battalions of the 501st. The latter was getting itself badly tangled in the snarl of traffic within the town, and since Ewell was not yet certain of how and where he would employ those battalions, he contented himself with the advance of the 1st Battalion and its supporting unit along the Longvilly road. On one occasion the men turned off by mistake towards Marvie, due east. But Ewell was able to set them right, and by 0730 in the morning, with the light just breaking, the situation looked fair enough.

In that region the Bastogne-Longvilly highway ran along

a valley dominated on each side by gently sloping hills. Those hills were partially covered with sparse vegetation, but the overgrowth offered little concealment. On this morning, however, the fog was dense. It was so thick that the left flank guards of the 1st Battalion by-passed two platoons of enemy infantrymen dug in on a hill in the vicinity of Bizory; though slight sounds carried distinctly on the damp air, neither the Germans nor the Americans became aware of each other's presence. Unsuspecting, the 1st Battalion marched straight towards the main body of the enemy.

The Germans, of course, were equally unsuspecting. Until that moment they had forced back the stubborn 28th Division, and the less stubborn, badly fragmented 9th Armored Division, without meeting heavily organized resistance. This had given the ordinary German soldiers new confidence; their morale was higher on the morning of December 19th than it had been since the invasion of the Normandy coast. In documents and letters later taken from German prisoners or from German dead, the enemy soldiers were writing home, "At last the war has become fun again." [1] They described the slaughter of armored and infantry divisions along the way as "a glorious blood bath" and prophesied to their families in the clean little towns of Germany that the European struggle would soon be at an end. Once again, evidently, it was *Deutschland über Alles*.

The first encounter with the deployed 1st Battalion of the 501st Parachute Infantry in the early hours of December 19th must have been a shock to them.

Contact was made at what seemed to be an enemy road block near the village of Neffe. The division reconnaissance platoon, which had somehow gone astray at the beginning of the advance, was on the point of overtaking the lead scouts of the battalion when, from the fog directly ahead, there was the unmistakable fast rattle of a German machine gun.

Almost to a man, the battalion went flat. With the first

[1] From a document taken by a 501st prisoner of war interrogation team.

sounds of fire the two German platoons which had been by-passed in the fog discovered their enemy in front and behind them. The confusion was so great that the German guns were quickly disposed of. However, the machine gun that had opened up at the crossroads and given the first alarm of the Bastogne siege, evidently outposted a lead element of considerable weight.

The valley road at that point did not pass through the center of the valley, but ran close to the rising ground on the left flank. Thus it was only on the right, where the valley sloped away to a small stream, that it was possible to deploy the men adequately. In keeping with McAuliffe's words, Ewell drily told the commander of the 1st Battalion, Lieutenant Colonel (then Major) Bottomly to "develop the situation." He himself found a stone house in a pocket of the hillside and established a temporary command post. Within a short time Bottomly reported to Ewell by radio that he was opposed by approximately two platoons of infantry and two Mark IV tanks. Ewell, to whom the report was put in the form of a question, told him to go ahead and fight his own fight.

The Mark IV tanks were firing, from a defiladed position near Neffe, straight down the highway. Consequently, the 57-mm. guns of the anti-aircraft company could not be brought to bear on them. And by ten o'clock in the morning, with no advance having been made on either side, the situation became a deadlock. Little more could be done just then; in Bastogne the 2nd and 3rd battalions still were struggling to get through the choked traffic of the VIII Corps, fleeing to the rear.

Off on the left flank of Ewell's position was a group of large farm houses in a broad valley. The valley ran down towards Neffe, but before it reached that village (held, Ewell judged, by the enemy) the ground rose up again to conceal the two villages from sight of each other. It occurred to Ewell that if the 2nd Battalion were to seize the town of Bizory, which lay in that direction, his men would be well situated to move onto the high ground adjacent.

Lieutenant Colonel Homan was in command of the 2nd Battalion. Implementing Colonel Ewell's orders as soon as he got free of Bastogne, he seized Bizory with no opposition and only a little fire from the direction of the deadlock at Neffe. During this time the 3rd Battalion, still in Bastogne, was trying to get out of town by an auxiliary side route. Ewell ordered the commander, Lieutenant Colonel Griswold, to strike for Mont, farther to the right of the forward positions then held by Bottomly and Homan. Ewell eventually intended to use Griswold's battalion in a flanking attack on Neffe, but he kept these intentions to himself. What chiefly concerned him was getting the battalion out of town.

Bastogne at that hour still was crowded with drifting and staring men. So great was the shock they had received that many of them were inarticulate. They trickled through the German lines in two and threes, making no attempt to organize themselves, refusing to be organized by anyone else. When they asked the paratroopers what they were doing, and the paratroopers replied, "Fighting Germans," they only stared. To them, at least temporarily, the war seemed lost.

Not all were like that, however. Some of the haggard, beaten men accepted a K ration, ate it silently, and then asked for a rifle. They were ready to go back and fight. Some of the armor was in good shape, and the morale of the armored men who elected to remain at Bastogne and fight it out was high. Among them, seven tanks and three tank destroyer crews organized themselves into a combat team and voluntarily attached themselves to the 2nd Battalion, while another platoon of armored infantry stuck it out with the regiment until the siege was lifted.

By noon of the 19th the situation was clearer. The 1st Battalion was halted at Neffe, fighting what Ewell thought was only a difficult road block. The 2nd Battalion had seized Bizory and was deployed on favorable high ground. The 3rd Battalion had reached Mont, but because the ground between there and Neffe was flat, and the enemy fire heavy, the soldiers had been unable to carry out the second phase of the order and sweep down on the road block at Neffe. By these three operations, however, a line had been stretched along commanding ground outside of Bastogne to the northeast. This was the critical and—as events later proved—decisive deployment.

Ewell decided to move his 2nd Battalion to Magaret, which would still further improve their position. He sent Colonel Homan with one company of men to secure the approaches to that town by seizing a small patch of woods on a long ridge above it. Homan did so, but was presently engaged along his entire front.

Company I had been separated from the 3rd Battalion and was making a reconnaissance of wooded areas to the front. It was ordered into the town of Wardin to investigate the reported existence there of an armored road block. The ill-fated company encountered the enemy in the town, but at 1500 radioed that its men were doing all right. When a company of volunteer tank destroyers arrived at Ewell's command post, however, he sent them to the 3rd Battalion to help out in case the group at Wardin needed support.

It was then 1600. Ewell had formed three battalions approximately abreast and in contact with the enemy all along his front. For the first time since the German break-through, the enemy was meeting a line of troops which refused to give ground.

At dark Ewell ordered the battalions to break contact and form to defend a general line along the high ground to the west of Bizory-Neffe and roughly parallel to this line to the southward. Taking his plan back to the red stone buildings where division headquarters had been established, he got McAuliffe's approval. On the way he assured himself, for the first time since daybreak, that Bastogne had not been seized.

Walking along the main street of the town, he met a sergeant of Company I.

"Have you heard about Company I?" asked the sergeant. "It's been wiped out."

Ewell, hurrying back to his radio, didn't believe it.

The town of Wardin lay on the extreme right flank of the Bizory-Neffe-Wardin line, which Ewell had formed on the commanding terrain northeast of Bastogne. Wardin was a small place of a dozen-odd houses, set at a little distance from one of the main roads entering Bastogne. Captain Wallace had taken his men of Company I into the village as part of the general reconnaissance ordered by Homan in compliance with Ewell's instructions. What ensued there was tragic.

When Wallace and his men entered the town, they encountered only a few Germans. Without much difficulty, they drove those men from the dreary Belgian houses and took possession. Wardin had strategic value and, though it was closer to the enemy than Bizory and Neffe, Wallace believed he could hold his place.

He and his men had been in the town only a short while, however, when a force of German armor appeared unexpectedly on the outskirts. As the tanks—they were Tiger Royals—spread out to prevent Wallace's force from escaping, the tank gunners opened fire point-blank. Under cover of this fire, a whole battalion of German infantrymen, who had all the ardor of their late successes, closed in to the streets. Wallace hastily withdrew part of his force to fight at the flanks of his command post and to keep one avenue of retreat open. The remainder of the Americans held out in the concealment of the houses.

The din was soon terrific—the fast rocketing "*whishtbang!*" of heavy-caliber shells at close range, the clattering of fallen rock, the explosions of bazooka shells, the rattle of small arms and the queer vibrating "*brrrrrrrp!*" of German automatic pistols. Bazooka gunners deliberately squatted in the open where they were plainly visible to the Germans and fired point-blank on the tanks. Soldiers in the houses held their positions until shells burst through the rooms and demolished the lower floors. Other soldiers snatched up the bazookas of men who had died.

House by house, fighting in a blaze of fire, the Americans retreated. The smoke of explosions from the tank guns clouded vision from one side of the street to the other. The Germans were systematically demolishing every house. Everywhere was the ammoniac stink of cordite; in the rubble of the demolished buildings hands, heads, legs protruded. Those paratroopers who still were alive fought their way towards Wallace and the command post. One youngster, running out into the center of the street, deliberately knelt in a furious rattle of small-arms fire and discharged a bazooka shell squarely into the lead tank. The tank was halted and, though the boy was dead an instant later, the rest of the oncoming armor was momentarily canalized.

Wallace, giving the infantryman's equivalent of "abandon ship," ordered the remainder of the men to split up—to get back to Bastogne singly or in pairs—any way they could.

On the street before the command post the men threw up a hasty tank obstacle. As the armor and the swarms of German infantrymen approached this final point, Wallace directed all the fire power at his disposal to cover the withdrawal of the men who were left. One by one, as the small-arms and heavy-caliber fire grew heavier, they passed through the barricade, Wallace urging them on. Then the officer ordered the men at the barricade, too, to fall back. A few of them refused. The final survivors of the trap of Wardin saw, as they looked back, the figure of their captain, still at the barricade, still fighting—the last they were ever to see of him.

All that afternoon and night the survivors trickled into Bastogne. At the regimental command post, a great room which had once been a school study hall was set aside for them, where they cleaned their weapons on the children's desks. They were very silent. A few of them sat against the wall, under a statue of the Crucifixion, with their heads in their hands.

Wallace, like many of his men, left a wife and child behind him. Of approximately 200 of his soldiers who had gone into Wardin eighty-three survived.

Undertones of tragedy marked the evening of the first day at Bastogne. As the light dimmed in the sky, the streets of town became deserted. The inhabitants disappeared into their cellars. In the great dark rooms of the regimental command post the only illumination came from the flicker of the squad cookers as the survivors of Company I heated their K rations. Nothing had been heard of a truck column bringing ammunition and other supplies to the town. Father Sampson was missing. And there were rumors that our division hospital, set up to the rear of Bastogne, had been captured.

The 501st Command Post was plainly visible from the enemy lines. With the exception of the church across the street, it was the most prominent building in Bastogne. Downstairs on the main floor were a dining hall, an immense cloister with Doric columns, a skylight, and an adjacent chapel. The chapel was used for a temporary aid station, while the cloister was designated for use by the company and regimental kitchens (if the equipment got through). The dining room, which occupied a wing of its own, was left to the Franciscan nuns, who were taking care of twenty or thirty very young, very curious children. It was interesting to note that, when the German artillery began to fall on Bastogne, those children disappeared underground with the nuns and did not reappear until three weeks later.

Upstairs in the seminary were dozens of connecting rooms, each of them piously decorated. Above the second floor were dormitories for the former pupils, while on the fourth floor was a vast chamber which had been occupied before the Ardennes break-through by VIII Corps military police. The haste with which the M.P.s had abandoned their quarters was evident in the discarded material strewn about the floors: paper-bound books, magazines, pin-ups, galoshes, webbing, blankets, even uniforms. The few of us who explored this room felt a little satisfaction in the debacle of the withdrawal—mute testimony of that upheaval of life which had come to a rear echelon when it had suddenly become a forward area.

By morning of the next day, December 20th, the temperature had dropped below freezing. There was little wind before dawn, and the unmoving blanket of clouds limited visibility in the darkness. The 501st men were in the same positions they had taken up at nightfall and not much had been done to extend the flanks. Though other units had

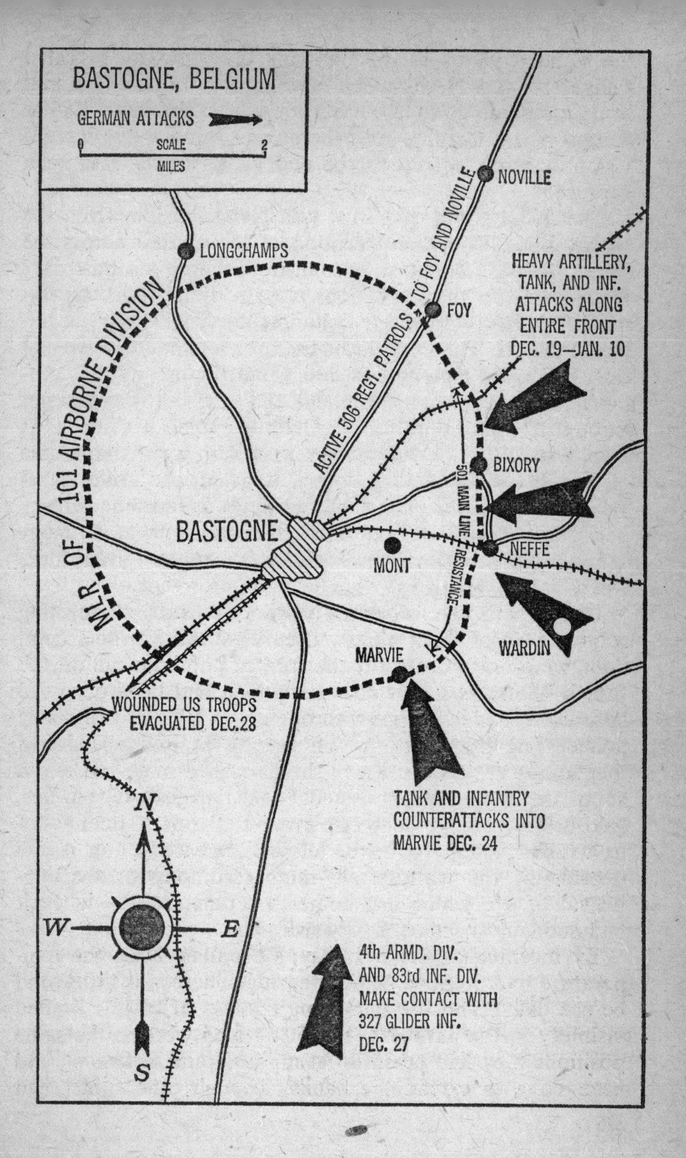
BASTOGNE, BELGIUM
GERMAN ATTACKS
0 SCALE 2
MILES
NOVILLE
LONGCHAMPS
TO FOY AND NOVILLE
FOY
HEAVY ARTILLERY, TANK, AND INF. ATTACKS ALONG ENTIRE FRONT DEC. 19—JAN. 10
101 AIRBORNE DIVISION
ACTIVE 506 REGT. PATROLS
MLR OF
BIXORY
501 MAIN LINE RESISTANCE
BASTOGNE
MONT
NEFFE
WARDIN
MARVIE
WOUNDED US TROOPS EVACUATED DEC.28
TANK AND INFANTRY COUNTERATTACKS INTO MARVIE DEC. 24
N
W
E
S
4th ARMD. DIV. AND 83rd INF. DIV. MAKE CONTACT WITH 327 GLIDER INF. DEC. 27

been brought up to either side, the 501st still was squarely in the line of the German advance.

One of the first moves made by McAuliffe, as an artillery commander, was to dispose his airborne artillery and tank guns in such a manner as to bring coordinated fire from all of the pieces on any one point of the line which he intended to "develop," or which was attacked by the enemy. Subsequently, when Bastogne was encircled, he was able to deliver the same concentration of fire on any point of the 360° defense. On the morning of the 20th, however, his main concern was the sector occupied by Ewell's regiment. And the honors of the day were about evenly divided between Ewell's men and McAuliffe's artillery.

The night had been reasonably quiet. From the Americans captured at Wardin the Germans had identified the division opposing them, and they evidently spent the hours of darkness massing their forces for a major drive. The much criticized G-2 of the Allied armies at the time of the Ardennes break-through was not the only one to be surprised in those days; documents later captured from the German staff revealed the enemy's astonishment of finding the 101st Airborne Division (which their intelligence had reported to be at Mourmelon, France) directly in the path of their advance at a key focal point of communications, a hundred miles from where they were supposed to be.

The first troubles on the 20th began at 0530, before there was light in the wintry sky.

East of Bizory, where Homan's 2nd Battalion men were deployed, was a rise of high ground. Between that high ground and the American front line was a clear field of fire, extending more than 3,000 yards. On that expanse, the only cover for an attacking enemy was the natural defilades where the farmland rose and fell. Homan's position was ideal for defense—so ideal, as a matter of fact, that, when an observation-post spotter who had field glasses reported that six enemy tanks were starting across the fields, accompanied by what he estimated to be a battalion of German infantrymen, the event took place at such a distance that the Americans, though alerted, could only sit by their guns and wait.

A scratch force of American tank destroyers had attached itself to Homan's battalion during the night. At word of the impending attack, the crews disposed their vehicles north of the village of Bizory on either side of a small road that was a key approach to the American lines. Meanwhile, Homan had notified Ewell about the approaching enemy; Ewell had notified Kinnard, and Kinnard, through McAuliffe, the artillery. One by one the guns within Bastogne were brought to bear on a predetermined coordinate—where, when the signal came to fire, their shells would drop in a screen across the oncoming Germans.

The expanse of ground in front of Homan was so great that the Germans advanced for a whole hour before they were close to the coordinate for the artillery barrage. During part of this time the men of the 2nd Battalion could keep them in sight, and, the nearer they approached, the brighter grew the morning. When the American machine gunners suddenly opened fire, the tank destroyers fired simultaneously, and, within an instant or two, in a curtain of artillery bursts, the German lines were struck squarely by hundreds of shells from McAuliffe's guns.

From full silence to the blaze of fire took only a few moments. The Germans still were at such a distance from Homan's men that the automatic weapons' fire had little visible effect. But so intense was the coordinated artillery fire from within Bastogne that the paratroopers, who had a grandstand view of the entire episode, witnessed the Germans begin to falter. Here and there, among the mushrooming clouds of artillery smoke, the tiny black figures stumbled and fell. Behind them one of the heavy tanks turned back towards its own lines—then rolled and halted. Two of the tanks were destroyed, and a third disabled.

The tiny figures of the Germans began to run. More and more of them fell. For twenty minutes the rolling barrage continued to pursue them. When it lifted, the only Germans who remained on the open fields were the scores of still bodies.

The shock of that first repulse must have been a severe one to the German troops. Until that morning they had met other pockets of stubborn resistance—the 7th Armored Division, whose soldiers had made a gallant stand at St. Vith, and the elements of the 28th Division already mentioned. But when the Germans, filled with confidence, attacked Bastogne on the morning of the 20th, they were repulsed not only with heavy casualties, but also by a group of organized soldiers who obviously intended to deny—to twenty-five enemy divisions—a critical road-net in the heart of the salient.

Towards midmorning of the 20th it started to snow. The German forces, under cover of thick woods to the northeast, began to shell Bastogne, devoting particular attention to the huge building by the church steeple.

This was the building which we had selected for a regimental command post. It was the largest command post any regiment could have had. It was five stories high and perhaps a quarter of a mile in circumference. The walls were about three feet thick. This was thick enough to withstand shellfire, but unfortunately, the operations offices had been selected in the very first hours, before anyone knew the direction of the enemy. When the lines were consolidated outside Bastogne, it was found that the Germans could—with good luck in their marksmanship—put artillery through the windows.

The snow came down steadily, gently. Soon it blanketed the bodies of the dead Germans at Neffe and those beyond Homan's positions outside of Bizory. The paratroopers were seeing the last bare earth they were to see for two months. Meanwhile, the shelling of Bastogne continued. The Germans regrouped for a concerted attack in force, and the fateful day was quiet.

The 1st Battalion, which had fired the first shots of the Bastogne siege, had been unable to seize Neffe beyond the turn of the valley road. Company B had successfully taken a house on the side of the critical Neffe road, and, from the windows of that house, the soldiers were able to command all the approaches to the battalion front. Machine guns were set up in there, while the infantrymen of the other companies dug foxholes and, where they could, lined the interiors with straw.

In Homan's area at Bizory, where the first enemy attack in force had been repulsed, there was no change. But at Griswold's 3rd Battalion, which had taken up positions at Mont, the 1st Platoon of Company B of the 705th Tank Destroyer Battalion had attached itself during the night. This was a valuable reinforcement. Griswold posted one of the vehicles at a bend in the Neffe road, where it commanded the stretch leading to that enemy-occupied town, and where it also commanded a draw leading off to the south. Another destroyer was placed to complement the fire of the first, while the second section of the platoon, from concealed positions, guarded the approach directly across the valley.

Everywhere there was silence. The skies were leaden; the snow came down steadily, almost audibly. No planes were in the air anywhere. At division headquarters, McAuliffe, in contact with General Middleton by radio, happened to remark that Bastogne would probably be surrounded.

The soldiers blew on their stiffening fingers and waited.

At seven o'clock a few shells fell in Bizory and Mont. These were followed by a few more and, shortly, by a great number. Finally, a heavy barrage dropped on all the critical points along the defensive line. So intense was the artillery fire from the German positions that within a few minutes every telephone wire connecting the battalions to regimental headquarters was severed.

When the firing slackened off, the German forces struck simultaneously in a two-pronged offensive against the 1st and 3rd battalions.

Bottomly, at the 1st Battalion, radioed Ewell that the enemy troops were charging straight down the highway. They came with the shouts and high morale of men convinced they were going through. Not even in Normandy had the paratroopers encountered such high morale. Bottomly reported to Ewell that it was too dark to see much, but that he could hear tanks coming along with the troops.

It was a bad hour for the regimental staff at Bastogne. On orders from someone, the records were packed, the equipment readied, the men dressed for retreat. If the two flanks collapsed . . .

The snow had ceased. The night was bitter cold.

There were eleven battalions of guns at McAuliffe's disposal within Bastogne. All eleven battalions dropped a "dam of fire" across the Neffe road, approximately 200 yards ahead of the town. It was the most effective American defensive fire during the siege. Three German tanks—two Panthers and a Tiger Royal—were struck almost at once; they had drawn up beyond the last houses in the village when they were hit, and there they stayed.

The short delay before the artillery barrage, however, had enabled a considerable number of German infantrymen to approach so close to the American lines that the greater number of shells fell behind them. Those men charged wildly towards the Americans, firing and shouting. Company B, posted in and around the house, on commanding ground at the side of the road, took the shock without yielding an inch of ground. The automatic weapons in the windows controlled the approaches so effectively that not a single German soldier got within bayonet distance of the American lines. Everywhere in the darkness the enemy troops stiffened and fell and died, and their blood spotted the snow. Weeks afterward they were still there, grotesque and stiff, the foremost bodies 300 yards in advance of the wrecked German armor.

The action in this area continued with intensity for some time. The soldiers were fighting in that bitter fume of smoke and sweat and cold where each man seemed hopelessly alone. There was no consciousness of cold or snow or wet clothes or hunger. When men are fighting each other, and the issue remains in doubt, there are only the simplest and most basic elements of human experience.

Meanwhile, the men of the 3rd Battalion were struggling to hold back a simultaneous enemy attack from a different quarter. It was evident that the Germans had abandoned their attempt to enter Bastogne across the wide field of fire opening down from Homan's positions, where they had failed that morning. The dual attack by dark left Homan's forces alone and evidently had the object of bending the two flanks of the 501st until those flanks collapsed and Homan was trapped in the middle.

The Germans attacking Griswold's forces also had supporting armor. But the enemy tank commander must have observed the tank destroyers behind the American lines, for his armor did not leave the concealment of a little wood just west of a château at Neffe. From that position the tanks could put down a base of fire for their advancing and—as events shortly proved—suicidal infantrymen.

The open and comparatively smooth slope which separated Mont and Neffe afforded a field of fire for Griswold's battalion almost as extensive as that which fronted the 2nd Battalion under Colonel Homan. In addition to this wide field of fire, the slope was crisscrossed with man-made obstacles—a checkerboard of barbed-wire fences erected by the Belgians to make feeder pens for cattle. The fences were in rows about thirty yards apart. Each fence was five or six strands high. Because of the manner of their construction, is was almost impossible to crawl underneath the fences: a man approaching Griswold's forces at Mont had to halt at each obstacle and climb through.

Whether the German commanders knew of the existence of these obstacles and decided to risk the attack anyway, or whether the leading enemy soldiers just stumbled onto them by accident in the darkness, will probably not be known. But the attack, once launched, had to be carried on. The German infantrymen ran forward with the same enthusiasm, the same wild yells and eagerness which had characterized all their offensive actions since the break-through. When they reached the fences, they simply climbed through. But it broke them.

As fast as they reached the obstacles, Griswold's machine gunners swept them down. The Germans were in great strength, and the forces behind, pressing upon the forces ahead, made a massacre inevitable. Bodies of the dead piled up around the wire fences, and the attackers who followed, climbing over those bodies, became bodies themselves a few steps beyond. The volume of tracer fire from Griswold's gunners was spectacularly intense; prisoners questioned later said that its visible effect, as much as the holocaust around the fences, was to them the terrifying element of the night attack.

What Griswold's men were facing was a whole German regiment—the 901st *Panzergrenadiers,* better soldiers than the *Volksgrenadiers* who had attacked Homan to no effect in the early morning. These Germans rushed towards the 3rd Battalion of the 501st with such high spirit that, despite the wire fences and the field of fire, Griswold was forced to regroup part of his battalion to reinforce his left flank. By the time he accomplished this, the action had become intense and the German casualties terrible. The total destruction of one side or the other was so imminent that the American tank-destroyer men, having no targets for their guns, fired the .50-caliber weapons from their vehicles, jumped out, and joined the infantrymen on the line.

By the time the German fire began to slacken off, the insane double attack of divisional strength had lasted four hours. It was close to midnight. Enemy dead were piled up in such numbers around the wire fences that even the German withdrawal was difficult. Around Neffe, where the other attack had taken place, the situation was much the same, and, though the casualties on the American side had been very heavy, the *Panzergrenadiers* had been decimated. Ewell's eye for ground had given the paratroopers an advantage they were never afterwards to lose.

As he remarked later: "I think that, as of that night, the 901st had 'had it.' They no longer had enough men to be an effective offensive force. They had been pretty well chewed up before they got to us, and we completed the job."

At the regimental command post, the staff unpacked to stay.

As everyone knows, the newspapers in the United States did not announce that the 101st Airborne Division had been cut off and surrounded by the enemy until a day or two before the relief of the besieged city. Oddly enough, most of us at Bastogne were almost as slow in getting the news.

Newspaper maps of front lines in a war usually show a salient in clear black, like a pool of spilled ink. The impression is that within that pool the land is thick with soldiers, that every square inch of terrestrial space has its allotted guardian. Nothing of the sort is true, of course. The breakthrough of the German tanks in Holland and their advance on Veghel through the heart of the enemy country were more typical than unique. Where the vehicles crossed the highway, and where they approached Veghel—both being guarded areas—they were engaged. But the remainder of their movements was through virtually deserted countryside, like the land on the road from Addeville to La Barquette.

Something of the sort was just as true at Bastogne. The first evidence of enemy forces to the rear of Bastogne came when a reconnaissance patrol engaged a small force of Germans on the road leading back to the hospital. In a few hours the enemy forces had moved elsewhere; but, as time passed, engagements on the roads to the rear became more frequent. McAuliffe at division headquarters knew that Bastogne would be ringed by the enemy, but at the respective regimental headquarters, and especially on the battalion lines, only rumors of the engagements to the rear reached the men. On the night of the 20th and the morning of the 21st the whole situation was in doubt. Yet the front lines of the German drive had already gone beyond Bastogne.

Von Rundstedt was aiming for Liége, where the largest supply dumps behind the Allied lines were situated. His plan was to seize those dumps and thus equip his army for the drive on Antwerp. Once Antwerp had been reached, the Allied forces would be split in half.

Nothing of this was known, however, on the morning of the 21st in Bastogne. After the Germans had fallen back, all was still and cold. The gentle descent of the snowflakes by the old church on the main street gave Bastogne the picturesque air of an old-fashioned Christmas card. By morning the snow had made the whole town clean and white—dangerously white for patrols; so Captain Phillips, with Lieutenant Frank as interpreter, ransacked the houses of Bastogne for bed sheets to use as camouflage.

That day—for the first and last time of the war—the operations offices of regimental headquarters moved underground.

A narrow corridor about ten feet below the surface of the earth, reached by a flight of stone steps, admitted to a series of cement-walled chambers underneath the convent command post. Each room was about ten by fifteen feet. When desks and chairs were put in, there was not much room to move around. The regimental commander, his executive officer, the adjutant, the intelligence officer, the operations officer, and their enlisted staffs were all crowded together into the connecting rooms. With the exception of the apartment in a private house across the street, occupied by the prisoner of war interrogation team, and with the further exception of a few aid stations, those underground chambers were the only warm rooms in Bastogne during the siege. They were not only warm, they were also safe. And consequently very crowded.

One of the last convoys to go through to Bastogne from outside brought the regimental kitchens. For lack of space in the forward positions the mobile stoves were set up—with nothing to cook—along the sides of the glass-ceiled cloister upstairs and beneath a huge statue.

The wounded who came from the lines were put temporarily in the cold chapel adjacent to the cloister. Major Carrel, the regimental surgeon, was ill, but Captain W. J. Waldmann of Bakersfield, California, a man with a high forehead and a grave manner, took his place. Operations and transfusions were performed by the yellow light of two gas lamps. The wounded men, wrapped in the few blankets on hand, were laid on the freezing floor of the chapel. As new casualties were brought from the lines, aisles were made between the litter cases. Soon the floor was covered with wounded men, who lay where they could see the crazy shadows dancing on the plasma tubes and the gas bottles for the lamps.

Presently, the enlisted men of the staff realized that no

wounded were being evacuated. And that was how the word of the encirclement finally spread.

Four German divisions and elements of three others faced the 101st Airborne Division when Bastogne was finally surrounded. Each of our men was outnumbered four to one. No one felt heroic about this, and no one made any speeches about it, written or otherwise. The troops were never called upon—as democratic statesmen are so fond of doing, especially after lunch—to give no inch of their embattled ground. Nor were they ever told that what they were doing was important, significant, or destined by any combination of circumstances to go down in military history. It was even doubtful that General McAuliffe's mimeographed Christmas message to the troops reached every foxhole.

But as soon as the word spread among the troops, both in town and on the lines, that the roads out of Bastogne had been cut off and the division surrounded, a curious, very subtle change took place in the atmosphere. It was difficult to understand. Perhaps it was this:

A certain good-natured rivalry had existed from the beginning among the various units of the division—the 501st, the 502nd, the 506th, the 327th Glider Infantry, the airborne artillery, and the others. In England, in Normandy, in Holland, in France the good-natured conviction of each unit that its own soldiers were the best had persisted. However, the various units as a whole considered themselves head and shoulders above the other divisions in the E.T.O.

So when Bastogne was surrounded, and the circle of the defense was manned, not by strangers, but by the "old gang"—the "Hell Raisers" of Newbury and Lambourne and Chilton Foliat and Littlecote and Greenham Common and Carentan and Eindhoven and Nijmegan—and we knew that the rear was protected and the flanks secured by what we considered the only kind of soldiers worth fighting with, the atmosphere in Bastogne became much as it would have been if someone had erected a sign on the highest point of town—*HOME STATION—SCREAMING EAGLES.*

No matter where the Germans attacked around the circle,

the men of the other units could say to themselves: "The Five-O-Deuce is getting it right now," or "Poor Sink. He's having a bad night." They could trust the 502nd or the 506th or any of the others. Those were not regiments a self-respecting 501st man would want to join, naturally (on account of Sink or Michaelis or too much "chicken," or any one of a dozen reasons), but they were a damned sight better regiments than any others in the E.T.O.

The stray units and fragments of units which had stayed to fight with us were not accepted just as additional fire power. By their free decision to remain and fight they were raised to the level of the airborne troops; were given, so to speak, honorary membership in the division. There were no strangers in Bastogne during the siege. Only after the siege had been lifted, and sad-faced, weary infantrymen of the relieving units filed by the hundreds through the ruined streets, did our men, and those who had fought with us, realize what had come to us for a little while and gone, and would never come again.

The day of the 21st was quiet for our regiment. The Germans had decided to abandon the attempt to gain Bastogne through the positions chosen by Colonel Ewell around Bizory, Mont, and Neffe, and were spreading around the town.

McAuliffe, worried by the dwindling supply of ammunition, and still in contact with higher headquarters by radio, asked for air resupply as soon as the weather cleared. He was promised it—*if* the weather cleared. But with the leaden skies over the town, as they had been closed over all of Europe almost without break since early November, there seemed little hope.

Captain Waldmann, working in the chapel hospital, knew that his supply of plasma would last only another day or two. Even by then, in spite of everything that he, Captain Axelrod, Captain Jacobs, and the other medical officers could do, some of the wounded had died. Outside in the courtyard, piled in the trailer of a jeep, were dead soldiers from the line, their bare legs, yellow in color, sticking out from under a frozen canvas cover. Everywhere, things were half-completed or not done at all. As the German shelling grew heavier and heavier, and the third night fell, the American artillerymen within the town counted their ammunition. On the lines the inadequately clothed men fought back strong, continual, probing attacks and counted their own ammunition. The situation at Bastogne that night and the morning of the 22nd was at its lowest ebb.

Around 11:30 in the morning of a dirty gray day—the 22nd—four tiny German figures waded up through the snow on the road from Remoifosse to the American lines. The soldiers of the artillery unit who had dug themselves into fortified positions along that sector drew a bead on the target. But they held their fire. The Germans were carrying a large white flag.

Word passed down through the front lines like an electric shock: the Germans wanted to surrender!

The road from Remoifosse happened to lead to Colonel Harper's medical station. There, to the astounded medics, the German group—a major, a captain, and two enlisted men—reported themselves in crude English and demanded to be taken to the commander of troops in Bastogne. Both officers were arrogant, and it annoyed them to be blindfolded. So Colonel Harper left them at his command post.

On the line many soldiers crawled out of their foxholes, stretched upright in full sight of the Germans across the way, and, for the first time since their arrival, took time to shave. Men of the other sectors were more cautious, but Colonel Harper's men knew they were safe as long as the German emissaries were inside Bastogne. So they relaxed and ate their K rations with legs dangling over the edges of foxholes.

Division headquarters had been set up above and below ground in a series of red-brick storehouses, not unlike garages, where the VIII Corps had had its own headquarters. German artillery shells had been falling on the brick houses at least once an hour. But during the presence of the German intermediaries the morning was still.

Colonel Harper and Major Jones took the surrender message to General McAuliffe. The note read as follows:

"The fortune of war is changing. This time the USA forces in and near Bastogne have been encircled by strong German armored units. More German armored units have crossed the river Ourthe near Ourtheville, have taken Marche and reached St. Hubert by passing through Hompres-Libret-Tillet. Libramont is in German hands.

"There is only one possibility to save the encircled USA troops from total annihilation: that is the honorable surrender of the encircled town. In order to think it over, a term of two hours will be granted beginning with the presentation of this note.

"If this proposal should be rejected, one German artillery corps and six heavy AA Battalions are ready to annihilate the USA troops in and near Bastogne. The order for firing will be given immediately after this two hours' term.

"All the serious civilian losses caused by this artillery fire would not correspond with the well-known American humanity."

And now let Colonel Marshall tell what happened:

McAuliffe asked someone what the paper contained and was told that it requested a surrender.

The General laughed and said, "Aw, nuts!" It really seemed funny to him at the time. He figured he was giving the Germans "one hell of a beating" and that all of his men knew it. The demand was all out of line with the existing situation.

But McAuliffe realized that some kind of reply had to be made and he sat down to think it over. Pencil in hand, he sat there pondering a few minutes and then he remarked, "Well, I don't know what to tell them." He asked the staff what they thought, and Colonel Kinnard, his G-3, replied, "That first remark of yours would be hard to beat."

General McAuliffe didn't understand immediately what Kinnard was referring to. Kinnard reminded him, "You said 'Nuts!' " That drew applause all around. All members of the staff agreed with much enthusiasm and because of their approval McAuliffe decided to send that message back to the Germans.

Then he called Colonel Harper in and asked him how he would reply to the message. Harper thought for a minute but before he could compose anything, General McAuliffe gave him the paper on which he had written his one-word reply and asked, "Will you see that it's delivered?"

"I will deliver it myself," answered Harper. "It will be a lot of fun." McAuliffe told him not to go into the German lines.

Colonel Harper returned to the command post of Company F. The two Germans were standing in the wood blindfolded and under guard. Harper said, "I have the American commander's reply."

The German captain asked, "Is it written or verbal?"

"It is written," said Harper. And then he said to the German major, "I will stick it in your hand."

The German captain translated the message. The major then asked: "Is the reply negative or affirmative? If it is the latter I will negotiate further."

All of this time the Germans were acting in an upstage and patronizing manner. Colonel Harper was beginning to lose his temper. He said, "The reply is decidedly not affirmative." Then he added, "If you continue this foolish attack your losses will be tremendous." The major nodded his head.

Harper put the two officers in the jeep and took them back to the main road where the German privates were waiting with the white flag.

He then removed the blindfold and said to them, speaking through the German captain: "If you don't understand what 'nuts' means, in plain English it is the same as 'Go to Hell.' And I will tell you something else—if you continue to attack, we will kill every goddam German that tries to break into this city."

The German major and captain saluted very stiffly. The captain said, "We will kill many Americans. This is war."

"On your way, bud," said Colonel Harper.[2]

The small party of the enemy, carrying their white flag,

[2] From *Bastogne—The First Eight Days,* by Colonel S. L. A. Marshall.

disappeared down the snowy road in the direction of their own lines. The USA troops climbed back into their foxholes.

And the threatened artillery barrage failed to materialize.

Shortage of ammunition, especially for the artillery, was McAuliffe's chief concern. That day the 463rd Field Artillery Battalion had only 200 rounds of ammunition.

McAuliffe passed the word to ration the firing to ten rounds per gun per day. He clarified his order for one artillery commander just before an enemy attack: "If you see 400 Germans in a 100-yard area, and they have their heads up, you can fire artillery on them—but not more than two rounds."

There was food—two boxes of K rations a day per man—but not for long. And the snow was blanketing the lines deeper. Already trench foot had set in.

Not enough maps, not enough ammunition, not enough clothing, not enough plasma, not enough food . . . What *was* there enough of?

Well, there was enough spirit.

And the next morning, after a night of heavy fighting in other sectors, the miracle happened. It was a simple miracle. Yet for a continent where months of winter had already grayed the skies day after day without change and would gray them again solidly for months and months afterwards, leaving only that one small patch of good weather in the dead center of a crisis, it *was* a miracle.

For the skies cleared and the sun came out.

And up from England by the hundreds roared the C-47 supply planes and the fighters—throttles open—destination: Bastogne.

"The fortunes of war are changing. . . ." It was a double-edged phrase.

The sun had not been up an hour before our first American fighter planes appeared. They were cheered by the frozen paratroopers at Mont and Bizory and Neffe and all along the lines—small silver planes which came swiftly from very high up and in a few moments were roaring in circles around the town, a thousand feet above the fox-holes. Men who had gone to sleep in covered positions underground were awakened by the familiar thunderous buffeting of air pressure cause by exploding bombs. Within Bastogne the few windows still unshattered shook and rattled and subsided and then shook again.

Those men who had a good view of the German lines—like Major Pelham, who occupied an observation post in a private farmhouse clearly visible to both sides—could watch the planes dive on some object behind the German positions, then pull up in a fine curve a few hundred feet off the ground, leaving behind, where the bomb struck, a perfectly-formed balloon of orange flame and black smoke which expanded soundlessly, brilliantly, and with spectacular beauty over the dazzling, snow-white hills. Moments later the sound would come.

The noise continued all day. Between the concussions of the exploding bombs we could hear the occasional *"whiff-fisssssss!"* of rockets from the Typhoons—a sound that brought to mind, all in a piece, the golden lines at Eerde and along the Neder Rijn. Close liaison was maintained by radio with the air support around Bastogne, and one infantryman, who reported five German tanks bearing down on his position, had six P-47s darting upon the tanks within a few minutes.

Close to the red-brick buildings which housed division headquarters was a gentle slope of hillside clear of shrubbery or trees. It was concealed from the lines by a higher rise of land beyond. This bare slope, dazzling white with snow in the sun, was selected as the drop zone for the C-47 supply ships. Division S-4, Colonel Kohls, placed Captain Matheson of the 506th and Major Butler of the 501st in charge of the bundle recovery, and notified each regiment to send five jeeps with trailers. Distribution of the parachuted supplies would be made directly from the field.

No hour had been given McAuliffe for the expected arrival of the C-47s. So from the break of dawn on a freezing crystal morning, December 23rd, Butler, Matheson, and the supply officers of the other units, each with a jeep of his own, stamped their feet, blew on their fingers—and waited. The rumor of an air resupply had reached the men on the lines, and, with the Germans virtually immobilized by the daylight bombing, they were having a quiet, cheerful morning. In straw-filled foxholes, dugout command posts, and farmhouses the American soldiers waited.

The first C-47s to reach Bastogne dropped parachutists. They were pathfinders out of England—men who had been called from classes at school several days before, and who had been waiting all this time for clear weather. They landed safely, set up radar sets—refinements of those which had been used in Normandy—and guided the resupply ships to the drop zone.

At 11:50 the planes roared in—241 of them.

What ought to be said is difficult to say. A tribute is an awkward thing. Even the men who felt like waving their arms and yelling did nothing at all except stare up in silence at the roaring planes. Bastogne vibrated with the thunder of American engines. These were the pilots, many of them, who had flown the division to the invasion of Normandy half a year before. They were the men who had been criticized or scorned by the parachutists for taking evasive action under fire—and who had then flown them to Eindhoven and Zon and Eerde and Veghel without mistake.

And now here they were again, the other half of the airborne equation, our young fellow countrymen, the youngest of all soldiers, sweeping in with their olive planes through the clear, blue December sky of Belgium, and low over the snow-covered hills, to resupply—in a town the world was watching—the same old gang.

Crowds of Belgian townspeople emerged from their catacombs under the houses to stare. It was difficult for us not to feel a sentimental pride of country. The equipment parachutes, blossoming over the white field where Butler and the other men waited to receive them, were green and blue and yellow and red—ammunition, plasma, food, gasoline, clothing. . . .

The planes made a circle of the besieged town and then turned away to the north, flying at an altitude of about a thousand feet. Flak had become heavy, but not a single plane took evasive action. The controls of one ship were shot away just as it swept, empty of its parachuted supplies, over the German lines. Its pilot had been gaining altitude. As the bullets struck it, a little wisp of brown smoke gusted out in a faint streak from its tail. Slowly the plane curled upon one wing and nosed down into a vertical dive. The airborne troops who watched, and who had ridden so often in the familiar C-47 cabin, could imagine the scene inside: the two American youngsters struggling with the controls, the cockpit windows showing nothing but up-rushing earth, the instinctive start backwards towards the cabin, and then . . .

A balloon of smoke and fire went up from the earth where the plane fell.

The drop zone was only a mile square. Yet 95 per cent of the 1,446 parachuted bundles were recovered. One hundred and forty-four tons of fresh supplies had come to Bastogne.

So speedily did the supply crews make distribution and load the bundles into jeeps (without stopping to detach the parachutes) that the artillery units were firing the new ammunition before all the bundles on the field had been recovered.

When the second aerial resupply was made, the ammunition shortage was no longer a problem. Gasoline had the lowest priority; since the division was not going anywhere, only 445 gallons were delivered. But food supplies, which had the second highest priority, remained far below the margin for safety, even after the deliveries had been made; the 26,406 K rations that had been dropped were, though impressive in figure, enough to feed the division personnel for only a little more than a day.

McAuliffe authorized foraging.

Troops like to forage, and nobody is better at it than the American soldier. An abandoned corps warehouse yielded 450 pounds of coffee, 600 pounds of sugar, and an equally large amount of Ovaltine. Most of those items were delivered to the aid stations for the use of the wounded. In an abandoned corps bakery, flour, lard, and salt were uncovered, while from a Belgian warehouse came margarine, jam and additional supplies of flour. Also found in the latter storehouse were 2,000 burlap bags. These were sent out to the front lines for the soldiers to use as padding for their feet.

The farms at the outskirts of town yielded potatoes, poultry and cattle, the staples most needed for the men. Because discipline and selflessness were at the highest during the siege, the soldiers who commandeered such items took them back to the kitchens at the regimental command post, instead of roasting or cooking them makeshift on the spot. As a result, the butchered farm animals were skinned and cleaned properly, and the meat was divided evenly among each of the battalion kitchens. It was not uncommon, in those uncommon days, to see the skinned, bloody carcass of a whole cow or a gigantic hog being hosed down by the cooks on the stone floor of the cloister at the regimental C.P., under a blue and gold statue of the Virgin Mary.

Oddly enough, the cooks themselves worked under intermittent shellfire. The glass ceiling of the cloister was also the roof of the building, and shells from the German guns to the northeast sometimes burst among the stone cornices. The KPs were kept busy sweeping away the broken glass. It is a statement of fact that no place in Bastogne could be termed a rear area. After the first German bombing, the town was sometimes more dangerous than the lines.

The fighting that took place on the 23rd and 24th, in different sectors of the all-around defense, was intense. The lines of the 501st Parachute Infantry underwent continual probing attacks by the Germans, especially each nightfall, but after the first two days the Germans had clearly abandoned the costly effort to enter Bastogne over the wide fields of fire which opened from the regimental positions. Division headquarters had no such respite, however, and for every six-hour period in Bastogne there were one or more attempts by the enemy to break through in force. Those who lived within the town seldom guessed how many men were dying in the suburbs to keep the streets empty of all but Americans.

McAuliffe had conceived the expedient of drawing a small reserve from each of the organizations on the line. These reserves were formed into a task force, with armor and tank destroyers, and were used as a mobile support, capable of moving to any sector of the line seriously threatened by an enemy attack. Ewell, copying the plan, created Task Force X, under Captain Frank McKaig and Lieutenant Ernest Fisher, to support his own battalions. For some reason, the Germans never attacked simultaneously on all sectors of the perimeter defense, so the mobile task forces were an effective device.

Approximately 2,000 civilian inhabitants of Bastogne remained in the town during the siege. They lived underground in mass shelters, one beneath a convent in the center of the town, another beneath the regimental command post. A few lived under their own houses. Those who lived in the great cellars of the two convents dwelt in conditions of indescribable filth. Old men, too crippled to move, sat in chairs at the side and stared into the darkness; young children crawled about the cement floors; men and women lay together on rough blankets or piles of burlap. At the regimental command post, this condition became such a threat to the health of the soldiers that at length certain male civilians were assigned the task of policing their own shelters and, under shellfire, of emptying the refuse outside.

An interesting, though rather ugly sidelight of life in Bastogne during the siege was the impossibility of digging slit trenches or making other arrangements for field sanitation. A large privy was dug in the courtyard outside the regimental command post, but because that area was under constant shellfire, few of the men would use it. In the beginning they utilized a large indoor latrine obviously built for school children. However, the plumbing froze after the first day; so in time the place was boarded up. From then on, at all hours of the day and night, soldiers could be found searching for unused toilets through the smaller rooms upstairs in the seminary.

The days and nights were bitter cold. Ewell authorized his men to wear whatever would keep them warm. That no loss of discipline occurred during the resultant individualism was a tribute to the discipline already ingrained in the troops. A few hours after the word had gone around, many soldiers appeared in civilian sweaters, crude blouses of parachute silk, and Belgian winter caps. One officer wore a Canadian combat jacket which he had saved from Holland. An enlisted man appeared at the command post in an army blanket, with holes cut for his arms and a rope binding it about his waist. He was the personification of the Sad Sack, but no one seeing the stubble of beard on his chin, the lines of weariness around his eyes, the tight, humorless slit of his mouth and the dirty hands cracked from exposure, gripping the one clean thing in his possession—his rifle—could have smiled.

The parachutes recovered from the equipment bundles were used to cover the wounded men. The command post personnel donated their blankets to the men on the line. Every civilian sheet and blanket in town had already been collected and put to use. Also every bottle of liquor.

On the afternoon of December 23rd, word came to Bastogne that Patton's armor was fighting its way to the besieged town. If luck held, Patton—with the division commander, General Taylor, in the vanguard—would reach Bastogne by Christmas Day.

Early in the evening of December 23rd, just after the winter darkness had fallen and a brilliant three-quarter moon lighted the snow-bound little town with a blue glare, Chaplain Engels, Lieutenant Peter Frank, Sergeant Schwartz and Sergeant Harvey were having a premature Christmas dinner in the second-floor apartment of the prisoner-of-war team, across the street from the regimental command post.

The chaplain had just come in from the lines, where the night was almost as quiet as it was in town. In the blacked-out, rickety apartment there were light and warmth. Lieutenant Frank, a Viennese by birth and an American by choice, had a flair for entertainment. He had set the supper table with linen, silver, wine glasses, plates, and candles—all (except the seminary candles) borrowed from the abandoned supplies of the house. Three bottles of looted wine were open on the sideboard; a stock of good Belgian cigars had been set out, and in the frying pan on the stove was steak, a gift from Chaplain Engels.

In half an hour the party had become merry and mellow. It is traditional with soldiers to feel more and more immortal as the wine is drained, and, the more immortal they feel, the more they toast each other's imminent death: this must be the root of that brooding melancholy which characterizes so many drinking songs. The officers and men toasted one another's distant wives and sweethearts, departed friends, and one another's lives and imminent deaths; they all toasted, in the old, old manner, confusion to their enemies.

"Gentlemen," announced Lieutenant Frank, "the Queen."

Everyone rose.

"Stalin," proposed Sergeant Schwartz.

"General Ike."

Glasses clinked.

"Benes . . ."

"McAuliffe . . ."

"Lady Macbeth . . ."

When the dinner was over and cigars had been handed around, the group, with Lieutenant Frank at the piano, sang Christmas carols.

They were midway through *Silent Night* when a buffeting of air pressure shook the floors and rattled the windows.

"Somebody's getting bombed," said Frank, pausing.

"Go on, Lootenant," said Harvey, " 'sh probably Berlin."

But a moment later a soldier put his head in the door. "German planes," he announced. "They're bombing the town."

There was a little silence. Then Frank said: "The hell with it. I'm staying here."

"Of course," said the chaplain, lighting a cigar.

But the next bomb exploded with such violence that one of the windows burst inward. The floors wobbled and shook. Plaster fell. Rushing to the door, the chaplain shouted the time-honored battle-cry of the infantry school—"FOLLOW ME!"—and fell head-over-heels downstairs.

The first bombs were dropped uptown in the vicinity of

a railroad overpass near division headquarters. An aid station was hit, killing most of the men and, with them, a Belgian girl who had volunteered to work as a nurse. Other bombs then struck the houses on the square below division headquarters, bracketing the group of shelters where the Belgian citizens had taken refuge and demolishing a memorial statue to the Belgian dead of World War I. One bomb had struck only fifty feet from the command post.

Another bomb tore through two floors of the command post itself and lodged—unexploded—in the ceiling of a potato cellar.

The force of aerial-bomb explosions defies description. Soldiers in Bastogne that night could tell by the rattle of anti-aircraft fire whenever the planes were coming to dive down. The small-arms fire always grew heavier as the plane reached the bomb-release point of its dive: this crescendo of noise had the same effect on the nervous system as a crescendo of drums. When the plane had swept by, the firing ceased, and then everyone knew that the bomb was on its way. Conversation ceased. Sometimes we could hear the high, whistling flutter of the descending projectile, and then death was very close.

Fires burned later in the town that night. Out on the lines, one or two of the battalion command posts had had near misses, but no one had been injured. Desolation gripped the upper regions of the town, however, and when the fires burned themselves out, only the charred skeleton of buildings remained around the main square. Bastogne, which had been untouched when the troops moved in, wore that ghastly air of desolation which had come to so many European towns in the war. In the still night a man walking past the ruins could smell the sickly-sweet odor of the untended dead.

This was Christmas, 1944.

Into the Reich

The day after Christmas, the first men from the 4th Armored Division drove into the lines of Bastogne; now it would be only a matter of hours before full reinforcements and supplies were rolling in. However, the 101st Airborne was not relieved; they were needed in Bastogne, now part of the front lines, and there they would stay until January 19th.

And now the bad weather, which had grounded the air forces during the whole breakthrough, lifted on December 25th; from then on the Allied air forces flew round-the-clock missions, smashing at the supply convoys and troop columns moving up. Weather continued good long enough for the Allies to force the Germans to keep pulling back their supply lines, to keep moving their rail assembly centers farther and farther back to escape bombing and strafing.

The Germans had gotten to within four miles of the Meuse River, but by the end of January the Allies had pushed them back to their original line of departure.

The Ardennes campaign was the last desperate convulsion of the Wehrmacht in the west; while the campaign delayed the end of the war, it cost the Germans tremendous losses in manpower and supplies. It also brought about a real crack in the shaky façade of the Allied Field Command. When the Germans drove their salient into the 1st Army, elements were split off to the north in Montgomery's sector; Hodges, commanding these elements, had little communication with Bradley. In the early stages of the breakthrough, Eisenhower decided the northern elements of the 1st and 9th Armies might be better attached to the command of Montgomery. This infuriated Bradley, and he told Eisenhower he would refuse to accept such an order, preferring to resign his command.

Bradley, incidentally, contends the tide had already been turned against the Germans before Montgomery committed British troops to action. Wilmot defends Montgomery—he was on his staff during the European campaign—by describing his strategy as waiting for the Germans to exhaust themselves in their drive. He assumed they were trying to reach Liége, he knew he was ranged in position to prevent its capture; Montgomery wasn't devoted to the American theory of constant offense as the best defense. Montgomery frequently delayed attack until he was sure he had the advantage.

With the Germans back to their original starting line by the end of January, SHAEF devised the following strategy: in the north, Montgomery was to strike across the Rhine and head for the Ruhr, the 1st Canadian Army attacking through the Reichswald Forest, and the 9th U.S. Army crossing the Roer River to join up with the Canadians. The 1st and 3rd U.S. Armies were also to strike for the Rhine in the south, but were not to cross over until Montgomery could also cross. Farther south, part of the 3rd Army and the American 7th Army were to hammer at the approaches to the Siegfried Line in an effort to break into the Saar, and push on as far as possible with an eye to an eventual envelopment of the Ruhr from the south. Predictably enough, conflict developed between Bradley and Montgomery once more. The Americans now had more divisions committed to the fighting than the British, and while Bradley and Patton accepted the strategy of Montgomery's striking from the north, they resented having to hold their own striking power until Montgomery had moved across the Rhine. In addition, the 9th Army was to remain under the command of Montgomery for this operation, and Eisenhower suggested that several divisions of the 1st Army might also be transferred to Montgomery, if his drive was successful.

Bradley and Patton agreed that if any more divisions went up to Montgomery, they'd never get them back, and so they decided to conduct an "aggressive defense." Montgomery's attack on Germany's Rhineland began on February 8th, when the 1st Canadian Army attacked the Reichswald. The Siegfried Line had been prepared as a major defense along the borders of Germany, but its line of fortifications didn't reach to the Reichswald, although the Germans had had time to prepare and utilize the forest's natural defenses. As in the Huertgen Forest, the Reichswald was the scene of bitter fighting. The Germans were able to throw in strong reinforcements here because they had let out the dams to raise the level of the Roer River, which would keep the American 9th Army from crossing the Roer to join the Canadians for two weeks.

The following selection from Lance-Cpl. R. M. Wingfield's *The Only Way Out* records his personal experience in the Queen's Royal Regiment of the 7th Armored Division, which fought its way through the Reichswald. Perhaps no other selection makes so vivid the dilemma of the infantryman—"*the only way out of the infantry is on a stretcher, or six feet under.*"

"HIDE AND SEEK" IN THE REICHSWALD

by Lance-Cpl. R. M. Wingfield

We waited on our start-line just inside the Reichswald. For the last few days we had had a very quiet time, the pleasant glades of the woods affording welcome peace and rest, apart from a few stray bullets from keen Canadian rabbit-hunters on our left.

Knowing Jerry as we did and the heavy casualties suffered by the Canadians, we realized that this quiet was suspicious. We were on edge, all dressed up for battle and nowhere to go. Two hours after we left, Jerry blew our part of the Reichswald to hell.

We breakfasted on "Armoured Pig" and "Armoured Dog." Pausing only to spit the "Yellow Peril" Vitamin C pills on to the growing pile round the corner from the cookhouse, we moved off.

The first German village we came to slowed down the advance. There were no snipers or mines, but an enemy village, the first we'd seen, was strange. Mostly from sheer curiosity, we examined and searched each house in the local Josef Goebbelsstrasse. Outside the village a farm was on fire and a poor old lady was trying, single-handed, to round up the panicky animals, the tears rolling down her old cheeks. Fraternization ban or no, our lads couldn't bear to see the old and weak in trouble. We trundled all the animals into a barn and slung some hay in with them. As we marched off down the road a quavering cry followed us.

"Danke! Danke!"

Now we moved into an entrenched knoll at the top of a road gradient to await further orders to advance. In an end-

This selection is condensed from the author's *The Only Way Out.*

less stream on the road passed section after section of Canadians of the Princess Patricia's Light Infantry. We could see them marching slowly and steadily down the road to Goch. This road stretched straight in front, a finger pointing into the heart of the German defences. Jerry tried to blast that road off the map. A dusty cloud flashed and puffed among the marching blobs. A section which had passed us jauntily ten minutes before vanished. The other blobs moved on steadily, passed into the drifting smoke and reappeared on the other side, never faltering. Another puff of smoke, this time much nearer, dirty yellow High-Explosive at its heart, appeared on the road in the middle of a section. The section fell apart like skittles. The survivors got to their feet. They moved on.

Now it was our turn to run the gauntlet. Once we hit the road we spaced out automatically. We reached the crater of the first shell. The hedge was spattered with strips of flesh and uniform. A white enamel mug danced pathetically on a windy branch.

Now we advanced cautiously through the town of Udem. The streets were choked with rubble and splintered timber. Our tanks slowly ground their way up and over the debris of homes, spraying before them with Besa. Snipers in the rubble bounced bullets off the tanks and some ricocheted near us. We left the cover of the tanks and took our chance in the open, dodging from cover to cover in the rubble. The tanks thrashed up clouds of dust and their steel bodies ploughed through a smoky, choking fog. Sniper fire turned from the fruitless task of trying to pierce the tanks half-hidden in the dust, and sought out the units following us. The old, chilling cry of "Stretcher-bearer!" echoed along what had been streets.

One sniper was spotted in the circular window of a church. A tank spat Besa fire at the wall. Puffs of dust spouted, moving steadily, inexorably up the building, inch by inch, flaming, leaping, leaden death. The sniper crouching in the circle was blasted to his feet, danced a jig on the bullets and slowly tilted and fell headlong, sprawling across the rubble.

He was soon avenged. A *"Panzerfaust,"* the German infantry anti-tank weapon like a flying gas-lamp, wobbled through the air and smashed into the back of the turret. Brown smoke gushed up from the turret and down the gun barrel, which drooped down lifeless. From the smoke the tank-commander spilled out of the turret. He was alone. We climbed up and dragged him from the smouldering steel. He wasn't injured, just dazed. We climbed up once more to rescue the others, but were stopped by a feeble cry from the commander.

"The rest have had it."

Tongues of flame came from the hatch. We backed away quickly and hit the ground as the tank "brewed up" with a muffled roar. Soon it was a mass of flame, rocked by the ammunition exploding inside the white-hot hull. A bursting shell blew the front away and we could see, silhouetted in the spitting flame, the driver sitting at his post, the hair on the back of the hands slowly burning.

"Let's get out!"

We did.

That night we dug in round the tanks against a glowing back-cloth of burning tanks and homes. We patrolled to flush any snipers. None of our troops was in the town, so we shot at anything that moved.

We waited. The tanks stood silent. Dawn came. The sun climbed. The morning was warm with a slight breeze—a nice day to die. The day's work was to advance still further to the Hochwald Forest. From Maas to Rhine the Germans had dug a huge anti-tank ditch. We had to capture and breach it.

Our tanks started up and we climbed aboard. This put us six feet off the ground, but we had to give the Jerry snipers a sporting chance after their splendid but vain efforts to penetrate the tanks. We stood there, shuffling and stamping our feet impatiently. No one spoke.

Finally we moved off to the open fields, swerved off the road into the country and on again. Immediately a Spandau burst bounced off the tanks. So did we. I heard the crack overhead and listened for the thump which always echoed from the gun itself. Got it! That clump of bushes! I told one of my riflemen to put five rounds of tracer into it. The other two section-commanders did the same. The criss-cross rounds signalled the target to our three tanks. They heeled as they turned and hosed the scrub with their three Besas. The bushes jerked and shook beneath the leaden flail. The machine-gun stopped.

We crept on, keeping to the hedges. To our right a farmhouse went on fire. From the blazing building spilled German Infantry, hands clasped behind their necks. One man came out by himself, a S.S. man, a leaping, hammering Schmeisser at his hip. He ran for a hayrick. Besa tracer stitched the air behind him. The earth at his heels boiled with dust. Now the Besa hit him and threw him into the haystack, which immediately "brewed up." The Besa cut off. Two German and two British Infantrymen rushed to save him. The heat was too great.

I got to my feet and my section followed me. We skirted the potato clamp cautiously. By now the smoke had drifted away. The fins of the smoke bomb stuck up from the ground. Standing on its head against the clamp was a German corpse. There was no trace of anyone else, just half a steel helmet lying by the two scorched divots of the bomb and grenade. We passed hurriedly. Ahead, up a slight gradient four hundred yards in front of us, was the anti-tank ditch.

There was someone in there.

We lay down to regroup. All was ready. There was only one thing left to do. No one wanted to give the order. I gulped and, turning to my section, shouted, "Fix bayonets!" That seemed to bring us all to life. I heard the nasty snick of the bayonets locking home. I pulled out the "Safety" of my Sten and stood up. Men to right and left stood up.

No one moved. We all stared at the ditch ahead. This was a bayonet charge. We had practised it before, stupid men in training trying to raise an empty scream while prodding a sandbag. This was no practice. It was the dread problem of "Him or Me," that problem which had never arisen yet and which we assumed would never arise. These men in the ditch were not going to give up easily. Oh God, let it be *him!*

I fingered my Sten, looked to right and left and set off at

a rapid walk. I glanced at my mate "Smoky" on my right. He licked his lips, grinned a dead grin and closed me to bring me under the protection of his bayonet. I should have to spray with my Sten and hope for the best.

The alignment was all to hell. I was leading an arrow-head. We broke into a trot, a run, a mad charge, screaming, yelling. One hundred yards away the lip of the ditch was lined with waving bits of white paper.

"So you're trying to pack up now, you bastards! It's too bloody late!" we roared and swept on. I sprayed a burst at the paper. It went down. Fifty yards . . . forty yards . . . thirty . . . twenty . . . and, with a wild yell, I was over and in.

The trench was ten feet deep. I hit the bottom with a crash and saw grey-green figures. I squeezed the trigger. Oh, God! A jam! Before I could shake out the cartridge a voice said:

"What the fornication do you lot think you're doing?"

We had charged our own "B" Company with an assortment of Germans varying from very dead to petrified with fright.

The next ten minutes, with the bubble of fear pricked, were spent in mutual recriminations, curses and remarks on the Higher Authority's ancestry. There might have been serious casualties, casualties which would have been unnecessary. Some stupid bastard had blundered. It was a bloody miracle we won the war when nobody knew where the hell anybody else was half the time.

In the middle of the curses and attempts to regroup, Jerry Defensive Fire came down. We hit the ground, "B," "D" and the German prisoners in a hopeless jumble. The gunnery was, fortunately, of a low standard as no shells came in among us. One straggler on the edge of the ditch was hit in the shoulder as he dived into the trench, rolling to the bottom in a shower of earth and stones. We bandaged him as neatly as we could. He didn't seem too bad, so we said how much we envied him, wrapped him in his gas-cape to prevent shock and gave him a cigarette. From the smile on his face we gathered that "Jack" was certainly All Right.

The barrage stopped.

That seemed to be the lot for the time being. We consolidated. I helped to booby-trap the trench with trip-flares and the inevitable tin cans. Two men took the only casualty to the Regimental Aid Post. We watched him go with envious eyes. The C.S.M. came round with the mail. The letters and parcels thumped unheeded on the ground. We were too busy doing the essential job—digging in. Slowly the trenches were dug out. The earth piled up on each side. The swinging shoulders and spades sank below the surface. Soon the trenches were dug and their parapets beaten flat. We replaced the turf as camouflage. The Bren was in the centre so that it could fire each side to protect the rest of the section and platoon. Grenades and clips of ammunition stood ready on the parapets. One at a time the men of the section went up and left their Bren mags with the gun. I stood my Sten magazines on the lips of the trench, open ends upwards, bullets pointing away. With one movement I could load and fire. I set to work with the cumbersome magazine filler to replace the burst I had given the German soil. There was only one round left in. I must have blazed off twenty-six rounds in my fright and fury!

The first shell came over as we settled down after the usual "stand-to." Everything happened at once. The shell's slathering scream came quickly, then the explosion, followed by the fluttering scythe of shrapnel. 88! My platoon was dug in well. Quickly I went the round of my section positions to see if they had enough food and cigarettes to last the night if the shelling persisted.

"Right, it seems to me as if Jerry's pulling out, but—take no chances! If and when the stonk stops, up with your weapons and all-round defence! That's when they start counter-attacks!"

I completed my round and dropped back into my trench. Smoky sat at the other end, his knees drawn up to his chin. His face would have made an interesting subject for a painter of the "Chiaroscuro" School. Each rising and falling circle of red from his cigarette showed a youthful face leaning on the dark wood of the rifle, a face streaked with dirt and sweat. The eyes were tired but calm, reflecting the quick

"Laugh and to Hell" resilience of the young. There was no trace of the introspective, brooding stare of the older members of the platoon. Maybe the Army *did* know what it was doing in ensuring a majority of youngsters in combat Battalions.

"Think they're pulling out, Corp?"

"Maybe! This stonk seems the usual racket, but if the barrage starts creeping that means trouble!"

Suddenly there flashed through my mind the warning in the sound-track of a "School of Infantry" film—*"Never* use an enemy's slit-trench and *never* dig near a prominent feature—Jerry's probably got it 'zeroed' for mortars!"

God! What a bloody fool I was! The slit-trenches of my section were all sited—by me—within fifteen yards of the anti-tank ditch! My own was within six feet! This was a hell of a time to remember! Too late to worry now. I had done the best I could think of at the time. The anti-tank ditch was well booby-trapped and it was unlikely that Jerry would start anything with the barrage still going strong.

The barrage slackened.

"O.K. Watch it!" I was pleased to see the speed with which those lads were up. These veterans of nineteen were no mugs. The barrage intensified.

A quavering voice from somewhere up on the earth began to sob, "Forty-two . . . Forty-three . . . Forty-four" with a shell-burst punctuating each number.

I shouted: "Stop that! The man in the trench with him—talk to him, tickle him, kick him, clock him—anything!—but stop him counting! He'll go bomb-happy!"

The noise stopped abruptly.

"How did you manage him?"

"Winded him! He's O.K. now."

"Right! Watch him!"

The shelling, with its monotonous beat, drugged us to silence. I sat, five feet down in the earth, staring—at nothing. The Sten, standing upright between my knees, shook with each concussion. I gripped it for something solid to cling to. A shell burst within a few feet and I looked up. In the bright flash I saw a small blade of grass on the edge of the trench, nodding gently in the steel breeze. I watched it, fascinated. "You're too small to be hit!" At that moment there was a thud and glow as a white-hot piece of shrapnel plunked into the wall of the trench and glared at me. I looked up. The grass was gone. Oh God! I turned on my side and tried to get my head lower. Many was the time that I'd wished the head and its brain Telephone Exchange were in the middle of the body to dodge high-flying bullets and shrapnel. Still, it would probably have been mangled by a mine, so what was the use of worrying.

My brain suddenly clicked back to the grass. The poor little piece of grass which points to *me* has gone. They'll never find my grave. *Grave!* I must snap out of it! Be *calm,* be *logical! Think! Think!* You're snug in the bullet-proof earth. You're safe in a trench four foot six down, two feet across and six feet long—just the dimensions of a grave! Shut up, you bloody fool! Think! *Think!* These are shells, not mortars! Their trajectory is almost horizontal, not vertical! They can't get you. Remember the bloke in "B"? He got a mortar bomb in with him. The bomb burst upwards and outwards. He was all right, I tell you, *all right!*

I settled down again. The shelling continued. I had a mad desire to get out and walk about in the night air. The shells wouldn't hurt me if I turned sideways. I imagined that I would be able to dodge the shrapnel as I tried to dodge raindrops as a child. Wouldn't it be better to nip up top and get "the chop" quickly and cleanly instead of having to face hell day after day! week after week—if you lasted a week? Don't be a fool, shrapnel's jagged. It would hurt like hell!

We slowly stood up. Our heads mounted into the dawn. It was a dreadful spectacle which met our eyes. The platoon area, no bigger than an average soccer pitch, was pitted with craters, interwoven, crumbling. Someone counted them. Over three hundred. I waited for the heads to rise from the earth.

No one was hurt.

It was a miracle.

We moved like automata back from the ditch and down the slope. We dug in to avoid any more shells and to silhouette the ditch and any attackers. The trenches were finally dug. We breakfasted. I don't remember what we had. No one else did either. I can remember drinking tea, but I don't know where it came from. That tea was the first thing we recognized in life. We were still awfully vague and dazed. We shaved. The wind, whipping the smooth cheeks, stung us to life. The shave wiped out the night's ordeal.

Throughout the day we waited. A runner came.

"Section-commanders to 'O' Group!"

"The Monmouths have bumped it again. They always do. The survivors are hanging on by their eyebrows. Some Companies are down to a dozen. They are approximately two miles to the west of us. We are passing through them at dusk. The plan is this. First, four flail tanks of 79th Armoured will clear the mines. We shall travel on tanks behind them, 'D' Company leading the Battalion, 18 Platoon leading the Company. Two hundred yards from the ditch, the flails will turn left and right and demine the approaches. The Infantry will get off the tanks and fan out into the fields. They will then advance to the ditch, which they will hold till the Engineers' Fascine tanks fill it in—then, back on to the tanks and keep going! The Yanks aren't very far away and Jerry is being heavily squeezed. Defensive Fire is expected to be heavy. (Much later we discovered that Jerry had 1,054 guns in the area.) Everyone to be as quiet as possible. Check ammo and food. Pull out of your present positions one hour before dusk and report here to Company H.Q. You will be taken by guides to the 15th/19th Hussars, who, as usual, will be our playmates. Off you go!"

We dispersed to pass on the information.

The comments in my section were very sarcastic.

" 'All ranks to be as quiet as possible'—with twenty-four bloody great roaring Cromwells, not counting those flail tanks with their bashing chains!"

"Usual muck-up! Why the hell can't we go over the part of the ditch we've captured here and take the bastards from the rear?"

"Steady on, mate, that'd be too easy. We might win the war, and that'd never do!"

"Think of it. A night attack with tanks. Those bastards are blind enough in daylight!"

"Cor! It'll be murder!" How right he was!

The hour of waiting was dreadful. We tried to occupy our time. We tried not to think. We all had premonition of trouble—big trouble. Our weapons were ready. We retested them. There was nothing to do. We talked. We smoked. The minutes ticked away. There was nothing to do. We looked to the west. We could see nothing. We could hear nothing.

A whistle blew from Company H.Q. Here we go! We put on our packs. The dry click of the metal buckles was the only sound. We moved back slowly, suddenly frightened of the ditch when we were to leave it. Any minute Germans might straddle the skyline.

"Don't worry, mates, we've got it covered," said a voice from behind. An evil-looking Vickers pointed from the scrub.

The light faded. Our feet moved automatically, left, right, left, right, winding through the wood. Our enemy was the weight of the pack, the stifling closeness of the pine forest, the unknown danger we had coming to us.

We came into a clearing. Stopped and silent lay the Cromwells, the crews sitting by the turrets, their boots tapping uneasily on the tracks. We moved past the sinister booms of the flails, their chains dangling lifeless, down the boom arm to the squat, steel boxes and on to the first Cromwell.

"O.K. Rex! Your section on that one!" God! We're the first in! We gingerly climbed aboard and settled with our backs to the warm exhaust-chute. The clatter of boots climbing on to the tracks and so to the armoured hulls faded down the line as the rest of the Battalion embarked.

We waited.

We waited a whole ruddy hour. By this time our bladders, distended by the tea and fear, were screaming to be let out. I asked for permission to dismount. No! We sprayed the surrounding area. We were easy.

We waited.

A faint squealing came from the interior of the tank. The Wireless Op. slowly got to his feet and climbed reluctantly into the turret.

"Move in five minutes!" The voice came hollow from the turret.

The rest of the crew came to life and climbed inside.

"Start up!"

A whine, a thunderous cough, and the tank trembled as the Merlin engine fought its way to full power.

From up front there came a deep roar and a clashing of whipping chains as the flails ground forward. We jerked back. We were off.

The night roared and snarled with the engines. Dust came back in choking clouds. We swayed and rolled on the pulverized track. My section moved up to the turret and held on to its solid, comforting coldness. . . . The tank-commander put his head out.

"Happy?" A chorus of groans greeted him.

"Rather you than me, mates!"

Yet we felt much safer than the tank crew behind their armour. An Infantryman may be more vulnerable, but he's a darned sight more mobile.

The tank column slowed and stopped.

"How's it going, mates?" asked a voice from below. We peered over the side of the hull. Two pale faces seemed to be resting on the ground. We shouted down from our height.

"You the Monmouths?"

"Yes."

"Had a good time?"

"Bloody awful, mates. We've been stonked and machine-gunned to hell. I think we're the only two left from our platoon. Didn't think we'd last out till you got here. I've never been so glad to see the dark. It's been very quiet for the last hour. You know what sort of quietness I mean. Best of luck, mates. You'll need it!"

We lurched on and stopped again.

The night was blasted by a sudden purple flash. The flails vanished in a roaring cataract of flame. I don't know to this day why they blew up. We had heard no shells.

I found myself with my section in a field twenty yards away. I don't remember getting off the tank. Our tank, stung to fury, blazed away with Besa tracer. The glowing beads sprayed at the trees, struck and whirled off, moved slowly left and right, up and down, blasting the whole of the front of the wood. We lay there with our weapons ready and pointing at the trees which leaped and dropped in the glare of the blazing flails. From our right a lazy burst of tracer sailed, a hundred feet up, over our heads. My Bren-gunner rose to his knees and hammered back.

Simultaneous with the last round of the Bren burst, I felt a searing pain start at my left hip, flash across and numb my right thigh. There was a shout to my left and the dull burst of a "36" grenade.

Then I knew.

"Christ! I've been hit!" I panicked. I'd been hit internally, so I should be bleeding from the mouth. I coughed into my hand. It was dry. Thank God! I felt better.

It was puzzling. I'd been hit all right, but apart from the first burning slash it wasn't too bad. I felt perfectly O.K. I was disappointed. No mortal agony, no frenzied writhing and no shattering pain churning my body.

A thump by my side and Smoky was there.

"Where've you been hit, Corp?"

"In the guts."

"Can you move?"

"I don't know. I'll try."

I tried to move my legs but my thighs and legs wouldn't respond. Oh, God! I'm paralyzed!

Smoky sat up, and once more I heard that chilling sound echoing, picked up and relayed into the distance:

"Stretcher-bearers!" Only this time it was for me.

I hoped that I would soon be out of it, and appealed to passing shadows to send the Medics when they could. All the figures were moving forward. All of them showed a morbid interest in where I'd been hit. To my shame, I found myself answering very proudly. I was the great hero. I'd been hit. They all told me how lucky I was. I suddenly realized that there would be no more battle for me. I felt fine.

Now I tried to move, with Smoky helping me. Each time I levered myself up, a pain shot through my guts. I still had no right thigh. I tried to remain calm and take stock of my position. I couldn't move. I was prone on the ground, so I should be safe from any more damage. Then I suddenly realized that I'd been hit when lying on the ground. Next time anyone said, "When in doubt, fall flat," I'd have something to say to them!

The greatest danger from wounds was shock. "Keep the patient warm," the book said. I rolled on to my back and unclasped my belt. A surge of warmth flooded through my abdomen and thighs. My right leg came back to me. I thought that it was only a temporary cramp which had attacked me and I tried to stand. The pain started at my abdomen and welled up over my body to my head and armpits. I felt sick. I lay down again, took my gas-cape off my belt, put it on and re-buckled the belt. The pain abated. So, in some way, my belt was acting as a partial tourniquet. I still didn't know what had hit me or where it came from. I had seen nothing.

A curious silence had fallen since I had been hit. It was broken by a sound from my left—a bubbly, heavy breathing which got hoarsely stronger and stronger—and stopped. Someone else had gone. A figure crawled across.

"Fred's had it! Hit through the lungs. What hit you, Corp?"

"I don't know."

"Maybe it was the machine-gun over by us. Just before Fred stopped his he'd slung in a grenade. It cut short a burst—but that burst got him."

A curious mutter arose from the ground and swelled to a shout—a pleading, cursing hubbub.

"They're leaving us! Come back, you cowardly bastards!"

The tanks were withdrawing. With them went our hopes, our prayers. The tanks moved slowly back, hosing the woods. Tracer faded and cut out. The last spinning burst ebbed and died and the tanks were gone. Their motors turned to a distant hum.

All around voices came from the darkness, discussing, despairing. Slowly, painfully, I crawled over to a dark mound on my right to draw comfort from a fellow sufferer. Smoky came with me.

"Pretty bloody, isn't it, mate?" No answer.

"I said, 'Pretty bloody, isn't it, mate?' "

Smoky touched the figure and recoiled. I didn't see his face. I wish I had. The man was staring straight ahead, his rifle gripped in his hands. He still said nothing. I moved round to his front and peered at his face. The pale forehead was stitched with four neat black holes.

"Get me out, Smoky, for God's sake!" I moved, half-crawling, half-carried by Smoky. I shivered and was sick.

Mere figures moved through us, another Company going forward. Suddenly tracer began to spray the area, probing towards the shadowy men. Some of them dived flat. One was late. The tracer vanished into the cardboard carton of P.I.A.T. bombs on his back. A split second of silence followed, then the most appalling crash and blossom of flame. I tucked my head to the ground, and round the edges of the steel helmet I felt the hot blast of the explosion hit my shoulders. Each of these six bombs could blow a hole in a tank. A body hit the ground heavily.

"Christ!" it said.

A miracle had happened. The man was only bruised by his long fall. There wasn't even a scorch on his battle-dress! Another man with him swore that he'd seen a blob sailing up in the air, turning over and over.

The man stumbled on.

A scuffing of boots sounded in the grass and a figure knelt by me—one of the Medics from Battalion H.Q. We recognized each other.

"Where have you got it?"

I tried to tell him with as much accuracy as possible. By the light of a blue shaded lamp he wrote my name, number, Company and where I thought I'd been hit.

"Do you want any morphia?"

"No, thanks. It doesn't hurt."

"Right! I'll take this back to the M.O. so that he knows what wounds to prepare for. We'll be back for you in half an hour."

"What's the time?"

"About nine o'clock." I'd been there for two hours already.

I turned to Smoky.

"Looks as though you can get moving. I'll be O.K. now! Thanks, mate, for staying with me."

"That's O.K., mate. You'd have done the same for me."

I would. "I'll try to see you again before they move you any further back." He moved away and his shadowy figure advanced to be lost in the wood.

I felt thirsty and tried to get at my water-bottle, but it was just too far away. The stretcher-bearer came back, looked at me, and without saying a word, took my Sten, dismantled it and threw the pieces away.

God! He thought I might commit suicide. Still, I suppose some people in their despair might do it. I had too much to live for. I also hadn't the guts.

"Don't drink," he said and walked away.

I didn't try to drink. I wondered whether it would be safe to suck a boiled sweet. Better not. It would be suicide to light a cigarette. Throughout the time since I had been wounded I had been mentally alert and I decided to try an experiment.

Many times I had heard that, in moments of danger, psychic messages could be sent to near ones. I concentrated very hard and tried to tell my mother that I had been hit. She heard me. There is no explanation.

There is also no explanation for the dreadful dream I had in Ypres.

I woke up one morning at two o'clock screaming. My mate asked me what was wrong. I dreamed that we had attacked a house. The Sergeant kicked the door open, threw in a grenade, and slammed the door. The grenade burst. The Sergeant kicked the door open again and dived flat. A machine-gun opened up and seven bullets hit me in the throat. I woke up screaming.

Two months later we attacked a house—*the house.* I was quite powerless to act. I was going to die and I couldn't do a thing about it. The Sergeant kicked the door open, threw in a grenade and slammed the door. The grenade burst. The Sergeant kicked the door open again and dived flat. So did I. The man behind me was hit seven times in the throat. The Sergeant killed the gunner.

In front I heard a sharp whistle, rapidly approaching, and over it went! The shell burst half a mile behind. I had been afraid of that. Defensive Fire, cunningly directed, was plunging into our supply route and rear areas. The stretcher-bearers wouldn't get through that lot. A universal groan from the other wounded told me that others had thought of that too. Patience! Patience!

The barrage moved slowly from the rear area. It was moving backwards and we were in the way. Now the shells burst among us, threaded their way back again and settled to a steady beat one hundred yards behind me. Our escape route to the rear was gone. We could only go forward.

The shelling stopped and figures appeared on the edge of the wood, coming towards us.

Counter-attack!

We could only play dead and pray. The men moved carefully between us.

"*Tot!*" said a voice.

Several things happened at once. At that moment a Vickers cut loose from behind. The tracers flared three feet overhead, stopped and went on again—but the beat of the gun hadn't stopped. One of the men's boots was right by my head when the burst started. A horrid sound, midway between a cough and a belch, and a body fell heavily across my legs, quivered, thrashed and lay still. His Schmeisser toppled across my shoulders, clouting me over the ear.

The Vickers stopped. There was a sound of running, weaving, dodging feet as the counter-attack melted back to the wood. A green Very light spun up the sky, poised, and fell. The shell storm burst with renewed fury. The counter-attack had failed. Jerry was pulling out. It was a question of waiting.

I wriggled clear of my burden. The night wore on.

Another danger came. Our own counter-barrage sparkled and crashed amid the woods. In its bright glow we saw branches chopped down and whirled away.

Then it happened. Our barrage corrected itself at the anti-tank ditch and slowly walked back—and back—*and back!* Thirty yards ahead a wounded man cried out. There was a cut-off scream as the body changed to a smoking crater. A steel helmet bowled off into the darkness.

God! Please, God! No more! *No more!* Save my miserable skin! I tried to deceive God that I was pleading for my family's sake. *He* knew better. So did I. The next shell bloomed ten yards ahead of me. Its scorching heat hit my shoulders and slammed me two yards backwards. A tiny piece of shrapnel spanged off my helmet. So these helmets were some use!

The shells plunged right amongst us. Their concussion threw me this way and that, forward and backward. The earth heaved. It shook. I seemed to bounce like a ball. I turned a complete somersault and landed on my knees with a crash. I buried my face in the ground. I closed my eyes. I daren't look any more. My helmet grated in the soil, dug itself a channel and was still. With my hands I gripped the turf, determined to stay down, to pull myself into the sheltering earth. Shells screamed and whooped, blew aloft. Earth pattered down. The groans stopped.

The warmth of the shells passed in front of me, moving further and further away. I looked up. Twenty . . . twenty-five . . . thirty yards away, on to the ditch and into the wood.

Tearfully I poured out my thanks to God in an agony of relief. I stretched my fingers. I flexed my limbs. They worked. I shook the earth from my gas-cape. The dry crackle of its waterproofing was the first new sound I was aware of. Our barrage was now fifty yards in front and the German shells were fifty yards to the rear. We were stuck in the middle. I wriggled to look round at the German corpse. He wasn't there. In the next shell-flash I saw him, draped like a rag doll, hanging on a hedge fifty yards away.

Muffled voices came from the field as the wounded checked to see how many were still alive. Someone said, in a quiet, calm, matter-of-fact way:

"There *were* forty, to my knowledge."

Someone else lit a cigarette. Those who could move crawled towards it for companionship. The black shapes slithered towards the red pin-point. I couldn't move.

A shell fell right in the middle of the group. I turned my head. I couldn't bear to look. When the roar died away, I did look. There was nothing. I stared at the wood and was sick. Two feet in front of my face a cigarette glowed.

The barrage seemed less violent. The noise changed to a steady rumble. Tracer jetted into the wood. Thank God!

The tanks were back! Ragged cheers broke out all over the area. There they were, the great steel bastards, moving relentlessly on, an endless train snarling into the heart of the forest.

The barrage stopped.

I heard the sound of boots scuffing on the grass.

"Here we are, mate! The sheriff's bleedin' posse always gets through!"

The stretcher-bearers had arrived.

"Room for one on top! Have the exact fare ready. Regimental Aid Post and all stops to Blighty. Fez pliz."

My face cracked into what I hoped was a grin. Strong arms lifted me on to the stretcher. Pain shot through me.

"Put me on my stomach, for God's sake!"

Slowly, gently, they turned me over. The pain vanished. I felt comfortable, secure. As we swung off across the field someone shook my hand warmly. I turned my head. It was Smoky.

"Glad to see you're out of it, Corp. Can I have the tin of soup you've got clasped to your manly bosom?"

I laughed and pulled the can from my blouse.

"So long, Corp. You're better off where you're going. You might like to know the rest of the section's O.K. Look after yourself, mate!" Smoky shook my hand again and left.

We picked our way carefully through the craters and down the track. We met no one. Ahead and to the right was a dimly lit door. My stretcher was put down on trestles. The hard wood bit into my shins and chest.

"O.K.," said the M.O., "turn him over!"

The pain must have put me out. I can remember someone asking for my field-dressing. I tapped my right thigh, and felt something move on there. When I came round, I could see the M.O.'s face, streaked with grime and sweat. There was a strong hospital smell. I felt cold at my stomach. I lifted myself on my elbow and stared at my stomach. No wonder I was cold. They'd cut all my battle-dress and underwear away from the knee to the chest. My field-dressing was round my right thigh. From the left hip across my loins was just a white field of gauze and bandage, slightly stained red.

The M.O.'s face appeared above me.

"What do you want doing with this lot?" He showed me a tin full of cigarette ends. I looked, puzzled.

"This collection was in your map pocket. There's a hundred and eighty of 'em."

I remembered. The nine hours' stonk last night.

"Chuck 'em away, please." A sudden thought occurred to me.

"What's the time, sir?"

"Three o'clock in the morning. You were picked up an hour ago."

I had been out there for seven hours.

The M.O. spoke again.

"Right, lad! You seem to be alert enough to learn what's happened. You've been hit by at least two tracers. They went in at your left hip and out at the right thigh. The hole was too big for one bullet, but they did you a good turn. The tracer powder cauterized the wound as it went through, so it's a clean hole. It's not my job to excavate, so I'm sending you to a Casualty Clearing Station. You mustn't drink till they know the internal damage. All your personal possessions are in this bag. Here you are. This will be a long job, son, but you'll be all right. Yes, Sergeant, give him a cigarette. Good-bye, son. Good luck!"

The cigarette tasted good.

Outside, I was lifted on to a Bren-carrier. The Padre sat there. I was scared.

"Don't worry, boy! I'm not with you in case you die on the way! I'm just coming down to the C.C.S. to see the rest of our boys. You're our last customer!"

The Bren-carrier throbbed, swivelled and turned on to the road. Its well-sprung movement carried me on a moving feather-bed.

The night was quite warm for February. A faint breeze blew.

So I left the Battalion.

I *was* "out."

Over the Rhine

Montgomery's armies were trying to break through to the Rhine in the north; at the same time columns from the American 1st Army drove to the Rhine, only to find that the Germans had blown its bridges. By March 7th, a dozen bridges across the Rhine had been destroyed

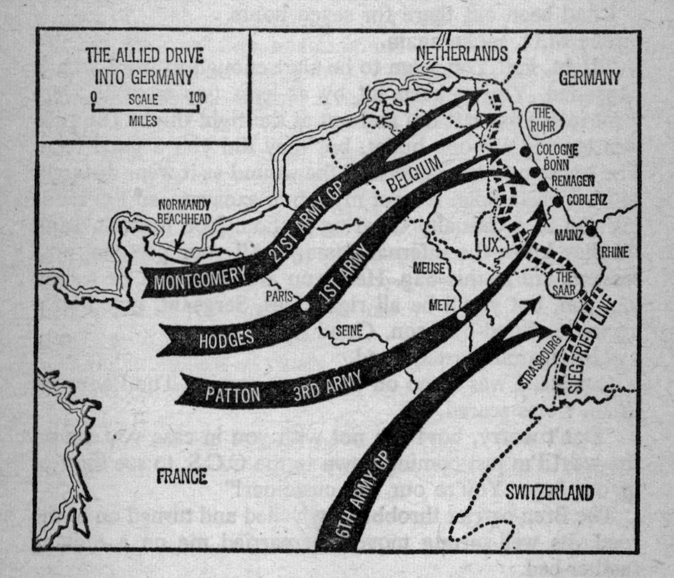

by the Germans. However, on the same day, the 9th U. S. Armored Division of the 1st Army, rolling into the hills above Remagen, was astonished to find the Ludendorff Railway Bridge still standing. The story of its daring capture follows, carefully prepared and researched by Capt. Hechler, one of the historians attached to the 9th Armored.

THE CAPTURE OF REMAGEN BRIDGE

by Capt. Ken Hechler

Late in the forenoon of March 7, a gray, drizzly day, a little group of American soldiers on the Birresdorf road near the abandoned R.A.D. camp above Remagen were talking excitedly. The Ludendorff Bridge was over a mile away, and Karl Timmermann and his men did not dream that it would still be standing when they reached it.

Timmermann and his second platoon leader, Lieutenant Burrows, were peering through field glasses at the distant bridge.

"Jim, look at those damn Krauts going over the bridge," said Timmermann.

"Hey, look at the cows and horses, too," Burrows said. "With all those people trying to cross over, that bridge would make a good target."

Burrows glanced around quickly for his mortar squad. "Amick," he yelled, "you and Mercadante set up and prepare to fire on that bridge." There was a hasty scuffling with the heavy base plates and stovepipe tubes as the men adjusted their mortars.

"Tim, I'm not so sure about this," Burrows said to his company commander. "Do you think our mortars will do the trick?"

"It sure tempts me."

"Let's plaster 'em, Lieutenant," one of the mortarmen called out.

"Well, we've got some heavy stuff back of us, and there's no sense in sticking a pin in their tail just to see 'em jump.

This selection is condensed from the author's *The Bridge at Remagen.*

Let's do it this way: get hold of Colonel Engeman and he can bring up his tanks and call for some artillery."

A runner took off to alert the task force commander about the big bonanza that Timmermann had found.

A few minutes later, Engeman roared up, followed by Major Murray Deevers, the commander of the 27th Armored Infantry Battalion, and Deevers' Operations Officer, Major Don Russell. They watched the procession of German troops, vehicles, and animals far below, making their ant-like way across.

"Let's lower the boom," Engeman decreed. A radio message flew out, and presently somebody shoved a reply into his hand.

"Damn. They won't fire the artillery. Claim there are friendly troops in the vicinity. How can I get it through their thick— Oh, what's the use! Murray, we've got to take that town, and it looks like the doughs ought to go down first and clean it out. I'll bring up my tanks to cover you. Let me know how you want to plan your attack on the town."

The minutes ticked by. The stream of traffic across the bridge slowed down. There was frustrating delay on top of the hill, as the debate proceeded on how to seize this tiger by the tail without inciting him to bite. Deevers spoke to the commanders of A and C companies, Lieutenants Timmermann and William E. McMaster: "Tim and Mac, you make a reconnaissance down into town and give me a report on how to go in there."

Timmermann and McMaster made their way a little over five hundred yards down the hill along a footpath into Remagen. They met no enemy fire, but they saw a lot of activity near the bridge and on the opposite side of the river. Timmermann paused a moment at the bottom, on the road entering Remagen, and contemplated a battered old sign: "Citizens and Friends: Preserve our parks." It had obviously been intended to restrain the out-of-town tourists from scattering papers. He laughed humorlessly and started climbing back.

On the road to Remagen lived Josef Büntgen and his wife. They were unwilling eyewitnesses, along with several

German soldiers quartered in the home, of the entry of the American troops into Remagen. Herr Büntgen was a very patriotic local official, heading the construction office in the town government. The soldiers and the Büntgen family watched the American troops at the top of the hill pausing to take stock and figure out the next move. They saw Timmermann and McMaster descend the hill to reconnoiter. They saw the terrifying tanks poised for combat. They could see American soldiers start to fix their bayonets at the top of the hill. A German sergeant took a moment to say goodbye to Mrs. Büntgen. He waved his *panzerfaust* and shouted: "I'm going out and knock off one of those tanks."

She tearfully argued with him: "Do that, and they will level all our houses and destroy the town."

"Lady, there's no better place to stop them than at the Rhine. Heil Hitler!"

(Later, the Büntgens saw the sergeant's body in a ditch, an unnamed and forgotten German hero who had tried to create his own Thermopylae.)

Timmermann and McMaster returned from their reconnaissance, and Timmermann got the nod from Deevers for the all-important task of breaking into Remagen. Lieutenant Jack Liedike's B Company followed, its mission to clear the southeastern part of town while protecting the right flank of the advance. Lieutenant McMaster's C Company was assigned to clear the northwestern part and protect the left flank.

Timmermann held a quick conference with his platoon leaders to issue the attack order, and singled out Lieutenant Burrows to point the assault with his second platoon. It was about one o'clock in the afternoon. He told Burrows to take the main road and work his platoon through the center of Remagen, hugging the buildings because of snipers. Sergeant DeLisio was to fan out along the river road on the left flank, crouching low along the river because the Germans could observe clearly from the east bank. Sergeant Chinchar's platoon was to capture the railroad station and move through town on the right flank of A Company before heading for the bridge.

Once Timmermann's men had started for Remagen, a

further series of developments put new life and speed into the attack. Major Ben Cothran, General Hoge's operations officer, had charge of moving the command post for the combat command on the morning of March 7. Because the main effort of the 9th Armored Division was to capture bridges over the Ahr, Hoge had stayed with the south column of his combat command and turned over to Cothran the job of moving his CP from Stadt Mechenheim to Birresdorf, three miles west of Remagen. Cothran, an adventurous officer, had been a newspaper editor in Nashville, and had a nose for news as it developed. After seeing the combat command's bag and baggage to Birresdorf, Cothran hopped into his jeep to find out how close to the Rhine Colonel Engeman's task force had come. He got the same tingling sensation in his spine as everyone else when he emerged from the woods and saw the Rhine and the intact bridge below. He looked just long enough to see the German vehicles streaming across and several locomotives on the other side of the river getting up steam.

"Don't you think we ought to bring some artillery down on all that?" asked Colonel Engeman.

"My God, I've got to get the Old Man," yelled Cothran, scarcely aware of the question.

He radioed to General Hoge, who tore across the countryside to the scene, arriving shortly after one o'clock. Things began to happen fast. The general stormed at the delay in taking Remagen. He told everybody in sight to take the town immediately. Speed, speed, and more speed, he raged, was the key to the whole operation. Colonel Engeman, who had been trying to size up the situation and make careful plans, was spurred into action and issued a series of decisive orders to his subordinates. Directly or indirectly, every man on the top of the hill felt the wrath of the general who demanded and got results.

Satisfied that his calculated display of anger had speeded up the operation and saved many precious minutes, General Hoge began to think about the bridge that, incredibly, still stood before his eyes. "You know," he said in rather subdued tones to Colonel Engeman, "it would be nice to get that bridge too while we're at it."

He quietly studied the procession of troops and vehicles crossing the river, and weighed the risks involved in trying to rush the bridge. An aide tapped his arm.

"Want me to drive back and tell General Leonard?"

Hoge continued to stare through his field glasses, and the aide waited apprehensively.

"We might lose a battalion," replied General Hoge, irrelevantly.

The aide shifted his weight to the other foot and tried again: "Do you see anything special?"

"Engeman, Deevers, Russell, get those men moving into town!" General Hoge barked, taking the field glasses from his eyes.

"Already on their way," the three replied, almost in unison.

It was true—Timmermann had already led his men down the hill and into Remagen. But the renewed interest up above speeded the attack noticeably.

Burrows' platoon had its biggest scuffle in the main square near the City Hall, where an automatic weapon momentarily slowed down the advance. As Burrows started to maneuver his men to flank the German gun, two of Lieutenant Grimball's tanks rumbled up and fired several 90-millimeter rounds into the square. The machine gun shut up suddenly. Grimball's tanks then intermingled with Burrows' second platoon of infantry and they pushed toward the bridge.

Timmermann's old platoon, the first, did not have too much trouble. Sergeant Chinchar proved an excellent interpreter of the frenzied remarks of Polish and Russian displaced persons and prisoners who were anxious to reward their liberators by indicating where the German soldiers were hiding.

The third platoon, headed by DeLisio, moved out rapidly under the aggressive leadership of the little sergeant.

"C'mon, you guys, just another town," DeLisio cried, waving his arm and giving a hitch to his M-1. His men fixed bayonets as they moved down the hill in single file past the stately St. Apollinaris Church. Bates, Foster, Plude, Kreps, Rusakevich, Pol, Rundbaken, Acosta, White, Kenny

—these were some of the men whom DeLisio led down to the river bank. They crept carefully along, squeezing close against the walls of buildings and keeping their submachine guns and M-1's cocked for trouble. From behind lace curtains, the apprehensive citizens watched. Some shivered. Some laughed and said: "Why do the Americans hug the buildings and move so slowly? There are no German soldiers left to fight!" If Company Commander Timmermann had overheard these remarks, he would have complimented his men for conducting themselves like the combat veterans that they were—sticking to the book, taking no chances.

DeLisio came to a road block which the Remagen *Volkssturm* had set up and then neglected to close. He posted four men at the road block and set up a machine gun 100 yards farther inside the town. It was a perfect trap, in which they caught a number of German soldiers trying to slip through town to get across the Rhine. All were taken prisoner.

Shortly after the road block had been set up, an excited American soldier dashed up to DeLisio and yelled:

"Joe, Sergeant Foster wants you on the double! He's got a German general."

DeLisio ambled down the street behind the messenger, and soon observed a very strange sight. Foster had the muzzle of his M-1 pressed against the stomach of a gaudily attired German, with elaborately braided blouse and trousers and enough "scrambled eggs" for several admirals on his hat.

"Here's yer general, Joe," Foster announced. "Now we'll find out the straight dope about that bridge."

"Lower your gun, Foster. Lemme see him," DeLisio began. He asked the prisoner a couple of questions in halting German, and then turned to the hangers-on from his platoon who had gathered to kibitz.

"General, my tail! You know what this guy is? He's the chief station agent for the railroad! Now scatter out, you guys, and let's check these houses."

The men took off, some sheepish, some laughing, and resumed the job of locating and silencing sniper fire. At several points civilians ran out and stopped American soldiers to point out cellars where German soldiers were hiding. Thoroughly demoralized, the Germans invariably surrendered without a shot; many of them realized the futility of resistance and some had even sent civilians to bring in the American soldiers. Still, it was not an easy job to clean out the town. Sniper fire rattled from unseen locations, some 20-millimeter German fire was landing in the town, and each quiet street carried the threat of a death trap at every corner.

Shortly after two o'clock, Timmermann's men had cleaned out enough of Remagen to turn their rifle fire directly on the bridge. Before they actually reached the bridge, the men saw a volcano of rocks and dirt erupt into the air—Captain Friesenhahn had exploded the preliminary demolition which gouged a crater thirty feet wide in the approach to the bridge.

Gradually, DeLisio, Burrows and Chinchar worked their platoons up to the bridge approach where they were joined by the tanks which had helped to clear out the town.

"Look at that hole," grumbled Grimball. "It's not enough that they want to blow the bridge, they won't even let us get near it."

Timmermann came up for a brief confab with his platoon leaders.

"Well, what're we goin' to do?" Burrows asked.

Across the river, they could see the German troops making frantic preparations to blow the bridge. Timmermann glanced along the bridge and clearly saw the wires and the telltale charges, ready to go off. Turning to his platoon leaders, he said:

"They'll probably blow it any minute now. Watch this—it ought to be good." He put his field glasses to his eyes and scanned the far bank. "They look like they want to get us out on the bridge before they blow it."

"Screw that noise," DeLisio said simply.

By three o'clock most of the infantrymen of A Company and the supporting tanks had taken up positions near the bridge. Myron ("Pluto") Plude, one of DeLisio's machine gunners, set up his gun and started throwing a few tracers across. The regular *thwump* of the tank cannon echoed against the Erpeler Ley across the river. Looking back at the top of the hill from which he had first seen the bridge, Timmermann could observe more tanks belching smoke as they threw their shells across the Rhine. Everybody was tense, waiting for the Germans to deliver the inevitable *coup de grâce* to the shaky bridge.

Alex Drabik, the shy, gangling butcher boy from Holland, Ohio, ambled up to the bridge and made one of his rare utterances to his company commander. "Lieutenant Timmermann, looks like we're gonna get some sleep tonight."

"Yeh, Alex," Timmermann answered. "We'll get some hot meals, too, and shack up here for a couple of days."

The same thought had been in General Hodges' mind when he told General Millikin that after joining up with Patton everybody could take a rest for a while.

Just south of Remagen, at Sinzig on the Ahr River, an incident occurred which had a profound effect on the tankers and infantrymen in Remagen. About the time that Timmermann's men were approaching the bridge in Remagen, a task force under Lieutenant Colonel William R. Prince, making the main effort of the 9th Armored Division, was meeting considerably tougher opposition in its attempt to seize the bridge over the Ahr. Prince's task force succeeded nevertheless in rushing the bridge before the Germans could blow it up. This notable feat was accomplished almost two hours before Timmermann led his men through Remagen to the bridge.

Colonel Prince's task force captured about 400 prisoners among the rabid defenders of Sinzig. His men also rounded up some *Volkssturmers* and civilians who were making menacing gestures. A couple of the civilians indicated that they had information "of great importance" which they would like to transmit to the American authorities. Lieutenant Fred de Rango, intelligence officer of the 52nd Armored Infantry Battalion, interrogated the civilians. Impressed with the attention paid to them, the civilians tried to enhance their own importance by giving a good story. They could not have made a better choice in their selection of subject matter: they told de Rango that the German command planned to blow up the Remagen Bridge at four o'clock on the dot.

De Rango received this information about half past two, and he naturally considered it to be of the greatest importance. Acting swiftly, he sent a priority radio message to Combat Command B headquarters, alerting them of this new intelligence. The message had an authoritative ring, and the combat command forthwith relayed it to Task Force Engeman. De Rango, feeling there was not a minute to lose and fearing that his radio message might have to pass through too many channels, also dispatched a special messenger to carry the news to Colonel Engeman. Soon the messages started to ricochet around Remagen as everyone hurried to inform everyone else.

The German troops at the bridge later swore their plan to blow the bridge had no set time schedule but hinged on the appearance of American forces. Furthermore, it seems scarcely plausible that civilians in a neighboring town would have detailed information on a secret military plan of this nature. Authentic or not, the news spurred the American commanders and troops to quicker action in order to cross the bridge before it was blown.

It was 3:15 when General Hoge received the message that the bridge was to be blown at 4:00. He immediately stormed down to give the word to Colonel Engeman. The scrappy Minnesotan already had the news, but General Hoge wanted action. "Put some white phosphorus and smoke around the bridge so the Krauts can't see what we're doing, cover your advance with tanks and machine guns, then bring up your engineers and pull out those wires on the bridge because we're going to take that bridge," General Hoge roared.

General Hoge champed nervously as the minutes ticked by. He directed Majors Deevers and Russell, the commander and operations officer of the 27th Armored Infantry Battalion, to get down to the bridge and order their men across. He turned again to Colonel Engeman: "I want you to get to that bridge as soon as possible."

Engeman bristled: "I'm doing every damn thing possible to get to the bridge."

General Hoge glowered. Without waiting for another word, Engeman started down the road in his jeep to Remagen. On the way he cut open his 508-radio and called Grimball: "Get to that bridge."

Grimball's rich South Carolina accent clearly pierced the static: "Suh, I am *at* the bridge."

Engeman told him to cover the bridge with fire and keep the Germans off it. He then sent a messenger to summon Lieutenant Hugh Mott, a platoon leader in Company B, 9th Armored Engineer Battalion. The pair met in the rear of one of the big resort hotels about two hundred yards from the bridge.

These were Engeman's orders: "Mott, General Hoge wants you to get out onto that bridge and see if it's mined or loaded with TNT, and whether it'll hold tanks. I'll give you fire support from my tanks and you'll have infantry scouts out there too." It was a tough assignment.

Lieutenant Mott, a tall, dark and cool-headed twenty-four-year-old from Nashville, swiftly got hold of the two most reliable men in his platoon—Eugene Dorland, a big Kansas stone mason, and John Reynolds, a little North Carolina textile worker. On their way up to the bridge, they saw the crater blown at the bridge approach, and when the smoke had cleared they jumped into the crater for protection. They also saw Majors Deevers and Russell talking with Karl Timmermann, and pointing at the bridge. Mott waved his two men forward with him.

Deevers and Russell had made their way independently to the bridge, and both of them made contact with Timmermann to give the tall Nebraskan the order to take his men across.

"Do you think you can get your company across that bridge?" the battalion commander asked.

"Well, we can try it, sir," Timmermann answered.

"Go ahead," Deevers snapped.

Timmermann took a split-second look at the bridge, the gaping crater at the approach, and the little knots of German soldiers making frantic preparations on the far bank.

"What if the bridge blows up in my face?" Timmermann asked quickly.

Deevers avoided Timmermann's steady gaze. He turned and walked away without a word. Timmermann knew then that this was a suicide mission. But he did not hesitate.

"All right," he barked to his platoon leaders, "we're going across."

Just as Timmermann was giving the order to cross the bridge, General Hoge back at the top of the hill was faced with a soul-searching decision. Hoge was jolted by a message from 9th Armored Division headquarters, ordering him to push south with all possible speed, objective unlimited, to link up with the 4th Armored Division of General Patton's army. The message gave him serious pause as he surveyed the bridge with his field glasses. In the light of this latest message, to concentrate on crossing the bridge instead of moving south would be a deliberate violation of orders from higher headquarters. Success might excuse such a violation; failure might mean a court martial and disgrace. Hoge could see that the Germans were preparing to blow the bridge. Suppose they blew it up while Timmermann's men were on it? Or, even worse, suppose they blew it after sucking across a large number of troops and vehicles?

General Hoge weighed his decision cold-bloodedly. He figured that he would lose no more than a battalion if the Germans blew up the bridge and cut off the first men who crossed. And if that happened there was still a chance that the men would be captured alive. Hoge also figured that he would lose no more than a platoon if the Germans chose to blow the bridge while Timmermann's men were on their way across. He made up his mind to go through with the crossing.

Back in West Point, Karl Timmermann's wife had given birth to a daughter who was now eight days old. General Hoge's command decision could not consider Timmermann's wife and baby girl, nor Drabik's eighty-year-old father in Holland, Ohio, nor Burrows' mother and father in Jersey City. Nor would Hoge, or Deevers, or anyone else in the world try to answer Timmermann's simple question: "What if the bridge blows up in my face?"

On the surface, Karl Timmermann tried to treat his mission as if it were a big lark. This was part of his art of leadership. While giving orders to his three platoon leaders, he casually passed out some candy he had "liberated" in Remagen. "Here, try one of these Kraut rock candies, and don't break your teeth," he said with a flip to Forrest Miner, an assistant squad leader at the edge of the group.

"Now we're going to cross this bridge before—"

A deafening rumble and roar swallowed up the rest of Timmermann's sentence. The German Sergeant Faust had set off the emergency demolition two-thirds of the way across the bridge. Able Company watched in awe as the huge structure lifted up, and steel, timbers, dust and thick black smoke mixed in the air. Many of the G.I.'s threw themselves to the ground or buried their faces in their hands.

Everybody waited for Timmermann's reaction.

"Thank God, now we won't have to cross that damned thing," Mike Chinchar said fervently, trying to reassure himself.

Johnny Ayres fingered the two grenades hooked onto the rings of his pack suspenders, and nodded his head: "We wouldn't have had a chance."

But Timmermann, who had been trying to make out what was left of the bridge through the thick haze, yelled:

"Look—she's still standing!"

Most of the smoke and dust had cleared away, and the men followed their commander's gaze. The sight of the bridge still spanning the Rhine brought no cheers from the men. It was like an unwelcome specter. The suicide mission was on again.

A thousand feet away, the German soldiers were working frantically around the far end of the bridge. They looked as if they were going to make another attempt to blow the bridge.

"Maybe they're just teasing us to get us out there and then blow us all to kingdom come," Sabia said. "I tell ya it's a trap."

Timmermann's casual air had disappeared. He had thrown away his candy and the grin was gone from his face as he strode up to the bridge. He saw at one glance that although some big holes had been blown in the flooring of the bridge, the catwalks were clear for infantrymen. The Germans were still in a frenzy of activity on the other side and on the bridge itself.

He quickly circled his arm in the air to call his platoon leaders together. Other men clustered around, eager and apprehensive. "O.K., Jim, Mike and Joe, we'll cross the bridge—order of march, first platoon, third platoon and then second platoon."

There was a moment of silence.

Timmermann turned to Burrows, cupped his hand, and said in a low tone: "Jim, I want your platoon to bring up the rear so we have an officer in charge of the last platoon across." Then, in a louder tone which everybody could hear: "And when you get over, Jim, take your platoon up that high hill on the other side. You know, the old Fort Benning stuff: take the high ground and hold it?"

There was no sudden rush to cross the bridge. To the tired, dirty, unshaven men it looked like sudden death. Stomachs were queasy, not only from some wine discovered in Remagen, but from fear.

Timmermann moved tentatively up to the bridge, and started to wave his arm overhead in the traditional "Follow me" gesture. A chattering of machine guns from the towers made him duck. Jack Berry ran up to one of the General Pershing tanks, located Lieutenant Jack Grimball, and pointed at the towers.

Grimball did not hesitate. His Pershing let loose a blast.

Mike Chinchar, leader of the platoon ordered to spearhead the crossing, was knocked off his feet by the concussion. So was Dean Craig. Chinchar and Craig had their faces buried in the mud by the blast. Sabia was lifted off his feet, and shook his head dazedly. Berry laughed uncontrollably as the trio staggered around, spitting out mud and trying to regain their equilibrium.

The tank shell opened a big crack in the tower, and the German machine-gun fire let up.

"Dammit, what's holdin' up the show? Now git goin'!" Timmermann yelled.

Big Tony Samele, who had been in the lead while the first platoon was cleaning out Remagen, turned to his platoon leader, Mike Chinchar: "C'mon, Mike, we'll just walk it across."

At this point, the battalion commander, Major Murray Deevers, called out: "I'll see you on the other side and we'll all have a chicken dinner."

"Chicken dinner, my foot. I'm all chicken right now," one of the men in the first platoon shot back.

Major Deevers flushed. "Move on across," he yelled, sharply.

"I tell ya, I'm not goin' out there and get blown up," the G.I. answered. "No sir, major, you can court-martial and shoot me, but I ain't going out there on that bridge."

While Deevers was arguing, Lieutenant Timmermann was using more direct methods: "Git goin', you guys, git goin'." He moved onto the bridge himself.

Chinchar shouted at Art Massie: "You leapfrog me up as far as that hole that's blown out." Massie had a quick and natural reaction: "I don't wanna but I will."

As they started out onto the bridge, suddenly the man who had been arguing with Major Deevers turned away from Deevers and joined the group from the first platoon which was moving across.

Timmermann's men had just started out onto the bridge when Lieutenant Mott and Sergeants Dorland and Reynolds of the engineers ran out to join them and started cutting wires connected to the demolition charges. The engineers were a doubly welcome sight, because the infantrymen had not expected them. When the big German emergency charge had gone off on the bridge Mott had decided that the main job of his engineers would be to locate and cut the wires to the other demolition charges. The three men joined Timmermann and his lead scouts just as they were starting across the bridge, and there was no time to coordinate any plans as the whole group surged forward.

The right side of the bridge was torn up by the German blasts, and so Chinchar's platoon started down the left catwalk. Here the men had some protection because most of the German rifle and machine-gun fire was coming from the stone tower on the far right end of the bridge. The fire had quieted down after Grimball's tank blast, but it started up again as the first infantrymen picked their way across.

When Chinchar's men were about a third of the way over, they came to a halt as the machine-gun fire intensified. The American tanks were still firing, but the German return fire from both the towers and the tunnel was growing stronger. Nobody dared move ahead.

From a half-submerged barge about two hundred yards upstream, the lead troops were getting more fire. It was not heavy and constant, but two snipers on the barge were beginning to zero in. There were no American tanks on the bridge, and so Timmermann ran back to yell to one of the German Sherman tanks at the bridge approach:

"How about putting something on that barge?"

The tank found the range and blasted the barge with its 75-millimeter gun until a white flag began to flutter.

"That's one thing they never taught us at Fort Knox," said a member of the tank crew later in reviewing his naval exploit.

Even with the barge menace removed, Timmermann faced a crisis. He ran forward to find that his old first platoon was frozen. The tank support was not silencing the opposition. The Germans were still running around on the far side of the river as though they were going to blow the bridge with the American troops on it. Timmermann waved for Sergeant DeLisio, leader of the third platoon.

"Joe, get your platoon up there and get these men off their tail," he yelled above the clatter of tank and machine-gun fire.

The little Bronx sergeant with the twitching mustache started weaving and bobbing across the bridge. One of the motionless figures hugging the flooring of the bridge grumbled as he passed:

"There goes a guy with more guts than sense."

If DeLisio heard him he gave no sign. Soon the rest of his platoon was starting over, and in a minute a few men from Burrows' second platoon had started also.

The reinforcements fired at the tunnel and the towers, and soon the enemy fire began to lessen.

Forrest Miner came up behind one of the men on the bridge and yelled:

"What's holding you guys up?"

"Don't you hear that machine-gun fire?"

"Fer cryin' out loud," Miner lied, "that's our own machine-gun fire coming from behind us."

The man looked incredulous and then hobbled to his feet with a blank and resigned expression on his face.

Above all the noise came Timmermann's constant: "Git goin', git goin'." The company commander was everywhere, spurring, encouraging, and leading his men.

DeLisio worked his way up to the first man on the bridge, a third of the way across, and shouted: "What's the trouble?"

"Trouble? Chrissakes can't you see all that sniper fire?"

"Why worry about a coupla snipers?" DeLisio laughed. "If this bridge blows up we've got a whole battalion on it. Let's get off. C'mon, guys."

DeLisio, of course, was exaggerating—there wasn't a whole battalion on the bridge, only part of A Company; but the psychology worked.

He helped uncork the attack. Other men with "more guts than sense" started to get up and weave and bob behind him.

Sabia started to run, but the bridge turned into an endless treadmill. His leaden feet got heavier and heavier, and he felt as if he had been running for hours and getting nowhere.

Ayres, his grenades and canteen bobbing up and down, suddenly wished he had not consumed so much wine in Remagen, and he vomited on the bridge. Through a blown-out hole in the bridge flooring he saw the swift current below.

"If I fall," he asked himself, "will this pack drag me under?"

Across the river, a German train steamed into view, chugging south.

Colonel Engeman, back in Remagen with his tanks, spotted the train and joyfully exclaimed: "Hallelujah! I've always wanted to fire a tank at a locomotive." Four or five tanks opened up. The firebox of the engine exploded. German troops started pouring out of the train, and set up positions to fire at their tormentors on the bridge and in Remagen.

DeLisio waved back for his support squad, led by Joe Petrencsik and Alex Drabik. Then he edged forward. Heavy fire started to come down on the bridge—20-millimeter shells from German anti-aircraft guns. Petrencsik with a sudden hunch yelled: "Duck!" DeLisio crouched, and something swooshed over his head and took a piece out of one of the stone towers.

In the middle of the bridge, Mott, Dorland and Reynolds found four packages of TNT, weighing 20 to 30 pounds each, tied to I-beams underneath the decking of the bridge. They climbed down and worked their wire-cutters hot until the charges splashed into the Rhine. Above them they heard the heavy tramp of the infantrymen and the hoarse cry of Timmermann which everybody had now taken up: "Git goin'."

Back on the bridge, Dorland started to hack away at a heavy cable.

"Why don't you shoot it in two with your carbine?" Jack Berry asked.

Dorland put the muzzle up against the cable, and blasted it apart.

By this time DeLisio had traveled two-thirds of the way across the bridge. The little sergeant had a theory that if you advanced fast enough you wouldn't get hit, so instead of hugging the bridge when the Germans fired on him from the towers, he simply ran on until he got behind the towers on the German side of the bridge. DeLisio chortled to himself at his good luck, until he looked back and saw that the German fire from the towers was still pinning down the men who were supposed to be following him.

Somebody yelled: "Who's gonna clean out that tower?"

DeLisio took the question as a challenge, and ran back to the tower where most of the fire was coming from.

He pushed aside a few bales of hay blocking the door to the tower. Just as he started into the door, a stray bullet went into the stone wall and ricocheted off. Sabia came up and yelled: "You're hit, Joe."

"You're crazy, Sabia. I don't feel nothin' at all."

Sabia insisted: "I saw that bullet, I tell ya I seen it go right through ya."

DeLisio ran his hands quickly around his field jacket, and finding no blood he brushed Sabia away and went on up into the tower.

Chinchar, Samele, and Massie then went up into the left tower. Everybody else moved forward. Many of them recalled what Nelson Wegener, DeLisio's old platoon sergeant, used to say after nearly every battle: "Guinea, you're one of the luckiest men alive. I dunno how you do it, but you always seem to get out of the toughest scrapes."

DeLisio started running up the circular staircase. There were three floors in the tower, and he couldn't take anything for granted. He heard machine-gun fire above him, and then it suddenly stopped. Had the Germans heard him coming, and was he heading into a trap?

He slapped open a steel door with the heel of his hand and burst in on three German soldiers. They were bending over a machine gun, as though it were jammed. There was an agonizing second as the three men jerked their heads around. DeLisio pumped out a couple of shots with his carbine, firing from the hip.

"Hände hoch!" he yelled.

The three Germans wheeled around with their hands in the air. DeLisio motioned them to one side with his carbine, and seizing the gun they had been using he hurled it out of the window. Men starting across the bridge saw the gun plummet from the tower and began to move with more confidence.

In his pidgin German and his sign language, DeLisio tried to find out if there were any more soldiers left in the tower. His captives assured him that there weren't. But DeLisio was skeptical and he motioned for them to precede him up the stairs.

On the top floor of the tower, DeLisio pushed the three Germans into a room, where he found a German lieutenant and his orderly. The lieutenant dived for the corner of the room, but DeLisio stopped him with a couple of shots. He took away the lieutenant's Walther pistol. Then he marched all five prisoners down the stairs and told them to proceed unescorted over the bridge to Remagen. They were the first in a long parade of German prisoners taken near the bridge.

Over in the left tower, Chinchar, Samele and Massie also tossed a German machine gun out the window and captured one cowering soldier. The flushing of the towers cost all of those involved the honor of being the first across the Rhine.

Alex Drabik, one of DeLisio's assistant squad leaders, had not seen him go into the tower and started looking for his platoon leader. He asked several people on the bridge, but nobody seemed to know. He made up his mind that there was only one thing to do.

"Let's go!" he shouted. "DeLisio must be over there on the other side all alone."

Drabik took off for the east bank, weaving and wobbling. Just before he got across the bridge he jounced so much that he lost his helmet. He did not stop to pick it up but kept running at top speed until he became the first soldier to cross the Rhine.

At Drabik's heels came the Minnesota plasterer named Marvin Jensen, repeating: "Holy crap, do you think we'll make it, do you think we'll make it?"

Drabik was the first man over, followed closely by Jensen, Samele, DeLisio, Chinchar, Massie, Sabia, a Missourian named Martin Reed and a North Carolinian named Joseph Peoples. A few seconds later Karl Timmermann, the first officer over, set foot on the German side of the Rhine.

Once over the bridge Drabik wheeled to the left, still looking for DeLisio, and raced about two hundred yards up the river road. The rest of his squad followed close behind, and he hastily set up a skirmish line in a series of bomb craters to ward off a possible German counterthrust.

The bridge itself was still a big question mark for the Americans. Every man that crossed it wondered if the Germans had yet played their final card. Were they saving up a more devastating stroke that would at any moment topple the entire structure into the Rhine? The three engineers, Mott, Dorland and Reynolds, methodically searched for the master switch that controlled the German demolitions. Near the eastern end of the bridge, Dorland finally located the box that housed the switch, went to work on the heavy wires leading from it, and blasted them apart with a few rounds from his carbine. A few minutes later, the three engineers came upon a large unexploded 500 to 600 pound charge with its fuse cap blown. Mott and his men examined it closely and found it correctly wired and prepared for detonation. Cutting all attached wires, they made it harmless.

At the Remagen end of the bridge, Colonel Engeman, Captain Soumas, and Lieutenant Miller drove their men hard to clear the way for tanks and vehicles. While Mott and his two sergeants were ripping out demolition wires and determining whether the bridge could hold traffic, other engineers checked the approaches for mines and pondered the problem of filling up the tremendous crater at the bridge approach. Miller finally called up Sergeant Swayne, whose tank was equipped with a blade to operate like a bulldozer, and Swayne began pushing dirt and debris into the big hole.

On the east bank DeLisio, who had stepped off the bridge shortly after Drabik, had already been sent by Timmermann on another trouble-shooting assignment. With four of his best men, the little sergeant crept forward to investigate the menacing railroad tunnel at the end of the bridge. None of the Americans knew how strong a force the Germans had hidden in the blackness of the tunnel. All they knew was that it gave the enemy excellent cover and concealment and that from it the occupants had ideal observation over the entire length of the bridge.

The five men moved forward cautiously, hugging the ground as shots rang out of the dark. When they reached the entrance, DeLisio fired two shots into the tunnel, and several German engineers quickly ran out, hands high above their heads, as if they had been eagerly awaiting this chance to give themselves up. Misled by the easy capture of this handful of the enemy, DeLisio failed to realize that there was a much stronger force deep in the tunnel. Moving his prisoners back, he reported to Timmermann that the tunnel looked clear and then joined Drabik along the river road.

Inside the tunnel, a German major and captain had received word shortly before four o'clock that the Americans had crossed the bridge. The news spread immediately through the milling throng of soldiers and civilians, and it became almost impossible to maintain even a semblance of order. Tank shells were bursting inside the tunnel, rifle fire was ricocheting off the walls, and three railroad tank cars were dripping gasoline that formed pools of potential destruction at the feet of the miserable tunnel occupants. Panic-stricken civilians were clawing at the soldiers to stop resistance. Except for the few prudent engineers near the entrance who had made the most of their opportunity to surrender to DeLisio's patrol, few of the terrified Germans were aware even that five Americans had come and gone.

By a little after four o'clock Timmermann had only about 120 men on the east bank. As an experienced infantryman he had recognized immediately from the other side of the river that the Erpeler Ley, the highest point in the immediate area, had to be taken fast. Summoning Lieutenant Burrows, he ordered him to take the second platoon up the precipitous slope. The heights of the Erpeler Ley, as well as the tunneled depths, had become crucial.

Burrows later said: "Taking Remagen and crossing the bridge were a breeze compared with climbing that hill." The lower slope was very steep, and the face of the cliff was covered with loose rock. Footing was slippery, and several men were severely injured when they fell. About halfway to the summit the Americans began receiving 20-millimeter fire. The trees were leafless, and there was little underbrush in which to hide. Silhouetted against the face of the black cliff, the climbing men were easy targets for the German anti-aircraft gunners. The Erpeler Ley quickly became known as Flak Hill.

At first the fire seemed to come from the west bank. Colonel Engeman sent one of his light tank platoons, under Lieutenant Demetri Paris, to clean out the pocket; but the anti-aircraft fire continued with such intensity that Burrows' men soon became convinced that it was coming from the northern part of the bridgehead. Some of them crawled around the nose of the bluff to the right to get out of the line of fire. Others slid or rolled to the base of the cliff.

Burrows' casualties mounted. His platoon sergeant, Bill Shultz, was severely wounded in the leg by a 20-millimeter shellburst. Ralph Munch and Frankie Marek took refuge in a small crater-like depression, and Munch had just moved to another spot when a mortar shell burst close to Marek and sent a piece of shrapnel through him below his lungs. Those men who finally managed to reach the top saw only a few small sheds across a field about a hundred yards away and a handful of German soldiers wandering around unconcernedly. Jim Cardinale, one of the American machine gunners, called excitedly, "Come on, lemme paste those guys but good."

"Shut up or we'll shoot you by God," one of the other men threatened in low but urgent tones. "We'll shoot you and push you off the cliff—you want to give our position away?"

Cardinale calmed down, and the Americans atop the cliff began a period of cautious and worried waiting. They could see numerous German infantrymen and vehicles in neighboring towns. At the base of the hill and along the side the firing got heavier. The enemy seemed to be moving in for a counterattack.

The advance guard of the Remagen crossing was in a precarious position. With no weapons more powerful than light machine guns, Timmermann called for his anti-tank platoon under Lieutenant Dave Gardner to come to the east bank, instructing them to bring as many of their .50-caliber machine guns as they could and employ them on ground mounts covering the roads into the bridgehead. Gardner's men also brought over four rocket launchers and set them up in pairs with the machine guns.

Timmermann then appealed for more men, more weapons and more support. The battalion commander, Major Deevers, sent over Lieutenant Bill McMaster's C Company, followed by Lieutenant Jack Liedike's B Company about half-past four. Their arrival eased the situation, but the battalion was still woefully weak and too strung out to present a very firm defense against a counterattack. Had German tanks struck at the flimsy American force between four and five o'clock, the Remagen bridgehead would certainly have been wiped out.

This possibility troubled Timmermann a great deal as he took stock of his thin line of men. It also troubled the men, and weighed heavily on the minds of the B and C Company reinforcements that came across the bridge. Everybody was either asking about the arrival of American tanks or fearing the arrival of German tanks. The sound of German vehicles came from neighboring villages. Patrols on the edge of the bridgehead confirmed the suspicion that German forces were moving up for a counterattack.

On the Remagen bank Lieutenant Mott and armored engineers were doing everything possible to make the bridge serviceable for tank traffic. Makeshift repairs were made in the shattered planking, but it soon became clear that the bridge would not hold tanks before dark.

The officers and men on the east bank chafed at the delay. They knew that infantry alone would never be able to hang on to their slim toehold. Runners started back across the bridge with urgent requests for help. Not long before dusk, the sight of these runners caused a flurry of uneasy excitement. The backfire of German vehicles in the distance started more rumors that Tiger tanks were moving toward the bridge. Along thousands of yards of thinly held front the troops were so widely scattered that many of them lost contact. Small groups drifted back across the bridge. In the space of an hour parts of the three companies on the east bank slipped back to Remagen in confusion and disorganization.

But the majority of the 27th Armored Infantry Battalion held on. Among those who remained were many who looked about for fellow Americans without seeing any; and the story later spread that only a few men had held the east bank of the Rhine on the night of March 7. Actually, the reinforcement of the bridgehead was resumed at dusk, and from then on throughout the night an almost steady stream of men crossed the bridge to bolster the defenses on the east bank.

The Enemy at Bay

It would be at least two weeks before the 1st Army could get permission to drive farther into the Rhineland from the Remagen bridgehead. But meanwhile Patton had got a division of his 3rd Army across the Rhine before Montgomery had. Even so, SHAEF was still holding out for Montgomery to launch the main drive at the Ruhr from the north. Now all that remained of the German forces west of the Rhine was in the Saar, and here Gen. Jacob Devers had Gen. Patch's 7th Army poised to drive through the defenses. Eisenhower wanted to clear the whole line west of the Rhine so there would be no bridgehead for a German counteroffensive. Bradley persuaded Eisenhower to let Patton strike across the Moselle River and wheel southward behind the Saar defenses, isolating the Germans in their Siegfried Line. The 1st and 3rd Armies were to conduct an encirclement of the Ruhr, while Devers pounded away frontally at the Siegfried Line.

The 7th Army began to cut into the tough Siegfried Line defenses, and met with desperate fighting. One of the assault regiments was the 274th, and one of its colonels, Wallace Cheves, has prepared one of the few histories, either regimental or divisional, that report the fighting from the perspective of the infantryman. The following chapter is a condensed version of the last bitter days of the fighting.

SMASHING THE SIEGFRIED LINE

by Lt. Col. Wallace Cheves

By March 2nd, the entire 274th Infantry regiment was looking down onto the vast plain which harbored the French border cities of Forbach, Stiring-Wendel and Neue-

Glashutte. In foxholes extending from Spichern Heights to Kreutzberg Ridge, nearly everyone of us had a grandstand view of the German fortifications inside the towns. The 276th had already taken most of Forbach after bitter house to house fighting. Stiring-Wendel and the cluster of small villages around it formed the last major barrier before the Siegfried Line and the Saar Basin.

The valley looked like a picture of peace and contentment, but to us who had to fight for it, it looked like the front yard of hell. The Germans had sowed a murderous crop of mines in the fields around the towns, and their field guns had every avenue of approach zeroed in. The 274th had one of the toughest jobs before it. We weren't just taking another town, we were cracking the strongest net of fortifications ever constructed by the human race. Our job was to breach the famed wall and establish a corridor through which our armies could race to the heart of Germany.

German artillery pounded the ridges with great ferocity. In addition, the infamous rocket gun, the "Screaming Meemie" or "Ole Rusty Barrel," was brought into action. It proved to be one of the most effective weapons the Krauts possessed.

"We could hear it fired in the distance," recalls Pfc. Harry Bealor. "It made a grating noise like the bark of a seal, or like someone scratching his fingernails across a piece of tin. Then for several seconds, everything would be quiet until it hit. The explosion sounded as though someone struck a match in the Krupp Works. You'd think the whole damn mountain had exploded. I've seen guys picked right up off the ground and thrown several feet through the air by the concussion."

By the afternoon of March 2nd, rumor that a full scale push was close circulated through the foxholes. TD's came up from the rear and poked their heavy guns out of the trees toward Stiring-Wendel.

"That's no good," swore Pfc. Ralph Schaefer as one of the iron monsters rolled up near his dugout. "Those bastards draw fire."

As if to prove he was telling the truth, a short time later

the hills were jarred by rockets and 88's. Every time the TD's moved, a half dozen more rounds would come in.

That evening company commanders and platoon leaders were called to battalion CP's to get attack orders for the morning. One paragraph in the attack order explained everything. It read:

"Attack H-hour from present positions. Overrun Stiring-Wendel, detaching units to clear the enemy from the city. Special attention to hostile positions covering the Forbach-Stiring-Wendel road. Continue the advance and seize that part of the Division Objective in Regimental Zone of Action. Organize and defend final objective. Mop up enemy within Regimental Zone by-passed during the advance. Relieve armored force blocking NE approaches to Stiring-Wendel. Maintain contact with 276th Infantry. Not less than one company will remain on Kreutzberg Ridge."

Colonel Conley chose Col. Boyd's second and Col. Landstrom's third battalions to make the main assault. Each had a company of French troops to mop up after it and take care of prisoners. The First Battalion was to remain on Spichern Heights and co-ordinate a defense there with the 275th Infantry. The big question then was which companies would catch the hell and which would be in reserve. In the Second Battalion, Fox and George were selected to make the advance with Easy in reserve, and in the 3rd Battalion, Item and King would assault, with Love in reserve.

It's hard to sleep the night before a big push. Most of us stayed awake all night trying to get our equipment ready, or just lay out under the stars thinking. Others gathered around in small groups and told stories far into the night. Still others, like Pfc. Bobby Hawthorne, threw a raincoat over the entrance of his foxhole to keep out the candlelight and read the New Testament.

In the early morning hours of March 3rd, while the moon was high, bathing the battlefield in a strange, ethereal light, we were quietly awakened by messengers from the CP. The empty dread that "this was it" arose in every man's mind. We crawled out of our blankets, slipped into our packs and waited. Sgt. Robertson of Item Company drew the first assignment. He was to go down to the little village of Sophia on the left flank and protect the main assault force against counterattack from that direction.

Back on the ridges, preparations for the attack were in full swing. It was a bright, clear spring morning, but the gaiety, the joy of being alive on such a morning was noticeably absent. In the trees above, birds were singing and darting back and forth among the branches. Some of us who took a few seconds off to watch the sun climb over the hills across the valley wondered if we would ever see the sun rise again.

By 0800 we were swarming through the woods heading for the line of departure. Companies F, G, I and K lined up to spearhead the drive. Tanks were to furnish support as soon as the roads into the town were cleared. Air missions were available upon one hour notice. Just a short time before H-hour, several squadrons of P-47's bombed and strafed the Metz Highway which was the main German supply route.

Promptly at 0817 after a ten minute artillery barrage, all units jumped off on schedule. All companies moved out abreast, keeping close contact, swinging slightly to the right and going down the hill. The 3rd Battalion went down on the left with Capt. Keith's Item Co. and Lt. Crowson's King Co. assaulting, Love in reserve. Col. Landstrom directed the entire battalion drive from a CP on top of Kreutzberg Ridge where the whole breadth of the battlefield could be observed.

Shortly after the drive got underway, King ran against a pillbox and a heavy minefield and was stopped cold. Item and Fox Companies, on either flank, were also forced to stop until the obstacles had been knocked out, to prevent a dangerous gap from forming. "King" fought hard to smash through, but death waited at the end of every step. Thousands of murderous shu-mines dotted the ground concealed under a few inches of dirt. One ill-placed step and a man's legs were blown horribly from his body.

"The machine gunners were out in front supporting the leading third platoon," said S/Sgt. Forrest Boughton. "We were trying to work forward to positions where we could button up the pillbox. Lt. Rytting was up forward on reconnaissance crawling around through the mines as calmly as though he were walking through a potato field back home in Idaho. War was a game to 'Riddle' as we called him. To him the only way to win it was to get in the thick of it and play hard. Physically, he was as big and tough as the West he came out of. When he came overseas he was the first one in the company to be battlefield commissioned. The bar didn't mean anything to him. He would have been leading if he were only wearing a Pfc.'s stripe. That's what he was doing when he went after the pillbox. He went up so close that he got down on his hands and knees and started crawling. He hadn't gone very far when the ground seemed to blow up from under him. We saw his leg go flying through the air and his whole body leap up and then roll on the ground. The pain and the shock almost paralyzed him. He never lost consciousness, though. He just lay quietly on the ground and waited for stretcher bearers to pick him up."

Fortunately both T-4 Kinsley, the platoon aid man, and a litter squad under Pfc. Dunning were close by.

"Going up to get Lt. Rytting was a dangerous job," said Dunning. "He was lying right in the middle of the mines. The guy who went after him stood a good chance of having the same thing happen to him. Kinsley took the chance though. He picked his way along, living a thousand years with every step he took. It's hell going through mines. It takes every gut a guy's got to move his feet.

"Kinsley reached Rytting's side safely and gave him a morphine injection to stop the pain, and then bandaged the stump of his leg as best he could. About that time we heard another explosion not far away and a cry for medic, and Kinsley started over to help. He only went a couple of feet when he himself stepped on a mine."

Kinsley tried to get up and walk on the stump of his leg but fell helplessly to the ground. Dunning heard him cry out and started up with his litter squad to get him. When they reached the spot, Kinsley was sitting on the ground trying to tie a tourniquet around his leg. One of the litter bearers tried to give him a shot of morphine but he couldn't push the needle through the skin.

"Kinsley grabbed the syringe out of my hands," said Pfc.

Tepper. " 'Give me that thing,' he said. 'I'll give it to myself.' Dunning and I fixed up the tourniquet and before we could help him, Kinsley climbed onto the stretcher himself. The pain must have been pretty bad. All the while we were carrying him back he kept saying, 'My leg is gone. I saw it fly through the air. I'll never be able to walk or finish college again.' We brought him and Lt. Rytting to the aid station together. Rytting was pretty far gone. He didn't want to leave the rest of his men. When they gathered around his litter to wish him luck he just said, 'You guys take it easy.' Then we carried him away."

In the meantime the pillboxes and mine field had brought the entire attack to a standstill. The halt was just what the Germans were waiting for. From OP's in town and the hills across the valley they had a perfect picture of us standing in the open near the base of the hill. Artillery, mortars, rockets . . . everything that the Kraut possessed was thrown at us. The earth was ripped and torn and the whole area pockmarked with shell holes. The trees were sheared down to shattered trunks. All along the line we clawed into the ground trying to escape the flying shell fragments. A thick, black, dry, suffocating curtain of smoke hung over the whole area. Every few seconds another shell would explode with a murderous red flash and send death-dealing shrapnel shrieking among the prostrate troops. It looked for a while as though the attack would end before it began. It seemed impossible that men could come out of the barrage alive. Yet, the battalion held its ground. There was no sign of a break, or a panic. Everybody just gritted his teeth and held on. "King" continued to hammer at the pillbox. Item started down the hill on the extreme left flank with the second platoon in the lead. Lt. Wilson, the company executive officer, declined to remain with the rear CP when the push started and joined Lt. Beck at the head of the column. The leading platoon was armed with three bazookas, several rifle grenades, a flame thrower and, in addition, each man carried a white phosphorous grenade.

The first barrage came in fast and caught the men off guard. Both Wilson and Beck kept the company moving, pushing down through the trees with scouts out. Enemy fire became more intense. A pattern of mortar shells exploded all around the platoon and the men dove into the ground. Recognizing the danger, Wilson immediately got the men to their feet.

"Beck, this is costing us lives," he said. "We'd better keep moving." So we drove on. We hadn't gone far when another concentration of mortars fell around us . . . this time with deadly effect. Lt. Beck, walking near the head of the column, was hit by a piece of shrapnel which punctured the phosphorous grenade he carried in his belt. A sheet of dazzling white flame enveloped and nearly consumed his body. In the same barrage, Pfcs. Paris, Harlen, Adams, Sanvas and Jessop were hit. Lt. Wilson led the rest of the platoon across an open fire break, through a net of barbed wire and into the trees on the other side. By this time the full force of the barrage was falling in back of us. Wilson's decision to keep moving had saved many lives.

Lt. Eblem's Fox and Lt. Cassidy's George Companies, moving down on the right flank of King, also came to a halt after they pulled abreast of the general line of attack. There, they too felt the force of the artillery barrage. All efforts were bent upon getting King through the mine field and net of pillboxes. Finally, about 1030, Col. Landstrom decided to bypass both pillbox and mine field, leaving them for Love Company, which was in reserve, to neutralize. Lt. Crowson then swung King wide to the left, leaving a large gap in the lines which was to be closed as soon as the mines were cleared.

A killing concentration of fire continued to pour in on King as it moved out from the foot of the hill. T/5 Jimmie Owen, medic for the first platoon, found himself with a double job after Kinsley had been evacuated. The whole forest rang with cries of the wounded and shouts of "Medic!"

"I emptied my medical pouches that day," said Owen. "I tried to take care of the worst cases first but there were so many I hardly knew which ones needed help the most. As soon as possible I got a line of walking wounded started back up the hill to the aid station. It was almost impossible to evacuate the serious cases. The casualty collecting point was in the edge of a woods clear at the top of the ridge. About two trips up that hill with a litter was all a guy could stand."

As the casualties began to mount, additional litter teams from our 370th Collecting Company were rushed to the 3rd Battalion aid station. By 0900 in the morning the wounded were streaming in. Most of them were numb from shock. The courage displayed by the men who had been hit was remarkable.

"No matter how bad they were hit they wanted us to look out for their buddies first," said Pfc. Monroe Gable. "I met M/Sgt. Lewis Ripley coming back from the front with a crude bandage wrapped around a hole as big as an egg in his elbow. His face was an ashen gray and he could hardly walk, but he refused to let me give him first aid or a shot of morphine. He told me to help the other boys first."

After King Company passed on, one squad of Love, supported by a tank, was dispatched to take care of the troublesome pillbox.

"While we kept the bunker buttoned up with rifle and machine gun fire, the tanks threw a couple of 75-mm armor piercing shells into the embrasure. After a while we heard the Krauts hollering inside and saw them stick a white flag out the door. We thought there were only a couple in there but it seemed like half of the Wehrmacht came streaming out with their hands up in the air. By the time it was all over we counted twenty-five scared Krauts."

The whole line of attack once again started to move forward, this time opposed by every bit of power the Germans could muster against it.

"We slipped and slid and dove for holes wherever we could find them," said Sgt. McNeely of Item Co. "Every time the rounds came in some one else would scream for medics. Lt. Wemple was hit in the ribs and Sgt. Hoot in the legs and stomach. Pfc. Ryan ran over to them and administered first aid but Hoot died on his way to the aid station. Everyone clawed the ground and waited in mortal dread that the next round would be for him. I saw Sgt. Harm picked up and thrown down again by an exploding 88 that dug holes all around him and then went sailing off into the air to rip off the branches of a tree that fell down on top of him. In the midst of the din I heard Lt. Wilson shout for us to move on again. Mortar and artillery rounds were coming in as fast as they could be shot out of guns. We wondered how long they could keep it up . . . and how long we could stand it. As we got in closer we could hear rifles beginning to fire. I knew we must be in closer now. Long bursts from our light machine guns and BAR's cracked nearby—followed by answering bursts from enemy Burp guns. There were a lot of pillboxes in front of us to be blown and a squad of engineers was following close behind us loaded down with high explosives. If one of their shape charges were ever hit it would have cleaned out an area of about 100 yards."

George Company had come all the way from billets in Etzlingen to take part in the attack. We moved up into the ridges and took up positions just to the right of Fox. Most of the men were fresh after a short rest in French homes and in spite of the seriousness of the situation, went into the attack with a cocky cheerfulness. Pfc. William Bloom was nicknamed "The Walking Pineapple" by the other members of his platoon. In addition to three fragmentation grenades tied onto his belt, he carried a white phosphorous grenade, a thermite grenade, and a Kraut flare pistol with 16 flares of different colors. Lt. Cassidy led off with the second platoon and followed a small trench along the crest of the ridges just before peeling off down the hill.

"We could hear King's boys running into a lot of trouble below us, and we were forced to hold up awhile," said Sgt. Robert Kirk. "King's casualties were streaming back, both on litters and on foot. The sight of them was enough to take the heart right out of a guy. Kraut artillery was falling as far back as we were and some of their boys were being hit again. We moved down along the trenches, sweating out heavy enemy mortars. Some of our own 4.2's were located just behind us and the Krauts were raking the area with counter-battery. Most of it was falling on us instead of on the mortars. After a while we were ordered to move up to a large cave which Lt. Cassidy was using as temporary Company CP. We started to dig in but the ground was so rocky it was almost impossible. About that time Pfc. Tice came up with orders to start moving again."

"It was then that the Krauts saw me," continued Tice. "I knew it was coming as soon as I heard the croak of a Screaming Meemie off in the distance. Everybody else heard it too, and just stopped in his tracks and wondered if it was coming our way. Then it hit. The first rounds struck a trench where the second squad was waiting and wounded Pfcs. Neagle, Malcolm and Daniels. The whole squad was nearly buried in the eruption of earth. Several rifles were smashed to pieces, Sgt. Dunbar was stunned by the shock but refused to be evacuated and helped reorganize the squad. We never lost our respect for the 'rusty barrel' after that. It was a killer."

After that first blast the Krauts let up on the fire somewhat, probably figuring that most of the target had been obliterated. Lt. Cassidy took advantage of the lull to make a reconnaissance down the hill with Lt. Sims and Pfc. Tice. About 150 yards ahead they found a heavily armed pillbox. The company then moved out with the third platoon on the left and the second platoon on the right. The advance was extremely dangerous because the Germans had excellent observation while our own visibility was blocked by a dense growth of trees. Enemy mortars again picked us up as we moved down the hill. Burst blanketed the whole area, falling with fatal suddenness upon the advancing platoons. Several men were seriously wounded. The rest darted from cover to cover never knowing who was going to be the next one wounded.

The third squad of the third platoon went forward to act as point. Suddenly, the scouts pushed out over the nose of the hill and were silhouetted against the sky. The Germans were waiting for them. Almost immediately a withering blast of machine-gun fire from a row of camouflaged bunkers in a wooded ravine below poured into them. Pvts. Flynn and Fixler were hit instantly. Pfc. John Hudak, acting as squad leader, came up to get his men out of trouble and in doing so was caught in a blast of automatic fire and killed. The rest of the squad hit the dirt and waited. After several minutes our artillery observer came up and directed a concentration of 105's on the bunkers and succeeded in forcing them to button up. We rushed in on the heels of the barrage and swarmed around the bunkers. Within a short time the occupants of several of them were flushed out with hand grenades. Several prisoners were taken . . . others stubbornly refused to come out and were blown up inside the pillbox. By this time the company had reached the edge of the woods and halted there until Lt. Cassidy could contact Col. Boyd and receive further orders.

On the extreme right flank Charlie Co. was pushing down the hill toward the small town of Golden Brahn through scattered resistance. During the early part of the attack German observers failed to see us sweeping down toward the village and the company was able to approach its objective undetected and thereby escaping the tremendous artillery barrage which was being poured into the other assaulting units. Soon after that, however, Sgt. Swinehart, who was near the point of the advance, seemed to jump into the air. A shattering explosion followed and a large cloud of dirt and mud flew into the air. The terrifying cry of "Mines" rang through the forest.

"We froze in our tracks," recalls Sgt. Hazelwood. "We didn't know how far we had gone into them and no one knew whether or not his next step would blow him into eternity. We then started moving to the left to get on a small road which we were pretty sure was clear. Every man walked with his heart in his mouth. Pretty soon we stopped again as an other explosion went off nearby. We saw Pfc. Leach, the medic, take off running through the mine field and knew someone else had been hit. Later we found it was Pvt. Kinney. We kept on going, feeling out every step until we finally reached the road."

We then moved down the left side of the road along a high stone wall which afforded some protection from mortar and artillery shells. Each man followed in the footsteps of the man in front of him. Pfc. Fulkerson, first scout of one of the squads, wandered slightly out of line and lost his foot in the explosion of a mine. We continued to move on until we reached the first outlying houses of the town. No hostile fire was met and at first it was believed that the Germans had pulled out and left the village to its fate. Hazelwood's squad cleared the first house without opposition. Sgt. Walker's squad worked around through a tank ditch to take the second house when our own artillery, late in coming in, began to fall dangerously close. Several members of the squad, who had advanced on the houses, were blown back into the ditch by the concussion. Word was immediately hollered back to "Lift that goddamn artillery."

Walker then went into the second house and fired his rifle down the cellar stairs into the darkness. His shots were answered by a scream and cry of pain. Several men were stationed around the outside of the house to block all and any chances of escape, and Walker, Martin, and Lloyd started down to blow the Krauts out. German artillery now began falling with deadly accuracy throughout the area. The windows of the house were blown out and shrapnel tore through the walls. Pvts. Swirepa, Shake and Reilly, standing outside in the yard, were wounded. All casualties were brought inside where they waited until late afternoon before they could be evacuated. The heavy artillery fire made it impossible to get them out during the day.

Germans could be heard moving around down in the basement. Pfc. Hays crept around the outside of the house keeping close to the walls until he came to a basement window with a stove pipe protruding from it. Hays glanced at the pipe and drew a grenade. Sgt. Yeryar saw him from across the street and shouted, "Hays, put that damn grenade away, I'm going to get a bazooka."

"I can't," replied Hays, "I lost the pin."

"All right, then, throw it."

Hays rolled the grenade down the stove pipe and ducked around the corner. In a few seconds, soot, pipes, stove and Krauts blew for half a block. Thirteen Germans, including one infantry Lieutenant, all black as the characters in a minstrel show, came up out of the cellar and surrendered. From them, Walker learned that there were no more enemy troops in the block. In rapid succession the next three houses were occupied. Strong points were established at the end of the street and the company waited there for reorganization and instructions for its next move.

In the meantime, Item and King companies were continuing to run the gauntlet of fire. Casualties were severe. Practically every non-com in King Company's third platoon had been hit. Conflicting orders and lack of leadership added to the chaos. Twice the company tried to pull out of position and assault and twice it was forced back. Item was driving through a woods thick with small fir trees and lofty pines.

"The only way we had a semblance of control was by constant yelling," said Sgt. McNeely. "The undergrowth was so thick we could hardly get through it. Sometimes we'd get caught in the bushes and have to back up and find a new way through. We found a few small caves that looked like they might be hiding places for Krauts so we dropped grenades in and moved on. Before long we drew near to the place where we knew a line of pillboxes was located. We got down on our stomachs and started to crawl toward them. Pretty soon we ran into a thick net of barbed wire. Apparently the Krauts were waiting for us to stop here like ducks in a shooting gallery because they had several machine guns all set up and as soon as we hit the wire they opened up. Lt. Wilson told us to hold our ground and to spread out so we could set up a base of fire. We got a bead on the Kraut guns and as soon as they opened up we let them have it. Everyone got pretty excited and started to yell—'Pour it on 'em. Give 'em hell! Let's show 'em there are some Yanks up here!' The Krauts must have thought that an army of 'banshees' was after them for soon all of the machine guns were silenced. I don't know if we killed them or not, but if they weren't dead, they were too scared to fire."

All this time Lt. Wilson was bringing up more men to build a stronger firing line. However, because of the jungle maze of barbed wire, which was undoubtedly thickly mined, he decided not to attack at this particular spot. There was no glamour, no dash about it when Lt. Wilson gave an order. He spoke with a quiet voice which encouraged rather than demanded.

"All right, boys," he would say. "Let's go around to the right now. Everybody up, come on, let's go."

We pulled back away from the wire and followed Wilson around toward the right flank.

"We went through the woods to the right until Wilson was satisfied that we had gone far enough," said Pfc. Corrigan. "Then he said, 'Okay, out of the woods and into the clearing, boys, just keep walking until fired upon.' "

We formed another skirmish line and headed toward the edge of the woods. As soon as we got into the clearing, machine guns opened up on us and everyone hit the ground. The only one left on his feet was Wilson. He just said, "That's all right, men, we'll just keep going. We'll cross this in short rushes. Come on now, let's go!"

One by one the men leaped up and dashed across the open ground in short bounds. Wilson remained on his feet among them, urging them on. "That's it," he would say when a man made a good rush. "About ten steps and hit the dirt!" Then he saw another that didn't quite satisfy him. "You there, soldier. That wasn't a rush . . . that was just a flop. Let's see you get up and give a good rush."

"It was one of the most amazing things I've ever seen," continued Corrigan. "He was standing up just like he was umpiring a training problem back in the states. I don't know how he escaped being killed. He was moving erect right in the middle of the enemy fire just as though bullets couldn't hurt him."

A huge tank trap was running down the middle of the clearing parallel to the railroad tracks.

"All right," said Wilson. "Let's see who's going to be the first man to hit that tank ditch!"

Driven by the sight of cover and protection from the deadly machine gun bullets, everyone raced low across the open ground and dove into the ditch. It was a huge excavation about twelve feet deep and ten feet wide. Wilson was one of the last to come sailing in from above. He soon saw, however, that unless we moved on, the attack would bog down there. Before he had time to take a breathing spell he was urging the men on again.

"Let's pull ourselves out of here," he said. "Up, now. Come on, let's get together and crawl out."

We slipped and slid and clawed and scratched at the

muddy embankment . . . pulling ourselves up and falling helplessly back. The greatest concentration of small arms fire against us seemed to be coming from the cellar window of one of the houses on the outskirts of town. As the men emerged from the trap they poured a heavy volume of rifle fire into the position. We crossed the railroad tracks with guns blazing.

"When we got close to the house the Krauts poked a white flag out the window," continued Corrigan. "When the guys saw it they only got sore. Everyone was for moving in and cleaning them out, but Wilson wouldn't let them. He told me to holler over that if the Krauts wanted to surrender they must come out with their hands over their heads and they wouldn't be hurt. I yelled at them across the street and soon after the first one came running over. He was a corporal and was sweating and trembling like he figured we were going to murder him right there in the street. I asked him where the rest of them were, and he said they were too afraid to come out of the house. I gave him one more chance to get them out in a hell of a hurry or else. Everyone was getting impatient and wanted to go over and blow them out with grenades, but Wilson wanted to take them alive if possible. Finally the corporal succeeded in getting them out. They were three of the most frightened men I've ever seen."

As soon as the Germans surrendered, Wilson went into the house to insure that it was all clear. Machine gun bullets were still ripping through the walls and knocking plaster all over the floor. At a signal from Wilson, Corrigan came running across the street and entered the house from a window on the side.

"We are being fired upon from the next room," said Wilson. "I want you to holler in there and tell them to come out and give themselves up."

Corrigan shouted but received no answer. Corrigan and Doyle then forced open the door and found the room empty. Then they realized that the fire was coming from one of the pillboxes they had bypassed outside. As the two men were standing there, Sgt. McNeely came running over from across the street to enter the house. As he was climbing through the window two shots rang out from outside and hit him in the head. He dropped to the floor, his feet still on the sill. Then he started gasping and coughing and

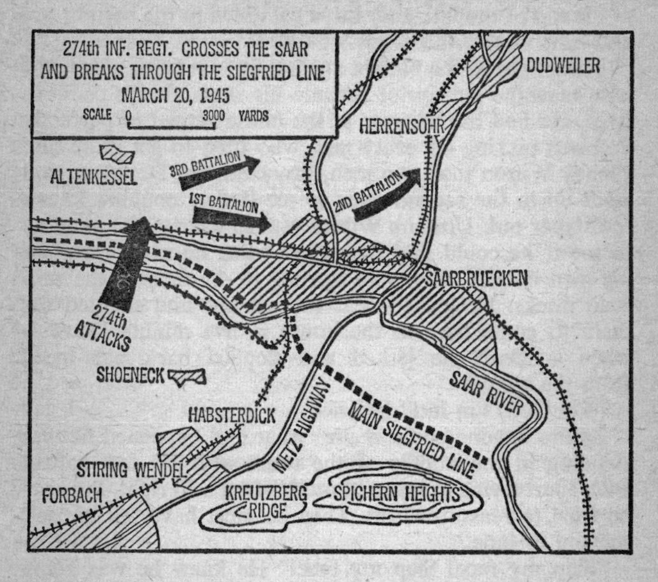

rolled back his half open eyes. Blood was coming from his nose and mouth. Corrigan and Doyle dragged him away from the sill.

"Don't worry, Sergeant," said Wilson. "We'll fix you up."

The three men took care of him as best they could until medical help arrived. In the meantime Wilson and Corrigan went down into the basement of the house to see if any more snipers were concealed there.

"I asked Wilson if I should toss a couple of grenades down before us," said Corrigan. "He said not to, though, because he didn't want to mess it up. So he went down first and walked right into the basement. If there had been anyone down there he would have made a perfect target. Luckily the place was deserted. When we made certain that everything was all clear we went upstairs. Just as we did so, one of the engineers who had accompanied us was shot in the hips and back as he was coming through the window. Of the twelve engineers who started out with us at the top of the hill, only three got down to the bottom . . . and now one of them was wounded."

The sniper in the pillbox apparently was using some sort of a machine gun pistol because his shots always came in twos. He had the window of the house zeroed in perfectly and was picking off every man who tried to get in or out. Finally Wilson took two men, Brancieri and Donovan, and went up to the second floor to see if they couldn't knock the sniper out. Upstairs Wilson walked over to the window to see if he could find the sniper when he saw several of his men outside who were starting to dig in near the railroad tracks. He leaned near the window and shouted for them to come over to the house in five minute intervals when suddenly he jerked and stepped back pale-faced from the window.

"My God, I'm hit!" he cried.

Before anyone could realize what had happened he was standing in the middle of the room with his feet spread wide apart trying to brace himself. "That's all right, I'm . . ." he tried to reassure them. Then he must have felt himself starting to fade.

"Slap my face! Slap my face!" He knew he was going but couldn't make himself accept the fact.

Brancieri struck him across the cheeks but his life had already drained from him. He fell to the floor and doubled up his legs and kicked a heavy oak table across the room. That was all. He was dead.

"When I went upstairs it was all over," recalls Corrigan. "I opened his shirt and found two small bullet holes just above his heart. There was not a trace of blood on the outside. He must have bled internally. I realized sooner or later he would have been killed but now that it happened none of us could quite believe it. I took the codes and overlays out of his pockets and looked at his AGO card. He was only 21 and as he lay there he didn't look anywhere near that. His hair was cropped close and he had no beard at all. He was just a kid, yet he proved himself to be the driving factor of the whole company. He was everything that could be expected of an officer and soldier. When he died, the spirit of the company died with him."

The rest of us set up a defense within the house and tried to establish contact with the units on the flanks. Wire and communications men from the Third Battalion headquarters valiantly tried to keep in touch with the attacking forces but their lines were pounded to shreds by the artillery. Cpl. Donald Frye tried to get down to us but was hit severely by shell fragments. Frye came all the way back to the top of the hill smiling as though nothing had happened.

No one believed he was hit until they saw the gaping holes in his shoulder and arms. Later on, Cpl. Norman Spencer and Stanley Daniels were hit while out on the lines. Spencer lost both feet at the ankles and Daniels had a large hole torn in his chest.

During Lt. Wilson's dash to the town, King Company was still fighting its way out of one of the most devastating artillery barrages it had ever undergone. The constant shrieking and hammering of the shells together with the sight of comrades being torn to pieces beside them had worn the men to the breaking point. No one was certain as to his objectives, but each knew that he could not last much longer where he was. Finally Lt. Edward Crowson took matters into his own hands, organized the remnants of his company and led them in a wild avenging charge into Stiring-Wendel. In a rage of madness the men swept over the open ground, across the railroad tracks and plunged into the first houses on the outskirts of town. Pfc. Charles Kocemba was one of the first to reach the buildings, followed closely by the slightly corpulent, but very aggressive Sgt. Dallas Waite. Waite peeled off and led an assault on the second row of houses while Kocemba followed the explosion of Pfc. Comer's grenade through a window. Not far behind came Lt. Crowson with a smoking rifle and a blazing cigar clamped between his teeth.

Crowson set up a CP in the house and then pushed on into the front rooms to observe up the street. There he was spotted by a Kraut sniper and received a painful bullet wound in the leg. Crowson merely took an extra long drag on his cigar and continued to direct the attack up the street. Tec. 5 Jim Owen, the medic, tried to get him to stop long enough so that he could dress the wound, but by the time he got a first aid bandage around it, Crowson was off again. Together with his Executive Officer, Lt. James DeLorme, who was also from North Carolina, the two drove the assault forward with the greatest amount of vigor the South has displayed since the Battle of Bull Run.

The platoons and squads separated and began to work their way up the streets toward the Metz Highway clearing the houses as they went.

"The Krauts had all taken off for the cellars," said Pfc. Warriner. "I heard a noise in the basement of the first house I entered so I yelled down in French for any civilians to come out. All I got for an answer was a low guttural, *'Geben Sie mir meine Pistole,'* followed by a shot. I tossed a grenade down the steps and when the thing went off a shower of canned fruits, smoked meats, and a couple of pickled Krauts came flying up. We moved on to the next house where a very pretty French girl threw her arms around me, gave me a big kiss and hailed me as her liberator. She told me that there were five Germans in the next house and said for me to go there and *'treiz les sales boches'* (shoot the filthy Germans). I got Sgt. Shahan and Sgt. Coleman to help me and we went over to the house and flushed them out of the basement with grenades and M-1s."

As soon as it had gained its initial objective, King company consolidated in the protection of the houses and took stock of its strength before continuing the attack. In the whole company only approximately sixty-two men were left. Its dead and wounded had been left behind to be picked up by the medics. Litter bearers worked back and forth through the mine fields all day long. The Medical Corps, as always, was performing its utmost and was taking more than its share of the casualties. In the afternoon Pfc. Carl Rylke was taking a litter team down the hill when he stepped on a mine and his left foot was blown off. The concussion threw him into the air and when he fell he struck another mine with his elbow and received serious wounds all over his body. Several German PW's were nearby and three of them were ordered to go to Rylke's assistance. All three of them, however, stepped on mines as they tried to get to Rylke. Again more prisoners were sent out to bring in the wounded men. This time they were successful and Rylke was brought in to the aid station unconscious and near dead. Several attempts were made to revive him by giving him blood plasma but each was unsuccessful and he died a half hour later. Lt. Zeling Cooper was hit while leading King's second platoon into the town and was lying out on the open ground unable to move.

"He laughed and joked with me all the while I worked on him," said Pfc. Monroe Gable. "It seemed like he was getting a big kick out of the whole damned thing. The Germans kept throwing more artillery all over the area where the wounded were. Cooper was already hurt bad and while he was lying there he was hit again. In spite of that he kept telling jokes and trying to keep up the spirits of the rest of the wounded. I knew we couldn't get them out of there for a long time. It was a pitiful sight. They were lying in the mud pleading for help and we had to pass on. Some of them had to lie there all night long before they could be evacuated."

During the night of March 3rd, Col. Conley reviewed the day's action. Our losses had been heavy, but we had succeeded in pushing a stubborn enemy back, the same 559th Division which only a few days before had been the aggressor. In forcing their retreat, we had come through extensive mine fields and barbed wire entanglements. Numerous trenches and concrete pillboxes had been overrun and captured by our assault down the hill. Another belt of the Siegfried Line had been breached, and our leading companies occupied houses along the outskirts of the town of Stiring-Wendel.

As the morning of the 4th dawned, leading companies once more drove forward through the town . . . this time supported by heavy tanks. Every building that was thought to contain German troops was pulverized by the heavy guns on the armored vehicles. The regimental anti-tank guns moved up and helped neutralize remaining pillboxes and fortifications. One of the gun crews found an old French lady and two young granddaughters living in a house they used as a billet. Although shells, rockets and mortars were raining down in that vicinity, she refused to leave, placing all her trust in the Lord, as she explained it. Several shells fell within six feet of the house and blew all the windows out but none of them were hurt and no shells hit the house itself. Right in the middle of the battlefield the woman did the men's washing and heated their rations . . . so completely did she ignore the horrors of war.

The assault companies jumped off around 0630 and proceeded rapidly through the town. Most of the German resistance faded before the onslaught of the tanks. Enemy artillery, directed from excellent OP's on the heights surrounding the northwest side of town, continued to rain down on the attackers, however, causing numerous casualties. While clearing the town many instances were seen of civilians, including women and children, firing on the American soldiers. Pfc. Bennett caught and killed one young boy sniping at a GI. This was a border town and German sympathies ran high. Some of the men found both French and German flags hidden in the homes they entered . . . one or the other to be displayed depending upon who was in control of the town. Some of our men claimed they had observed houses flying the Nazi Swastika from up on the hill . . . but when they entered the town they saw the tri-color of the French hanging from the same pole.

All companies made steady progress through the town finding scattered points of German resistance. Lt. Cox's Easy Company moved into town and took over a sector of houses from Fox and George. French troops followed the Americans into the town and were taking over and occupying the houses after they had been cleared. Easy cleared houses all day without suffering one casualty. "That's the way I like to fight this damned war," remarked Pfc. Haley. Mortar and artillery fire kept them jumping in and out of houses all through the day, however, and often the men tore out walls to pass from one house to another to avoid going out in the shrapnel littered street.

By the end of the second day we had crossed the Metz Highway, and most of the town was in American hands.

Only the large and heavily defended Simon Mine still held out. Companies and platoons selected quarters and set up OP's from which they could observe to the front and both flanks. The Germans continued to pound the positions with artillery and rocket fire but casualties were slight. Snipers continued to fire from different quarters of the town long after it had been cleared and taken. Vehicles could only reach the positions at night after racing down a 1,500 yard stretch of highway under direct enemy fire.

That night Lt. Peterson, 3rd Bn. S-4, was leading a group of jeeps up with chow for the third battalion but after searching vainly through a vast network of streets he was unable to find any of the companies he was looking for. Finally he saw what he believed to be a guard standing in the shadow of the doorway of one of the houses.

"Where's the K Company CP?" he asked.

The guard stepped out of the doorway and came over to the side of the jeep like he hadn't quite understood.

"Vas ist das?"

For a fraction of a second Peterson stared petrified. Then there was a resounding roar and a clashing of gears as he threw the jeep in reverse and went sailing down the streets backwards.

Wire sections were having a difficult time maintaining communication with the attacking units. Artillery kept tearing up telephone lines at regular intervals. Losses in the 3rd Bn. section were especially heavy.

The Simon Mine was now the big obstacle upon which the regimental attack was centered. For several days it had been shelled and bombed but still the trapped Germans inside of it showed no signs of surrender. Time and again attempts had been made to take it by storm but each assault was driven back. A huge steel wall surrounded the place topped by a net of barbed wire. Tanks attempted to blow holes in the walls but were driven off by enemy anti-tank fire. It was estimated that approximately three to four hundred civilians were being held prisoner deep down in the shafts. A large Red Cross flag hung from one of the entrances but any attempt to enter there was met with a hail of machine gun fire.

On the afternoon of the 5th a huge column of men was seen streaming toward the American line from the direction of the German lines. At first it was thought that a large scale German counterattack was being launched.

"They were straggling for miles all up and down the Metz Highway," said T/Sgt. James Wilson. "They seemed to wobble over the road like they were drunk. Some of them would fall to the ground and then drag themselves up again with a great effort. Then we found out that they were Russians who had escaped from a large prison camp on the edge of town. Most of them were in a pitiful condition. They had not had anything to eat for days and were so weak and emaciated they could hardly stand up. When the Germans saw them getting away they turned machine guns on them and killed a lot of them. Others wandered into the mine fields along the road and were blown to eternity. Still they kept coming towards us. Those who were too weak to walk just fell along the side of the hill and lay still. The rest of them came plodding on. They were so hungry they would scrape the empty cans our K rations were in, even when they were infested with ants and flies."

"We got the German prisoners to help them back," continued Pfc. Hershey. "It was nothing to see half a dozen of them sprawled on the road half dead from hunger and exhaustion. We gave them all the rations we could spare but they didn't half go around. We put some of them in trucks and sent them back to the rear where they set up special camps for them."

On the morning of the Sixth, Lt. Doane's Love Co. was ordered to attack the Simon Mine on the battalion left front. King was to furnish fire support from Neue-Glashutte and Item would be in reserve.

"We pushed through the woods up to the outside of the factory," remembers Pfc. Robinson, "and captured 12 prisoners and two machine guns there, but were then driven back by heavy machine gun fire from pillboxes hidden in the trees and from fire from the Mine itself. Every time we withdrew to let the artillery pound the factory, the Krauts would go down into the underground passages of the place and wait until the shelling was over. Then they would come up in time to catch us as we started to assault."

"It was impossible to attack the building from the side," continues Sgt. Gray. "We had to hit it head on because there was a deep sludge area around the sides. Tanks tried to come up but were knocked back by Kraut anti-tank guns. By taking it in rushes we got to within 50 yards of the outside wall. Then the Krauts turned everything they had on us. The whole company was pinned down."

Sgt. Cathey spotted one of the machine gun positions and tried to bring fire on it. He called Pfc. Bissenger to come up with a bazooka, but before Bissenger could get into position to fire, a sniper shot him through the chest and he died about fifteen minutes later.

We continued to press the attack but stubborn resistance made it impossible to get beyond the iron fence. Pfc. Wagner was shot through the head and killed and Pfc. Zoebelein lost a foot when he stepped on a mine.

"When he saw it was impossible to go any further, Sgt. Cathey went back to bring up a tank," said Sgt. William Smith, "Cathey rode on top of it up toward the wall right out in plain sight. When the tank got up to the wall Cathey jumped over and started going after a German machine gun nest. The tank fired four rounds with its 75-mm cannon and then the Germans hit it with a bazooka round. Not much damage was done but fragments from the shell flew off and hit Cathey. The tank then took off in reverse as fast as it could go and left Cathey lying there wounded inside the factory wall. When the Krauts saw him alone they started firing at him with machine guns and hit him again in the arms and legs."

It was almost certain suicide to attempt to rescue him. German guns fired at anything that moved inside the wall. Outside, the whole company was pinned down by fire. Nevertheless, Pfc. Lawrence and two others risked certain death and went up through the curtain of fire and dragged Cathey back to a ditch inside the wall out of the line of fire.

About two hours later Sgt. Kohn sent a litter squad to bring out the wounded man. Three times the squad attempted to get to him but three times it was driven back by hostile mortar, rocket and tank fire. The next time Kohn started out alone.

"I climbed over the wall only to drop in a tangle of barbed wire on the other side," said Kohn afterward. "I tore my clothes to pieces but finally pulled myself free and got over to where Cathey was lying. I told him to lock his arms around my neck and I would drag him away.

" 'I can't,' he replied. 'Both of them are broken.'

"Then I ripped his shirt up the back and tied it around my neck and started dragging him toward the wall. Mortar shells were dropping all around and a German tank had come to within fifty yards of us. Cathey was suffering pretty bad from the pain and I had to tell him to quiet down or he would attract the Kraut's attention to us. When I got him to the wall both of us got caught in the barbed wire. I pulled and jerked on his clothes until they were nearly torn off him but finally tore free. Then I lifted him to the wall and dropped him to litter bearers on the other side. The wire tore my Red Cross brassard off my arm and I picked it up and held it between my teeth. Going over the wall, though, I started to cuss and lost it."

The litter bearers from the 370th Medical Bn. took care of the rest of the evacuation by waving a Red Cross flag to see if it would be fired upon. When nothing happened a litter team was led across the field and brought Cathey back to the aid station.

The whole time we were in Stiring-Wendel the Krauts continuously hammered the area with artillery. Thousands of rounds pounded this small town daily and our own 882nd Field Artillery expended itself trying to neutralize the enemy artillery pieces with counter-battery fire. We had heard that the Germans would not fire if we kept our liaison cub planes up in the air to spot them, so our "cubs" practically lived in the skies. This did no good either and we finally resigned ourselves to fate and decided that the German artillery was just another part of the Seigfried Line, guns imbedded in concrete with only the muzzles projecting. We had also heard that the Germans were short on ammunition, but during this period they were outshooting us 5 to 1—and we were throwing every round of ammunition we could get our hands on.

Capt. Keith's Item Company led the 3rd Battalion march towards Schonecken, to be followed later by King and Love Companies. Keith moved his men out early in the morning and kept going all day. No contact was made with the enemy, however; so late in the day, Keith decided to hold up and then resume the pursuit in the morning. The company pulled into an old barn and settled down in the mouldy hay and cow dung to get a few hours' rest before driving on in the morning. Shortly afterwards, though, word arrived that the chase would continue without stopping.

"We hardly got our eyes shut when we were shaken out of the sack to start on again," said Sgt. Bailey. "This time our objective was Schonecken. The way out from the barn was a zigzag course around mine fields and finally out to the road again. Lt. Westbrook went out in front to find the best route for the company to follow. He took one squad and had just about made it into the town when the squad ran into some barbed wire. They stopped there because everybody suspected they would run into something out of the ordinary ahead. It was still pitch dark so Westbrook got down on his hands and knees and crawled under the wire and started feeling around with his hands. Pretty soon he touched a boxlike object.

" 'Mines,' he said."

After waiting for a short time to figure out what to do next, they decided they had to find a route through for the rest of the company. So they continued crawling forward, feeling the ground as they went. Every time someone would come to a mine, he would feel around it, remove the detonator and then dispose of the explosive charge and the box. They were small yellow "shu" mines designed to blow off the foot or leg of anyone who stepped on them. It was a ticklish business crawling through a mine field at night deactivating mines as you went. Foot by foot, mine by mine, they finally made it. They continued on into the town and found that the Germans had deserted it. Then Westbrook said he would need a good man to go back and guide the rest of the company up. He asked Bob Doyle if he would be willing to go back.

"Why, hell yes," answered Doyle, his voice disguising the natural fear any man would have had to pick his way through a mine field at night. Bravery wasn't lack of fear, but the control and overpowering of fear.

Walsh volunteered to go back with Doyle, and the two of them set off through the mines. When they got to the field they made a guess as to where Westbrook had crossed, and started the blind groping and feeling. It was necessary to mark a path so the rest of the company could find it, so they left trails of tooth powder on either side of them. Before they got across, the tooth powder gave out, despite their careful efforts to conserve it. They crossed the rest of the way and found the company still in the barn where they had left several hours before.

Capt. Keith thought that the tooth powder trail would not be enough to get the men safely through the field so he asked Doyle if he could mark a clearer lane. Finally, Yarus, the Commo. Sgt. brought out a roll of toilet paper. Doyle went back to mark out the field while Walsh stayed behind to guide the company through. He picked out his earlier powder trail and marked off the rest of the path with toilet paper. Walsh soon brought the rest of the company down and the entire unit crossed the field despite the darkness without casualties. Then we proceeded into Schonecken.

The company stopped for about an hour in the middle of town, but since we met no resistance, we were ordered to keep going.

"King" then passed through Schonecken and continued down the road heading for the Saar River. Morning dawned with a bright warm sun creeping above the horizon. The streets were crowded with civilians shouting "*Vive l'Amérique*" and "*Bravo,*" but most of the men paid little attention to them for most of them had said the same thing to the Krauts when they marched through the town a few years before. Streets were littered with propaganda leaflets. Some of them warned that the terrible Siegfried Line was just ahead and the men defending it were bold and brave and that no Yank would cross it and live. Most of the men tossed them aside and vowed they would hang their washing on the vaunted Line.

The 274th had surmounted another hurdle in its struggle to crash through the Siegfried barriers and was now across the border facing the last line of pillboxes. On the left in the 3rd Bn. sector, the Saar River afforded a natural barrier between us and the last line of defense. On the right in the 1st Bn. sector, a formidable thick layer of protruding concrete dragon teeth ran continuously across the front. Ours was a tough assignment, and much of the success of the Seventh Army depended upon our ability to complete the cracking of this wall and thereby opening the strategic Metz Highway N 3 over which the Army could travel to the heart of Germany.

The plan was again for the 70th Division to make the main effort, with the 63rd Division on the right prepared to exploit our successes. The 274th was to continue spearheading the Trailblazer drive. The 276th Infantry had kept abreast of us but the 275th had remained in defensive positions on the right ever since the capture of Spicheren.

Both Army and Corps Headquarters were pressing hard so General Barnett ordered Col. Conley to attack without delay. We were not prepared for a river crossing; therefore Col. Conley chose Major Cantrell's 1st Bn. to attack on the right through the dragons' teeth.

Neither were we prepared for a land assault on the Seigfried Line. Self-propelled guns were not available and our supporting tanks had not been able to negotiate a route forward to our foremost positions.

Baker Company was selected to spearhead the attack. The ground ahead was covered with cleverly concealed pillboxes and long rows of dragons' teeth. There didn't seem to be much hope for Capt. Mitchell's men. It was flesh and bones against concrete and steel . . . truly a modern mechanized war.

"We were told that each pillbox was manned by about 17 men," said Lt. Chappel of B Co. "Most of them were supposed to be transfers from the Luftwaffe. It made no difference whether they knew anything about infantry tactics or not. All they had to do was sit inside the thick concrete bunkers and pull the trigger of a machine gun. It was sure suicide to cross the flat fields swept by perfect enemy fire, but orders were orders and we were going to try it. Our artillery turned loose an all-out barrage to help knock out the enemy bunkers, but they did no good. Even our '8' shells failed to dent the fortifications. I don't think they even shook up the occupants, and we might as well have saved our ammunition."

"My platoon jumped off first," said S/Sgt. Rysso. "I had two squads forward and one back. As soon as we started to move the Krauts threw over a lot of artillery and mortars, but most of it fell in back of us. Pfc. Condict was the first man over the knob of the hill in front of the Line. When he came back, he was sweating and his face was pale. 'It's going to be rough,' was all he said. We kept going until the two leading squads were at the top of the hill. We could all see the dragons' teeth, pillboxes, dugouts, and trenches from there. The hill was completely bare and we stood out in plain sight like sore thumbs. The Krauts couldn't help but see us. They waited until we were out on the flat ground in front and then cut loose.

"Nicokoris, a lead scout, hit the ground and then got up to run to some barbed wire, where he hit the dirt the second time. He didn't get up again. Penland ran up to help Nicokoris and tried to find out where the worst fire was coming from. He got as far as a small mound of earth when the Krauts turned on him. Dunn came up beside Penland behind the mound. Every time they tried to move, the Krauts started cutting off the top of the mound with machine gun fire. The Germans could see every move they made. Before long the mound was riddled and the men thought the bullets would soon be coming through it.

"The rest of the squad flattened on the ground squeezing into every little depression that could be found. The Krauts mistook several piles of manure for men and blasted hell out of them. We were completely pinned down. We called back for artillery on the pillboxes. It came over but just bounced harmlessly off the sides. We were told over the radio that tanks would soon be coming up. Five came, but one's gun jammed and it turned around and went back. When the Krauts saw the tanks, they opened up with all the 88's and machine gun fire they had."

Nicokoris stirred a little out on the ground when things got worse. He had been hit in the chest the first time. Then he tried to pull himself back toward the mound where Penland was, but was hit again in the arm. When the tanks came up, he was wounded a third time by 88 fragments.

"I saw Frazier get it while he was running to get behind one of the tanks," continued Sgt. Penland. "An 88 burst nearby and got three of them. Palmer fell to the ground and tried to get up but the Germans opened up on him again. We later found him dead, riddled with machine gun bullets. Rakowsky was hit and knocked to the ground, but he got up and joined the rest of the boys behind the tank. Those who weren't wounded got behind two of the tanks and started firing at the pillboxes. After about 15 minutes the tanks decided to withdraw because they claimed the ground was too soft and they couldn't get across the dragons' teeth anyway. When they pulled back the infantrymen were left exposed to the murderous fire out in the open, so we took to the cover of a line of trees behind the hill."

"Once we had reached temporary safety I started to reorganize the men we had left," continues Sgt. Rysso. "Dunn made two attempts to go out into the field to get the wounded but was driven back by machine gun fire. Then Newton, the medic, went out, accompanied by Penland, Dunn, Boering, and Mann. Strange to say they drew no fire even though they were plainly visible to the Germans. They found Palmer dead, Casto with a broken leg, and Jannick unconscious with a hole in his head. He was still wearing a packboard with four bazooka rounds in it. Cuervo and Condict were also lying on the ground badly wounded. Newton did what he could for the men. He gave them all a shot of morphine and then waited for litter bearers to come up."

The platoon then withdrew farther back to a row of trenches, leaving Penland and Newton to take care of the wounded. Just about that time, two short rounds of American artillery came over and appeared to fall right in the middle of the wounded lying on the hill top.

Penland immediately yelled at Rysso who was not far away, "Tell those bastards to lift that artillery! It's falling among our own men!"

Rysso was already shouting the same thing into the radio.

Just then three wounded men were seen coming out of a low row of shrubs near where the shells were falling, helping each other back. It was later learned that they were Andrews and Helaszek, supporting Darling between them. Suddenly another round came over and made a direct hit on them. The story of the tragedy can best be told by Penland:

"Two artillery shells whistled across the top of the hole Newton and I were in and exploded only a short distance away. I could see that they landed right among our wounded still lying in the field. Out of the corner of my eye, coming from the left, I saw two men supporting a third coming toward the shell crater. I glanced about and recognized Andrews on the right, supporting Darling who had been wounded in the right thigh. I did not have time to tell who the third man was, but was later told it was Helaszek. I just got out the first word of warning 'Get down!' when a large caliber shell screamed over very low and hit directly on the three men. I saw a tremendous flash of fire and a fearful cloud of black smoke. Pieces of men's bodies came flying through the air. The concussion blew off my helmet and threw me to the bottom of the crater which was filled with mud and water. One man's horribly torn body flew over my head and hit in the water beside me. Newton was standing beside me nearest the shell and was blown down into the water. I grabbed him to keep him from sinking under. He was covered with blood from the men who had been hit by the shell. I asked him if he was hit. He said he didn't know and crawled over to help another man who was pushing himself toward the water with only his legs. This was probably Helaszek who later was found dead in the hole.

"I looked around and saw just a man's chest and hands

sticking out of the water. I grabbed to pull him out, thinking that possibly he might still be alive and was drowning. When I got him out, though, I saw he was mangled and dead so let him slip back into the water. While Newton was working on the wounded, I went back to the platoon and assembled it. I could only account for ten men. Litter bearers eventually came up but were driven back immediately by fire from the Germans. They waited until after dark and then picked up all the wounded they could find."

In the morning Lt. Chappel went out to the shell crater to identify the bodies. He was able to pick out Helaszek by his dog tags and Darling by a letter. Throughout the day American artillery shelled the sector with 155's and 8-inchers.

The next day, March 16th, TD's and tanks moved up into the woods where they could bring direct fire on the Siegfried fortifications. Captain Murphy, Bn. S-3, reconnoitered forward positions to determine whether TD's could knock out the pillboxes in co-ordination with the infantry assault. Later it was decided to use 8-inch guns. For several minutes the huge guns rained hell on the fortifications. Direct hits were scored on several of the pillboxes. Often the powerful shells were seen to glance off the concrete structures and go sailing off into the air or explode harmlessly leaving nothing but a dent in the side.

During the night "B" and "C" Companies sent patrols out to inspect the damage. Both received small arms and machine gun fire. They reported several direct hits on the bunkers directly to the front.

That night a reconnaissance party went down to the woods in the 3rd Bn. area to observe enemy fortifications on the other side of the river. It was discovered that the primary firing lanes of the bunkers were facing up and downstream. Farther to the rear, however, were more installations from which cross fire could be maintained over the river. These showed signs of activity and the apertures were blackened to indicate use.

From interrogation of prisoners it was learned that six enemy troops manned each bunker armed with a heavy MG and 6,000 rounds of ammunition. Each fortification contained enough food to last the crews two weeks. It was also learned that our artillery had had little effect on the structures and they were operating as strongly as before.

During this time our 3rd Bn. was holding down a long line abreast of the Saar River. A tall, 150-foot water tower was used by Colonel Landstrom as an OP and by artillery observers to bring fire on targets across the Saar. A large gap formed on the right while the 1st Bn. was trying to break through the Siegfried defenses. The Battalion's mission was to patrol the river for crossing sites and locate the occupied pillboxes. It soon became apparent that all pillboxes were occupied and there was one every one hundred yards.

All the power the 70th Division could mass was brought up along the lower bank and turned upon the impressive fortifications on the opposite side. Against us was the most powerful section of the most elaborate system of fortifications ever built in the history of the world. Pillboxes blocked the way miles in depth. No one tried to think of what could happen while we floundered around in the water right in front of these electrically controlled guns on the other side.

Patrols moved at night between adjacent units. An "Item" Patrol was going down the main drag in pitch blackness when someone heard voices a short distance away. The patrol hit the ground and listened, feeling sure that the Germans had come across during the night and were digging in on the American bank. The men crept closer until they could see the dark figures digging in a heavy field gun. One of the patrol members exclaimed, "The bastards even brought artillery across!"

Then one of the voices was heard to say, "Aw, Sonubabitch! Bringing a man out in the middle of the night." . . . They were Americans, a TD outfit emplacing their guns.

By the night of March 18th, armored spearheads from the Third Army had punctured to within 60 miles of Saarbrucken and were menacing the German right flank. It was believed that the enemy might withdraw during the night under the threat of being surrounded and cut off.

The original plan had been for the 276th Infantry to

make the initial assault crossing and all anti-tank guns in the area had been placed under that regiment's control to support the operation; however, plans were being changed now and it looked as though the 274th would spearhead again.

Col. Landstrom asked for permission to fire on the pillboxes across the way with these anti-tank guns. Permission was delayed until 1720 in the afternoon because clearance had to be obtained from the 276th. Finally it came, and Major Greenhalgh relayed the message over the phone, giving the OK to fire:

"All right, out there, shoot everything you've got. Start whenever you want to and don't stop till it gets so dark you can't see."

That was all the anti-tank and TD gunners were waiting for, along with the cannon company gunners. The whole southern bank of the river opened up with a furious barrage. Some of the guns went at the pillboxes while others lambasted factories and possible OP's farther back. This was the first time our guns ever had good direct fire targets. Plaster and concrete flew all over the other side of the river. After a half hour's pounding one of the gunners saw a white flag waving from the steeple of a church which the Germans appeared to be using as an OP. The gunners just dropped the next round below the flag and by slightly raising each succeeding round, raised the banner right up into the sky. As soon as the barrage lifted, however, the ever present machine guns still returned fire from the pillboxes.

During the night the 289th Engineer Bn. brought up 38 boats to carry the 3rd Bn. over the river. Regimental S-3 told Col. Landstrom he would have 2,000 rounds of artillery to back him up on call. At 2010, Col. Conley contacted Col. Landstrom on the phone and said:

"The Commanding General expects us to cross tonight. You are to select the time for crossing. If you need any assistance, it is ready on call. If you are successful, the 2nd Bn. will follow you."

Higher headquarters still believed the enemy had retreated. We disagreed, and on the night of March the 19th they were still blazing away. Col. Landstrom summed up his ideas on the subject as follows:

"If we start across, we will complete it. I am not in favor of patrols. Prefer to go all out. The time for crossing will be sometime between midnight and daybreak. We are still receiving fire from enemy 50 and 88-mm guns. This points to same resistance as before."

The night of March 19th was quiet and peaceful. The warming winds of spring swept up from the south and sent patterns of ripples twinkling in the starlight on the river. In foxholes along the shore the men looked up at the sky and waited.

The Last of It

The 274th Regiment jumped off at dawn, March 20th. The crossing had been feared, but the 3rd Army's roll-up of the defenses behind the Saar River made the German positions untenable; they withdrew bare hours before the 274th and the rest of the 7th Armored Division managed the crossing. With few losses, they continued into Saarbrücken.

The Americans kept breaking through the Rhine defenses, establishing more bridgeheads; by the end of March Hitler could see the end in sight. But he refused to give up. The Fuehrer commanded the German people to carry out a scorched earth policy. There was no hope for them at this point anyway, he announced, so the Allied victory must be made as costly as possible. Hitler had led his people to disaster; he was now determined to lead them to destruction. Many, still mesmerized, followed him, but the German field commanders secretly worked to undermine this order.

By April 18th, the Americans had scored a crushing victory, the 1st and 9th Armies completing the envelopment and capture in the Ruhr of more than 300,000 German troops, together with the armament factories that fed the German war machine. This was a greater loss than the Germans suffered at Stalingrad.

The Americans now streaked across central Germany, reaching the Elbe River and holding a line there. They were to wait for the Russians to close in from the east, by previous agreement. In northern Germany, Montgomery had moved north from the Lower Elbe, sealing off the coastal ports. On April 30th, the Russians were fighting their way through the rubble of Berlin. Hitler had already shouted that the German people were unworthy of him, and on the 30th he abandoned them, via suicide—to the intense relief of the German generals. They had followed Hitler's last-ditch orders long after all reasonable hope of resistance was gone. Now they could make peace. They had to.

Early on May 7th an armistice was signed at Rheims between Germany and the Allies; the terms were unconditional surrender, and delivery to the Allies of all the German forces on all fronts.

The military war in Europe was over. Its destruction to life and property staggers the imagination.

The Battle of the Atlantic cost the Allies more than 20,000,000 tons of merchant shipping, in retaliation for which 781 German submarines and their crews were sent to the bottom.

Army casualties in Europe were over 700,000. The infantry, representing only 20% of the U. S. overseas forces, absorbed 70% of the casualties.

The U. S. itself extended lend-lease aid to Allied countries, including Russia, in the amount of almost fifty billion dollars.

Such statistics are chosen at random. Perhaps they mean little to the reader, perhaps even less to the fighting man. What of him? Would his many sacrifices be forgotten, washed over by the cold war?

Eric Sevareid said, in one of his broadcasts to the nation:

> War happens inside a man. It happens to one man alone. It never can be communicated. That is the tragedy—and perhaps the blessing. A thousand ghastly wounds are really only one. A million martyred lives leave an empty place at only one family table. That is why, at bottom, people can let wars happen, and that is why nations survive them and carry on. If, by the miracles of art and genius, in later years two or three among them can open their hearts and the right words come, then perhaps we shall all know a little of what it was like.